Springsteen as Soundtrack

Springsteen as Soundtrack

*The Sound of the Boss
in Film and Television*

Caroline Madden

McFarland & Company, Inc., Publishers
Jefferson, North Carolina

LIBRARY OF CONGRESS CATALOGUING-IN-PUBLICATION DATA

Names: Madden, Caroline, 1991– author.
Title: Springsteen as soundtrack : the sound of the Boss in film and television / Caroline Madden.
Description: Jefferson : McFarland & Company, Inc., Publishers, 2020. | Includes bibliographical references and index.
Identifiers: LCCN 2020000434 | ISBN 9781476672854 (paperback : acid free paper) ♾ | ISBN 9781476637877 (ebook)
Subjects: LCSH: Springsteen, Bruce—Criticism and interpretation. | Motion picture music—History and criticism.
Classification: LCC ML420.S77 M3 2020 | DDC 782.42166092—dc23
LC record available at https://lccn.loc.gov/2020000434

BRITISH LIBRARY CATALOGUING DATA ARE AVAILABLE

ISBN (print) 978-1-4766-7285-4
ISBN (ebook) 978-1-4766-3787-7

© 2020 Caroline Madden. All rights reserved

No part of this book may be reproduced or transmitted in any form or by any means, electronic or mechanical, including photocopying or recording, or by any information storage and retrieval system, without permission in writing from the publisher.

On the cover: Tom Hanks as Andrew Beckett in the 1993 film *Philadelphia* (TriStar Pictures/Photofest)

Printed in the United States of America

*McFarland & Company, Inc., Publishers
Box 611, Jefferson, North Carolina 28640
www.mcfarlandpub.com*

For Mom and Dad
Thank you for always supporting my dreams

Table of Contents

Acknowledgments	ix
Preface	1
Introduction	5
Baby It's You	17
Mask	33
In Country	43
Philadelphia	63
Dead Man Walking	76
No Looking Back	91
The Sopranos	102
High Fidelity	117
Prozac Nation	132
Reign Over Me	148
The Wrestler	159
Show Me a Hero	173
American Honey	191
Chapter Notes	205
Bibliography	221
Index	229

Acknowledgments

This book would not have been possible without the unending love and support of my mom and dad. I cannot thank them enough for everything they've done for me. I also have to thank my amazing grandparents. My tremendous editor Charlie Perdue and the entire team at McFarland & Company have been a joy to work with, and I am incredibly grateful for their help in bringing this book to life. I would be nowhere without the tutelage of my phenomenal professors Dr. Tracy Cox-Stanton and Dr. Chad Newsom at the Savannah College of Art and Design's cinema studies program—they shaped my writing and taught me so much about the film medium. Enormous gratitude also goes to Jon Landau for the opportunity to interview him and to Alison Oscar and Laura Kraus at Jon Landau Management for their assistance. Thank you to John Sayles for speaking with me about his beautiful film *Baby It's You*, to Meredith Atkinson for coordinating our correspondence, and to Irv Slifkin for kindly connecting us. In addition, thank you very much, Mrs. Nay Wasicsko-McLaughlin, for answering my questions about Nick.

My research journey led me to some incredible Bruce Springsteen resources. Eileen Chapman, director of the Bruce Springsteen Archives and Center for American Music at Monmouth University in Long Branch, New Jersey, generously provided me with the majority of the academic articles I reference in this book. The collection is a treasure trove of Springsteen materials that fans and scholars alike could spend an eternity inspecting. I credit Philip Sobell's blog (http://www.sandlercruise.blogspot.com), a collection of Springsteen references in film, television, and more, as the initial inspiration for this project. Eddy Wehbe at *Springsteen Lyrics* (http://www.springsteenlyrics.com) provided much-needed lyrical information and translations. *Brucebase* (http://www.brucebase.wikidot.com) is a virtual Springsteen encyclopedia helmed by Pete Russell and many other contributors. The site is an abundant reservoir of performance dates, facts, and (best of all!) transcriptions from concert performances that were all a great aid to this project. Ken Rosen's blog *E Street Shuffle* (http://estreetshuffle.com/) was a fantastic resource with in-depth analyses of both popular and rare Springsteen recordings. I'd also like to thank the New York Public Library of Performing Arts for providing me with an early draft of *Prozac Nation* as well as a quiet haven in which to write.

Stan Goldstein is the preeminent Springsteen expert, and I am deeply appreciative of the materials he provided and questions he answered during my research and conception of this project. I highly recommend his wonderful book, *Rock & Roll Tour of the Jersey Shore* (co-authored with Jean Mickle).

In April 2017, I spoke at Monmouth University's "Bruce Springsteen's *Darkness on the Edge of Town*: An International Symposium," organized by Kenneth Womack. My panels "Springsteen and Film" and "Springsteen in the Movies" with Alex Biese, Irv Slifkin, Joe

Amodei, and Shawn J. Poole were an indelible part of my writing and research process, and I am greatly appreciative of their feedback and our engaging discussion. Shawn was gracious enough to send me several resources that were a terrific aid to my work, and I thank him and *Backstreets* for their support. Very special thanks to Chris Jordan of the *Asbury Park Press* for helping spread the word early about this project. Thank you so much, Debra L. Rothenberg, for the publishing advice; see her marvelous photography in *Bruce Springsteen in Focus 1980–2012*.

I am extremely grateful for my early readers Candace E.C. O'Brien, Brandi Lucier, and Michael MacCambridge. My fellow Savannah College of Art and Design alumni Joshua Ward, Juliette Faracone, and Candace E.C. O'Brien were kind enough to assist me in finding some much-needed articles, books, and citation information. Kate French-Morris helped me compile Springsteen's copious songs about cars and the road. She is an engaging scholar with a focus in American literature, music, and landscape whose work I very much look forward to seeing more of in the future. Special thanks to Judy Hancock for sending me *Down Thunder Road* and always providing sweet encouragement. Thank you, Cassidy Quinn Deegan, for letting me bounce ideas off of you and all the *Springsteen on Broadway* adventures!

Everyone has their own "how I fell in love with Bruce Springsteen" story. Mine began in 2003 when I started listening to *The Essential Bruce Springsteen* (2003) with my mom in the car (thanks for the copy, Uncle Craig!). I remember playing "Mary's Place" and "Dancing in the Dark" on my Walkman on the bus heading toward my own New Jersey Catholic school. However, it wasn't until high school, when I read Elizabeth Wurtzel's book *Prozac Nation*, that I became a full-fledged prisoner of Springsteen's rock and roll. I listened to the songs she referenced, such as the Hammersmith version of "For You," "Stolen Car," and "The Promise." Their aching beauty lit my soul on fire, and I began to truly understand the soul-transmogrifying power of Springsteen's music. Bruce Springsteen closes out his Broadway show with the supplication "I hope I've been a good traveling companion." His music has been my greatest traveling companion—a friend that will always be there for me no matter how rough the road gets. I cannot thank him enough for all the joy he's brought me and the sadness he's gotten me through. This book is for him.

Preface

It was thanks to my discovery of Philip Sobell's blogs *Bruce@Movies* and *Bruce@TV* (written under the alias of Sandler Cruise) that this book was initially conceived. Sobell compiles Bruce Springsteen references found in the soundtracks, dialogue, props, and background images of various films and television shows. Around the same time that I found these blogs, I browsed Springsteen's IMDb page and was surprised to learn that his music had been included on the soundtrack of more than two hundred films and television shows. There appeared to be an abundance of media that not only had a diegetic Springsteen connection but also was directly influenced by his music and star image in a significant way. In addition, I began reading critical analyses of his work and noticed that there was much conversation devoted to the literary, biblical, and political aspects of Springsteen's musical oeuvre but little to none on his relationship with cinema—a considerably crucial influence on his songwriting. If Springsteen was such an integral component of so many films and television shows, why was no one discussing it? Watching the various films and television shows I found on Sobell's blogs and IMDb.com, it occurred to me that an investigation of how Springsteen's music intersects with the moving image would be noteworthy. With this book, I aim to fill the gap in Springsteen scholarship regarding the use of his music in films and on television.

As my chapter on *Mask* (1985) indicates, Springsteen is extremely particular about which projects he permits to use his music. According to his manager Jon Landau (whom I was fortunate enough to interview), Springsteen especially prioritizes "a personal connection, an appreciation of the material, and admiration for the director" and reads all of the scripts that pass his desk for soundtrack consideration.[1] For his original compositions such as "Streets of Philadelphia," "The Wrestler," or "Dead Man Walkin'"—songs specifically written for a film—"it's about finding his own point of view and can he write a song that gets the job done?"[2] Springsteen is one of the few musical artists with an auteurist sensibility, lending his voice only to works that align with his canonical ethos and interests. I employed this kind of scrutiny when selecting which films and television shows to discuss in the following chapters. This book is not a comprehensive study of all filmic works that include Springsteen on the soundtrack, but rather an in-depth intertextual analysis of thirteen that inoculate constitutive thematic concerns in his oeuvre.

Presented in chronological order, each chapter is devoted to a specific film or television series that includes Springsteen on the soundtrack and represents a fundamental theme or cultural context found within his musical corpus, including (but not limited to) religion, race, masculinity and femininity, working-class politics, 9/11, depression, and Vietnam. Many of these subjects have previously been discussed in Springsteen scholarship, but they have rarely been applied to the representation of his music within the cinematic medium. The Springsteen texts I discuss range from his pre–record deal output to the majority of his albums after his 1973 debut *Greetings from Asbury Park, N.J.* to his 2016 memoir *Born to Run* and the 2017–2018 Tony Award–winning pièce de résistance *Springsteen on Broadway*. The candid revelations made in Springsteen's memoir about his inner emotional life and personal inspirations behind his songs engender an intriguing new outlook on his vast musical landscape and its intertextual relationship with cinema. Additionally, I consider extratextual elements such as the historical and social contexts of Springsteen's stature as an American artist and popular culture icon, tying his autobiographical circumstances, star image, and personal credos to the film or television series in question.

Springsteen asserts that, throughout the years, he has "tried to think long and hard about what it means to be American: about the distinctive identity and position we have in the world, and how that position is best carried. I've tried to write songs that speak to our pride and criticize our failures."[3] In *Springsteen on Broadway*, he proclaims, "I wanted to know the whole American story.... What did it mean to be an American and to be a part of that story? ... I wanted to be able to celebrate and honor its beauty, its power." Since Springsteen so eloquently probes the niceties of quotidian American life, it seemed important that my film selections do so as well. Therefore, the cinematic works I study in this book are located in Springsteen's own Asbury Park, New Jersey; New York City's neighboring concrete jungles; the deep South; the desolate Midwest of his *Nebraska* (1982); and California's arid mountainscapes found in *The Ghost of Tom Joad* (1995). I wanted this book to examine narratives that stretched to every corner of Springsteen's promised land, as he is the prevailing voice of its majesty and foibles. Springsteen is the country's shining lodestar, and his music guides these thoroughly American cinematic stories.

"Like so many American film directors and authors, Springsteen uses the American landscape as the canvas on which he inscribes his characters' journeys," Colleen Sheehy surmises.[4] The workaday leading characters of the films I have chosen seem torn from the pages of a Springsteen songbook: Jersey Shore teenagers, highway travelers, criminals, downtrodden waitresses, repairmen, Vietnam veterans, 9/11 widows, and more. Often, these Springsteenian figures contemplate urgent American issues such as post-war and post–9/11 trauma, the social class divide, and the fragility of democracy. They all struggle to make ends meet while holding on to their illusive hopes and dreams. In more than half of the films I study, the leading characters have an ardent intra-diegetic connection with Springsteen that propels them to actively engage with his music. That so many protagonists make their Springsteen affinity known within the diegesis is what separates him from other musical artists and their representation in cinema, speaking to his universal appeal, fervid fandom, and ability to emotionally connect with his audiences in such a profound way.

I approach this book from the soundtrack studies tenet that the soundtrack is an integral component of the filmic text with the ability to structure the temporality of the mise-en-scène, vocalize a character's inner thoughts and emotions, conjure a particular mood, and define the time period and milieu. I examine how Springsteen's songs operate as both diegetic source (music emitting from an object within the film itself) and non-diegetic score (music that is not present in the action or story space, typically in montages or credit sequences). Within the discipline of cinema studies, the soundtrack has been examined through a variety of theoretical frameworks, but there is an opportunity for an extensive study on how a particular musical artist has been represented in motion pictures across time. In scrupulous Springsteenian fashion, I have curated a collection of films and television shows from the 1980s to the present that speak to definitive aspects of his work and encompass the thematic concerns that have since come to define him as an American musical luminary. The decades-long marriage of Springsteen's incredible music and cinema is ripe for intertextual analysis, and it is my hope that this book will provide an engaging glimpse of how his songs shape narratives, define the inner lives of characters, and affectively captivate spectators.

Introduction

From storm-tinged and rattlesnake-ridden deserts housing downtrodden garage mechanics to the carnival fantasies of the Jersey Shore boardwalk guarded by greasers and lusty dive-bar waitresses, Springsteen's imaginative and evocative lyrics craft an eclectic tapestry of rich landscapes and complex characters. Although many critics examine Springsteen's corpus through literary frameworks—such as Roxanne Hardt and Irwin Streight of *Reading the Boss: Interdisciplinary Approaches to the Works of Bruce Springsteen* going so far as to equate him with William Shakespeare and *New York Times Magazine* calling him "Steinbeck in Leather"—I contend that he is primarily a cinematic writer. While Springsteen often cites musicians and authors as inspirations (such as Woody Guthrie, Elvis Presley, Jim Thompson, and James M. Cain), movies and filmmakers remain some of his most formative influences, particularly the western and road genres. Springsteen's love of cinema shapes his songwriting style and musicality, accounting for his work's exceptional functionality within the filmic medium. Directors are drawn to his music as soundtrack because of its uniquely cinematic aesthetic.

The maverick director Jonathan Demme declared Springsteen the "greatest American filmmaker who has yet to make his first film."[1] Like film itself, the epic arcs of Springsteen's narratives plumb the psychological depths and minutiae of human nature to reveal the extraordinary art in ordinary life. He consciously writes images as he describes the action, locales, and characters' inner thoughts and dialogue with a detailed script-like quality that animates in listeners' minds like brilliant CinemaScope. Jon Landau affirms Springsteen's "ability to make his lyrics flash before your eyes as if they already were films—very few people have done anything like that, and none have done it better."[2]

Springsteen's settings—whether they be the sun-dried tranquility of the Midwestern plains, the salty-aired, candy-coated mirth of the Asbury Park boardwalk, or the bohemian vibrancy of Greenwich Village—"seem like they were filmed on location, or maybe it's just that the settings feel like the characters themselves. Springsteen is a compulsive recorder of detail—the sheets 'damp with sweat,' the girl 'bopping down the beach with a radio,'" Ariel Swartley writes.[3] His banal protagonists, from the humblest of factory workers to hopeful Mexican immigrants to the devilish Charlie Starkweather, are also brought to life in this vivid and punctilious mode, with Springsteen fully inhabiting their internal geography as if he were an actor. Discussing the killer characters on *Nebraska*, David Burke argues that "we buy into Springsteen as psychopath just as we buy into Robert De Niro as Travis Bickle or Marlon Brando as Colonel Kurtz. This is Springsteen as method singer."[4] Burke's observation of Springsteen as "method singer" accurately describes his performance approach of emotional identification with *all* of his characters, good and bad, mobilized by his intimate use of first-person narration to not only speak in their voice but also inhabit their inner being.

Springsteen even describes his songwriting technique using filmic language, suggesting that he views his own work not as literary text but as a sonic mode of cinema. He told Chet Flippo of *Musician* that he wanted his songs "to kind of just pan out and be very cinematic."[5] "There's no settling down, no fixed action. You pick up the action, and then at some point—*pssst!*—the camera pans away, and whatever happened, that's what happened. The songs I write, they don't have particular beginnings and they don't have endings. The camera focuses in and then out," he continued elsewhere.[6] Springsteen cemented this idea of his music as cinema in *Rolling Stone*: "Part of the thing is that when I write the song, I write it to be the movie—not to make a movie, to be a movie."[7] Using his descriptive lyrics and evocative instrumentations as a camera to construct motion pictures in the heads of his listeners, Springsteen asserts himself as a musical auteur.

As with any notable auteur, Springsteen has a distinct style and dominant thematic preoccupations that run throughout his canon. He explicitly sought to emulate director John Ford, who could "depict almost identical situations a dozen times and yet make each one of them different."[8] "I became fascinated with John Ford movies in the fact that they were all Westerns. I watched the early ones and the late ones. It was fascinating to me how he'd film the same scene—a dance scene or a confrontation—and make it different in every picture," Springsteen told Robert Hilburn.[9] Springsteen's work is decidedly Fordian in its continual reshaping and expansion of the same narratives and themes throughout diverse songs across the years. "There was a lot of continuity in [Ford's] work. I liked that. You go back to the previous movie and have a clearer understanding of where he was coming from. What he was saying in this film was changing the shape of what he said in another one," he observed.[10] Springsteen upholds this idea of continuity by tracking the evolution of his characters as they age, following them not just as teenagers or in their twenties "but into the middle parts of their lives, into their forties and on. The idea was to draw my own map and maybe help other people draw their maps."[11] In the vein of Ford, each album Springsteen releases comments on and metamorphoses the ideas of its immediate predecessor. He particularly uses the generic framework of the road movie to trace the arcs of his characters: they continually bound across the highway, but their destination and what they are in search of transform with each ensuing record. Romantic teenage tramps become malcontent spouses fatuously circling the Circuit or rebels on the run from state troopers; as they grow older, a wreck on the highway forces them to confront their waning mortality before they finally settle in domestic bliss with their lonely valentine.

Westerns were a staple for most little boys who grew up in the 1950s. Springsteen's mother's bedtime story *Brave Cowboy Bill* first sparked his love of the genre, a fascination that is particularly present within his early music. The periods of 1972 and 1973 saw Springsteen recording numerous songs inspired by the western genre with the familiar iconography of blazing shoot-'em-ups, majestic and expansive plains, spur-booted cowboys with a quicksilver shot, tense town square confrontations, and gusty canyon winds that howl like coyotes. "Cowboys of the Sea" reimagines Jesse James as an underwater rider among seaweed-stitched stallions and mermaids. James appears again in "The Ballad of Jesse James," a sharp, bluesy glorification of his and Billy the Kid's courageous conquest of the Wild West. These seminal western figures also appear in films such as *The Left Handed Gun* (1958) and Howard Hughes' *The Outlaw* (1943).

"Evacuation of the West" is a lament for the cowboys of old who were ousted from Texas after the industrial revolution. Springsteen's sweeping sound mourns their former glory after their guns rust, ponies collapse, and the desperate loneliness of the dangerous western landscape kills them. He paints a vivid backdrop of a swollen, angry red sun hanging low in the sky over the bitter, dark earth. "Saga of the Architect Angel" has the soft toe-tapping rhythm of a saloon ditty. Springsteen spins an intriguing tale of a duel between the manic Brooklyn Kid and the Architect Angel. Like the rapid cuts of a Sergio Leone showdown, the music quickens with each half-step during Springsteen's recounting of the skirmish imagined with a cinematic flair: the Architect Angel stands strong and holds a staff high up in the air, his gun glistening like the sun as he draws and speedily slaughters his opponent. The song's final lines are reminiscent of Ford's *How the West Was Won* (1962). "Ballad of the Self-Loading Pistol" details a man's confession to his father of a murder and robbery he happily committed. The second verse describes a familiar western genre portrait of a sundown shoot-out in the middle of the town square, with the victim's screaming widow and enraged brothers running after Springsteen's outlaw. "Ballad of the Self-Loading Pistol" ends with an iconic western image of the outlaw riding off into the sunset, crossing the border with a rifle on his shoulder and renewed by the intoxicating pleasure of blood on his hands.

Springsteen also incorporated the western genre into his later music. "This Hard Land," an outtake from an unreleased 1982 album that later appeared on *Tracks* (1998), is a warm, spirited tale of friendship and searching for a promising future on the frontier wrapped in an affectionate Copland-esque country melody as majestic as the Great Plains.[12] *Devils & Dust* (2005) features "Black Cowboys," about a young black boy growing up on the hard New York City streets who reveres the western movies that play every day on television and loves to read books about black cowboys on the Oklahoma range. Rainey would have appreciated the early 1920s and 1930s pictures that depicted these black cowboys, such as *The Bull-Dogger* (1921), *Harlem on the Prairie* (1937), and *The Crimson Skull* (1922), before the glamorized Hollywood visions of an all-white west dominated the 1940s and 1950s. As an adult, he travels across the country to make his boyhood cowboy dreams come true. In *Working on a Dream* (2009), Springsteen evokes the Technicolor absurdity of Ennio Morricone's spaghetti western themes in his tongue-in-cheek epic "Outlaw Pete," about a baby who does a three-month jail stint and grows to be a killer and thief murdered by a bounty hunter. Previously, in 2007, Springsteen won a Grammy Award for Best Rock Instrumental Performance for his reinterpretation of Morricone's infamous *Once Upon a Time in the West* (1968) opening.

But there is one western that impacted Springsteen the most and serves as a personal touchstone: Ford's notorious *The Searchers* (1956). The musician saw a reflection of himself in the trope of the "individual traveler, the frontiersman, the man in the wilderness, the highwayman, the essential American adventurer, connected but not beholden to society" manifested in John Wayne's curmudgeonly cowboy.[13] Springsteen often compares his young adult life to the iconic final shot where Wayne, as Ethan Edwards, stands shadowed in the doorway looking into the house with his niece and her family nestled inside—a poetic, lonesome image of a reclusive desperado unable to assimilate into the quiet normalcy of domesticity. Much like the Comanche corpse he found earlier in the film, Ethan is fated to "wander forever between the winds" alone. "At the end of the film John Wayne has some realization as he reconstitutes that family that he can't join it. His inability to do that resonated with me," Springsteen told Nicholas Dawidoff of the *New York Times*.[14]

Ethan's ostracization from others resonated with Springsteen because, as a touring rock star, he "spent 20 years playing on the road with no real home life or connections except when I played at night. Once I walked off the stage I didn't know how to do it, be part of it. Too much fear. I didn't have confidence that I could be accepted in the real world outside my work."[15] For Springsteen, the idea of home filled him with "distrust and a bucket load of grief."[16] Like Ethan in *The Searchers*, he had convinced himself "that homes were for everybody else."[17] In his memoir, Springsteen imagines his life as a movie in which he plays an isolated but emancipated drifter wandering the dusty backroads of America perennially in search of adventure. Unbeholden to anyone, his heart belongs to the highway. "I lived that masterpiece for a long time," Springsteen writes.[18] He saw himself as a road movie character, the later incarnation of a cowboy like Wayne's Ethan, whose singular obsession with the guitar and touring life prevented him from forming any meaningful social and romantic relationships. He believed he was content to rove the country untethered by the burdens of domesticity for the duration of his life.

During his mid-thirties, Springsteen faced his fears and adhered to the societal conventions of family life he had long avoided by marrying Julianne Phillips, a substantial life change that was reflected in his music, particularly the western-inspired road movie narratives. The highway in "Thunder Road" that once enabled Springsteen's young greaser to live out his frontiersman fantasies became the site of a despairing midlife crisis for Billy in "Cautious Man." Written during his strained first marriage, the ballad questions the rugged individualism of Springsteen's *Born to Run* (1975) characters as the song's narrator faces the temptation to desert his new bride for the solitary comforts of the open road. Nearly twenty years after his long-standing marriage with Patti Scialfa, *Working on a Dream* champions the significance and beauty of staying rooted in one place and growing old with a partner. The romantic tramp of "Born to Run," modeled after Wayne's rover, evolves to celebrate fidelity's tough realities. *The Searchers* spoke to Springsteen's misanthropic "on the outside looking in" self-perception and can be considered one of his most enduring influences. Springsteen's auteurist songwriting in the vein of Ford—a constant reformulation of analogous themes—outlines his life's journey and private metamorphosis from lonely rock star wanderer without a map to family man with a destination. Unlike Wayne's character, however, Springsteen was able to cross that threshold into the pleasures of domesticity.

Westerns influenced much of Springsteen's early music, but it was not until he was under the tutelage of Jon Landau, a former film critic for *Rolling Stone*, that he began to seriously consume films as a muse and openly infuse a cinematic style into his writing. Landau began introducing his protégé to a variety of films, stoking the flames of his artistic inspiration while instructing him to shed the marble-mouthed flourishes of *Greetings from Asbury Park, N.J.* (1973) and *The Wild, the Innocent & the E Street Shuffle* (1973) in favor of a more sonic grandeur with romanticized lyrics that describe the expansive action as it unfolds. Landau told me that from the late 1970s on, Springsteen "was constantly looking at and thinking about film and how it could enhance the sound pictures he was trying to create" (meaning the kind of picture that the sound of the record suggests).[19] During a panel at the 2017 Tribeca Film Festival, Springsteen described the sound picture of *Born to Run*: "And then, the basic sound was widescreen! Up until then it [our sound] was like a very local form of filmmaking, but once *Born to Run* hit it was widescreen, it was something that gave you a sense of wide open spaces and a life outside of New Jersey."[20] The kind of sumptuous sound picture Springsteen creates in *Born to Run* is informed by his New Jersey milieu and 1950s road movie iconography of surly teenage greasers, drag racing, and muscle cars. "*Born to Run*? Cinematic. Cinematic. And it came from life experience of being in Asbury on a Saturday night looking at the circuit with the hot rods going round and round every Friday and Saturday night, so that life was there in front of me. But it also came from every

B-hot rod picture," Springsteen affirmed at Tribeca.²¹ The title *Born to Run* even sounds like the name of one of those hot rod B-pictures, containing the same filmic grandiosity found in the album's thrumming rock and roll. "At first I thought it was the name of a movie or something I'd seen on a car spinning around the Circuit, but I couldn't be certain. I liked the phrase because it suggested a cinematic drama I thought would work with the music I was hearing in my head," Springsteen wrote in his lyric book *Songs*.²² He incorporates the B-movie's flashy panache and panoramic thrills into his bombastic, Spectorish sound and high-octane narratives of hemi-powered drones rambling down the sprawling highways and cagey backstreets of Jersey.

Springsteen frequently borrows film titles for his albums, songs, and lyrics. Sometimes these titles have little connection with the content and iconography of the song, selected instead for their bold, pictorial allure. "All That Heaven Will Allow" from *Tunnel of Love* (1987) evokes the painterly Douglas Sirk melodrama *All That Heaven Allows* (1955), another soapy canvas of romantic relationships. Springsteen borrowed from the Wyoming western *The Wild and the Innocent* (1959), about a mountain trapper who falls for a runaway saloon girl, for his second album *The Wild, the Innocent & the E Street Shuffle*, although, as a portrait of New York's melting pot vibrancy and languid summer nights on the Jersey Shore, the latter has more of a dramatic, *West Side Story*–esque jazzy flair. The jaunty "Ramrod," about a joy ride with a blue-jeaned dolly, is also the title of a grim western noir starring Veronica Lake, where the title refers not to the ecstasies of hot rodding and sex but to the ranch foreman whom Lake's conniving vixen deceives. Robert Altman's whimsically pointed neo-noir *The Long Goodbye* (1973), starring Elliot Gould as a private investigator implicated for the murder of his best friend's wife, slightly departs from Springsteen's *Human Touch* (1992) song of the same name, which is centered on a man's difficult quest to overcome his frailties and longing to escape the drudgery of his stagnant existence.

Landau says "Point Blank" from *The River* (1980) "oozes with the feelings of a great film noir" in its shadowy, descending cyclone of sounds: the dark, trailing piano lines, crashing cymbals, and rolling organ. Springsteen's deadpan vocals accentuate this dismal tale of petty lies and imbue his monochromatic ballad with a taut cynicism in line with John Boorman's disorienting noir *Point Blank* (1967), about a double-crossed man seeking revenge on the band of gangsters who stole his money. Yaky Yosha's *Dead End Street* (1982), the first film to include Springsteen's music on its soundtrack, uses "Point Blank" to heighten the noirish qualities found in its dismal mise-en-scène of the tumbledown Israeli streets. The lead character Alice is a seventeen-year-old prostitute who mirrors Springsteen's lonesome, desperate girl on welfare who grew up fast; she, too, dreads each tomorrow and feels as if she is dying with each breath—eventually committing suicide by the film's end. Springsteen returned to the film noir genre for his full-throttle tirade "Murder Incorporated," lifted from the 1960 film of the same name that also focused on America's entrenched violence and corrupt injustices.

Springsteen and Landau searched through film critic Andrew Sarris' index *The American Cinema: Directors and Directions, 1929–1968* to name what would eventually become *Darkness on the Edge of Town* (1978). Landau was intrigued by Frank Borzage's romantic melodrama *History Is Made at Night* (1937), a title that fit the album's use of nighttime as a symbol of the only time when the malcontent protagonists find freedom from their mundane blue-collar lives and the darkness that lies within their hearts. Springsteen was drawn to Frank Capra's breezy bank drama *American Madness* (1932), a title perfectly suited for an album filled with choleric characters roaring down the interstate with demons running around their heads, lost in the dark heart of their country's broken dreams—a title that would encapsulate Springsteen's searing depiction of blue-collar America's disaffection and pain during the 1970s.

"Thunder Road" lifts from the hot rod B-movie *Thunder Road* (1958), starring Robert Mitchum as a Korean War veteran in charge of his family's secret moonshine business. Like Springsteen's roadrunners, Mitchum's Lucas is a lone wolf who "roars down the hottest highway on earth," as the tagline states, in order to evade the restrictions of authority. Director Arthur Ripley's taut, energized style, balanced with a quiet solemnity and retrospection, has the same freewheeling exuberance and simmering mystique as *Born to Run*. "It's a great noir picture, and I saw all of those at the time. So a lot of it came out of that, too," Springsteen noted at Tribeca.[23] Aside from its pulpy drive-in aesthetic of souped-up, rumbling drag cars and neon-lit turnpikes, *Born to Run* has tinges of film noir in its tenebrous depictions of New York City, particularly in the song "Meeting Across the River," which Springsteen's former manager Mike Appel likened to Jules Dassin's noir classic *Night and the City* (1950), about a small-time grifter struggling to ascend the ranks of the criminal hierarchy. We hear its mysterious noirish sound in the tentative trumpet opening and somber piano. Arthur Penn's masterpiece *Bonnie and Clyde* (1967) is a potent mixture of Springsteen's favorite genres: the road movie and film noir. "Highway 29" from *The Ghost of Tom Joad* evokes the film's splashy violence as Springsteen's pair of outlaw sweethearts tiptoe around blood-covered bodies in order to pick up the stolen money strewn about the floorboards. In the harrowing final verse, the bank robbers' attempt to hop across the country's border results in a cataclysmic car crash; they lie among the windshield's razor-sharp broken glass, the bitter wind and pungent smell of spilled gasoline whipping through the snow-covered air, a haunting image that brings to mind Penn's unrelentingly violent ending, in which the bullets rip through Bonnie and Clyde's bodies, turning them into flopping rag dolls.

As much as B-movies inform the sonic architecture of *Born to Run*—its bright, melodramatic sound and the swift, splashy vignettes of cars, sex, and rock and roll—Springsteen wanted his songs to eclipse the genre's simplicity and flamboyant clichés, and he continually rewrote them in order to avoid falling into those traps: "The initial lyrics would have been like 'bad B-picture,' where I always thought the end product was supposed to be kind of 'good B-picture,' and then imbued with a certain spiritual thing," Springsteen explains in the *Wings for Wheels: The Making of Born to Run* (2005) documentary. His songs transcend the B-picture by delving deeper into the psychological complexities and motivational forces driving his protagonists, exploring what makes them run and why. Landau says that *Born to Run* was the "height of one style of visual songwriting, ending with the masterpiece that is 'Jungleland.' You can literally 'see' every line of that the exquisite lyric. After that one, an artist could only downsize his scale because the vision couldn't get any more majestic."[24] *Born to Run* dazzles with an unparalleled celluloid vibrancy in its detailed and fanciful focus on rumbling engines, the soft, glistening summer rain beading on the arms of a barefoot girl, mist-covered amusement parks, and massive highways that stretch as far as the eye can see.

Springsteen scales down the lyrical grandiosity of *Born to Run* in *Darkness on the Edge of Town*, using hard-boiled lyrics and a stark, austere sound that evokes the film noir genre. Springsteen cites Jacques Tourneur's tale of a small-town gas station attendant with a corrupt history *Out of the Past* (1947), Ripley's tantalizing post-war melodrama *Gun Crazy* (1950), and the eminent noirs *The Postman Always Rings Twice* (1946) and *Double Indemnity* (1944) as inspirations for *Darkness*, drawn to the genre's depiction of alienated men and women navigating a bleak, hopeless, and morally corrupt world. These themes manifest throughout the album in his somber stories of factory workers going deaf from the din of their thankless jobs, a near-suicidal hot rodder gratuitously driving down Kingsley Street, or a son trying to escape the original sins of his forebears. Photographer Frank Stefanko punctuated the record's stark noir aesthetic with the album cover portrait of Springsteen standing in front of ghostly pale blinds and washed-out floral wallpaper, a living embodiment of the shabby, tumbledown environments that house his *Darkness* characters. Donned in a leather jacket and white T-shirt with a fixed, befuddled gaze, Springsteen personifies his forlorn protagonists and taps into the steely, impenetrable star image of James Dean in *Rebel Without a Cause* (1955) or Marlon Brando in *The Wild One* (1953).

On May 5, 2005, during his *Devils & Dust* solo tour stop in Oakland, California, Springsteen introduced "Racing in the Street" with a reference to Monte Hellman's road movie *Two-Lane Blacktop* (1971), which has palpable parallels to the nomadic dirge. Both center on inert souls whose hollow lives revolve around racing their hot rods. Hellman's and Springsteen's vacuous protagonists have virtually no identity outside of their all-consuming love of running their cars down the strip, an activity that defines their entire mental and emotional being. The names of Hellman's lead characters are not human but mechanical—the Driver, G.T.O, and the Mechanic—signaling how deeply their selfhood is tied to mobility. They persistently offer lengthy, tender soliloquies about the inner workings and idiosyncrasies of their beloved automobiles. Similarly, Springsteen's stirring ballad opens with the narrator's detailed gawking at his cherished 1969 Chevy shining beneath the bright 7-Eleven parking lot lights: the 396 engine, the fuelie heads, the Hurst on the floor. He and his friend Sonny built this formidable machine piece by piece with their own bare hands, endowing the narrator with a strong sense of pride and ownership. They race virtually everywhere they can, from the secluded fire roads to police-patrolled interstates, caring little for consequences when they are under the intoxicating spell of gasoline and burned rubber. In "Racing in the Street" and *Two-Lane Blacktop*, drag racing is the only thing that makes the protagonists feel truly alive: the thrum of the engine, shifting of gears, and foot ramming the gas pedal provide an invigorating thrill unmatched by any facet of ordinary life.

The races these detached figures participate in are half-baked attempts to fill their internal void with some sort of aim. The winner obtains the loser's car in the competition between the Driver and G.T.O., while in "Racing in the Street" a literal woman is at stake; after defeating the dude from Los Angeles and his Camaro, Springsteen's narrator claims her as his trophy. But in the mundane throes of his everyday life following the thrill of the race, he deserts her, opting instead for his revered automobile—his only true source of pleasure and sanctuary from the complexities of the adult world. Springsteen's rider, the Driver, and G.T.O. all refer to their true prized possessions with female pronouns, neglecting the flesh-and-blood women before them. In *Two-Lane Blacktop*, the unnamed Girl whom the highwaymen meet during their travels is excluded from the ritual of their races, their passionate enthusiasm for cars overpowering any sexual or even interpersonal relationship possible with her.

These vagabonds understand, relate to, and love cars better than people—an idea made clear in the Driver's confession that he willingly left behind a socially acceptable job and family life and in Springsteen's heart-wrenching final verse of "Racing in the Street." While the song's narrator races in the summer night's invigorating swelter, his deeply depressed wife sits alone on the porch, ruefully waiting either for him to return or to learn that he has perished in a crash. She is completely alone with her broken dreams while her husband fecklessly chases the former glories of his youth. Devin Faraci of *Birth.Movies.Death.*

compares *The Searchers'* ending, with Ethan standing in the doorway, to Hellman's finale of G.T.O thundering down the interstate until the film negative bubbles and melts away, thereby trapping him in his nomadic isolation for all eternity. Springsteen has also referenced the other Hellman films in his concert monologues, such as *Cockfighter* (1974) and the western *The Shooting* (1966), both about lonely men engulfed by their obsessions—a common theme in his work.

Pictorial detail, dramatic plots, and bold images appear throughout *Darkness on the Edge of Town*, making it one of Springsteen's most filmic albums. Landau contends that "'Darkness on the Edge of Town' has one of Bruce's deepest and most visual lyrics of all, 'The Promise' feels like a song about a movie that has already been made, and 'The Promised Land' is cinematically based from first line to last."[25] The title of "Darkness" holds the stygian intrigue of a film noir, and its lyrics evoke the genre's notorious use of voiceover narration—the cynical inner thoughts of a weatherworn character alienated by society. Springsteen crafts monochromatic images of the long, dark shadows from the trestles ridden by rambling racers that lie far beneath the stately homes in Fairview where folks with the good life reside. The psychological profundity that Landau attributes to this song lies in the middle verse, where the narrator bemoans the gnawing secret that continues to drag him down unless he sets it free. We all carry something dark and frightening inside of us—an insecurity, fear, or trauma—that we bury because we cannot face the consequences of the truth. "The Promise" has a lush, scopic sound that paints a kinetic picture of the withered Route 9 down which the narrator drives his Challenger, past the dead ends and bad scenes of the two-bit town he and his friends Billy, Johnny, and Terry occupy. The haunting, emotional intensity of Springsteen's Thunder Road wails have a cinematic flourish that recalls the flicks at the drive-in frequented by the narrator. Landau's reading holds true in "The Promised Land," from the picturesque opening of the narrator whizzing across the Waynesboro county line with the radio playing to the dusty speedway churning beneath his tires, up until the ending, when he drives into the giant cloud rising on the edge of the desert. From the dashboard we see the terrifyingly monstrous and roaring twister that threatens to engulf him. These songs are more examples of Springsteen's striking widescreen visions.

One of Springsteen's favorite movies of the 1970s was Paul Schrader's neo-noir *Taxi Driver* (1976), which operates in the same vein as *Darkness on the Edge of Town* to articulate the era's misery. The hermetic psychopath Travis Bickle lives out his twisted John Wayne fantasy as he tries to save women from the scum-lined streets of a decrepit and decaying New York City. Springsteen's solitary and purposeless racers in *Darkness* echo the troglodytic Travis and his desperate need for interpersonal connection. Like Travis, the strung-out loner of "Streets of Fire" aimlessly wanders the nighttime streets and surveys the strangers who live around him with disgust, similar to the animals Bickle despises—the "whores, skunk pussies, buggers, queens, fairies, dopers, junkies, sick, venal" who inundate his filthy metropolis like a flood pouring in from an open sewer. In his memoir *Big Man: Real Life & Tall Tales*, Springsteen's longtime saxophonist Clarence Clemons stated that Robert De Niro's infamous "You talkin' to me?" line was inspired by Springsteen's October 16, 1975, performance at the Roxy Theatre when he responded to fervent "Bruuuuuce"-ing with a cheeky "Are you talking to me?"

Schrader also wrote and directed Springsteen's other favorite 1970s film, *Blue Collar* (1978), about automobile factory workers waging war against the inflation, unemployment, and dishonesty that pervaded working-class America during that time period. In this radically volatile film, Schrader perfectly captures the lives of those suffocated by the pressures of economic oppression. *Blue Collar* is another strong influence on Springsteen's *Darkness on the Edge of Town* and his depiction of working-class despair. In the early 1980s, Schrader sent Springsteen a draft of his latest script, *Born in the U.S.A.*, about a struggling Cleveland bar band. Schrader re-christened his film *Light of Day* (1987) after Springsteen copped the name for the title song of his bestselling album. As repayment for purloining the title, Springsteen penned the film's rip-roaring finale song "Light of Day," performed by leads Michael J. Fox and Joan Jett. During his *Born in the U.S.A.* superstardom, Springsteen worked with Schrader's *Obsession* (1976) collaborator Brian DePalma—the director of some of his favorite films, including *The Untouchables* (1987) and *Scarface* (1983)—for his "Dancing in the Dark" music video.

Springsteen's grim tone poem *Nebraska* holds the kind of cinematic quality "where you get in there and you get the feel of life. Just some of the grit and some of the beauty," as he told Chet Flippo.[26] That grit is found in the title song based on Terrence Malick's part noir, part lovers-on-the-lam road movie *Badlands* (1973), a hauntingly poetic reinterpretation of Charles Starkweather and Caril Ann Fugate's killing spree across the Midwest during the 1950s. Springsteen's first description of the naïf Caril (called Holly in the film) twirling her baton on the front lawn is taken directly from Malick's dreamy slow-motion shot. Starkweather (renamed Kit) is played by Martin Sheen, who embodies the sullen allure of James Dean in *Rebel Without a Cause* with his swooping coif, jeans and white T-shirt, and dangling cigarette. Springsteen imbues the laconic sadism and chilling misanthropy of *Badlands* within the flat, dour musicality of his *Nebraska* album and its disturbed characters who maim without hesitation and believe they are better off dead. His apathetic singing style in "Nebraska" expresses Kit and Holly's nihilistic detachment from the heinous crimes they commit, a vacuous savagery that is merely the result of a vague meanness in the world.

For the songs "Used Cars" and "Mansion on the Hill," Springsteen returns to the memories of his youth. "The music is very childlike and mystical. On the record I used a glockenspiel. I think I was interested in an aural projection of the Robert Mitchum film *The Night of the Hunter*, which is kind of this horror story told from a child's perspective," Springsteen explained.[27] A reference to *The Night of the Hunter* (1955) also appears in Springsteen's "Cautious Man." Akin to Mitchum's character, Springsteen's narrator has love and fear (instead of love and hate) tattooed over his knuckles—a representation of the two disparate paths he faces. Will he succumb to his commitment anxieties and abandon his wife or see his relationship through? These nostalgic, reflective narratives in *Nebraska* also evoke Robert Mulligan's transcendent film adaptation of *To Kill a Mockingbird* (1962). Like Scout, Springsteen's adult characters confront the dark realities of their upbringing. We imagine "Used Cars" and "Mansion on the Hill" with the same Gothic formal qualities as the aforementioned films—the skewed angles from a child's vantage point, the stark and slanted shadows. Springsteen projects onto our mind's eye a kind of black-and-white Midwestern milieu in these drowsily astral songs. The dark, steel gates that surround the Babylonian mansion seem mammoth to the boy and his sister as they lie in a giant cornfield, and from their short height they can just barely make out the faces of gaping neighbors from their window as their Pa winds down Michigan Avenue in a "brand new used car," a parade that fills them with shame. For "Mansion on the Hill" in particular, Springsteen wanted to evoke the poetic surrealism of the *The Night of the Hunter* scene when the little girl runs through the woods.

During the conception of *Nebraska*, Springsteen saw John Huston's surreal adaptation of Flannery O'Connor's novel *Wise Blood* (1979). The Catholic author soon became one of his most significant literary influences. Huston's absurdist dissection of morality about a choleric fake preacher who rails against those who believe in God, an afterlife, and sin is felt in the senseless and depraved world that holds Springsteen's unhinged characters, who, correspondingly, cannot find any reason to live or reason to believe in anything.

Aside from films that influence his songs, Springsteen's diegetic characters often reference the act of watching movies as an escapist vehicle from the mundane realities of their working-class existence. They strive to emulate the stars they idolize on screen, but buying into the fantasy that cinema sells often has dangerous consequences for their well-being. The narrator of "Backstreets" and his friend (or lover) Terry imitate the swaggering ambition of their on-screen heroes. Springsteen's despondent mechanic in "The Promise" regrets following his dreams like the hot rod matinee idols he venerates on the drive-in screen. The girl in "Be True" and "Mary Lou" is so enraptured with faultless leading men that she cannot have an authentic relationship in the real world. "Fade to Black" uses the cinematic fade as a metaphor for the end of a relationship between two people who met during a matinee screening. With a voice as drab and mechanical as the camera technique he describes, Springsteen pictures the scene of this breakup with a shot of the camera panning onto the glum, empty aftermath of the couple's heated squabble before slowly pulling back to the dissolve that marks their separation. The sparkling Hollywood dreams of the real-life 1920s silent film star and dancer Camilla Horn, known for F.W. Murnau's *Faust* (1926) and Ernst Lubitsch's *Eternal Love* (1929), lose their luster in Springsteen's short 1972 folk outtake "Camilla Horn." Basking in the faded glory of the fans who once asked her to bless and caress them, Horn drowns her sorrows at the bar after realizing she will never be the next Greta Garbo like she was promised. The central thesis of these songs is that cinema often perpetuates unrealistic expectations about life, love, and ambition. Springsteen's quotidian protagonists discover that they cannot measure up to those they are enamored with up on the screen. Instead, they must face the complexities of human nature that Hollywood glosses over with shiny smiles and neatly packaged finales.

Cinema is one of Springsteen's most significant influences. Not only do many of his songs contain references to certain films or the act of watching films, but his music also evokes the mise-en-scène of the great American film genres: the hypersonic thrills of B-movies, the elliptical gloom of film noir, the pastoral grandeur of the western. I believe that Springsteen's deep relationship and emotional identification with cinema, and how that manifests within his lyrical text—the intricate depiction of his character's internal lives and worlds, his full embodiment of their emotions, the poetic situations he details, and his auteurist sensibilities—is what enables his work to function so well as soundtrack music and accounts for why nearly two hundred filmmakers have been driven to include his music in their stories. Like the best films, Springsteen's songs balance an epic scope with a captivating simplicity that refracts the inordinate pains and pleasures of quotidian American life—our euphoria and tragedy, fatalism and desire, ambition and rage, sorrow and yearning.

Hearing Springsteen in Film

As previously noted, music in cinema is divided into two categories: non-diegetic and diegetic. Diegetic music emanates from an object source within the story that the characters can hear and engage with (radio, record player, car, live musician, etc.), while non-diegetic score overlays the image, functions as an editorial comment, and does not originate within the film's world. Claudia Gorbman, author of *Unheard Melodies: Narrative Film Music*, believes film music should remain unobtrusive and "unheard," "much like [how] the editing of a film is inconspicuous…. Music should be accessible but out of sight, like the reverse side of the image."[28] This idea of non-diegetic score as more of a suturing device, something to gently bind the images together or modestly accompany the visual narrative, directly opposes the use of a soundtrack compiled from popular preexisting music that automatically demands attention in its recognizability.

Jeff Smith avers that pop/rock scores carry "associational baggage for the spectator and not only [is] this potentially distracting but these associations might also clash with those established by the narrative."[29] Anahid Kassabian calls such associations "affiliating identifications," meaning the emotional and cultural dialogue that popular music already has with an audience.[30] Classical scores have assimilating identifications with the spectator because, as orchestrations, they effortlessly blend into the background and are generally unfamiliar prior to viewing. According to Smith, the spectator's relationship with a popular song—their emotional connection to the lyrics, knowledge of its cultural history, or familiarity with the artist—disrupts their immersion into the film's diegesis. This book challenges Smith's ideals by examining how the soundtrack, particularly that of Bruce Springsteen, serves as an intrinsic component of the film text. Our affiliating identifications with Springsteen's work, star image, and personal life heighten our relationship with and understanding of the film and television show being discussed.

I study how directors consciously use Springsteen as both diegetic source music and non-diegetic score in order to establish the milieu, welcoming the associational baggage that comes with Springsteen's worldwide notoriety and storied career. The rhythms and melodies of his songs structure the temporality and form of specific film sequences. Most important, his lyrics articulate protagonists' unspoken feelings and psychological states not made explicit in the dialogue and visuals. Springsteen's inward songwriting style, often sung in the first person, is perfectly suited to this function. "You're hearing character's thoughts—what they're thinking after all the events that have shaped their situation have transpired. So I try to get that internal sound, like that feeling at night when you're in bed and staring at the ceiling, reflective in some fashion," Springsteen told Will Percy.[31] He "wanted the songs to have a kind of intimacy that took you inside yourself and then back out into the world."[32] The intimacy found in Springsteen's music mobilizes the spectator's emotional identification with the cinematic characters.

David R. Shumway argues that the use of popular music in film "has changed the relationship between music and image … unlike the classically inflected scores of yore, rock soundtracks are meant to be heard."[33] Shumway's proposal prompts the larger question: What do we gain by closely hearing and interpreting popular music soundtracks? This book specifically asks: What do we gain by hearing Bruce Springsteen's music as soundtrack? How does his music and personal history intersect with and augment the visual language, mood, and spirit of a particular film or television show? What makes his expression of their themes so compelling? How do his lyrics communicate the internal depths of characters? Why do the protagonists emotionally relate to him?

Director John Sayles, whose film *Baby It's You* (1983) is examined in the next chapter, says, "Music added to the images can reinforce, underline, counterpoint, or deny what is happening on the screen…. When it works movie music is like a natural voice, like the only sound the picture up there could possibly make."[34] This book will explore how Springsteen is unequivocally the natural voice to conduct the flow and feeling of the moving images or to channel the ideals of the particular films and television shows I have chosen to examine.

Sayles also noted in my interview with him, "Music and movies is a kind of alchemy. You think you've got the perfect song for a moment and then when you edit it together the song overpowers the moment. One of the things with Bruce or any kind of good songwriter is sometimes the song is so powerful that you forget about the movie."[35] Although Springsteen's extraordinary music is exceptionally potent, his inclusion on the soundtrack is not meant to take away from the film, but rather to reinforce and develop the movie's message and significance. This book presents the efficacious amalgamation of sound and image within the context of Springsteen's magnificent body of work. My goal is to demonstrate how Springsteen's songs are not distractions, but rather a captivating and unique intertextual device. Gorbman attests that "music, like the caption, anchors the image in meaning, throws a net around the floating signifier; assures the viewer of a safely channeled signified."[36] The use of Springsteen's music anchors the film image in a wealth of intertextual meanings that have long been unexplored.

Baby It's You

Before John Sayles directed Springsteen's music videos "Glory Days," "Born in the U.S.A.," and "I'm on Fire," he was one of the first filmmakers to include his music in a film. *Baby It's You* feels like a Springsteen song come to magnificent life in its New Jersey maximalism, early 1960s iconography, class divide narrative, and idealistic-turned-disillusioned protagonists.[1] Writer and director Sayles shot all throughout Springsteen's motherland, from Cliffside Park to Fort Lee and Hoboken (where Sayles was born) to Jersey City, Lawrenceville, and Newark. He tells the story of Jill Rosen and Albert "Sheik" Capadilupo, Jewish and Italian teenagers from opposite sides of the Trenton tracks, mediating the difficult transition from high school to college and adult life in 1966 with non-diegetic anachronistic Springsteen songs. While Sayles does include songs from the appropriate time period, he specifically chose Springsteen's work "so that it wasn't just another nostalgia soundtrack."[2] Sayles noted in an interview I conducted with him that the 1950s and 1960s songs come from within his filmic world, "whereas the Bruce songs are more like a comment on what is going on in that world" (namely, Jill and Sheik's reluctant and precarious shift into adulthood).[3]

Alex Woloch argues that *Baby It's You* consists of "a series of embedded ruptures: in the production of the film (between director and studio), in the form and genre of the film (between the first and second halves), in the plot of the film (between high school and college), and finally in the romantic rift between the two lovers that rests at the heart of the film's imagined story."[4] Woloch neglects to mention another integral rupture: between the period and Springsteen music. These fissures situate *Baby It's You* as an anti-nostalgia film, opposing others, such as *American Graffiti* (1973) and *Grease* (1978), that present the 1950s and early 1960s in a static and romanticized light. Through the magic of celluloid, *American Graffiti* immortalizes the mythical summer of 1962 and the innocence of pre–Kennedy assassination life, as the recent graduates are free to do nothing but race cars, visit the drive-in, obsess over girls, and listen to radio disc jockeys. The audience does receive a textual coda summing up their lives after the film's conclusion, including the loss of one character in Vietnam, but director George Lucas never visualizes these darker circumstances. At the end of *Grease*, which on the whole is a saccharine pastiche of the 1950s, Sandy and Danny wave to the camera as they fly away in a magical car—no telling what awaits them when they land. Unlike *Baby It's You*, these films permanently fix their teenyboppers within an ephebic temporal space before they must face adult responsibilities.

Nostalgic discourses burgeon when the present is considered the demise of an enshrined past. The loss of the Vietnam War, economic collapse, Watergate, and unemployment propelled films and television shows of the late 1970s and 1980s, such as *Happy Days* (1974–1984), *Laverne & Shirley* (1976–1983), *Diner* (1982), and *Back to the Future* (1985) to look back fondly on the era of post–World War II prosperity. The first half of *Baby It's You* shares their glossy sheen and humble pie portraiture in its familiar iconography of jukeboxes, muscle cars, diners, and *Patty Duke Show*–esque schoolgirl skirts and cashmere sweaters, but there is grittiness in the cinematography and an underlying melancholy that allows it to avoid the nostalgia genre's syrupy trappings. During the second half of the film, Sayles presents the generational shift of the late 1960s into a more psychedelic and free-spirited ethos when Jill encounters hippies and bohemian artists at Sarah Lawrence. Sayles crafts an eloquent piece about the serpentine chrysalis of adolescence by formally and temporally splitting the narrative between Jill and Sheik's high school and post-graduate experiences, a unique division that cements *Baby It's You* as one of the most authentic and vulnerable coming-of-age films ever made. *Baby It's You* opposes the nostalgia genre's monolithic and mawkish views of yesteryear by displaying how life outside the safe confines of high school does not necessarily offer happiness and satisfaction, and how the events of our teenagehood shape our lives without defining its end.

Baby It's You marked the first time that the notably independent filmmaker Sayles had creative input from a studio, and his tense collaboration with Paramount nearly resulted in the erasure of what makes the film so extraordinary and the burial of the finished product. The studio executives were not pleased with Sayles' initial screening of the film, expecting a nostalgic teen sex comedy in the vein of the popular *Porky's* (1981), *Fast Times at Ridgemont High* (1982), and *The Last American Virgin* (1982). They deemed *Baby It's You* an overly long downer and suggested that the second half in which Jill attends Sarah Lawrence and Sheik moves to Miami after high school be reworked or cut, prompting Sayles' threat to remove his name from the film and abandon the project entirely. Sayles was adamant that he would not create another nostalgia film, and his decision to move beyond high school walls and explore how Jill and Sheik's former relationship affected them in the real world was key to his vision. "As far as Amy [Robinson] and I were concerned, the only thing that made it interesting was that it did go on to college and that it wasn't just another nostalgia piece," he affirmed to Kenneth M. Chanko in *Films in Review*.[5]

The quintessence of *Baby It's You* lies in this narrative divide, which Sayles elaborates on in *American Film*:

> It follows these characters over two big hills. One is from 1966 in Trenton, New Jersey to 1967 at Sarah Lawrence, which was a huge jump in what was expected of somebody who was young. Jill, the female character, goes from a high school in which getting good grades and being straight makes her popular to a time and place where you need to be just the opposite to be accepted. The other big jump is from high school, which is the last bastion of true democracy in our society, where you have classes and eat lunch with the guy who's going to be picking up your garbage later in life, to the year after, when she goes to college and [Sheik] runs into the fact that he's going nowhere. It's about class in America, and where the divisions are. It's about how certain things are possible in high school, but when people enter the real world, they become impossible.[6]

Sayles uses the soundtrack to emphasize his class concerns and the couple's discordant relationship. The girlish, sugary pop songs of Dusty Springfield's "You Don't Have to Say You Love Me," the Supremes' "Stop! In the Name of Love," and the Dixie Cups' "Chapel of Love" match Jill's innocence, her desire for a storybook romance, and the narrow life expectations available for women at the time—namely, marriage and babies. These songs are juxtaposed against the swinging orchestrations of Frank Sinatra that Sheik loves (and the kind of outmoded music that Jill's parents listen to). *Baby It's You* asserts itself as an anti-nostalgia film by avoiding an overreliance on golden oldies to evoke the era and using Springsteen's non-diegetic music from the 1970s. New Jersey's chosen son serves as the perfect vocal conduit for the working-class loner Sheik, who dreams of something more: girls, cars, and stardom.

The chronological placement of Springsteen's music, moving from his debut *Greetings from Asbury Park, N.J.* to *The Wild, the Innocent & the E Street Shuffle* to *Born to Run* and, lastly, *Darkness on the Edge of Town*, reflects the sunder of Sayles' film. Like Sayles, Springsteen structures his work around the dissolution of his protagonists' quixotic dreams, their youthful aspirations giving way to the lugubrious realities of maturity once they leave their corybantic nights of bar hopping, flirting, and racing behind for the working life. The freewheeling, sprightly joy of Springsteen's early music accompanies Jill and Sheik's high school hijinks while the darkness that flecks the Spectorish bombast of *Born to Run* presages the false hopes, emotional turmoil, and failed dreams that constitute the film's latter half. After *Born to Run*, Springsteen says, "I left behind my adolescent definitions of love and freedom—it was the dividing line, from here on in it was going to be complicated"; these conflicts also appear in the album's sequel, *Darkness on the Edge of Town*, where he found his "adult voice."[7] As Springsteen notes in his memoir *Born to Run*, with *Darkness* he "was on new ground and searching for a tone somewhere between *Born to Run*'s spiritual hopefulness and seventies cynicism…. I wanted my characters to feel older, weathered, wiser, but not beaten. Their sense of daily struggle increased; hope became a lot harder to come by…. I steered away from escapism and placed my people in a community under siege."[8] Sayles uses the melancholic *Darkness* to buoy Sheik and Jill's struggle with the real world's harsh truths as they grow older. Sheik finally grasps that he will not become the next Frank Sinatra; Jill is no longer the perfectionistic, prim theater star she once was; and they will not end up together. *Baby It's You* and the chronological Springsteen soundtrack present mirror images of one another: both move from the nostalgic visions of teenagehood to the adult complexities of class, work, and love.

What attracted Sayles to Springsteen's music was its balance between hope and doomed romanticism while avoiding bubblegum sentimentality, thereby appealing to his narrative of kids with very different futures whose relationship was not heading toward the typical happy ending of a nostalgia film. Sayles noted in my interview with him:

> High school is where you have these kind of *Romeo and Juliet* romances that the world just kind of shakes its head and says, "Well that's totally inappropriate, and that's not going to last," and usually it doesn't, but because teenage romance is really intense at the time, I felt like Bruce really had a handle on the hopes of kids. Even if they live in a shitty neighborhood and they never get to enter the door of the mansion on the hill, they have the same hopes and dreams and romantic fantasies and stuff like that. Even though they usually didn't get them, there's something heroic about their efforts to get them despite knowing how the world works.[9]

There is a sense of uplift even in the most despairing of Springsteen's lyrics, and this resilience motivates his musical bildungsromans. Springsteen's vibrant and dramatic songs underscore Jill and Sheik's passionate affair as it goes from infatuation to disenchantment, a love that shapes their self-knowledge and acceptance that life is not a fairy tale. The chronological placement of the Springsteen soundtrack is an essential intertext that aids our understanding of the film as an antithesis to the nostalgia genre. Midway through *Baby It's You*, Sayles pans across a slogan on the Lower Trenton Bridge that reads, "Trenton Makes. The World Takes," a phrase that encompasses the marrow of Sayles' narrative. Sayles and Springsteen explore what happens when teenagers forged on the hangdog streets of Jersey enter the disappointing world of adulthood that quenches their romantic ambitions. *Baby It's You* has all the beauty and grit of the best Springsteen songs, drawing on the prevailing tenets of his canon in Sheik's working-class frustration, the couple's yearning to break free from their current circumstances and make their dreams come true, the crushing disappointment when those attempts fail, their continued perseverance and belief that it is still possible, and their final acceptance of change with grace.

From Hot Rods to Heartbreak

Springsteen's early albums *Greetings from Asbury Park, N.J.* and *The Wild, the Innocent & the E Street Shuffle* largely consist of "party songs, bar band music, and solid rock with classic anti-authoritarian themes that aren't dark and introspective. It is the voice of adolescents avoiding and rebelling from authority so that they can go out and have some fun—a truly 1950s-1960s theme," and Sayles reflects this tone in the first half of his film.[10] Springsteen's zesty tales of innocents searching for freedom from the confines of society and stringent rules of the adult world perfectly accompany Jill and Sheik's teenage escapades of hot rod racing, visiting nighttime Jersey hotspots, and skipping school. Despised by his teachers, kicked out of his former school Saint Anthony's (a mysterious incident that tantalizes Jill and her giggly friends) and forced to attend an entirely new school during his senior year, the swaggering Italian American greaser Sheik fits within the Springsteenian paradigm of rebellious outsider. He purposefully segregates himself from his peers and lower-class status by dressing in sophisticated suits, slicking his hair back, and carrying himself in a dignified manner—personifying the big band–era refinery of his idol Frank Sinatra. Sayles signifies Sheik's isolation in the shots of him standing alone in the hallway after the bell rings or walking in the opposite direction from the rest of his classmates entering the building for first period.

"It's Hard to Be a Saint in the City" from *Greetings* introduces the spectator to Sheik and self-referentially asserts his character traits. The song's punchy pace motivates the visual grammar of the sequence, as Sayles frequently cuts to a new shot on the downbeat. The tentative guitar strumming underscores the opening shot of Sheik gazing into his reflection through the glass of the cafeteria doors while coiffing his pompadoured hair, "slicked sweet" to perfection. Satisfied with his appearance, Sheik opens the door directly as the piano melody unfurls in a jubilant spiral. As if they can hear the sprightly music accompanying the mysterious new kid's sudden entrance, the other students questionably glance up at the sharply dressed Sheik, much like the cripples and sisters in Springsteen's song who marvel, "Don't that man look pretty?" With the same leather skin and "diamond hard look of a cobra" as Springsteen's street-cool kid, Sheik surveys the room in search of Jill with a steely side-to-side glance. Sayles cuts to a wider shot of Sheik strutting down the cafeteria immediately after Springsteen's first line and the ensuing piano flourish. Springsteen's jaunty rhythm and quickened acoustic guitar tempo propel Sayles' leftward pan that follows Sheik's walk across the cafeteria. Like a flashy supernova, Sheik emerges from behind a structural beam in the next close-up shot, a determined man on a mission.

This sequence establishes Sheik as a Springsteenian character: a young, dark, loner in search of his ideal car and girl, a poser mimicking the secure masculinity of Hollywood heroes like Marlon Brando and James Dean, the notorious lothario Casanova, or (in Sheik's case) Sinatra. Sheik admires Sinatra's smart taste in the "best clothes, best cars, best women" and for being a man who knows what he wants and gets it. He specifically turns to Sinatra's slick, old-fashioned style and quintessentially New Jersey manhood in order to rise above his meager background; he believes that looking and behaving like someone not blue-collar will bring him good fortune. Springsteen's renegade energy and exuberant rhythm in "Hard to Be a Saint" drive Sheik's monarchical preening; he walks around as if he owns the place, suavely stealing a freshman's French fry and pointing at someone off screen in acknowledgment. Akin to Springsteen's wannabe saint, Sheik beams with a self-assured bravado, takes pride in his appearance, and struts like a peacock throughout the aisles of the cafeteria instead of the hard New York City streets. When the top of the second verse fades out at the end of this sequence, Sheik spots Jill alone at a table, presumptuously sits beside her, and asks her out on a date.

"The E Street Shuffle" from *The Wild, the Innocent & the E Street Shuffle* accompanies the couple's awkward first date, where the seeds of the class differences that will eventually sever them are laid out. Jill waits apprehensively beneath a streetlamp next to a storefront, uncomfortably ogled by a group of black men, two older white gentlemen, and a man in a car who winks at her, assuming she is a street walker. She feels out of place on Sheik's tumbledown turf. Sheik eventually saunters up in a chic tan wool coat, walking because, unlike Jill, he cannot afford a car. "You look really pretty," he says, and the compliment ushers in the funky introduction of horns, bass, and chicken-scratch guitar. The 1970s-style groove of the cornet and baritone saxophone grows louder after Sheik offers his hand to Jill; then Sayles cuts to an exterior wide shot of Joey D's—a two-bit joint not unlike Easy Joe's in the song or others that Springsteen frequented along the Jersey Shore. The handsome Sheik is the schoolboy pulling out all the stops this night, and the song's hearty vitality expresses his desire to impress Jill and assimilate her into his environment. Sayles' sequence consists of several point-of-view shots of Jill hesitantly appraising the dive bar filled with rugged, scrubby Springsteenian characters such as teenagers making out, blue-collar workers drinking beers, and members of the mafia. These are the classic tramps and E Street brats of Springsteen's songs—kids with nicknames like Power, Little Angel, and Weak Knees Willie. Sayles' character Rat shares the same name as the protagonist in "Jungleland," and his girlfriend Joanne, with her long earrings, heavy eyeshadow, teased bouffant hair, pale lipstick, and leather jacket, is the kind of female greaser Springsteen encountered during his adolescence. The hip, wild vibes of "The E Street Shuffle" embody the bar's celebratory atmosphere and Jill's sense of awed fascination with this enigmatic space far removed from her own prudish world. "Unchained Melody" by the Righteous Brothers diegetically drowns out Springsteen's bop after Joanne selects it from the jukebox.

Jill and Sheik fit the rah-rah and greaser social dichotomy of the late 1950s and early 1960s that Springsteen experienced in his youth and discusses in his memoir. Sheik is reminiscent of the greasers who sashayed through the halls of Springsteen's Freehold High School with their pristine suits, precise grooming, and perfect coal-black pompadours. There was one in particular, Tony, who was similarly "attired impeccably in a three-quarter-length black waistcoat, with an Italian sex god's face out of every good little cheerleader's wet dream. He wore it like a king."[11] Springsteen encountered these "sharkskin-suit-wearing, see-through-nylon-socking-clinging-beat-your-ass-with-an-Italian-shoe, pompadoured, preening, take-more-time-to-get-ready-for-school-in-the-morning-than-my-auntie-Jane, fight-you-at-the-drop-of-a-hat, Italian-descended, don't-give-a-fuck-about-you" figures throughout his schooldays and at the teenybopper clubs, pizza joints, and beaches where he performed gigs all across New Jersey.[12]

Greasers like Sheik, according to Springsteen, "were the kids destined to live the decent hardworking lives of their parents ... the future farmers, homemakers and baby makers, if they could scoot through these few years of wild pounding hormones without getting hurt or hurting someone else. If they could keep out of jail for this short stretch, most would go on to be the spine of American society—fixing the cars, working the factories, growing the food and fighting the wars."[13] They were rebellious loners who lived hard and fast because they had nothing to lose. This lack of a promising future fuels Sheik's continual defiance of his teachers' rules, reckless driving, and petty crimes. Teachers worry that Sheik is a bad influence on Jill—especially her drama director, who warns her not to betray her talent "for the sake of a few careless adventures."

Sheik's shabby home life reflects Jill's remark that he looks like he should be "selling used cars or stealing them." He occupies cramped, tacky quarters with a doting mother and hectoring father constantly bickering over the din of the television among the plastic-covered furniture and kitschy decorations. By contrast, Jill is solidly middle class and lives in a comfortable, stately home that doubles as an office for her doctor father. She embodies the rah-rahs whom Springsteen encountered during his performances on the beaches near Jersey's Sea Bright, Middletown, and Rumson areas—prestigious and exclusive neighborhoods with palatial estates and private beach clubs. Springsteen describes rah-rahs as the "jock, madras-wearing, cheerleading, college-bound, slightly upscale teen contingent who were the homecoming kings and queens and who lorded it over most local high schools. I'm sure they continue to do so today as 'preps' or whatever their latest nom de guerre is"—those who had money and did not let you forget it.[14] Jill's parents are affluent enough to fully fund her Ivy League education and allow her to pursue her theatrical aspirations without financial worries. Jill and Sheik's class identities affect their motivation to achieve in school. Since Sheik is resigned to the lower class and knows that he cannot afford college, he does not pursue education or extracurriculars with vigor, whereas Jill is thrilled to attend college and gain a deeper knowledge of drama and the other subjects she loves. The film's poster, a re-creation of Jill and Sheik's yearbook photos listing their extracurriculars, emphasizes their differences in both enthusiasm and opportunity: Jill is a high achiever with the credits of president of the Drama Club, cheerleading captain, Debate Team, chief editor, National Honor Society, and Glee Club, while Sheik is only the woodshop monitor.

The stark class divide between Jill and Sheik is easily forgotten during a pleasant interlude that takes place in the tranquil seaside locale of Asbury Park, a key environment in Springsteen's personal and musical geography. Sheik encourages Jill to skip school, and the two of them travel down the pine-laden New Jersey highways to the destination seen on a colorful billboard promising rides, shell games, pinball, and prizes at the Palace Amusements. The use of "Stand by Me," with its lush strings, wistful beat, and Ben E. King's velvety vocals, lends the montage a sense of romantic longing. They drive along the sunny but deserted boardwalk before parking and walking past the fortune teller Madame Marie and Convention Hall—other important icons in Springsteen's lexicon—with their reflections bouncing off the Kohr's ice cream window. Sayles captures the dazzling blue sky, billowing surf, vivid sea-foam green funhouse, and giant Ferris Wheel in crisp, clear shots with a painterly precision that endows the sequence with nostalgic lyricism.

After they cross the glistening beach that Sayles frames in a gorgeous wide, deep-focus shot, the director shows Jill and Sheik facing one another at a cinderblock window with the whirling ocean behind them like the canvas of a gorgeous landscape painting. Jill worries that Sheik will be kicked out of school, but he doesn't care. She also frets about his lofty artistic dreams, reminding him that "nobody sings like Sinatra." "You think Frank wants to hang around somebody who's copying his style?" he retorts (an ironic defense because he

Jill (Rosanna Arquette) and Sheik (Vincent Spano) walk along the Asbury Park boardwalk (www.photofestnyc.com).

eventually obtains a job as a dishwasher lip-syncing Ol' Blue Eyes' songs). Their rendezvous ends at the Roadside Diner in the town of Wall, where Springsteen filmed his "Long Walk Home" music video. Like Springsteen himself, diners are ubiquitously New Jersey icons. The couple dances to Sinatra's warm "Strangers in the Night" on the jukebox in the middle of the tile floor beside the booths and counters before Sayles cuts to an exterior shot of the tiny diner shaped like a trailer home, with their silhouettes in the window moving under the bright fluorescent lights that slice through the evening's darkness. This abrupt transition cuts off the romantic music for the sounds of traffic rushing by, symbolizing the harsh reality that awaits Jill and Sheik in the real world.

Amusement parks are fantastical spaces of harmony and joy where men, women, and children of all races and class standings can savor thrilling pleasures. For one afternoon, Asbury Park enables Jill and Sheik to ignore the boundaries of class and happily coexist away from the regimentation and judgment of their teachers, classmates, and parents. Yet the wintry haze that grips the empty boardwalk and the high school sweethearts' fretful conversation about the future endows this seemingly utopian sequence with a subtle melancholy—perfectly capturing their impossible but ineffable love.[15] Their jaunt reflects Springsteen's quixotic valentine to the shore "4th of July, Asbury Park (Sandy)." With a piano that sounds like the fireworks that sparkle in the night sky, accompanied by a carnivalesque accordion and a mournful vibrato, Springsteen bids farewell to his boardwalk life and the titular Sandy whom he promises to love forever even though he will never see her again. Springsteen explains, "I used the boardwalk and the closing down of the town as a metaphor for the end of a summer romance and the changes I was experiencing in my own life"[16]—a conceit that readily relates to the imminent demise of Jill and Sheik's relationship as the end of school approaches. Some of the Asbury locales in the romantic ballad—dusty arcades, the beach, the Casino, the pier, the boardwalk, the Circuit, and Madame Marie—appear in Sayles' film. *Baby It's You* also uses the Asbury Park boardwalk as a symbol for one last goodbye to youth and the end of a romantic relationship. The Asbury Park sequence is sweet and tender, but there is an underlying sadness, as this excursion is one final moment of pure delight before the graduation that looms around the corner tears Jill and Sheik apart.

"She's the One" from *Born to Run* marks Sayles' segue into the darker latter half of the film, moving from the disappointing end of Jill and Sheik's high school experience and relationship into their even more dispiriting adult life. Most of *Born to Run* is a pastiche of Springsteen's childhood musical influences from the 1950s—Elvis Presley's seductive croons, Phil Spector's crystalline sound, Roy Orbison's operatic romance—that matches the time period of *Baby It's You*. Springsteen manifests this milieu on the album's cover image by donning an Elvis fan club pin and *Rebel Without a Cause*-esque greaser jacket. The album once again focuses on the rebellion and revelry of teenagers, but it is not as overtly joyous as the majority of *Greetings from Asbury Park, N.J.* or *The Wild, the Innocent & the E Street Shuffle*. As in Sayles' film, in *Born to Run* Springsteen explores the dichotomy between what is flesh—our meager reality—and fantasy—the dreams of youth we fruitlessly chase. The record's duality is perfectly suited for Sayles' gloomy prom night sequence, which precipitates the film's thematic and temporal shift.

There is a tension between the romantic lyrics of "She's the One" and the darkness that infuses the entirety of *Born to Run*. In spite of the record's unabashed starry-eyed visions of wanderlust and finding a love that's real, there is a sense of doomed romanticism that runs through it, as Sayles says.[17] Springsteen moves from the amusements of the Jersey Shore and the wonder of the open road to the oppressive nine-to-five grind in "Night," with a boss man who endlessly gives him hell, and then down into the gritty and dangerous gutters of New York City in "Meeting Across the River," where hoods prepare to do a job for their mafia connection. A rampant unease defines the latter song as the narrator nervously stuffs a gun in his friend Eddie's pocket and reminds him that this dicey task is their last chance to prove that they are worthy allies. In Springsteen's soaring chef d'oveure "Jungleland," which closes the album, police officers chase (and eventually gun down) the gang member Rat. The surrounding city dwellers ignore the wailing ambulance that carries his broken body from Harlem, a tenebrous scene that reflects Sheik and Rat's criminal escapades on prom night during the "She's the One" sequence.

Prom night is typically presented in the nostalgia genre as the most pivotal evening of a teenager's life and often serves as the climax of the film, but Sayles subverts the genre by placing this event midway through the film and separating his couple after Sheik gets in trouble at school and is banned from attending prom. Instead, Springsteen's love song propels a rather dismal chain of events in which Sheik must flee Trenton in order to avoid arrest and Jill's friend attempts suicide. *Born to Run*'s alchemy of somber and romanticized emotions fuels the "She's the One" sequence in *Baby It's You*.

The sequence opens with a close-up shot of Rat fittingly wearing a cartoon rat mask; he stands in the middle of a tuxedo shop with his back toward the camera. Sayles pans right, following Rat's head turn, to Sheik in a wolf mask rummaging through the cash register, a smooth movement buoyed by David Sancious' swirling piano. Between Rat and Sheik stands a male mannequin wearing a tuxedo with a corsage and a sign in the distant window that reads "Prom Special"—glaring reminders of what Sheik has been denied on this night. Springsteen's passionate portrait of an elusive woman made of soft French cream expresses

Sheik's own enraptured visions of Jill, a refined overachiever who is just as unattainable as Springsteen's angel. "She's the One" emerges from Sheik's internal pain as he is barred from being with Jill on this critical night.

The store owner flicks on the bright fluorescent lights, and the gangly pair turn, point their guns at him, and quickly flee to the Ratmobile parked outside—a massive black automobile with painted flames on the side like Springsteen's own 1957 Chevy Bel Air.[18] Sayles increases the song's volume to match Sheik and Rat's adrenaline while they make their escape. Their departure opens with the camera fixed on the car's hood, looking into the front window at the harried boys and the nighttime Trenton landscape rushing past them. Sayles then cuts to Jill driving her rambunctious and inebriated friends to Joey D's, their carousing covering Springsteen's husky vocals. Not only is Jill irritated by their behavior, but she is also upset at having to attend prom with someone other than her boyfriend. A cop car rushes past her with its siren wailing, likely on the way to pursue Sheik.

Springsteen's deep-throated "Hey!" and quick patter of drums cues the next cut, where the bopping Bo Diddley beat kicks in and pulls the Ratmobile around a corner into the frame of the dark city streets, with the crash of drums and whirling piano bringing the car chase to explosive life. The song's deep, driving blues, thrumming percussion, and twinkling piano fuel the exhilarating rush of the renegades' chaotic getaway; it also adds a manic energy to the Ratmobile's crash into a fence, followed by the boys scuttling away from the cops who have caught up with them. Sayles' "She's the One" sequence brings to mind the urban ballet "Jungleland" at the end of Springsteen's *Born to Run* album in its familiar iconography of fog spliced by halogen lights, blood and glass, dark streets, chain-link fences, wailing cherry tops, and a roadster's screeching tires. Only Sheik is lucky enough to elude the cops and run off into the night. But Springsteen continues to taunt him until the song's

The suave Sheik (Vincent Spano) inside the prized hot rod The Ratmobile borrowed from his friend Rat (www.photofestnyc.com).

slow fadeout, promising that Sheik will never be able to shake Jill's hold on him no matter how far he runs.

The lovestruck narrator of "She's the One" idolizes the mystifying unnamed girl with shining eyes like the midnight sun—she is so enchanting that only an anomaly can describe her. Her kiss, love, and tenderness have the awe-inspiring ability to fill his languorous summer nights and, most important, rescue him from the world's bitterness. Sheik similarly views Jill as a beautiful beacon of hope that keeps the dismal realities of his dead-end job and lost dreams at bay. Springsteen's narrator is absolutely enthralled by this spellbinding long-haired beauty, and his wish that "she'd just leave me alone" is also Sheik's lament. Sheik engages in this criminal activity to try to forget about Jill and the night he is missing out on, but still she haunts him like a specter. This line also prefigures the hold Jill has on him long after they graduate, symbolized by the yearbook photographs of her that decorate his ramshackle Miami apartment. Worn down by the grind of his restaurant job and the frustrated realization that he will not achieve stardom, Sheik nostalgically believes that Jill is the only one who can bring him happiness and the same contentment and self-assurance he once had in high school. However, in the same way that the song's narrator is intimidated by the nameless girl's immaculate perfection and devilish imperceptibility, Sheik fears that Jill is far too out of his league and that their class divide will always keep them apart.

After successfully evading the cops, Sheik enters a train station and purchases a ticket for Miami, abruptly leaving before graduation and without saying goodbye to Jill. This action initiates the midway fade to black that codes *Baby It's You* as part of the anti-nostalgia genre. Sayles then fades in to a shot of Jill walking with her parents on move-in day at Sarah Lawrence, wearing a crisp white skirt and suit jacket with her hair pulled up in a refined twist. From the first sight of a boy walking down the hall with barely a towel on, it becomes immediately clear that college is vastly different from her sheltered, prissy life in Trenton; Jill has never been in such close proximity to a man in such an exposed state of undress. When Jill performs an excerpt from her high school play *The Time of Your Life* by William Saroyan (an ironic title that points toward Sheik's eventual romanticization of their high school past and Jill's secret longing for the comfortable familiarity of her Trenton life after experiencing the confusion of college) during theater class, her teacher condescendingly asks whether she was in the dramatics club. "I was president," Jill proudly replies. He encourages her to forget everything she learned in high school and start over, rejecting the more affected histrionics of her high school training for his raw, emotionally vulnerable, and experimental teachings. Utterly desperate to adjust to the rituals and mores of her new social life, Jill gradually begins to change by wearing jeans and fancy fur coats and smoking cigarettes in order to fit in with her new friends. Her roles as a rich daddy's girl and Little Miss Perfect, which made her so popular in high school, do not help her in college.

During a double date with Ivy League boys, Jill gets wildly drunk for the first time, laughing like a hyena when she relays a manic monologue about the Ratmobile and dating Frank Sinatra (aka Sheik) before vomiting profusely. Depressed and hungover in the hallway, she decides to call Sheik, someone from her old life whom she does not have to perform for and who understands who she truly is. "I've been sort of bummed out. It's different here.... I don't know how you're supposed to act," she confesses. Sheik, however, basks in his Floridian happiness; he tells Jill that he is performing his act and encourages her to visit him. After making her way to Miami during one of her school breaks, Jill sees that Sheik's routine is nothing but lip-syncing Frank Sinatra songs one night a week to sad, lonely old people in a gaudy restaurant where he also moonlights as a dishwasher. When Sheik attempts to impress Jill over fine dining, she notices that he still clings to a wide-eyed, innocent belief that he will eventually achieve fame. "I think back on Trenton sometimes, it's like years I spent in prison," he spits out, a line that recalls Springsteen's infamous "Born to Run" lyric about teens springing from New Jersey's industrial, domineering cages onto Highway 9. For Sheik, Florida embodies everything he has ever hoped for and is far removed from the draconian shackles of his former life.

The trip culminates in Jill and Sheik finally sleeping together in an achingly tender scene, their smoothly taut tan bodies melting into one another, coolly lit against the night sky—a years-long sexual tension concluding at last in a sweet, fervent release. After their long-anticipated coitus, Jill gazes despondently outside Sheik's window at the silhouette of a palm tree swaying in the breeze and the light from a Technicolor blue and pink neon sign and bright yellow headlights of cars rushing by, cutting through the venetian blinds to illuminate her tears. In this moment, Jill realizes that their romance is best left in high school. Now that she knows what it is like to make love to Sheik, there is nothing tying her to him but the empty vestiges of a shared past. She is ready to move on and into her new life.

When Sheik drops Jill off at the airport the next morning, he cannot believe that she is actually going to finish college and subtly entreats her to stay in Miami with him. Jill hurries the conversation along, wanting to sever ties with him as quickly and kindly as possible. She hastily promises to write in a flat, artificial voice. Sayles frames the former couple from the perspective of their reflections in the window to signal their disconnection and then cuts to a completely transformed, curly-haired Jill in hippie garb smoking pot with her friends. Abandoning her former rah-rah identity, Jill performs these disparate roles of beatnik, debauchee, flower child, and New Jersey turncoat like the great actress she aspires to be.[19] The grungy sounds of Velvet Underground play in the background to signal Jill's transformation. She uses Sheik as a scapegoat to ditch her past life, calling him a "fucking loser" who was obsessed with her every move, downplaying the authenticity of their former love for one another and turning someone she truly cared about into a quirky anecdote.

Jill's friends in the pot circle groan when she tells the story of Sheik's fake kidnapping for the umpteenth time. That petrifying altercation occurred shortly after they began dating. As portrayed in the first part of the movie, Sheik decides to watch Jill at one of her rehearsals. Embarrassed after he witnesses her fumble and receive directorial critiques, Jill begs him not to return, a request that escalates into a larger argument about how mismatched they are. "I don't want you to wait for me after school. I don't want you driving by my house at night. I don't want you to call me. I've had nothing but trouble ever since I met you!" she shouts. To Sheik, this last remark indicates that the chasm between their classes is too great for Jill to handle. "What do you think, you're too fucking good for me?" Sheik furiously bellows while throwing her books to the ground. He taunts the posh Jill when she walks away in a huff: "Turn your little chin up in the air. Go home to daddy!"

After failing to apologize to her at school, Sheik grabs Jill and her friend walking down a storefront block and throws them into a shiny black roadster. "You're gonna end up in jail! And when they let you out, they're gonna give you a job picking up garbage!" Jill screeches after Sheik declares that they have just been kidnapped. Rat then hands Sheik a gun and waves it in the girls' faces before humbly confessing that they borrowed the car from Lester at the bowling alley and have to return it by midnight (a fact that Jill particularly finds amusing in hindsight when she repeatedly relates the story to anyone who will listen). After the initial terror of the situation dissipates, Jill forgives Sheik and kisses him in the backseat.

Aside from turning this experience into an anecdote she can share at parties, hangouts, or virtually any nerve-wracking social situation at college, Jill also uses the tale for a cathartic acting exercise, tearfully relating how Sheik was such an asshole to make her fear for her life. But she candidly admits that there was a tinge of excitement beneath her terror. Jill constantly tells this yarn because it is the only zany and thrilling occurrence in her formerly priggish life.

"We're not in high school anymore"

Eventually Sheik's blissful Miami fantasies give way to harsh reality when he becomes painfully aware that he will never escape his blue-collar roots, despite the American Dream's promise that hard work will earn him a better living than what his parents have. This shift in Sheik's outlook mirrors the experience of Springsteen's protagonists in *Darkness on the Edge of Town*, the partying teens wearied by the working-class life and their inexorable personal issues. Sayles appropriately uses a *Darkness* song to accompany the dissolution of Sheik's romantic dreams, his sobering realization that he is nothing but a dishwasher and a pale imitation of his idol in a faux fancy restaurant for retirees. Although he and Jill have not been out of school long, they are already confronting the glaring differences between their new and old lives and have lost their innocence from the first half of the film, voiced by Springsteen's earlier albums. The furious "Adam Raised a Cain" accompanies Sheik's regretful comprehension that not only has he turned into a version of his father—his greatest fear—but Jill has also exceeded his grasp.

"Adam Raised a Cain" is Springsteen's volcanic censure of father/son relationships inspired by his own contested entanglement with his father. Douglas Springsteen was both his son's hero and his greatest foe—a taciturn, volatile despot whom young Springsteen yearned to emulate and please, only to be constantly met with cruel silence, verbal abuse, and outright disdain. During his igneous stage monologues, often before "Adam Raised a Cain" or a raging cover of the Animals' "It's My Life," Springsteen recalled his father stewing in the dark kitchen while nursing a beer, beaten down by the Freehold blue-collar grind and his psychological demons. In these tales, Springsteen would often try to creep stealthily by in order to avoid his father's critical, hot-blooded tirades against everything he hated about his son: his fucking guitar, his hair, his friends. The acrimonious pair would often erupt into tempestuous screaming matches, forcing Springsteen's mother Adele to intercede.

Our first and only glimpse of Sheik's father occurs early in the film, when he sits sternly on the couch drinking and hypnotically staring at the television, which plays a violent program with resounding gunshots. The couch in Sheik's stifling household functions as the Springsteen kitchen table: an epicenter for fathers to brood about their broken lives and holler at their sons, the eye of the storm brewed by their quiet vehemence and bitterness. Mr. Capadilupo's sofa occupies the space between the two doorways that respectively hold Sheik and his mother, symbolically positioning him as the locus of the household so that his wife and son must constantly orbit around his turbulent hostility. After Sheik puts on a particularly spiffy suit that his mother has carefully ironed for his date with Jill, his father threatens to rip his lungs out if it was purchased with money earned through mafia connections. Sheik insults his father's meager profession and chides that he would never be able to afford this suit. "One of these days, Mr. Big Shot, you're gonna find yourself flat on your ass, spread out on the sidewalk," Mr. Capadilupo retorts. Although Sheik's family life and paternal relationship seethes with a quieter acrimony, both he and Springsteen occupy oppressive homes that are like a minefield, where each step they make could awaken the simmering vitriol of their rancorous father figures. "Long as I don't end up like you," Sheik acidly retorts to his father before leaving, a wish that he does not end up fulfilling.

Springsteen's sizzling rocker about an internecine paternal war articulates Sheik's fear that by sharing his father's blood, he is bound to his same miserable working-class fate. He loathes the domineering chains of his lineage, believing that his low-class family weighs him down and prevents him from transcending his social echelon and being the kind of respected, urbane individual he longs to be. Like Cain, he was born into his fate—the fate of being nobody. Sheik's discovery that the restaurant has replaced him with a real singer, someone who possesses the tangible talent he does not have, ignites his fury and cues "Adam Raised a Cain" on the soundtrack. Without this creative outlet and small taste of his biggest dream, he is nothing but a scanty dishwasher—a position no loftier than that of his garbageman father.

The "Adam Raised a Cain" sequence opens with Sheik smashing plates on the ground and kicking them aside to the sound of Springsteen's furious guitar licks. This is the humiliated Sheik's dramatic way of quitting and thus abandoning his dreams of becoming the next Sinatra. Sayles focuses on Sheik's shoes in a backward tracking shot as he walks out of the kitchen, his coursing vexation only communicated by the fierceness of his gait. The kitchen workers angrily curse in their native tongue after he storms out of the frame. Springsteen's razor-sharp, piercing guitar conducts Sheik's frantic return to his apartment to collect money and clothes. After ripping down his posters of Jill, he goes outside and steals a car so he can travel to Sarah Lawrence and see her again. The camera zooms out on Sheik speeding the convertible down the street and then cuts to a profile shot of him cruising along the coast with the wind whipping his hair before panning out onto the dashboard, where the highway stretches out before him—all very Springsteenian images of mobility and road travel.

The song's forceful drums and bass-heavy beat, paired with Springsteen's deep, gravelly intonation, propel the montage of Sheik crossing state lines, growing wearier with each mile, making his way through Georgia and up north toward New York. He stops his focused journey to change a tire, matching Springsteen's exact drumbeats in short and quick cuts that epitomize his anxiousness to reach Jill. Another montage follows where Sheik pays a toll, turns the headlights on, and changes lanes in the middle of the night. Sayles notes that he used the lashing percussion of "Adam Raised a Cain" as a way to "keep [Sheik's] anger going through the whole sequence and have that feeling of 'I'm going to get there.'"[20] In other words, Springsteen's dynamic sounds and inflamed emotions motivate the sequence in a forward motion, inducing Sheik's movement closer and closer to Jill. The song's rasping furor, combined with the kineticism of Sayles' road montages, conveys the cyclone of feelings roiling through Sheik: the disappointment that he is turning into his father and his crippling fear of the future.

These Springsteenian images of mobility encapsulate the masculinist ideals of Springsteen's road songs, where women and automobiles are powerful objects that deliver men from their dismal working-class conditions. The car provides the literal vehicle for Sheik's means of escape from Miami's sunny sorrow. Like the majority of Springsteen's characters, Sheik's journey is made alone; all that is missing is the girl in the passenger seat. He also objectifies Jill as someone with the talismanic ability to facilitate his happiness and self-actualization. Sheik undertakes this voyage to Jill because she is a nostalgic icon of his halcyon past, a time when he still had his show business ambitions and was free to race cars, chase girls, and roister around town. In other words, Jill represents the past that he is now desperately determined to get back. He naively believes she is the only unvarying thing in his protean world. If only he can reach her and be with her again, then everything will be as good as it used to be.

Sayles interrupts "Adam Raised a Cain" with a short scene of Jill on her hallway payphone receiving the news that her date will not be able to attend the upcoming dance with her. "It's not like the senior prom or anything," she dismisses, referencing the significant teen ritual that so deeply disappointed her.

The cacophony of keening guitars and choir of anguished moans in the third verse accompanies Sheik's bleary-eyed driving through the familiar industrial fortresses of northern New Jersey. The Statue of Liberty rises on the distant horizon of the cotton candy-colored sunrise, beckoning Sheik toward Jill. Springsteen's discordant agony increases as Sheik nears his breaking point, reaching a fever pitch when Sheik finally arrives at Sarah Lawrence. The pace of "Adam Raised a Cain" quickens when Sheik aimlessly wanders the cafeteria in search of Jill. Springsteen's fiery lyrics feel as if they are exploding out of Sheik. The gruff yowls and choleric repetition of the song's title capture Sheik's outrage as he ransacks Jill's room, the sight of her birth control especially upsetting him. These foreign objects are so distant from the innocent, preppy Jill he once knew. He has no idea who Jill has become; she has changed, and he wasn't there to see it. Sayles explains, "Everything that he sees around him is a reproach. This school, these girls, this world that he is not going to be accepted in. What are these posters? What are these clothes? What the fuck is she doing in this world that won't let me in?"[21]

"You know, to me, in both 'Saint in the City' and 'Adam Raised a Cain' are kind of [Sheik's] attitude at the moment; there is this kind of class anger in him when he goes to this world that he can have no part of. He goes up to Sarah Lawrence and thinks, 'What the fuck is going on here?' and he's just pissed off there's no room for him in that world," Sayles noted in my interview with him.[22] The "It's Hard to Be a Saint in the City" sequence demonstrates how Sheik is easily able to infiltrate Jill's world within the enclosed and democratized confines of high school, unlike this new adult life, where they are separated by many states and the differences between their classes are more clearly demarcated. Sheik comes to Sarah Lawrence in order to woo Jill as he did in the high school cafeteria, believing that the adult responsibilities of college and jobs "don't mean shit" as long as they love each other, but the gulf between them—geographically, economically, and psychically—is far too wide, and he feels like an invader inside her Ivy League citadel.

More to the point, they cannot be together because Jill does not love him. Her confession sends Sheik into a flurry of outrage that sparks his blue-collar insecurities. He accuses Jill of turning against him "on account of where I'm gonna end up." "I ain't ever gonna be anything! I'm gonna end up like a fucking garbageman like my father!" he bellows while desperately pacing back and forth, an internal cauldron of ire and heartbreak. Actor Vincent Spano does an impeccable job of portraying Sheik's painful comprehension that he will likely never transcend his class like he envisioned during high school. It is fitting that in this scene Sheik's usually pompadour-ed hair is disheveled and his crisp white shirt rumpled, the élan of his high school style completely absent. When Jill reminds him of his singing aspirations, he shouts, "Don't fuckin' talk down to me!" and storms out of the room.

While Sheik cools down on the stairwell in her dorm hallway, Jill quietly reassures him that she does love him but not in a romantic way. "I'm trying to be somebody up here, and I'm a complete washout," she confesses through tears. She is trying to be someone who is completely different from the proper girl she was in Trenton, a vastly different world that Sheik embodies and reminds her of. Although she is currently trying on different identities like an actress changing costumes, Jill believes that she cannot grow into the person she will become with Sheik—a remnant of her old life—by her side. "What do you want from me? You want me to quit school and get married to you and have kids?" she demands, and Sheik replies, "What is so awful about that?" "That's not who I want to be! I don't know what I want to be, but it's not that," Jill sobs. Sheik wants Jill to adhere to his Italian old-world values, the post–World War II expectation for women to settle down immediately after high school, but Jill is on the cusp of the women's movement and wants something more for her future.

Jill fears that if she marries Sheik, she will become an embittered and lonely housewife who gave up on her theatrical aspirations, much like the miserable woman with vacant eyes and an empty soul in "Racing in the Street," the spiritual sequel to "Thunder Road" and "Born to Run" found on *Darkness on the Edge of Town*. Jill still sees her future as full of possibility and hope and does not want to be tied to her past in any way. The *Darkness* album perfectly buttresses this final half of *Baby It's You* because Springsteen revises his *Rebel Without a Cause* romanticism and wistful sentimentality of *Born to Run*. Like Sheik, in *Darkness* Springsteen's male heroes' expectations for life completely fall apart, their youthful reveries of finding love and speeding out of town giving way to endless, monotonous days in factories or nine-to-five jobs and crippling depression. The road is not a liberating space but instead where they face harrowing twisters or spin fruitlessly in circles. No longer "born to run," Springsteen's *Darkness* protagonists suffer from a nihilistic emptiness, an acute pain in their hearts that they need to carve out with a knife, the heavy weight of their secrets dragging them down, and a lonely internal darkness that incites their desire to let go and die.

In the final arc of *Baby It's You*, Sheik attempts to re-create the youthful, romantic ethos of "Thunder Road" and "Born to Run" by offering Jill the chance to run away with him, but he comes up against the despairing adult realities of class and broken dreams found in *Darkness on the Edge of Town*. In the vein of Springsteen's forlorn hot rodders, Sheik objectifies Jill as his redeemer, someone to provide him with the emotional stability and joy lacking in his post-graduate life. He nostalgically believes they can rekindle what they once had in high school if only she would climb into his front seat so they can drive off into the horizon together. But Sheik's proposal is only a means for him to navigate his feelings of loss in adulthood. He believes that by claiming Jill as his prize once more, he will be able to rise above his mortifying class position. The narrator of "Racing in the Street" literally won Mary/Wendy in a race against a dude from Los Angeles, but instead of successfully transporting her to his coveted place in the sun, they reach a dead end. Like Sheik, the racer acts in his own best interests and ignores his girl's thoughts and feelings. When the "Racing" narrator sees his wife, the former vision on the porch blithely dancing to the radio, now confined to a rocking chair and wishing she were dead, he understands that his idealistic, adolescent dreams of escapism in "Thunder Road" and "Born to Run" were detrimental to both of them. Treating her not as a person but as a trophy to be won led her to a despairing and lonely existence. He fails to notice that she is no longer a cheerful girl enamored with his nimble street racing, but rather an older woman frustrated by his lack of growth and stability, someone who needs him by her side and not out in the streets. Springsteen subverts the nomadic thrills of his *Born to Run* songs in the protagonist's realization that winning both this woman and the race did not lead to eternal bliss, because she is deeply unhappy and he still ineffectually roars down the interstates or fire roads in the summer heat to ward off his demons and briefly forget about the blue-collar grind. In this way, the use of a *Darkness* song for Sayles' denouement presages Jill and Sheik's doomed fate should they choose to elope together. As in "Racing in the Street," the couple's connection is only based on a flimsy nostalgia for the past.

"When we were in high school—" Sheik pitifully remarks before Jill yells, "We're not in high school anymore!" This line lands with a blunt thud and brings Sheik to the disquieting realization that he cannot recapture the former glories of high school and that Jill has evolved beyond him. By the end of their torrid argument, his romantic vision of her as a magical remedy for a better life disintegrates and he sees her as her own transformed woman for the first time. They stare at one another for a few beats, slowly taking in their silent, mutual understanding that their lives have fundamentally changed and paths have split apart. This honest and emotionally propulsive scene of reconciliation and acceptance defies the nostalgia genre in its depiction of a high school courtship's dissolution and the protagonists' desire but ultimate failure to recapture the past.

During the film's moving and bittersweet finale, Sheik and Jill experience the prom moment they never had. The scene opens with a hippie grunge-style band informing the audience that they are going to indulge a "weird request" to play "Strangers in the Night." Sayles glides his camera through the other dancers giving the band questionable looks before landing on a close-up of the former couple warmly dancing in a loving but wistful embrace, knowing that this may be one of their last moments together. The camera circles around them in a flushed haze until Sinatra's version of the song enters non-diegetically and drowns out the diegetic band. This change from Jill's progressive, modern stoner rock to Sheik's vintage, big band crooning embodies the ruptures of Sayles' anti-nostalgia film as a whole. *Baby It's You* asserts itself as a film divided within the rifts between its characters, narrative, form, and soundtrack. Unlike many couples in the nostalgia genre, Jill and Sheik have not found, as Sinatra sings, a love that will last forever. After this night, it is likely that they will never see each other again. However, through their relationship they have found personal acceptance and understanding that the past belongs in their high school memories.

Springsteen's music guides Sayles' anti-nostalgic rhetoric and vocalizes the inner emotional lives of his self-questioning New Jersey teenagers. Sheik in particular, a working-class loner who in the face of adversity learns to reject his nostalgic dreams, embodies Springsteen's characters. Each Springsteen song attaches to a significant moment in the couple's relationship: Sheik asking Jill out, their first date, the night of the prom, and asking her to run away. Sayles chronologically places Springsteen's songs to trace their painful breakup and evolving confrontation with the real world. Through its division of the first and second halves, *Baby It's You* disrupts the virtues of the nostalgia genre, pushing past high school's safe spaces to confront the audience with an imperfect adult world where teenage dreams do not come true, relationships may not last, and life will not be like the songs you once listened to on the radio.

Mask

Mask is based on the true story of Rocky Dennis, a teenage boy with severe facial differences caused by craniodiaphyseal disease, and Rusty, the wild, loving mother who raised him. The film marked director Peter Bogdanovich's "spectacular and long-awaited comeback to mainstream filmmaking after a decade of succès d'estime and critical box-office failures."[1] A commercial and critical triumph, *Mask* was one of Universal Studios' biggest hits and reestablished Bogdanovich as an American film luminary. However, he renounced the theatrical version of the film and sued Universal Studios for $11 million because the Springsteen soundtrack was replaced with Bob Seger without his consent.[2] Universal argued that they could not afford the $1 million permission price tag and the unprecedented 25 percent shares of videocassette sales for Springsteen's camp. According to Bogdanovich, Springsteen loved how the film used his music—so much so that he was crying after the private screening he attended—and wanted to support it despite the contractual hurdles, offering to donate half his salary to Rocky's mother and the other half to her favorite charity.[3]

According to producer Frank Price, when Bogdanovich handed in the Springsteen-scored final print, financial agreement for the use of his music had not yet been established. "I raised the red flag with Bogdanovich the first time the singer's name was mentioned in pre-production meetings.... I mentioned that we'd failed previously to strike a deal on using his music for a film, and that it might be a problem," Price recalled.[4] Price also noted that Bogdanovich and producer Martin Starger were always aware of the Springsteen problem but "refused to ever consider alternatives."[5] Bogdanovich refused to consider alternatives because he deemed Springsteen's music utterly integral to his directorial vision, and its removal, as he said, was "like cutting an arm off as far as I was concerned."[6] The studio heads took it upon themselves to insert Seger's music in Springsteen's place when the settlement fell through without informing Bogdanovich, who was away on vacation at the time.

Renowned directors such as Billy Wilder, Hal Ashby, Frank Capra, John Cassavetes, and Francis Ford Coppola co-signed an open letter objecting to the censorship of Bogdanovich's film, declaring the replacement of Springsteen a "clear violation of the director's artistic and expressive intentions."[7] What enraged Bogdanovich the most about Universal's erasure was that it was a betrayal to the real-life Rocky, who "loved Bruce Springsteen, but didn't even know Bob Seger"—Springsteen was his favorite singer.[8] It was not until the release of the 2004 "Director's Cut" DVD nearly twenty years later that Bogdanovich was able to have "the version we made and the version we wanted to put out there" seen by audiences.[9] For Bogdanovich, there was no *Mask* without Bruce Springsteen, and the effect of his music on the film was "incalculable because of his brilliance as a songwriter. That's why I wanted him in the first place."[10]

The Springsteen soundtrack serves as the film's emotional and thematic framework.

Not only do his songs locate Rocky and Rusty within their working-class environment, but "Bruce's music was a very eloquent statement of Rocky's own hopefulness" and tenacity.[11] Bogdanovich translates Springsteen's blue-collar malaise to Rocky Dennis' struggle with his disease, employing the soundtrack as narration of his inner thoughts and feelings on love, adjusting to a new school, heartbreak, and wanderlust. Rocky transcends his dismal realities through the resilient ethos of his rock and roll idol. Such thematic impact is completely lost with the replacement of Seger. The fact that Bogdanovich was willing to risk his reputation and sue a major studio in order to preserve Springsteen's music positions *Mask* as the ideal model to consider how the soundtrack is an indelible part of auteurial intent and the filmic text.

The Outsiders

"When you listen to Bruce's music, you aren't a loser. You are a character in an epic poem about losers," Jon Stewart said in his speech for Springsteen's Kennedy Center Honors ceremony.[12] Losers, misfits, outcasts, and loners populate Springsteen's canon, characters always "on the outside looking in" at the picturesque lives of others who have found the kind of kinship and prosperity they crave. Springsteen follows drifters rumbling down deserted highways in search of someone who won't look through them as if they are an apparition, doleful teens abandoned by their lovers traipsing the boardwalk in the midsummer heat, and overtaxed blue-collar workers ogling beautiful women in the hopes that they can muster the courage to talk to them. Springsteen's self-professed "lonely rider" of "Thunder Road" identifies with Roy Orbison's heartsore croon and pursues Mary with fervid desperation; he willingly admits that he is no swaggering hero and his dirty-hooded car is a meager offering for the possibility of redemption, but he is determined not to become another loser trapped in his soporific town. The musical bookends in *Mask*—"Badlands" and "The Promised Land"—feature dispirited young men worn down by the working-class grind with no control over their leaden lives. Through such lonesome souls, Springsteen "examines the tension between individuality and community ... the figure of the outsider is an individual who can never be part of a community, and this unresolvable detachment is the real cause of tension."[13]

Springsteen personally identifies with this tension: "I've always been fighting between real isolated and looking to make some connection," he confesses, a battle that was forged during his tumultuous childhood.[14] "Growing up, I felt invisible," Springsteen admits, "and that feeling is an enormous source of pain for people," a pain that would go on to inform his music.[15] An extremely bashful boy with few or no friends, young Springsteen rarely spoke, and on the rare occasion that he did, he would not look anyone in the eye. In the Peter Ames Carlin biography *Bruce*, Springsteen's mother Adele recalls witnessing her withdrawn son standing against the fence by himself and not playing with the other children during recess.[16] "It was like I didn't exist. It was the wall, then me," Springsteen explains.[17] Springsteen's oppressive home life, parochial school, and hometown left him "alienated and socially homeless."[18] When not dodging the ire of his irate, manic-depressive father castigating him for being an "outcast weirdo misfit sissy boy," he endured "rude, predatory, and unkind" bullying from his teachers and peers at the Catholic school St. Rose of Lima.[19] Schoolmates nicknamed him "Blinky" because of his anxious compulsion to blink hundreds of times per minute. The severe nuns subjected him to cruel physical abuse: "I'd have my knuckles classically rapped, my tie pulled 'til I choked; be struck in the head, shut into a dark closet, and stuffed into a trash can while being told this is where I belonged," Springsteen reminisces in his memoir.[20] When an eighth-grade Springsteen was banished to a first-grade classroom as punishment, one of the students slapped him in full force across his face, leaving the teenager "shaken, red-faced and humiliated."[21]

During his late teens and early twenties in the 1960s, Springsteen embraced the counterculture movement that swept his local haunt Asbury Park, adopting a bohemian style and spirit that was at odds with his hometown's conservative ideologies. In the unreleased ditty "Freehold," Springsteen describes his birthplace as a "redneck town" with bigoted inhabitants who look down on those "different, black, or brown" and possess a particular desire to kick his ass. The radical transformation of Springsteen's hair from a Beatles-esque shag to a lengthy flower child flow and his colorful, wild-patterned clothes ostracized him even further from his blue-nosed community. He was asked not to participate in his high school graduation ceremony and received complaints about his reticence and hippie mien during his brief stint at Ocean County Community College.

Music gave Springsteen the fellowship and acceptance he could not find growing up in Freehold. He bonded with other local musicians who shared his nonconformist nature and cultivated a galvanic sound and stage presence that hurled him into local bar band celebrity. The thrum of his guitar, hot footlights, and roar of the crowd was all Springsteen needed to transform from a timid maverick into a convivial rock and roll superhero. As Christopher Sandford writes, "Offstage, he was a narcoleptic loner. But once on the boards, it was like a case of possession: he was a dazzling physical presence, a comic delight, an imaginative treat, a raconteur, wit, and above all, vivid embodiment of the music."[22] But no matter how much he sparkled on stage, Springsteen was still an introverted misanthrope in his daily life—often to the point of emotional damage. Torn between dueling compulsions for solitude and freedom and commitment and stability in a romantic relationship, Springsteen habitually used music as a balm for his lack of meaningful connections. This enduring sense of isolation informed his work's thematic concern with marginalized individuals. In *Mask*, Springsteen's music resonates with Rocky because it astutely captures and is inspired by the kind of loneliness the teenager faces on a daily basis due to his disease.

Rocky faces loutish voyeurism instead of ignorance and bodily harm: the incessant gazes and hushed snickers of his peers, as well as brusque questions about his possible intellectual disability. Bogdanovich conveys Rocky's alienation through distanciated shot/reverse shots from the perspectives of both Rocky and his classmates. Through these subjective shots, the spectator identifies with both the curious classmate thinking "Who is this strange boy with the facial deformity?" and Rocky's sense of constantly being stared at. Rather than fading into the background as if he were a specter like young Springsteen, Rocky's facial differences make him a highly conspicuous target for ridicule. Luckily, Rocky is not as crippled by timorousness as Springsteen was in his youth and is able to withstand derision with a bit more bluster. Both Rocky and Springsteen rely on their mother's love to shield them from a "world so deadly and true," as Springsteen sings in "The Wish," his mellifluous ode to Adele. Rusty's strength enables her son to withstand his maltreatment with wit and fortitude.

In a canon that forces listeners to identify with social pariahs, Springsteen explores the most recherché of characters: circus performers. With Little Tiny Tim, the Human Cannonball, Strongman Samson, the fat lady Missy Bimbo of "Wild Billy's Circus Story" and Mary Queen of Arkansas, Springsteen examines "the seduction and loneliness of a life outside the margins of everyday life," exotic figures whose bodies disrupt societal norms in their smallness, elasticity, superhuman muscularity, fatness, and gender ambiguity.[23] There is a sequence in *Mask* that incorporates this kind of carnivalesque iconography to correlate the human outsider figure with the "freak" and "monstrous." Rocky, Rusty, and the biker gang visit an amusement park funhouse, its interior a claustrophobic, sensory-overloading phantasmagoria. Beneath the flashing lights, Rocky gazes into the funhouse mirror that warps his image and magically reveals the "normal" boy trapped beneath his facial differences, bringing to mind Springsteen's crazy 5-D mirror in "Tunnel of Love." This bizarre space of the fairground accents Rocky's otherness.

The monstrous intertext appears in the *Mask* mise-en-scène when James Whale's *Frankenstein* (1931) plays in the background on the television in Rocky's living room, a nod to Bogdanovich's frequent on-set reference to *Mask* as the "Universal family monster movie."[24] However, *Mask* was inspired by a subversion of the creature feature narrative: *The Elephant Man* (1980), the chronicle of a nineteenth-century man named Joseph Merrick (renamed John in the movie) with similar facial differences to Rocky who was exploited by the circus in a freak show exhibit before meeting the gracious Doctor Frederick Treves. Had Rocky been born in Merrick's time, he might have experienced a similar fate; one could picture him exhibited as "The Lion Boy" because his mother says he looks like he "was a lion in a past life but something got left over." Bogdanovich's former lover Dorothy Stratten, a gorgeous *Playboy* centerfold tragically murdered at just twenty years old, was fascinated with Merrick's story. Bogdanovich discerned that Stratten's interest in *The Elephant Man* stemmed from her keen understanding that "extraordinary beauty sets you apart as much as extraordinary grotesque does."[25] Stratten struggled to cope with society's obsession over her looks in the same way that Merrick and Rocky do. "There was a remarkable contrast in my mind between the grotesqueness of John Merrick and the beauty of Dorothy Stratten. Dorothy's beauty singled her out as much as his ugliness did him," Bogdanovich says.[26] Existing on the fringes of a society and pining for interpersonal connection and affection, the insulated Merrick and Frankenstein are magnified versions of the outsider character found in Springsteen's music whom Rocky acutely identifies with.

Rocky Rises Above

Mask opens to the quiet sound of chirping birds as the camera meticulously pans left across the San Gabriel Mountains that lie beneath a scopious sky to unveil the bustling urban freeways that cleave the roaming hills dotted with homes and condominiums. A cacophony of traffic noises—whirring airplanes, the whine of rushing tires, and honking horns—pierce the arid desert air as the pounding drums and opening lines of "Badlands" from *Darkness on the Edge of Town* faintly emerge beneath the din. After a wide shot of a highway nestled between two hills, Bogdanovich cuts to a closer shot of Rocky's street, where the mountains shepherd the neighborhood like watchful gods. "Badlands" amplifies on the cut and continues to rise as we draw closer to its source: Rocky's tiny bungalow home. The camera crawls through his backyard swing set to reach his bedroom window, where Springsteen's paen blares from Rocky's boombox, the sound getting louder and louder as we draw near. According to Bogdanovich, this telescopic opening forces spectators to wonder who the boy listening to Springsteen is.

At first Bogdanovich shrouds Rocky in shadow, bifurcates his image through window panels, and views him only from his side or back. This gradual reveal of his facial differences enables the spectator to comprehend that Rocky is just a regular teenager who happens to look out of the ordinary.[27] Bogdanovich eases into a full view of Rocky's disfigurement through an over-the-shoulder shot of Rocky observing himself in the mirror and putting on a jean jacket that evokes Springsteen's *Born in the U.S.A.* tour costume. Such a matter-of-fact visual technique brilliantly dispels "all potential on the audience's part for feeling sorry for Rocky by swiftly winning them over to his side."[28]

The opening sequence establishes Rocky's main fourteen-year-old male interests: road trips, Springsteen, and baseball. Pinned to Rocky's wall are his 1955 Brooklyn Dodgers baseball card collection and a poster of his musical hero Springsteen. Rocky draws a circle on a map of Europe, marking his dream destination for his future motorcycle journey. In true Springsteenian fashion, Rocky yearns for the autonomy of mobility. Rocky bops around his room along to the vigorous drums of "Badlands," then swiftly locks eyes with his reflection in the mirror and proudly pantomimes strumming a guitar, imitating Springsteen's commanding stage presence. These minute gestures were completely improvised by actor Eric Stolz while Bogdanovich played the song live on set. In this instance, the soundtrack directly informs the on-screen performance, and the studio's removal and replacement of the song with Seger's "Katmandu" completely ruptures its intertextual connotations. The simplistic lyrics of Seger's Nepalese dreams and overview of American locales he will miss during his travels may align with Rocky's desire to see the world outside of his California home, but the bouncy and humorous song has no genuine emotional core. There is nothing about Seger's song that attaches to Rocky's emotional experience beyond his European aspirations, which is only a small aspect of his story. Springsteen's "Badlands" encompasses the credo of Bogdanovich's film: perseverance through adversity.

Introducing *Mask* with "Badlands" establishes Rocky as a heroic character with the same unrelenting endurance in the face of soul-ravaging despair. "Badlands" launches with a hypersonic drum riff that crashes into a galvanizing piano and electric guitar melody—a euphoric instrumental opening that immediately rouses the listener. Despite the images of violence, fear, and destruction—"trouble in the heartland" foretold by the absence of light and a guttural sickness so potent it evokes the annihilation of a car collision—the narrator conjures the heart and soul necessary to reign over his fate; he no longer passively awaits a moment that "just don't come" or incessantly relives the "same old played-out scenes" of his mundane existence. Through these lyrics, Springsteen implores Rocky not to waste time waiting for his dreams to come to fruition or for the acceptance of his judgmental peers. The Boss assures his teenage fan that life is his for the taking, no matter what ailment he suffers from. While the narrator of "Badlands" pursues a singular face that is not looking through him and a space where he does not feel so invisible, Rocky faces a public that cannot see beyond his facial malformations. Their consternation and ridicule could easily prostrate him, but, like Springsteen, he pushes until it is understood that he is no different from anyone else and should be treated with the same deference. Preparing for his nerve-wracking first day at a new school with his hero's perfervid anthem, Rocky absorbs the "Badlands" virtues of love, faith, and hope by treating even the worst of his objectors with kindness and not succumbing to the disparity of his illness.

Rocky's plucky and devoted mother also embodies the essence of Springsteen's "Badlands." She influences Rocky to withstand his illness with gaiety. Anyone who treats Rocky as anything less than a normal boy must face her minacious wrath. When an inexperienced doctor informs Rusty that Rocky's "prognosis is not good. We feel that life expectancy is—"

the mother and son robotically finish the end of his sentence for him: "three to six months." They have heard it countless times. Rusty then launches into brassy monologue: "You're not gonna really give us that number again, are you? You know, for 12 years I've been listening to you guys' bullshit. First you told me he was retarded. Then that he would be blind and deaf. Then you told me that he'd never be able to do what regular kids do. If I had dug his grave every time you geniuses said he would die, I'd be eating fucking chop suey in China by now. Anything else?" Rocky peppers his intense doctor's appointments with beguiling mirth, cheekily referring to calcium—the stimulus of his craniodiaphyseal dysplasia—as his "pal" and feigning a cure from the "water in Azusa." The teenager faces his illness by emulating his two personal heroes, Springsteen and his mother, and their "refusal to accept life's meanest fates or most painful limitations."[29] Despite the perpetual stares, eating alone at lunch, peers asking him to take off his "mask," or being labeled with slurs for the intellectually challenged, Rocky never yields to cynicism or despair and never lets his disease define or limit him. As film critic Thomas J. Harris explains, "Rocky's whole existence was predicated on his not feeling sorry for himself, so that he could thereby maintain the high spirits which enabled him to 'make himself well' over and over again."[30] Rusty and Springsteen teach Rocky to "spit in the face" of his personal badlands and know that it is not a sin for him to be glad that he is alive in spite of his disease. In this way, "Badlands" rises above being a mere introductory track—it defines Rocky's entire characterization.

"Racing in the Street" buoys Rocky's desire to motorcycle across Europe. He hits "play" on his boombox as his friend Ben, who also intends to join the excursion, excitedly sets up their new map. Springsteen's downcast vocals are barely audible as they fervently chart their journey, speaking hurriedly over one another. Bogdanovich centralizes the map between the silhouetted backs of the boys' heads and then slowly pulls closer to symbolize its arresting lure. During this shot, the instrumental coda of "Racing in the Street" amplifies, the song's meditative longing underscoring the friends' elegiac wanderlust. "It's virtually impossible to put a Springsteen song in a scene where there's dialogue because you're not listening to the dialogue, you're listening to him singing," Bogdanovich says, elaborating on his decision to focus on the song's piano instrumental section rather than the verses or chorus.[31]

"I want to go to every place I've ever read about," Rocky sighs dreamily as he traces the route with his finger, trailing through Rome, London, and Budapest. The specific use of this song to underscore a sequence in which the characters fantasize about the potential of the open road encourages the spectator to engage with Springsteen's depiction of mobility. For Springsteen, the car (or, in Rocky's case, the motorcycle) is the cardinal icon of his oeuvre, the vessel that holds the dreams of his disenfranchised characters and empowers them to flee their stultifying blue-collar towns. Trading the car for a motorcycle as his means of liberation from a judgmental society, Rocky envisions himself as an autonomous Springsteenian drifter on a quest for selfhood on the open road. However, the song's melancholic tone and status as a requiem for the freewheeling ethos of "Born to Run" foreshadow Rocky's unfulfilled dreams; sadly, he will pass away before he can ever embark on his long-awaited trek. In one of the film's most moving final moments, after Rusty discovers that Rocky has died, she replaces the tacks onto the map and tells him, "Now you can go anywhere, baby."

"Thunder Road" undergirds Rocky's heated quarrel with his mother after she refuses to listen to his English class poem, preoccupied with her preparations for a night of drug-addled debauchery. Rusty ignores Rocky's pleas to join a rehabilitation program, provoking his venomous reproach: "All you care about is getting loaded and laid." In a rare moment of pure malice toward her beloved son, Rusty rips his treasured baseball card and slaps him. Bogdanovich's unhinged camera frantically follows behind Rocky until he slams his bedroom door and immediately flicks on his stereo to blast the roaring middle of Springsteen's "Thunder Road." This kinetic cinematography embodies the dynamism and drive of Springsteen's restorative melody. The paen's rousing tenor relieves the quiet, strained tensions of the argument between mother and son. Springsteen's line "the night's busting open" accompanies the sound of Rusty's squealing tires as she races off to her bacchanalian rendezvous while Rocky places tacks onto his map, yearning to "case the promised land" just like Springsteen. He dreams of escaping on the open road, where Springsteen promises heaven is waiting on the tracks.

Seger's "Rock and Roll Never Forgets" in the theatrical version completely eradicates these subtexts. Its narrative of a weathered old man trying to recapture his 1950s-era adolescence in the sounds of a local rock and roll bar band opposes the starry-eyed dreams of youth in "Thunder Road." Rocky stands before the same metamorphic precipice as the recently graduated Mary and her guitar-playing savoir, where a future of infinite possibilities and a highway as voluminous as the universe awaits him. Although its toe-tapping rhythm is pleasurable, Seger's song does not have the same rapturous uplift as "Thunder Road," which removes the sting of Rocky's argument with his mother. "Rock and Roll Never Forgets" in no way connects to Rocky's nomadic dreams or his experience as a teenage boy.

The first of two uses of "The Promised Land" expresses Rocky's "desperation about women for the first time," Bogdanovich says in the DVD commentary.[32] Rocky's sexual frustrations exacerbate his insecurities about his facial differences, so he asks his mother if he can meet with a plastic surgeon. Not sensing his despair, Rusty casually remarks that they need to wait another two years for his bones to stop growing. "Don't you understand anything, Mom? It's girls!" Rocky shouts before storming off and slamming his bedroom door off screen. The heartfelt drums coming from his bedroom immediately cue Rusty's rummaging through the household in search of money. In a rather unconventional parental gesture, Rusty hires a prostitute to sleep with Rocky, but he kindly rejects the offer and informs the girl that he envisioned losing his virginity with someone he loves.

Bogdanovich's selected snippet of "The Promised Land," from the choleric second verse into the chorus, voices Rocky's pain. Although we do not see Rocky place the cassette into his player once he enters the sanctity of his bedroom, we can surmise that the song functions diegetically in the same way as "Thunder Road"—namely, to soothe Rocky's rage and channel his churning emotions. Springsteen uses evocative violent and suicidal imagery to express his garage mechanic's profound anguish: left blind, cold, and weak, he yearns to "explode and tear" apart his town and remove his pain from his heart with a knife. It is an agony so potent that even the abandoned and feral dogs who howl on Main Street identify with him. These lyrics histrionically convey Rocky's lovesick heart and aggravation that he cannot be a normal boy who has no problem getting the girl. Like Springsteen's incensed Utahan, Rocky longs to declare that he is not a boy but a man in control of his own destiny; he wants to break free from the shackles of a disease that infantilizes and desexualizes him. Rocky identifies with the protagonists' struggle "to live the right way" because he strives to maintain a sanguine spirit in spite of his disease. "The Promised Land" likewise attaches to Rusty's on-screen actions to suggest that she also identifies with the song's vexations. She mourns the fact that her son must face this significant adolescent crossroads with such a polarizing abnormality.

Rocky's female troubles soon reach a new level when he takes a job as a counselor for blind children and teenagers and falls for one of the campers: the sweet Diana, a fair-haired girl who reminds him of *Alice in Wonderland*. Springsteen's "The River" plays for only one line; yet it captures the melodrama of Rocky's post-summer romance blues. The sequence begins when Rocky's friend Ben walks across the yard and peers into his bedroom window. Springsteen's dirge emits from the boombox, but Rocky is not there to listen. He sits with his shoulders slumped at the kitchen table across from his mother while the song softly whispers in the background from his bedroom. Rocky wonders why Diana's mother always says her daughter is out when he calls each day, but his farewell to her at camp should have made it clear. During that scene, Bogdanovich held on a short close-up of Rocky hesitating to walk over and meet Diana's parents, dreading their reaction to his mangled face. His worst fears were confirmed when he was met with speechless and appalled stares. Assuming that Rocky took advantage of their daughter's disability, they gave him a cursory excuse about hitting traffic and briskly whisked her away. Rusty encourages her son to call Diana again, but Rocky just slams the phone down in frustration and weeps in his mother's arms, a tender image that embodies the aching grief of "The River."

Bogdanovich selects the bleakest verse of "The River," wherein the narrator describes his incessant return to the coveted river—the mythical site of his rhapsodic courtship and lost youth. Now that he is older and married to his high school sweetheart, the love they once shared has run dry. Rocky is similarly nostalgic about a past love and mourns his physical separation from Diana, opposing the emotional separation in Springsteen's moving ballad. Bogdanovich specifically synchronizes "The River" with Ben's arrival because he delivers a piece of disheartening news that renders Rocky's dreams defunct: he will not be able to accompany Rocky on their European excursion. Losing Diana and the promise of his European trip—the two intrinsic motivational forces of Rocky's young life—plunges him into an emotional nadir in line with the song's protagonist. Lastly, Springsteen's melancholy elegy ushers in the final act of the film in which Rocky's illness worsens.

Rocky has a self-reliant homeopathic method of "making himself well" that cures his sadness and splitting headaches: all he has to do is close his eyes and conjure treasured memories. When Rocky dances with Diana at a summer New Year's Eve party, he wistfully remarks, "Man, do I have a great one to use now … a great thought. My mom taught me when things get rotten, I should think of a good memory." He gives the same advice to the forlorn prostitute Lorrie: "When something bad happens, you gotta remember something good." Rocky echoes these lines when he bids Diana a final farewell; contradicting the escapist spirit of his beloved "Thunder Road," he says, "We can't run away, Diana. But we can sort of run away in our minds. We can remember camp, the mountains and the ocean … especially New Year's Eve." Through this innate positivism, Rocky is able to keep the physical and emotional hardships of his illness at bay. But soon his headaches intensify, eroding his usually ingratiating attitude and culminating in a rare physical altercation. On the first day of high school, an onlooker sneers, "If that's a mask he's wearing, I sure wish he'd take it off." Slamming the boy to the locker with a resounding thwack, Rocky acidly grits through his teeth, "I'll take my mask off if you take your mask off, you son of a bitch!"

Makeup designers Michael Westmore and Zoltan Elek, who won an Academy Award for their work in *Mask*, signified Rocky's interior degradation with a transformed pallid and worn exterior. During a party at his house, guests urge Rocky to sing a song with his mother, but he is too fatigued and retreats into his room. Bogdanovich's lingering close-ups of Rusty and Gar (Rusty's boyfriend and Rocky's quasi-father figure) bidding Rocky goodnight code the scene with a somber finality, as if they discern his flagging mortality. The subsequent scene of Rusty discovering her son's death is especially moving due to Cher's raw performance.

Had Rocky been alive in 1984, he would have been thrilled to see his hero catapulted into the pop culture firmament by the *Born in the U.S.A* phenomenon. The album's title song launches from the chorus during a dissolve shot of Rusty replacing the tacks on Rocky's map that shifts into her car driving down a cemetery road. Bogdanovich links this dissolve specifically with "Born in the U.S.A." to "signal to the audience that it was not 1980 any longer but now, four years later," after Rocky's death.[33] "Without that transitional device, a lot of people thought it was Rocky's funeral and wondered why there weren't more people there. So, the emotional impact of the picture was damaged as a result," Bogdanovich carps.[34] This scene is the only instance in the film where Springsteen's music does not come from Rocky's tape player. Instead, "Born in the U.S.A." plays diegetically from Rusty's car radio to signify the idea that she now carries her son with her wherever she goes.

A close-up of Rusty's halcyon smile as she recalls the fond memory of her son's poem precedes the final frame of *Mask*: a wide shot of Gar kneeling beside Rocky's grave next to Gus, one of Rocky's dear motorcycle gang friends, underneath the towering trees, with Rusty beside him toward the far left. The vivifying introductory harmonica riff to "The Promised Land" accompanies the fade to black, and the song continues throughout the end credits montage. This montage not only acknowledges the actors' exceptional work but also enables the spectator to recover from the film's lugubrious conclusion.[35] Bogdanovich carefully selected scenes in which each actor was interacting with Rocky as "a way of keeping him alive, bringing him back, [and] make the audience not so depressed."[36] The director drove around listening to Springsteen in search of the perfect song for his film's denouement. When he landed on "The Promised Land," he was so overcome with emotion that he had to pull over to fully absorb its mesmeric power. "I thought it was a really powerful way to end the film," he explains on the DVD commentary.[37] Not only would "The Promised Land" provide a "strong, uplifting ending," but it was the "absolutely perfect song to express Rocky's indomitable spirit."[38]

"The Promised Land" crystallizes Rocky's ability to endure his disease with intrepidity. After toiling in his daddy's garage, Springsteen's mechanic blazes down a "rattlesnake speedway" chasing a far-off, hazy mirage that represents the freedom he pines for. Blinded by his ennui and on the verge of exploding into thousands of crestfallen pieces, the unvenerated narrator hopes that he will be able to take charge and control his fate. Such ambivalence manifests in a piercing guitar break that ushers in "a saxophone that is not soaring but looking onward to a destination that is made home with a triumphant harmonica solo."[39] This stirring instrumental bridge is the sound of the narrator gaining the courage to head straight into the harrowing storm, where only those who have the "faith to stand its ground" can withstand its destruction. During his legendary concert on November 5, 1980, at Arizona State University, Springsteen engaged every molecule of his body in his performance of the song—thrashing his fists, arms, and legs to the drum's inspiring rhythm and repeatedly raising his defiant fist in the air to grandly declare his unwavering credence in a promised land—an image that mirrors the *Mask* poster of Rocky with his fists lifted in exultation. During the 1980 performance, when Springsteen launched into the harmonica coda, he hunched down into the instrument and blared as if his very life depended on it, dramatizing his character's vigor. Backed by the beatific sounds of an angelic choir, the jubilant coda successfully marshals him onto the other side of the tempest.

Seger's "Roll Me Away" serves as the end credits song in the theatrical version, and while its lovely piano flourishes and driving tempo are invigorating and its road narrative harkens to Rocky's nomadic dreams, it hardly holds the same emotional and thematic resonance as "The Promised Land." Trading brews in a roadside bar and hitching a ride on a two-wheeler has nothing to do with Rocky's journey. Seger's celestial descriptions of starlight, mountaintops, hawks flying in the sky, and rolling into the sunset conjure a peaceful feeling after the revelation of Rocky's death, and we imagine that Rocky was able to live out his roadside fantasies in the afterlife, but "The Promised Land" articulates the driving force of Bogdanovich's narrative: hope that there can be triumph amid the greatest difficulties. The Springsteen finale establishes *Mask* as a story of "what Rocky and his mother truly believed in—pressing on," says producer Martin Starger.[40]

Through Springsteen's ratifying anthem, Rocky repudiates those who bully and judge him for his distinct exterior. With his ability to "make himself well" and focus on good thoughts, Rocky has the faith necessary to stand his ground against the burdens of his debilitating disease. Rocky adheres to Springsteen's command to "blow away" what breaks his heart and the lies that leave him "nothing but lost and brokenhearted," believing that he is not worthy of life or happiness because of his disease. "The Promised Land" perfectly encapsulates what Starger considers Rocky's core essence: "Everyone has something about themselves that they feel inferior about—whether it's not being smart enough, pretty enough, athletic enough. Rocky personifies those problems and shows us that what you really are is what's inside. He had every reason to feel sorry for himself but didn't. He just went out there, faced life and helped others do the same thing."[41] The beauty of Springsteen's "The Promised Land" lies in the narrator's grit; although he has profound doubts, he firmly believes there is a promised land waiting on the other side of the perilous storm, and he doughtily persists and passes through, a coup underscored by Springsteen's rhapsodic instrumental passages. Springsteen uses the dark cloud metaphor to assure Rocky and his listeners that they have the will to survive even in the most despairing of circumstances.

With the exception of the second use of "The Promised Land," Springsteen's music in *Mask* always functions as diegetic source music, primarily emitting from the boombox of a teenager who idolizes him. Rocky explicitly chooses to play Springsteen's songs during key moments in his life: preparing for his first day at a new school, dealing with one of his biggest fights with his mother, confessing his lifelong dream, and recovering from his first breakup. Seger's biker aesthetic aligns more with Rusty and her weatherworn friends; it does not capture Rocky's being or the film's overall themes. On the "Director's Cut" DVD commentary, Bogdanovich reveals that he lost footage of Rocky gazing longingly at his Springsteen poster the night before he died. Perhaps the ailing teenager knew in this moment that he would never be able to listen to his musical hero again, and so he gave him one last look. This scene would have been a sublime visual expression of Springsteen and Rocky Dennis' intimate connection already established on the soundtrack. Bogdanovich fought hard to preserve the music of Springsteen because it superbly encapsulates his protagonist's characterization and narrative themes. *Mask* aptly demonstrates how the removal of a particular soundtrack choice can completely alter the cinematic body and interfere with directorial vision, as well as how Springsteen's music can be a personal touchstone for characters within the film diegesis.

In Country

Directed by Norman Jewison, *In Country* (1989) is based on Bobbie Ann Mason's 1985 novel of the same name. The coming-of-age story revolves around seventeen-year-old Samantha Hughes during the summer after her high school graduation in the small town of Hopewell, Kentucky. Torn between attending college and settling down with her boyfriend, Sam contemplates her future and reflects on her family's recent past. She yearns to decipher the mystery of her detached and troubled Vietnam veteran uncle and to learn more about her father, Dwayne, who died in the war before she was born. She actively questions and analyzes the male Vietnam experience and longs to understand the perspective of the veterans in her community, despite their continual denial of allowing her entry into their psyche. Sam's uncle Emmett secretly wrestles with the symptoms of post-traumatic stress disorder, refusing to divulge his triggers or wartime experiences. Sam's father remains an illusory figure, kept largely hidden from her life until the moment her friend Dawn finds a box of his letters, photographs, and war memorabilia. Irene, Sam's mother, rarely discloses information about Dwayne since she was only married to him for a few months before he was sent off to war. Sam spends the summer trying to solve the mysteries of the Vietnam experience and the patriarchal figures in her life.

The aberrance of the Vietnam conflict stood in stark contrast to the jingoistic ethos of World War II. A senseless and futile war, Vietnam disrupted a culture that once prided itself on being the locus of virtue and righteous victory. American soldiers became baby killers intruding on another country's fight instead of superheroes rescuing the nation from the evils of Nazism. On the home front, Americans lost faith in the institutional powers—the government and the military—that they once revered. The vitriol of protesters and feelings of betrayal from disenfranchised veterans imbued the nation with violence and rage. Unlike World War II veterans, Vietnam veterans arrived home without any celebration or official welcome; there was a deep shame and regret surrounding the failed war, and Americans wanted to swiftly forget their involvement. Vietnam veterans were expected to put their wartime experiences behind them and assimilate quickly back into society; the fact that many were psychologically and physically unable to do so resulted in their further marginalization. They were labeled social misfits, stereotyped as potentially dangerous men with violent tendencies that threatened to erupt at any moment, and made scapegoats of the country's vexations with the war and its loss.

In Mason's novel, Bruce Springsteen is a key icon that facilitates Sam's perception of Vietnam and masculinity. The teenager frequently mentions her crush on him and ogles his "Dancing in the Dark" music video. Springsteen's denim jeans "as tight as rubber gloves" and dancing "like a revved-up sports car about to take off" turn her on, and she dreams of being pulled out of a concert crowd to boogie with him like Courtney Cox.[1] But more than his appealing physicality, Springsteen's music touches Sam's soul. "Somehow there was a secret knowledge in his songs, as though he knew exactly what she was feeling," Mason writes.[2] One of those feelings is her confusion about Vietnam and need to understand what her father, Uncle Emmett, and all the other veterans in her hometown went through. To Sam, Springsteen's plangent protest anthem "Born in the U.S.A." is about a beleaguered veteran whose brother "gets killed over there, and then the guy gets in a lot of trouble when he gets back home. He can't get a job, and he ends up in jail."[3] The gargantuan powerhouse helps her comprehend America's disdainful mistreatment of its soldiers after a war that divided a generation.

Although Norman Jewison's film adaptation removes many of the Springsteen references from the novel, Sam cites him in a significant monologue, he appears on two large posters in Sam's bedroom (promotional photos from *Born in the U.S.A.* and *Tunnel of Love*, the latter of which depicts a smoldering Springsteen holding a bouquet of roses), and the moody "I'm on Fire" (one of the seven Top 10 hits from the *Born in the U.S.A.* album) features on the soundtrack three times. The film departs from the novel by shifting the time period from the summer of 1984—coinciding with Springsteen's career zenith—to 1989. This decision removes the popular culture immediacy of his inclusion in the text. During 1984, Springsteen skyrocketed from cult darling to household name and achieved colossal, worldwide fame. It was a time when young girls like Sam Hughes would have been acutely aware of and avidly imbibing his work.

The incorporation of "I'm on Fire" and other Springsteen allusions in Jewison's *In Country* invoke the intertextual connections between the singer, Vietnam, and the 1980s sociopolitical milieu—namely, the conservative wave helmed by President Ronald Reagan and its reactionary gender ideologies focused on the remasculinization of the Vietnam veteran. Reagan misread Springsteen's patriotism, his use of American flag iconography, and the hypermasculine, aggressively heterosexual image of his pumped-up hard body as analogous to Reagan's jingoistic vision of the United States. Sam sees her Uncle Emmett in the protagonist of Springsteen's misinterpreted juggernaut "Born in the U.S.A." and other veteran characters. Her favorite rock star's work fuels her obsessive curiosity about the Vietnam veterans in her family and community. As a teenager during the war's escalation, Springsteen had an extensive history with Vietnam—narrowly avoiding the draft, witnessing the deaths of his friends and neighbors, and later grappling with survivor's guilt—which he has chronicled throughout his musical oeuvre, live performances, and memoir. As outsiders and non-participants in the Vietnam War, both Samantha Hughes and Bruce Springsteen empathize with and strive to understand their family and friends who have endured the horrors of battle and returned with dreadful psychological and physical afflictions.

Father Figures

The first instance of "I'm on Fire" occurs directly after the opening scene of Sam at her high school graduation. The ghosts of Vietnam haunt this sequence, as the ceremony marks another milestone in Sam's life that her father has not been there for; the older Sam gets, the more Dwayne has missed. Sam's grandmother, Mamaw, points out her son's absence, and Sam replies that she can feel her father's eyes on her from heaven. Separated from the rest of the family, Emmett watches Sam receive her diploma before he suddenly hears the voices of his dead friends and becomes wrapped in a violent wartime flashback. The graduation ceremony causes Emmett to reflect on where he was around Sam's age, facing possible death in the balmy wilderness of Vietnam and then dealing with mental and physical illnesses following his homecoming.

Sam is eager to memorialize the occasion with a family portrait, gathering her mother, grandparents, aunt, cousin, and stepsister around her before dragging the brooding and resistant Emmett to join. Bright yellow headphones are wrapped around her neck above her gown, indicating her close connection with the Springsteen music that follows in the next scene. Just as the shutter clicks and the film's frame becomes the still image, the alluring opening chords to Springsteen's "I'm on Fire" begin to play. Jewison then cuts to a shot of marble statues in the shape of stalwart Confederate soldiers from the Civil War—symbols of the white nationalist conservative values found in America's heartland that President Reagan upholds. Unlike Vietnam veterans, who fought for another country's cause that few Americans supported, these soldiers stood for what they believed to be a righteous cause to defend and honor their land. A crane shot reveals the sprawling, quiet cemetery with its lush green grass and tall, billowing trees. Sam jogs beneath the pale sunrise in between the statues and gravestones. The close-up of her sneakers pacing down the asphalt matches the anticipatory rhythm of Springsteen's throbbing drums and simmering bass line. In a wide shot, Sam sprints beneath a passing freighter on top of a bridge that overlooks a dusty and dingy path. Towering steel power plants loom in the corner of the frame before she passes a group of construction workers digging in the dirt with dusty shovels and tending to a concrete mixer. They tip their hard-hats and yell out in appreciation of her young, slender, and tan body.

In the next shot, Sam scampers down a suburban road, with a barking puppy disrupting the halcyon morning atmosphere. The spires of a courthouse peek over the trees in the far distance. Sam finishes her run up to a tiny diner with a giant, supercilious rooster statue in mid-strut adorned on top. Only the final verse of "I'm on Fire"—with Springsteen's vocalizing and sonorous repetition of the song's title—plays over Sam's jogging journey through her insular hometown. Springsteen connects to this bucolic Americana milieu; each space Sam passes by—a post-industrial factory, a diner, a cemetery—resembles the low-class, homespun locales featured in Springsteen's songs, reflecting his upbringing in the hermetic town of Freehold, New Jersey. Both Sam and Springsteen experience the devastating ramifications of Vietnam within their close-knit communities.

Each instance of "I'm on Fire" occurs before a significant moment in Sam's struggle to bond with her uncle and the other veterans. Over breakfast at the diner, Sam attempts to infiltrate Emmett's group of friends who spend their time trading war stories, trying to converse with them as if she were a fellow war buddy. Yet her sincere and incessant questioning about their combat memories is met with sarcastic jokes and the same mantras: "You ain't never going to understand it. You don't want to," and "Well, you weren't there. So you can't understand it." To the veterans of *In Country*, Sam will never fully grasp what they have endured because she is an outsider, a naïve little girl unworthy of their attention because she did not directly experience the traumas of war. Their hushed secrecy and staunch refusal to reveal their disturbing wartime memories simply because of her gender and youth frustrates Sam throughout the film. When Sam asks Emmett's veteran friend Tom, "Why don't any of the vets I know get along with women?" she bluntly acknowledges their emasculated insecurities; left with broken bodies and fractured psyches, the veterans view themselves as despised, enfeebled emblems of a tumultuous society unworthy of interpersonal relationships with women. Emmett and his friends try to conceal their pain from women and the rest of the public in order to project an image of strength and virility that was stolen from them by the war, but Sam sees through this puissant façade. "Don't be macho and pretend," she scolds Emmett after he downplays the impact of his sickness.

The group's isolated natures cause the entire town to spread malicious gossip about the state of their mental health: "Well, you know what they say about Emmett," Sam's boyfriend Lonnie remarks. Hopewell views Emmett and his friends as gelded weirdoes who oddly keep to themselves. When Lonnie chastises Sam for hanging out with Emmett's peculiar circle, she replies, "What do you think they're going to do? Snap and hold me hostage?" Sam recognizes the social stereotype of the mercurial Vietnam veteran as a savage, vexed psychopath, a cliché that Hollywood transformed into a marketable villain during the late 1960s and 1970s in the exploitation and horror genres. Vietnam veterans were dangerous snipers in Peter Bogdanovich's *Targets* (1968), ruthless rapists in Elia Kazan's *The Visitors* (1972), deranged, barbaric hog riders in the motorpsycho cult classics *The Born Losers* (1967) and *Angels from Hell* (1968)—titles indicative of the societal disdain expressed toward veterans at the time—and a mohawked insomniac with frenzied John Wayne fantasies in Martin Scorsese's legendary *Taxi Driver*.

Despite Sam's driving need to have a realistic understanding of her father's wartime experience, she is blinded by childish notions of him as an innocent, virtuous victim, perceiving him as someone who naïvely went to Vietnam and died. Sam initially sees her father as a celebrated romantic war hero with a good, honest heart. She pins Dwayne's photograph onto her mirror and speaks to it: "You missed Watergate, *E.T.*, the Bruce Springsteen concert. God, you missed everything. You were just a country boy and you never knew me." Defining him as a "country boy" emphasizes her view of Dwayne as the embodiment of wholesome heartland version of America, a beacon of innocence harshly persecuted after being thrown unwittingly into the dangers of Vietnam. The image of her father becomes as revered as that of the pop star—akin to the Springsteen posters that loom over her—an unattainable figure of purity and goodness that is constantly present but ultimately unreachable.

Sam's allusion to Springsteen in her monologue as one of the seminal events in her life affirms his importance to her and ushers his music onto the soundtrack once again. The hypnotic opening chords of "I'm on Fire" return during a gradual close-up of Dwayne's military portrait. The dignified snapshot of Dwayne in his majestic uniform slowly fades out onto a shot of his daughter running with her Walkman—a visual symbol of his overwhelming, spectral presence and intertextual connection to Springsteen. Sam jogs past a brick wall and into the government building seen in the background of the opening sequence. In a sullen, deep-throated croon, Springsteen asks his little girl whether her daddy is home or if he left her all alone. Although Springsteen is using the word "daddy" in a sexual manner to refer to the girl's (possibly older) male lover, the insertion of this opening line directly after Sam's monologue about her own absent father conspicuously invites the spectator to read it as a direct inquiry from Springsteen to Sam about Dwayne. Jewison consciously emphasizes these specific lyrics after an intimate scene about her paternal conflicts to insist that through his death, Sam's daddy has indeed left her all alone. The sequence ends after Sam enters the building to meet Anita, a spirited blonde nurse who used to date Emmett. Sam asks Anita to accompany her uncle to the local dance supporting Vietnam veterans, a gesture that would help him reclaim his lost sense of masculinity. Sam dances along to the tune on her Walkman in an upbeat way that is incongruous with Springsteen's smoldering tempo, and the song fades out when she removes her headphones.

The smoky bass line of "I'm on Fire" punctuates Emmett's long-awaited visit to the doctor about his headaches, rashes, and insomnia, which Sam suspects is a result of exposure to Agent Orange. Springsteen's moody closing chords overlay a languid zoom into a double shot of Sam and Emmett in the front seat of the car, removing Sam's misogynistic boyfriend Lonnie from the frame (sitting in the driver's seat). Eliminating Lonnie from the shot unites the uncle and niece currently contemplating the ramifications of Vietnam on their lives. Sam can sense the profound psychological and physical anguish that her taciturn uncle conceals. While lovingly adjusting Emmett's collar, she optimistically assures him that "there's gotta be a way" to heal his pain despite the doctor's insipid advice to merely wash his face more.

This tender image of Sam and Emmett fades into Sam listening to Springsteen's steamy purr on her headphones while running toward Tom's ramshackle auto shop past a series of mailboxes and tangled knolls of grass. Like Springsteen in the "I'm on Fire" music video, Tom is a garage mechanic who is working on a car for Sam. The song's pulsating sexuality and reference to a paternal figure precipitates Sam's complex erotic relationship with this significantly older Vietnam veteran. She attempts to sleep with him after a dance held by the local community's Veterans' Association, but he cannot perform; his combat memories are far too great for him to surrender himself to physical pleasure. In the novel, Mason makes it clear that the war has rendered Tom completely impotent. There is an incestuous subtext to Sam's sexual pursual of Tom because she uses him as another way to get to know what her father went through in the war.[4]

Mason heightens Springsteen's relationship to Tom's character. She writes that Tom resembles Springsteen, especially his smile, which drives Sam's attraction to him. When Sam watches the "Dancing in the Dark" music video, she pities Tom because he has a limp from the war: "It made her sad. She kept thinking about what it would be like to dance with Tom. He had said she was cute. But he could never move with Bruce Springsteen's exuberant energy."[5] Mason makes Tom the same age as Springsteen in order to demonstrate the differences between a man who has been tarnished by the Vietnam War and one who has not.

"I'm on Fire" describes a torrid summer night of unbridled ecstasy. Sam connects to the song's carnality in her hankering for Tom, but she also relates to the narrator's mental unrest, his desire to have a knife cut open his skull and excise the thoughts that barrel through his head like a freight train. The sensual song's sense of looming anxiety and longing for something that is so close, yet so out of reach, connects to Sam's yearning to comprehend what the men in her life went through during the war. The chugging backbeat matches the shots of Sam's rhythmic running, a physical action that brings her closer to the knowledge of her family and community. Jewison continuously places Springsteen's suffering ballad directly before scenes where she makes small steps toward better understanding the Vietnam experience.

Uncovering Uncle Emmett

The withdrawn Emmett ensconces himself within the hermetic world of his home, mindlessly consuming *M*A*S*H* and Pac-Man or doing mundane chores. He much prefers the company of his cat Moonpie or the various rabbits he tends to. This isolation worsens his depression and post-traumatic stress disorder. Emmett's struggle with mental illness brings to mind Springsteen's *Born in the U.S.A.* B-side "Shut Out the Light," a despairing ballad about a veteran's corporeal and psychological homecoming struggles. During the pained chorus, the tormented veteran Johnson "Johnny" Leneir cries out for his mother to mollify his agonizing shakes and nausea. The pitch-black twilight terrifies him, and he begs for her not to "shut out the light," a fear that stems from his skirmishes on the battlefield, bringing to mind the opening scene of *In Country*, where soldiers stand shrouded in the black darkness of night. The only salvatory light is the explosion of enemy bombs that illuminates the dense rainforest behind them. A wide shot shows the American soldiers distracted by a rocket flare shooting across the sky while the Viet Cong mysteriously rise from behind the rice paddies. Jewison crafts an unnerving moment when their machine guns flash and pummel the unsuspecting soldiers with bullets, though no sound is heard.

The blackness of a mighty southern thunderstorm reminds Emmett of his conflict in the roasting jungles of Vietnam and triggers his PTSD. With each flash of lightning, Jewison intercuts Emmett's horrifying memories of burning bodies and stentorian explosions. He whimpers and trembles in fright as Sam wraps her arms around him, mirroring Johnson and his mother in Springsteen's forlorn song. This image reappears later in the film after Sam's failed sexual encounter with Tom. While the pale summer moonlight shines down on them in bed, Tom entreats the teenager to hold him real close, just like Springsteen's narrator asks his mother to throw her arms around him. Sam's maternal gesture keeps Tom's haunted recollections of combat at bay after he confesses, "My mind takes me where I don't want to go."

For Sam, Emmett and Tom are living embodiments of Springsteen's despondent blue-collar protagonist in "Born in the U.S.A." because they deal with the same post-war struggle to find employment and social acceptance ten years or more after the war. "Born in the U.S.A." portrays a damaged man discarded by the world before he is even able to get on his feet. Springsteen equates the Vietnam veteran with the abject, bestial figure of a cowardly and beaten dog to signify his demasculinization and societal repudiation. Emmett covers up from society like the pusillanimous canine by refusing to divulge his internal conflicts, rejecting women, and concealing himself within the lonely confines of his home. Tom's broken body—his impotence and limp—externalizes Vietnam's ruin of red-blooded American manhood. Emmett and Tom have also spent the last decade furiously "burning down the road" in search of something that will give their lives meaning outside of their arresting traumas.

The opening lines of Springsteen's plangent anti-anthem situate the veteran within a "dead man's town," a destitute space dominated by the twin industrial poles of a refinery and a penitentiary. The cinematic Hopewell echoes this downtrodden locale. Sam encourages her uncle to take a job at the local tire plant—a Springsteenian blue-collar occupation and just about the only opportunity available in the picayune town—but Emmett would rather live on disability than take a job away from a man who has a family, an indication of just how limited positions are in this community. Although Sam's boyfriend Lonnie does not have the burden of being a veteran, the only job in town he can find is as a supermarket box boy, which he eventually quits. "Well, I walked in there this morning, and I looked in Quinnie's face, and I thought to myself, 'I do this for thirty years, and I'm going to look just like Quinnie,'" he explains, a statement that echoes the purgatorial factory life Springsteen depicts in his despairing working-class odes such as "Factory" and "Youngstown." Caught in a "hometown jam," the narrator of "Born in the U.S.A." has only two options: imprisonment or enlistment. When he returns home from his tour of duty, the refinery has no jobs left and his VA man cannot help him. For the narrator and many other young men like

Emmett, Tom, and Sam's father, there were no other options in their hardscrabble town but to go to war.

Most infantrymen in the Vietnam War were recruited from underprivileged communities like Hopewell and Springsteen's Freehold because of the college draft exemptions that allowed affluent upper- and middle-class men to avoid the war. Springsteen admonished this discriminatory policy in a *Rolling Stone* interview with Kurt Loder: "I remember thinkin', like, what makes my life, or my friends' lives, more expendable than that of somebody who's goin' to school? It didn't seem right."[6] He also astutely pointed out the racial disparity of the draft, noting that his bus to the Newark draft board was filled with "sixty, seventy percent black guys from Asbury Park" because most people of color were from lower-class backgrounds.[7] During Sam's visit to the Vietnam Veterans Memorial in Washington, D.C., at the end of the film, she remarks that the majority of the names inscribed are all podunk "country boys," simple and uneducated men like those in Hopewell.

These men were not only poor but also young and naïve. In *In Country*, Sam asks her uncle how old he was when "he went over there," and he replies, "About a year older than you are now." Seventeen-year-old Sam is astonished to learn that she is nearly the same age as Emmett and thousands of other young men who went overseas and faced death, and she cannot imagine having to experience such a harrowing predicament as a mere teenager. Springsteen says that at the same age, "I didn't even know where Vietnam was. We just knew we didn't wanna go and *die*!"[8] He recalls his enthusiastic Castiles bandmate Bart Haynes jesting behind his drum kit in his dress blues, "'Here I go, goin' to Vietnam'—laughin' and jokin' about it. And he went, and he was killed," becoming the first soldier from Freehold to die in the war.[9]

By the end of *In Country*, Sam obtains her father's diary and travels to the Cawood pond in an attempt to re-create the sweltering tropical landscape of Vietnam. She reads a passage that describes Dwayne's unremorseful killings of the Vietnamese enemy. Up until now, the letters she read were only about fraternizing with his war buddies or fantasizing about home. It never occurred to Sam that her father had to kill. Sam spends the entirety of the film trying to determine why the Vietnam veterans she knows are so troubled and to get them to share their experiences, but when the grim truth of Vietnam is exposed, she recoils, frightened and upset; it tarnishes her idealized image of the innocent country boy. She tells Emmett that she doesn't want to listen to his Vietnam stories and that she doesn't like her father anymore. Sam's narrow-minded rejection of Dwayne angers Emmett, and he finally reveals the agonies he has spent the film covering up; he confesses that he still feels the spirits of his fallen friends and veterans all around him:

> And they're all still alive. You know that? In my head. They're all sitting around a village that's all burnt out, eating ham and waiting for a Huey to come and evacuate us. They got a dead VC propped up against a hooch with a cowboy hat on and cigarette stuck in his mouth. They're all wondering, where's ole Emmett? How's he doing back in Hopewell? And they're wondering why I ain't out there with them. Waiting for me. I'm just hanging on here with every bit of strength I've got. Christ, it exhausts me. I ain't got nothing left. Not for you, or Anita, or anybody else. There's something wrong with me. Like there's this hole in my heart. There's just something missing, and I can't get it back. Out there with them. I'm already half dead.

Just as Lonnie remarked earlier in the film, mentally Emmett is "still back in Vietnam."

Emmett's monologue is a deft expression of the post–Vietnam malaise that affected countless returning American soldiers. Springsteen chronicles this despair in "Vietnam," an early version of "Born in the U.S.A." and "Shut Out the Light." Set to a rockabilly backbeat,

Springsteen's male narrator caustically gibes that he "died in Vietnam." He returns home to widespread unemployment and the news that his sweetheart ran away with a rock and roll singer. All he sees when he passes the windows of Main Street is the reflection of a stranger, for his memories, hopes, and fears have all been left in Vietnam. He returns to America a hollow shell left to wander the streets of his hometown like an apparition—forgotten and unseen. In the same way, Emmett's life ended in Vietnam and he has been nothing but a phantom since his return. The loss of his friends and the traumatic violence of war damaged Emmett so much so that he was unable to make lasting connections with anyone on the home front. Through the candid revelation of her uncle's internal miseries, Sam is finally able to register the impact of the veterans' wartime experiences and their need to cover themselves with silence and hostility.

"Born in the U.S.A."

After attending Springsteen's August 25, 1984, *Born in the U.S.A.* tour concert at the Capital Centre in Landover, Maryland, Republican reporter (and Ronald Reagan's unofficial re-election campaign advisor) George Will published an article "A Yankee Doodle Springsteen" in the *Washington Post* praising the rock star for championing traditional American values. He wrote, "I have not got a clue about Springsteen's politics, if any, but flags get waved at his concerts while he sings songs about hard times. He is no whiner, and the recitation of closed factories and other problems always seems punctuated by a grand, cheerful affirmation: 'Born in the U.S.A.!'"[10] Like many other right-wing listeners, Will did not recognize the biting satire of Springsteen's patriotic chorus. Although Springsteen did use a mammoth American flag as a stage backdrop on both his album cover and the concert stage during the stadium leg of his *Born in the U.S.A.* tour, it stood not as a symbol of blind nationalistic worship but as a reminder of how far political leaders had strayed from the values the country was founded on. President Reagan also touted Springsteen as a conservative hero by mentioning him during a campaign speech in the musician's home state: "America's future rests in a thousand dreams inside our hearts. It rests in the message of hope in the songs of a man so many young Americans admire: New Jersey's own Bruce Springsteen. And helping you make those dreams come true is what this job of mine is all about."[11] Springsteen's scathing response to his September 21, 1984, audience at the Pittsburgh Civic Arena was that Reagan should start listening to *Nebraska*, which featured stark tunes about socioeconomic injustice without the distracting pop hooks of "Born in the U.S.A."

The original version of "Born in the U.S.A." is an austere and intimate acoustic ballad punctuated by aching wolf-like howls that could have easily fit on *Nebraska*, but the genius of the final song lies in its thundering instrumentals that envelop a tension between desperate, tragic verses and a rousing chorus. The galvanizing refrain often overshadows the somber body of the song and causes some more casual or conservative listeners to misinterpret it as a patriotic anthem. These vacuous fans completely misunderstand how Springsteen's clever protest only works within his grandiose framework. "Born in the U.S.A." was consciously crafted "as an indivisible, but inherently conflicted, whole," with the strains between its doleful lyrics and booming bombast, its solemn stanzas and anthemic chorus, a shrewd articulation of the Vietnam veteran's societal alienation and internal despair.[12]

"Born in the U.S.A." opens with the explosive smash of Max Weinberg's drums and the dazzle of Roy Bittan's synthesizer—euphoric sounds that belie the dismal introductory images of a deserted town and cowering beaten dog. If this is a song venerating the pomp of American mythos, the opening lines are an incredibly morose way to start. Upon returning home after killing legions of faceless yellow men to whom he is indifferent, Springsteen's despondent veteran cannot find a job at the local refinery or through the VA. The hiring man flippantly refers to him as "son," "as if he were a lost child or if he were asking for something unreasonable."[13] "Don't you understand?" he pleads, knowing that any excuse he tried to offer the veteran about the lack of employment opportunities would be futile. Springsteen's soldier realizes that society has abandoned him like a mangy stray. Would he have been better off dying along with his brother in Khe Sanh, the most gruesome and pointless battle in the war's history? There soldiers defended a worthless piece of ground for two months against constant barrage of savage assaults—which transformed the perimeter into a sea of rat-chewed bodies—only to be suddenly dismissed and the fort subsequently destroyed and abandoned.[14] Springsteen references this particular battle to emphasize the horrifying senselessness of the war. The verse closes with a snapshot of the brother embracing a Vietnamese woman, two enemies united in spite of bloodshed—an image of peace that flies in the face of the Reagan era's xenophobic ideals.

The brazen chorus between the acidic verses is not a proclamation of triumph, as George Will vapidly misconstrued, but of fury and confusion. Springsteen sings "Born in the U.S.A." with a gravellier rasp than usual, the voice of a worn-down man who identifies with a defeated, scruffy mongrel. He snarls the refrain with the same bitterness as his veteran, who discovers that despite serving overseas and sacrificing his life, he has been denied the rewards and protections he was promised as an American citizen. Forsaken and alone, his homeland is no longer a source of pride and comfort. The continual affirmation of his birthplace condemns the United States instead of celebrating it. Over and over again, Springsteen insists that America has betrayed the birthright of its people. Springsteen pounding his fist in the air to each drum effusion is not a gesture of earnest nationalism but of hollow misery; his "Born in the U.S.A." character sardonically salutes a country that does little to care for veterans like him. Being "Born in the U.S.A." means nothing.

Springsteen's says his "Born in the U.S.A." protagonist longs "to strip away that mythic America which was Reagan's image of America. He wants to find something real, and connecting. He's looking for a home in his country."[15] The majestic sounds of the E Street Band embody a chauvinistic America that boasts of its idealistic glories while at the same time abandoning veterans in need. Springsteen's howling screams in the song's denouement capture the devastation and wrath of thousands of men and women who were forgotten and scorned by their native soil. They cry out in search of that bond, for some leader or citizen to recognize and empathize with their pain. "Oh my God, no," Springsteen moans as the veteran crumbles into despair, haunted by the memories of combat and dismayed by the alienation of his homecoming. He finds himself left lost in the midst of a spiritual crisis, "like he has nothing left to tie him to society anymore. He's isolated from the government, isolated from his family, to the point where nothing makes sense," as Springsteen told Chet Flippo.[16] The neglected soldier roars beneath the pompous synthesizer sounds of victorious patriotism, fighting to be heard above the E Street Band's bombastic din and refusing to be kept silent and invisible. Springsteen will no longer let him be ignored. These haunting caterwauls in the coda rupture any possible nationalistic reading of the song. With his juggernaut "Born in the U.S.A.," Springsteen ingeniously envelops dolorous reflections on post–Vietnam American injustices—the veteran's struggle to find employment, societal abandonment, loss of fellow soldiers—within anthemic instrumentals to critique the

1980s political landscape. Narrow-minded conservative listeners could not hear beyond these monumental sounds or comprehend the social satire behind his seemingly jingoistic chorus.

The Broadway version of "Born in the U.S.A." radically transforms the anti-anthem into a sinister and deeply mournful southern-style requiem. The song becomes a gritty blues whine with minimal guitar mewls that Springsteen growls in a quiet, half-spoken word. This veteran has been burning down the road for forty years now, and you can hear the exhaustion in his voice, for he no longer has the energy to even sing the melody. Springsteen's hunched and lonely figure on the expansive stage, shadowed by the dusky stage lights, appears like a ghost who has been wandering his country for decades in search of a recognition that will never be found. There is no fist pump, no massive American flag backdrop, and no deafening drums. His action of stepping away from the microphone to fill the small theater with his frayed voice adds a solemn vulnerability to this tale of a browbeaten veteran with nowhere to turn. In this muted and seething performance, there is no mistaking Springsteen's intentions with the song.

Although the connection is made clearer in the novel, as filmgoers we can assume that Sam listens to the entire *Born in the U.S.A.* cassette on her Walkman and has a relationship with Springsteen's most controversial song. She does not misread it as an anthem of blind nationalistic pride—she perfectly cognizes its true meaning as an elegy for a country that failed its young men and women by forcing them to fight a foreign war that few supported and then leaving them to fend for themselves after returning home. Throughout the film, Sam complains about the silence surrounding Vietnam. "My mom acts like the Vietnam War was back in the Dark Ages," she says. Uncle Emmett, Tom, and the other veterans in her community simply pal around and refuse to reveal their emotional wounds. Sam is moved by the emasculated discontent of disenfranchised American soldiers that Springsteen captures on "Born in the U.S.A.," the same kind that she sees in Hopewell every day. Like Springsteen, Sam recognizes that the ramifications of Vietnam are not in the distant past but painfully in the present. Veterans may have been "burning down the road" for the past ten or more years, but that does not make their problems any less pertinent.

"The Rambo of rock and roll"

Springsteen used "Born in the U.S.A." to challenge the Reagan administration, which he staunchly opposed, but his message got lost in the song's gargantuan sounds and his appropriation of Americana iconography. During a 1984 interview for *Rolling Stone*, Kurt Loder asked Springsteen for his thoughts on Reagan's bid for re-election, to which Springsteen responded, "I think he presents a very mythic, very seductive image, and it's an image that people want to believe in. I think there's always been a nostalgia for a mythical America, for some period in the past when everything was just right. And I think the president is the embodiment of that for a lot of people. He has a very mythical presidency."[17] In his persona of "football hero, good soldier, faithful cowboy," Reagan used his presidency to turn back the clock and detach America from the divisive chaos of the 1960s and 1970s—an era filled with protests, radicalism, and violence spurred by the anti-war, civil rights, and second-wave feminist movements, as well as a declining economy, increasing unemployment, and post–Watergate distrust of the government.[18]

By using repeated phrases such as "renew the American spirit," "the rebirth of American tradition," and "recapture our destiny," Reagan's speech "Time to Recapture Our Destiny" asked his country to return to the imagined, romanticized past of the placid 1950s, a time when America was the greatest military power on the planet, nestled in its booming economy and the birth of suburbia.[19] Reagan wanted to reclaim the lost patriarchal mores of that era—the masculine might that guided the nuclear family and sustained the armed forces. Since the loss of Vietnam was a stain on the fabric of our nation's triumphant military history, the jingoistic ideologies of Reagan's white, male America worked to reinstate the lost masculinity of the male veteran, fallen confidence in American individualism, and resilient militarism.

This artificial chimera of a tranquil pre–Kennedy assassination America appeared in Reagan's "Morning in America" television advertisements, a quixotic collage of utopian suburbia set to wistful music. In this sequence, surrounded by manicured lawns and white picket fences, a businessman heads to work in his station wagon, a teenage boy completes his morning paper route, and a young, white heterosexual couple celebrates their Christian marriage. The maudlin montage ends with a giant American flag waving in the breeze that takes up the entire frame, not unlike the opening of Springsteen's "Born in the U.S.A." music video.[20] Springsteen openly condemned the eerily saccharine commercial: "And you say, well, it's not morning in Pittsburgh. It's not morning above 125th Street in New York. It's midnight, and, like, there's a bad moon risin.'"[21] For him, "Morning in America" presented a hackneyed pastorality that belied what was truly occurring in America at the time: economic disparity and an ignorance of marginalized people that he chronicled in his albums.

Part of Reagan's campaign to rectify the recent past was to restore the reputation and value of the American soldier in what Susan Jeffords defines as the project of remasculinization. He issued a public pardon of the Vietnam veteran, declaring him the "heart, spirit, and the soul of America."[22] The weak losers who were once rejected, spat on, and denied were reborn as formidable, laudable men defending their powerful nation with a mighty heroism. However, Emmett does not adhere to the pattern of remasculinization because his narrative arc climaxes with a moment of forthright vulnerability when he reveals how Vietnam affected him. *In Country* hinges on Emmett's confession as the climactic moment, a revelation in which he does not perpetuate the toxic ideologies of hypermasculinity by internalizing his emotions. The final shot in the film shows Emmett alongside Sam and Mamaw rather than leading them, a position that insists they will equally embark on their journey navigating post–Vietnam America and there is more than solely Emmett's patriarchal self-actualization at stake.

Sylvester Stallone's aggressive vigor and cartoonish muscularity in the souped-up action flick *Rambo: First Blood Part II* (1985) embodies Reagan's herculean vision of masculinity in post–Vietnam America. The *Chicago Tribune* named Springsteen "the Rambo of rock and roll" due to his similarly sculpted brawn accentuated by a bandana wrapped around his brow, further contributing to his false alignment with Republican values. Springsteen and Stallone's ostensibly white, heterosexual hard bodies were inextricably bound with American values, their bulging muscles embodying a masculine power that was missing on a national level after the failure in Vietnam.

Reagan chastised the feminine characteristics of weakness, non-aggression, and negotiation that drove the government's approach to the Vietnam War, observed in Congress' failure to back up its actions and the frequent decisions to retreat as opposed to defeat. "We should have asked for a declaration of war and called it a war.... Everyone thought that you have to fight a war without winning it or you might find yourself in a bigger war. Well, maybe General MacArthur was right, there is no substitute for victory," Reagan seethed, promising a more hard-lined, bellicose militarism in line with hypermasculine values.[23] After Rambo asks, "Do we get to win this time?" he provides Reagan with the kind of victory he wanted. The incensed soldier rewrites America's loss in Vietnam by bravely traversing the mysterious labyrinth of the Vietnamese jungle to vanquish the enemy as his country should have done all those years ago. With his ninja-like assassination skills and sinewy physique, there is no question of Rambo's masculinity, and he enables the Vietnam veteran to finally reign triumphant and return to his exalted position in society.

Conservative audiences saw in Springsteen's Grecian physique a fulfillment of Reagan's male ideal akin to Rambo. "There is not a smidgen of androgyny in Springsteen," George Will proudly declared in his article (a dig at gender-fluid artists of the time such as David Bowie and Prince).[24] The wholesome Americana of Springsteen's stage iconography—his short hair topped with a trucker's cap, plain white T-shirt and denim jeans, the elephantine American flag backdrop, and impassioned fist pumping on the robust chorus "Born in the U.S.A.!"—seemed to embody Reagan's virile homespun patriotism. Sam from *In Country* scrutinizes Springsteen's all-American *Born in the U.S.A.* album cover—the close-up of his denim-clad derriere with a baseball cap in the pocket and his shapely body "facing the flag, as though studying it, trying to figure out its meaning. It is such a big flag the stars don't even show in the picture—just red-and-white stripes."[25] Reagan and his right-wing faction saw Springsteen as a real-life, musical Rambo who wanted his devotees to love their country as much as he loved it. While Springsteen does care about what it means to live in America, he does not view his country through starry-eyed imaginings of bucolic mornings, nor does he mobilize a mindless machismo to defend it. His sensitive depictions of the Vietnam veterans' plight do not support Reagan's romanticized visions of a newly minted dauntless soldier and reveal the devastating extent of their continual suffering. On *Born in the U.S.A.*, Springsteen stands before a prodigious emblem of his country, lost in the expanse of its epic promise, before he pulls back this star-spangled curtain to reveal the foibles behind Reagan's mythic America.

Vietnam in Springsteen's Life and Music

Vietnam has been an overwhelming presence in Springsteen's life, from his days in the Castiles to his *Springsteen on Broadway* production (2017–2018). Springsteen was part of the "Vietnam Generation," where the war was an "inextricable and unavoidable part of American social, cultural, and political life," its chaotic brutality flickering on the television every night.[26] As he noted in an interview with Phil Sutcliffe, "In the States in the late '60s, if you weren't involved in protesting against the War and what the government was doing and the way the culture was changing, people thought there was something wrong with you. So that was bred into you and I carried that along with me."[27] Springsteen saw young men from his neighborhood be shipped off to Vietnam never to be seen again, or else returning with debilitating physical and mental injuries. As he says in "The River" preamble on the *Live/1975–85* album, "[A] lot of guys went, and a lot of guys didn't come back. And the lot that came back weren't the same anymore." The draft and deaths of his bandmate Bart Haynes and hero Walter Cichon in combat were dramatic and pivotal events in Springsteen's life that affirmed his liberal political ideologies and led to a decades-long exploration of Vietnam in his work.

After dropping out of Ocean County College in December 1969, Springsteen was no longer eligible for a college deferment and was swiftly summoned by the draft board for a physical. In his memoir, Springsteen recalls his turbulent emotions while reading that fateful, ominous summons: "I felt cold in my stomach. Not shocked, but momentarily gut-punched by the real world hitting hard. I was chosen to be a player in history, not of my own accord or desire, but because bodies were needed to stem the perceived Communist menace in Southeast Asia. My first thought was, 'Is this real? And what does it possibly have to do with me, my life, my ideas?'"[28] Springsteen quickly concocted a plan to avoid the draft: "In my travels I had met and talked to young men who'd fed themselves fat, starved themselves skinny or mutilated extremities."[29] Another friend bathed in milk and let the stench ferment for three days. Springsteen also recognizes the classism of the draft process and its ill effects on working-class communities like Sam's Hopewell. The privileged few did not have to resort to violent, self-flagellating means of avoiding the American military's clutches. He writes, "I heard about the wealthy with their doctor notes specially designed for remaining stateside and safe at home. I didn't have the recourse to anything so extravagant."[30]

Along with his fellow musicians "Mad Dog" Vinnie Lopez and Little Vinnie Roslin, Springsteen traveled to the Newark draft board and played the part of a "mumbling, bumbling, swishing ... freak on LSD" well.[31] He checked off all the alarming boxes, letting the recruiters know "they're trying to corral a drug-addicted, gay, pathologically bed-wetting lunatic who can barely write his name."[32] However, it was ultimately a concussion injury from a motorcycle accident when he was seventeen that gave him a 4-F (physically unfit) classification.

This is the same motorcycle accident that Springsteen memorably recounts in the opening monologue to "The River" from the *Live/1975–85* album, an incident that burst the simmering tensions between him and his domineering, hot-tempered father. Their already heated relationship turned apocalyptic when Douglas Springsteen took advantage of his bedridden son and invited a barber to chop off the young man's emasculating lengthy locks. Fed up with his son's lofty guitar ambitions and hippie attitudes, the elder Springsteen would incessantly barrage his son about his future plans. "I can't wait till the army gets you, when the army gets you they're gonna make a man out of you. They're gonna cut all that hair off and they'll make a man out of you," he would seethe. Springsteen's long hair was the external expression of his countercultural ideals. As a World War II veteran, Douglas bitterly resented the younger generation's pacific attitudes.[33] In his mind, a true red-blooded American male would defend his country no matter what and not run from combat. Douglas Springsteen thought the army would instill the patriotic and hypermasculine ideologies he valued and tried in vain to impart on his sensitive, bohemian dreamer of a son. For him, war was a boy's passage to becoming a man, and manhood was inextricably tied to violence and the ability to conquer an enemy. Springsteen's "The River" soliloquy closes on a tender note: when he told his father he had received the 4-F classification, Douglas managed to eke out a quiet but elated "That's good." As the perennial target of his father's disdain, this was Springsteen's gratifying proof that his father at least cared enough about him to fear his possible death in Vietnam.

Throughout Springsteen's long-haired days with his band Steel Mill, he engaged in several anti-war causes at Monmouth College.[34] On October 15, 1969, the band performed as part of the Moratorium to End the War in Vietnam. The following month, Steel Mill appeared in the campus' Vietnam Peace Offensive, returning again in December for a benefit concert to bring anti-war speakers to campus. They performed highly politicized and scathing anti–Vietnam songs penned by Springsteen. These gritty protest anthems have the same sort of brute honesty and indefatigable spirit as any of his later studio compositions. In "The War Is Over," backed by the band's signature psychedelic blues sound, a wailing young Springsteen uses a Middle Ages milieu as an allegory for the Vietnam conflict. The political leaders of the United States become tyrannical kings and queens distracted by farcical court jesters, ignoring the revolution brewing outside in the sounds of screaming children and the thousands of innocents they "murder in the name of freedom." In the vein of the American government, the despotic rulers of this kingdom "pledge allegiance in the face of a bomb," privileging their bloodlust for war over civility and peace. Springsteen spits this line out in a gurgling rage before launching into an elongated and howling guitar solo underscored by Danny Federici's wild organ.

"All Man the Guns" juxtaposes its straightforward pace and glassy vocals against harrowing lyrics about a "God-fearing patriotic man" horrified by the impending trials of battle. The night before he leaves for Vietnam, he has a nightmare about thundering cannons that jolts him awake, screaming in his urine-soaked bed. Despite his insistence that he would "fight the fiercest battle" and "cross the roughest land" for his beloved Mary, he is terrified that he will not return from Vietnam's tropical maze of horror. The narrator's fanatical need to win the war and come back as quickly as possible opposes his jingoistic Christian values; rather than bravely defend God's country for as long as needed, he is petrified and wants to hide within the safe confines of his home.

One of Springsteen's most audacious and withering censures of the Vietnam War is "America Under Fire," which brutally critiques the government's willingness to turn a blind eye to the harsh realities of the war and its calamitous consequences on veterans and their communities. The darkly misanthropic lyrics paint an apocalyptic vision of late 1960s and early 1970s America that eerily belies the smooth tempo. Springsteen envisages a country full of "conquered freak soldiers," blind and "viciously insane men" holding a cane and a cup while begging for money on street corners. These veterans returned from their tours of duty only to find that their hometowns cared little about their absence. Instead of being celebrated for their sacrifice, their neighbors regard them with the same disdain as before they left. The sweet, doting, and virtuous women they left behind "have all turned into whores," and even the bands they listened to have not improved. Left thunderstruck and alone, these Vietnam veterans find no credible reason for "all this madness and sorrow" and decide their participation in the war was utterly futile.

Midway through "America Under Fire," the instrumentals slowly unwind into a carnivalesque rhythm that signifies the absurdity and frivolity of war. Springsteen compares the bombs' behemoth boom to a clown's "big red balloon" and depicts bright rockets bursting and shattering the earth, "making the little girls cry." All the audience of this demented circus can do is laugh as airplanes barrage them with gunfire, napalm, and other weapons of mass destruction. Springsteen critiques traditional society's perverse willingness to equate such savage annihilation with masculinity in his Norman Rockwell–esque portrait of a mother and father kissing and shaking the hand of their son in his military uniform. The father proudly congratulates his newly minted soldier son on becoming a man. Here Springsteen boldly questions whether violence—particularly the massacre of innocent children and their families—should be what defines manhood. Steel Mill simultaneously duets eerie renditions of "America the Beautiful" and the *Mickey Mouse Club* theme song to highlight the farcical nature of the country's involvement with Vietnam, situating the men in power as boorish children playing with toy soldiers.

"Clouds" is an excerpt from one of Springsteen's auctioned-off notebooks from 1968. There is no official recording, but it is possible that Springsteen played this song during some of his acoustic shows that year. The lyrics are a heartbreaking portrait of a young Vietnam soldier on the precipice of death. Glancing up at the serene clouds languidly crossing the sky offers him an ephemeral refuge from the frenzied cries of war that rack his brain. It seems as if it has been a thousand years since he has been home with his loved one, whom he dreams of in the twilight. The more he strives to stay alive, the more his sanity wanes. Paper flags flying over the swath of soldiers' graves surrounding him are eerie reminders of his endangered mortality. Why must he give up his life for this unjust cause? What mistake was made to lead him here? He cannot fathom why he and thousands of other young men must sacrifice their lives for such a fatuous endeavor.

Springsteen returned to his exploration of Vietnam just a few years later on his 1973 debut album *Greetings from Asbury Park, N.J.* "Lost in the Flood" presents a soldier's homecoming to a ravaged and anarchic American landscape "as foreign and threatening as any battlefield."[35] Gunner wanders alone in an opiate haze through a burning and depraved metropolis littered with pregnant nuns and savage gangs staging shoot-'em-ups in the middle of the Bronx streets. He uses the sweet release of narcotics to dull his senses and avoid his painful combat memories. "Lost in the Flood" thunders with a resounding rage, the jagged crescendo of pounding drums, piercing guitars, and churning keyboards evoking the intensifying flood that submerges society. This flood symbolizes the degradation of Vietnam-era society, which swallows the veteran whole. Gunner fought in the war for the betterment of his country, but he regrettably returns to find it plunged into turmoil. Disillusioned by America's loss of innocence, Gunner intentionally catapults his Chevy stock super eight into a hurricane, his lifeless body smacking on the pavement "with such a beautiful thud."

In 1981 at the Sunset Marquis hotel in Los Angeles, Springsteen met the prolific paraplegic Vietnam veteran and anti-war movement leader Ron Kovic just a few months after he had purchased Kovic's best-selling memoir *Born on the Fourth of July* on a road trip during a pit stop at an Arizona drugstore. Kovic invited Springsteen to visit the Venice Veterans Center, a tense and somber experience that Springsteen recounted in his Broadway show:

> I'm usually pretty easy with people. I'm a bit like my mom, I can kind of talk to anybody. But once at the Center, I didn't know exactly how to respond to what I was seeing. My own life seemed simply frivolous in the face of some of the problems that these guys were having: the homelessness, the drug problems, the post-traumatic stress, young guys my age dealing with life-changing physical injuries.... I didn't know what to say to these guys. So I just listened.[36]

Springsteen was touched by the veterans' hardships and wanted to honor these men who paid body and soul for their country and received nothing in return. He collaborated with Bob Muller, head of the Vietnam Veterans of America, on a benefit concert for the foundation, which was floundering due to the lack of governmental support.

Muller's introduction before the performance held at the Los Angeles Memorial Sports Arena on August 20, 1981, recalls the societal disregard of the veteran's plight that Sam witnesses in *In Country*: "[T]here was a lot of controversy and a lot of pain surrounding the tragedy of Vietnam and because of that, a lot of people are trying to forget it and pretend that it never happened.... But tonight is the first step in ending the silence that has surrounded Vietnam."[37] The leader of Sam's local community center similarly reflects on the sparsely attended Veterans' Awareness dance: "Well, I thought more would come. Hardly anybody showed up who wasn't in country. People just don't care, I guess. As far as they're concerned Vietnam never even happened." An exasperated Tom tells Sam that she "might as well stop asking questions about the war. Nobody cares. Nobody gives a shit." Sam retorts in frustration, "Well, I do. My daddy died over there and I want to know what happened to him. God, nobody will tell me anything."

Springsteen uses the analogy of a dark alley to articulate America's suppression and ignorance of the Vietnam veteran:

> It's like, when you feel like you're walking down a dark street at night, and out of the corner of your eye you see somebody getting hurt or somebody getting hit in the dark alley, but you keep walking on because you think it don't have nothing to do with you and you just want to get home. Well, Vietnam turned this whole country into that dark street, and unless we're able to walk down those dark alleys and look into the eyes of the men and the women that are down there and the things that happened, we're never gonna be able to get home.[38]

Sam's hometown of Hopewell, Kentucky, is that dark alley. Her entire community, including her own mother, ignores the traumas of the local Vietnam veterans because they are "emblems of a failed war that America would rather forget."[39] "They all act like there's some big, deep, dark secret or something," Sam bemoans. Rather than confront the pain of a dissentious time period, it was easier for Sam's hometown to ignore what the veterans went through and continue living as usual. As Dave Marsh explains, "[t]he war had revealed a massive split in American society, and acknowledging the vets' existence could tear it open again."[40] Sam wants to shine a light down that dark alley and uncover the truths of Vietnam in order to help her family and friends heal their physical and mental wartime maladies.

The knowledge that he was tasked with lifting disconsolate spirits and illuminating the decades-long oppression and struggles of Vietnam veterans who were in the audience weighed heavily on Springsteen and accounts for the magnificence of what has become one of his most legendary performances. In the recordings, Springsteen and his E Street Band barrel through the songs like a high-speed locomotive. The stunning set list is an emotional odyssey that promotes steadfast perseverance in the face of adversity. Springsteen's lyrics take on a greater emotional resonance in light of the Vietnam veterans' presence. In "Prove It All Night," his doubt that dreams will ever come true transforms into a bitter, incensed condemnation of his country's failure to live up to the romanticized American Dream for its soldiers. The final lines of "Darkness on the Edge of Town" blaze like they've never been heard before as Springsteen ardently beseeches veterans to stand proud, make themselves known, and refuse to surrender. The "pulling out of here to win" lyric from "Thunder Road" envisages a roseate future, assuring veterans that they will find the justice they seek and overcome their greatest traumas. Springsteen's agonized moans in the denouement of "Jungleland" lament the thousands who lost their lives in Vietnam or who returned home and continued to suffer. The concert's crown jewel is Springsteen's hauntingly raw performance of "The River." He sings in a brittle voice of immensurable despair, fully inhabiting the role of a young man from the same impoverished background as many of the battered veterans who sat before him. Springsteen was supposedly so overcome with emotion that he had to stop singing. In the end, "A Night for the Vietnam Veterans" saved Muller's organization from financial ruin, brought more awareness to the mistreatment and dire state of America's veterans, and went on to become one of Springsteen's greatest artistic triumphs. "Without Bruce Springsteen, there would be no Vietnam veteran's movement," Muller declared, and the organization would not have been brought into the national consciousness.[41]

During the period of 1981 to mid–1984 for the *Nebraska* and *Born in the U.S.A.* albums, Springsteen frequently explored the theme of Vietnam in his songwriting, likely inspired by his interactions with Ron Kovic, Bob Muller, and the other wounded veterans he met in Venice. "Highway Patrolman" from *Nebraska* is a hushed meditation on the frailty of familial ties that features a disturbed Vietnam veteran whose experience during the frenzied and senseless war aggravates his rebellious tendencies, unlike his strait-laced policeman brother who received a farm deferment. The tenebrous *Born in the U.S.A.* outtake "Shut Out the Light" poignantly captures the anxieties of a veteran's homecoming, "surviving the war and coming *back* and not surviving."[42] In this song, immediately after the airplane wheels touch down on the blacktop, Springsteen's veteran Johnson "Johnny" Leneir buries himself in the dark corner of a local bar on Main Street. Johnny does not return home as the hero he was expected to be; instead, he lies paralyzed, staring at the ceiling in the middle of the night, tormented by his memories in country. The "Welcome Home Johnny" banner that his family made, which stretches across the porch, and the glistening chrome of his Ford, newly polished by his brother Bobby, seem to mock him—images of comfort and joy that now appear anything but. Despite the affectionate warmth of his mother, brother, wife, and children, he feels nothing but emptiness, manifested in Springsteen's monotonous rhythm and flat vocals.

The extra verse that Springsteen later omitted references drug addiction—a significant problem for Vietnam veterans. After supper, Johnny locks himself in his bedroom and shoots up, dulling his senses and silencing his mental demons. In addition to his nightmares and PTSD, the nightly shakes and sweats he suffers from can be read as symptoms of heroin withdrawal. The heartrending song ends with Johnny standing in a nameless Maryland river overlooking his brightly lit hometown, dreaming "of where he's been," perhaps back in Vietnam so that he may be united with his fellow soldiers who truly understand him, echoing Emmett's confession at the end of *In Country*. Although Johnny had "gone and done his best" just as "the other before him" who fought in World War II or the Korean War, he was not met with the same societal support. Despite his caring family, his psychological wounds are far too deep, and he succumbs to dangerous, all-consuming habits. He wades further into the water as it rises above his chest—an image not of baptismal renewal but of suicide.

The *Ghost of Tom Joad* outtake "Brothers Under the Bridge" is a somber, half-whispered ballad about a group of homeless Vietnam veterans living in an underpass near the San Gabriel mountains. Springsteen's unnamed narrator addresses the daughter whom he abandoned twenty years ago. He recounts his time as a naïve young soldier marveling at how the streets of Saigon carried the same Coke machines as his hometown, an icon of the faraway comforts of American suburbia that he sorely missed. Shortly after he returned home, he realized that he could no longer function in mainstream life and retreated into the Santa Ana desert. With no possessions or close human relationships, all he does is try to survive in the dangerous territory where his friend Billy Devon recently burned to death from the dry brush. In the final verse of his monologue, the veteran recalls being "just a kid" when he returned from the war in 1972, before his daughter's birth. During a Veterans' Day parade, he stood in his dress blues next to her mother, watching the bright red, white, and blue pomp pass him by. He knew he should feel the swell of pride and familial comfort, but "something slip[ped]." No longer present, his sanity snapped and psychological well-being unspooled, severing him from his family for the rest of his life. "Brothers Under the Bridge" is an absolutely devastating ode to post-war loneliness. It brings awareness to the thousands of homeless veterans who occupy America and their acute struggles with mental illness.

Although the song "Nothing Man" is included on Springsteen's post–9/11 opus *The Rising* and appears to be from the perspective of a firefighter or rescue worker, it was originally written about a Vietnam veteran. The unnamed narrator's "brave young life" was "forever changed" by the travesties of war, but his friends and neighbors act as if nothing has changed, echoing Springsteen's "America Under Fire" lyric about the countrymen who "look just as they did before." These lines speak more to the post–Vietnam zeitgeist of ignorance and shame rather than 9/11, which was a devastating catastrophe that could not be ignored and inspired a communal fellowship among Americans. The Nothing Man's companions refuse to acknowledge his pain because they, like many of the characters from *In Country*, wish to pretend the Vietnam War never happened. After fighting in a needless and abhorred war, the only heroism the Nothing Man can lay any claim to is in his willpower not to commit suicide with the gun resting on his night table. Springsteen's voice aches with the bottomless hurt that drives this rueful line. The title of this poignant ballad connotes a Vietnam veteran more than a 9/11 rescue worker—men and women heralded for their heroic sacrifices during such a confounding tragedy. By contrast, Vietnam veterans were broken symbols of a dark war and divisive time period in American history. They were willfully forgotten and shunned, made voiceless apparitions through America's hatred and ignorance. They were the nothing men.

Inspired by Springsteen's own visits to the Vietnam Veterans Memorial in Washington, D.C., "The Wall" from the *High Hopes* (2014) album is Springsteen's softly bitter elegy for his New Jersey bar band hero Walter Cichon, front man of the Motifs and the first true star Springsteen had ever been close to. Cichon served as a rifleman in Kontum Province, South Vietnam, and suffered a head wound on March 30, 1968. Shortly after, he was deemed "missing in action"; his body was never recovered. The song's narrator condemns the wealthy heads of state who sent his young friend to die and now leisure idly "in rich dining halls." The recollection of his buddy laughing in his Marine uniform is a direct reference to Springsteen's Castiles bandmate Bart Haynes joking before he left for Vietnam, a place he could not even pick out on a map. Springsteen's taut guitar strums and mournful organ interlude evoke the "hard tears" that pour from his eyes as he touches the pitch-black stone in a gesture of mourning while the closing trumpet evokes the funereal "Taps."

In the final scene of *In Country*, Sam and Emmett travel to the Wall. As Springsteen's song reminds us, this monument is an important symbol of remembrance and honor that allows people to reconcile, or at the very least confront, their post-war pain and anxieties. The dog tags, wreaths of flowers, and bright red ribbons that litter the ground before the great black stone in Springsteen's dirge mirror *In Country*'s cinematography as the camera glides over the various gifts left by mourners on the memorial's ground. Emmett places his dog tags within the crack of the Wall, finally free of his own survivor's guilt. Like Springsteen's narrator, he places his hand on the hard memorial in a quiet and reflective repose, a moving image that unites those left behind and the spirits of the fallen. In the third stanza of "The Wall," Springsteen wonders whether his departed friend's eyes "could cut through that black stone" and recognize him after all those years, a line that recalls Sam's action of leaving a gift for her father; by placing her high school graduation portrait at the foot of the memorial stone, Sam "closes the spiritual gap that she has increasingly felt since graduation and completes literally as well as symbolically the family portrait."[43] In his letters, Dwayne often wrote to Irene that he couldn't wait for her to send him a picture of Sam. This act fulfills his wish, allowing him "to see" the picture of his child. Through these rituals of leaving behind gifts, Emmett and Sam are free to leave the conflicts of Vietnam behind them.

"When I go to Washington … I'm glad that Mad Dog's, Little Vinnie's, and for that matter my name isn't up on that wall, but it was 1969 and thousands and thousands of young men to come would be called, simply sacrificed just to save face for the powers at be, who by

Sam (Emily Lloyd), Emmett (Bruce Willis), and other mourners pay their respects at the Vietnam Veterans Memorial in Washington, D.C. (www.photofestnyc.com).

then already knew it was a lost cause.... So I do sometimes wonder who went in my place, because somebody did," a doleful Springsteen confesses during *Springsteen on Broadway*, suggesting that some semblance of survivor's guilt has weighed on him throughout most of his life. Springsteen's decades-long exploration of the Vietnam veteran experience, from his early band Steel Mill until his residency under the footlights of Broadway, affirms that it has. Vietnam was a titanic event that shaped Springsteen's life and his work. His Vietnam veteran characters are inspired by the damaged soldiers of his Freehold hometown, the activists Ron Kovic and Bob Muller, and the countless others he met in Venice and elsewhere. Their mistreatment was evidence of a failed American promise to protect and care for its citizens. The social disdain and neglect they received upon their homecoming revealed an uncharacteristic American callousness that Springsteen detested and challenged. Throughout his illustrious career, Springsteen has offered a sensitive and considerate examination of the Vietnam veteran's ennui and encouraged his country to see them as broken men who did not deserve to become symbols of America's humiliation—men who should be embraced, commended for their sacrifices, and absolved of their suffering.[44]

Generations Apart

During the 1980s, when *In Country* takes place, "Born in the U.S.A." dominated the airwaves and caught the attention of the fictional Samantha Hughes, a teenage girl doing everything in her power to learn what the Vietnam War meant to her family, community, and country. In both the book and the movie, she wonders what happened over there to affect her uncle and his friends so strongly and shroud them in secrecy. Springsteen aids her in this process, a male voice that conveys the pain and trauma of the veterans Sam strives to understand. Jewison includes some of the Springsteen allusions from Mason's text because he recognizes the significance of Springsteen's relationship with Vietnam and the 1980s American political landscape. Like Sam, Springsteen was an outsider who tried to make sense of a war he did not directly participate in. She is drawn to Springsteen because he articulates the turmoil of Emmett and Tom's enigmatic generation, as well as the tensions of post–Vietnam America during the 1980s, and refuses to let the perspectives of those who served in Vietnam be silenced any longer.

Philadelphia

Philadelphia (1993) was the first mainstream Hollywood film to tackle the AIDS crisis, nearly a decade after the disease's emergence. It tells the story of Andrew Beckett, a high-profile attorney fired for his illness, and the only lawyer who will represent him in suing his former firm is the homophobic Joe Miller. Springsteen's song for the film, "Streets of Philadelphia," went on to become a critical and commercial success, garnering significant radio play, four Grammy Awards,[1] and an Academy Award for Best Original Song. Director Jonathan Demme made *Philadelphia* "for the malls" in order to challenge and "reach the people who couldn't care less about people with AIDS," particularly those victims in the LGBTQ community.[2] Demme's rather lofty goal was to unravel homophobia, which he considered the adverse "fabric of American society."[3]

Most of the scripts that originally passed Demme's desk about the AIDS epidemic centered on its heterosexual victims, and although their stories are equally valid, the director wanted to contribute to positive queer cinematic representation. Demme was driven in part by a need to atone for his past. Demme's *Silence of the Lambs* (1991) was condemned by AIDS activist Larry Kramer as "one of the most virulently and insidiously homophobic films ever made" due to its unfavorable depiction of a transgender character, the serial killer Buffalo Bill (aka Jame Gumb).[4] Kramer and other gay rights advocates argued that Demme framed Gumb's gender identity as a terrifying pathology, enabling him to fulfill the transgendered killer trope (see *Psycho* [1960], *Freebie and the Bean* [1974], *Cruising* [1980], and *Dressed to Kill* [1980]).[5] Such criticisms served as a personal and professional wake-up call for Demme and motivated him to helm screenwriter Rob Nyswaner's *Philadelphia*. *Philadelphia* became a milestone for LGBTQ on-screen representation in mainstream cinema.

Philadelphia was released in the midst of the underground New Queer Cinema movement in the early 1990s. Born from an "outrage about the public response to the AIDS crisis" (or lack thereof), the independent features of the New Queer Cinema movement, such as Stephen Frears' *My Beautiful Launderette* (1985), Todd Haynes' *Poison* (1991), and Gus Van Sant's *My Own Private Idaho* (1991), were authentic depictions of queer identity with a brazen "in your face attitude."[6] New Queer Cinema boldly subverted "the unspeakable nature of homosexuality in post–World War Two Hollywood films."[7] Classic Hollywood cinema had established a connotative representation of queer men and women in which the details of their sexuality were kept out of sight and rarely spoken of.[8] Within these films, LGBTQ identity was restricted to scatters of subtext and innuendo, with the characters having "empty, lonely, pitiful, and all too often deadly" lives or serving as objects of disdain and ridicule.[9] Juan Botas, a late friend of Jonathan Demme who was diagnosed with AIDS and served as the subject of the documentary *One Foot on a Banana Peel, the Other Foot in the Grave: Secrets from the Dolly Madison Room* (1994), shrewdly pointed out that queer characters in such films were relegated to being ridiculous comic-relief caricatures, demented killers, or dead.[10] "It's very hard growing up gay and being exposed to all these stereotypes," Botas remarked.

In his bid to appeal to conservative heterosexual audiences, Demme sacrificed the kind of nuanced and unabashed depiction of queer characters found in independent New Queer Cinema for a portrayal that, despite his best efforts, relies on connotation nearly as much as the films of classic Hollywood. Demme completely erases Andrew's sexuality in the lack of genuine physical intimacy between him and his partner Miguel. Although they dance and Miguel kisses Andrew's hand, they never kiss on the lips as a typical couple would, especially when one of them was dying. Tom Hanks, who plays Andrew, glibly argues that such an action would have been a distractive keystone, the only aspect of the film that spectators and critics would focus on.[11] Perhaps what Hanks really means is that he did not want to kiss a man, a preference that co-star Denzel Washington also reportedly adhered to. Demme likewise cut a sequence of Andrew and Miguel lying in bed together. Screenwriter Ron Nyswaner (who is gay) argues that "its point was so obvious that it was offensive to put it in. Politically it would've worked, but not cinematically."[12] While the scene does include incredibly hackneyed dialogue, the quotidian images of the couple exchanging "I love you" and snuggling would have added a sense of verisimilitude to their romantic relationship. But Demme succumbed to his fear of alienating traditionalist spectators with the sight of two men sharing tender physical expressions of their love for one another. He told Anthony DeCurtis of *Rolling Stone*, "When we see two men kissing, we're the products of brainwashing—it knocks us back 20 feet. And with *Philadelphia*—I'm sorry, Larry Kramer—I didn't want to risk knocking our audience back 20 feet with images they're not prepared to see."[13] As part of targeting the masses in the malls—spaces that strongly oppose the tiny art houses of the New Queer Cinema movement—Demme had to sanitize his gay characters' sexuality.

For lesbian director Rose Troche, *Philadelphia* is not a gay film "but a tidy representation of gays, a safe film that straights could embrace because everyone knows Tom Hanks is straight. There's no way that film would've done what it did if they'd cast a gay man in the lead."[14] Indeed, Demme capitalized on Hanks' affable star image as the quintessential American Everyman in order to placate his mass market audience. "When you cast Tom Hanks, you don't have to try to get your audience to like the character," he explains.[15] In the documentary *The Celluloid Closet*, Hanks elaborates on how his nonthreatening on-screen persona helped draw audiences: "People with AIDS make me nervous, but Tom Hanks is saying yes to it, so he wants us to come." His mere presence incites favorable spectatorship, enabling those who are insensitive to AIDS and homosexuality to bear witness to the sufferers' plight. Hanks constructs Andrew as a "starting pitcher"—hard working, good natured, and pragmatic—the kind of guy you could "watch the Super Bowl with."[16] In other words, Andrew passes as straight and adheres to the conventions of traditional masculinity, thereby erasing—or connoting—his gay identity in order to mollify the film's orthodox heterosexual consumers.[17] Larry Kramer accused Hanks of embodying a bland "noble gay white hero trope" because his character was "an utter cipher. I couldn't tell you anything about him—opinions, beliefs or even whether he's gay."[18]

Springsteen acknowledged in his interview with *The Advocate*—his first time speaking openly about the LGBTQ community and with a queer publication—that Demme "wanted to take a subject that people didn't feel safe with and were frightened by and put it together with people that they *did* feel safe with."[19] The director approached Springsteen in the same vein as Hanks because he also "identified with a testosterone, machismo kind of thing," thus providing the unconverted straight men in the audience with a pair of shoes they "could feel comfortable inside."[20] The ideal of walking in someone else's shoes, of ushering his audience into the worldview and circumstances of a disparate person's inner life through his words, is a perfect fit for Springsteen's songwriting style, as reflected in his use of first-person narration in "Streets of Philadelphia." "You can't tell people what to think. You can show them by saying, 'Put on these shoes, walk in these shoes.' People then recognize themselves in characters whose lives on the surface seem to have no relation to theirs," Springsteen elaborates regarding his lyrical approach.[21] Through the vessel of Springsteen, the rugged quintessence of American manhood, Andrew's queer life becomes identifiable and the spectator shares in his feelings of loneliness and despair.

Specifically placing "Streets of Philadelphia" within the film's opening title sequence immediately anchors the spectator in the subjective consciousness of someone with AIDS who knows their life is slipping away, thereby allowing homophobic audiences to emotionally identify with Andrew from the beginning. "Streets of Philadelphia" not only constructs the opening montage but also expresses specific moments in the rest of the film. Countering the critical contention that Springsteen universalizes the language of the song so that the narrator could be suffering from any terminal illness, I will demonstrate how "Streets of Philadelphia" abounds with images of AIDS that Demme realizes in his film. For Springsteen, his musical contribution to *Philadelphia* was a chance to "clarify my own feelings about gay and lesbian civil rights" and connect to his LGBTQ fans in spite of his "very heterosexual, very straight" image.[22] However, further examination of Springsteen's extra-diegetic concert performances and other songs points toward a queer aesthetic that contrasts Demme's—and Springsteen's own—contention that he is a paragon of robust heterosexual masculinity.

The City of Brotherly Love

Demme wanted the "most up-to-the-minute, guitar-dominated American rock anthem about injustice" for his opening montage, "a hard rocking song to placate and reassure the young hetero males in the audience."[23] He first contacted Neil Young for a piece in the vein of "Southern Man," but Young composed the doleful "Philadelphia," which was better suited for the final memorial sequence. Demme then requested a "kick-ass" anthem from Springsteen, who returned with the soul-stirring "Streets of Philadelphia," leading the director to quickly abandon his ideas for the film's introduction.[24]

Philadelphia begins with the sound of a metronomic hip-hop drum beat against the company credits and introductory black screen. An angelic and moody synthesizer reminiscent of a church organ conducts a fade in to a long shot of the Philadelphia cityscape. These oscillating chords, "melancholy, reflective, and metaphoric of the protagonist's societal alienation," propel the camera's steady zoom into the Benjamin Franklin Bridge before Demme cuts to closer shots of the skyscrapers, welcoming the spectator into the "City of Brotherly Love."[25] Accompanied by Springsteen's lachrymose instrumentals and voice of "spiritual stillness," these otherworldly aerial images of Philadelphia "exude a foreboding feeling."[26] The birthplace of America sits under God and his watchful eye. Although the city holds enormous promise for the up-and-coming Andrew, it will ultimately abandon him.

The title card overlays a shot of Philadelphia City Hall, with its statue of the city's founder William Penn adorning the top, a symbol of the white heterosexual masculinity that defines America's institutional forces. Despite its simplicity, the title *Philadelphia* holds great significance: it points toward the birthplace of American democracy and its moniker "the City of Brotherly Love."[27] Positioning the title over the image of City Hall signals how the film will question America's commitment to its credo "liberty and justice for all." If the city that preaches brotherly love persecutes and abhors Andrew for his sexuality, how can we as a nation say that we stand for the fair treatment of all our neighbors? The space of Philadelphia should embody our nation's intrinsic values of equality, security, and freedom for all its citizens, virtues passed down from the founding fathers who once roamed the city's municipal vestibules.[28] That Andrew's firing, such a flagrant obstruction of justice, occurs in the heart of America is unforgivable.

Demme uses a definitively American space riddled with historic civic symbols to critique the authenticity of the country's ideologies and failure to embrace queer citizens within the national sphere. He accentuates his interrogation of national beliefs by using a thoroughly liberal American musical icon on the film's soundtrack. Springsteen's epic and extensive musical vision of his country stems from an interest "in what it means to live in America. I'm interested in the kind of country we live in and leave our kids. I'm interested in trying to define what that country is," as he told Scott Pelley.[29] Both Springsteen and *Philadelphia* seek to hold America to its promises by truly accepting the LGBTQ community as an essential part of the nation's identity.

"A wholeheartedly Eisenstienian 'intellectual montage' over which the opening credits are superimposed" follows the long shots of the city.[30] It has a punchy pace that smoothly glides through an American menagerie literally on the streets of Philadelphia: people dancing or playing in a park, cushy suburban homes, firefighters, dockworkers, dilapidated and graffiti-ridden buildings, waiters in an upscale restaurant, winding soup kitchen lines, a homeless person sleeping in a pile of leaves, and schoolchildren visiting the Liberty Bell. The camera races past a mural depicting Pilgrims, Native Americans, and immigrants overlooking the Statue of Liberty. This painted presence of the nation's early settlers alludes to the country's puritanical history that modern conservatives use as a basis for their discrimination; they make signs that say "Adam and Eve, not Adam and Steve" and reference the Leviticus 18:22 passage ("Thou shalt not lie with mankind, as with womankind: it is an abomination") as evidence for God's hatred of homosexuals.

This quintessentially American locale serves as the backdrop for Andrew Beckett's turmoil. Most of the grounded opening shots could be read from Andrew's point of view; he is both the song's narrator and the montage constructor as he observes the bustling activity on the streets and avenues of Philadelphia. The metropolis' vivacity overwhelms him while his body gradually erodes. Yet there are also moments when people break the fourth wall and wave at the passing camera, greeting the spectator instead of Andrew. Richard C. Cante narrowly argues that this documentary-like referentiality is an odd choice that disrupts the narrative's spatiotemporal logic, but the characters' welcoming nature warmly invites wary spectators into the controversial subject.[31] By gazing into the camera and addressing the spectator head on, the smiling figures on screen are no longer fictional characters but the embodiment of one's neighbors, family, or friends. Demme uses this docu-style opening to inform spectators that *Philadelphia* is not just a narrative concocted by the Hollywood machine; rather, it reflects a tangible, immediate event, and people with AIDS are human beings who live among them. The sounds of the city and its people bleed through Springsteen's soundtrack—clapping hands, barking dogs, clattering pots and pans, the rush of traffic—

thus adding a sense of realism. Overall, Springsteen's heartfelt composition delicately buoys the smooth cinematography, crafting a poetic opening sequence that immediately fixes the spectator in its emotional resonance. While a rocker like "Southern Man" certainly would have given the montage a buzzing enthusiasm, Springsteen's ethereal elegy mourns America's lost ideal of liberty and justice for all and is an impeccable depiction of the spiritual vulnerability and social loneliness Andrew feels due to his imminent death. Its languorous, staid tempo; Springsteen's quiet, soporific vocals; and the surrounding spiritual choir that resembles a host of angels all evoke Andrew's plight as a man who has reached the end of his life and is struggling to hold on.

The music video for "Streets of Philadelphia" borrows heavily from the film's beginning. Directed by Jonathan Demme's brother Ted, it went on to receive the MTV Video Music Award for Best Video from a Film. Springsteen continues the film's documentary approach by looking into the camera while he sings live. He appears with a shaggy goatee and grungy clothes, bundled in a sweatshirt and leather jacket, similar to Hanks' look in the middle of the film. Instead of subjective shots of the city, we observe the song's narrator (embodied in the figure of Springsteen) plod along the smoky and trash-hewn sidewalks. The video contextualizes the song's ideal of "what it's like to feel very connected to a place but to simultaneously feel so radically alienated as to be, in effect, not there at all" in the image of Springsteen trudging with his head facing the ground in a defeated stance while no one acknowledges his presence.[32]

In between shots of Springsteen, the music video inserts a close-up of Andrew standing dejectedly on a street corner. Ted Demme lifts this image from the film's second non-diegetic use of "Streets of Philadelphia," an alternate version of the song with saxophone and harmonies by Ornette Coleman and "Little" Jimmy Scott. The haunting choral vocalizations underscore Andrew's most defeated moment, when his case is rejected by Joe Miller (along with every other lawyer in Philadelphia). During their meeting, Joe cannot hide his homophobia, offering Andrew scraps of insincere sympathy, flippantly regarding his deadly illness as "a bitch," and refusing to shake his hand out of fear that the disease can be contracted by mere touch. While Springsteen's hypnotic drum loop backs the keening vocals, Demme focuses on Andrew in an extreme close-up as he pushes back tears and stares into the distance in disbelief. The blurs of nameless faces obscure the frame for the few seconds that they linger and the law office's door continually revolves behind him—a symbol of life's perpetual motion while Andrew slowly withers away. Springsteen's song acutely expresses Andrew's "hopelessness through a recognition that there will be no saving grace, whether it be supernatural, medical, or communal," and the "overwhelming loneliness that results from physical immiseration and social invisibility."[33] In this brief scene, Hanks magnificently portrays Andrew's profound despair and cognizance of his mortality.

Communion

Analysis of "Streets of Philadelphia" is often divorced from an intertextual study of *Philadelphia*, but closer examination reveals how Springsteen infuses moments of Demme's film into his song. A dirge sung in a dying breath from Andrew's perspective, "Streets of Philadelphia" is a tender expression of the character's battle with AIDS. Critics such as Robert Kirkpatrick argue that Springsteen universalized the lyrics of "Streets of Philadelphia" to ensure that it "would receive wide airplay and, thus, spread the message of the film (albeit indirectly) to help 'Philadelphia' to play in Kansas,"[34] but this contention overlooks just how Springsteen captures the physical and emotional realities of AIDS, echoing numerous scenes in *Philadelphia*. Springsteen may not sing the word "AIDS," but he doesn't need to—the nature of the disease permeates his text.

Reading "Streets of Philadelphia" through the lens of Andrew's point of view establishes the addressee in Springsteen's lyrics—the brother to whom he relays his inner turmoil—as Joe Miller. *Philadelphia* uses the character of Joe to "chart out different positions vis-a-vis homosexuality from ignorance to humanist enlightenment."[35] Conservative spectators identify with Joe's homophobia and (hopefully) learn from his journey toward acceptance. Through Joe's eventual embrace (or, at the very least, tolerance) of the LGBTQ community, Demme holds up a mirror to the audience and asks them to do the same. Several scenes designate the extent of Joe's bigotry. While cooking dinner for his wife in his stately suburban home, the site of their heterosexual domesticity, Joe swishes around with his hands on his hips, assuming the pose of the "sissy" homosexual stereotype—the frilly floral print apron he dons punctuating his effeminate performance. In a high-pitched voice, he mockingly ponders how gay men have sex: "Don't they get confused? Is that yours or mine?" Joe continues, "I don't want to be in bed with anybody that is stronger than me or has more hair on their chest than I do. You can call me old-fashioned or conservative—just call me a man. Besides, I think you have to be a man to really understand how disgusting that whole idea is." Such dialogue brings to mind Quentin Crisp's comment in *The Celluloid Closet*: "Mainstream people dislike homosexuality because they can't help concentrating on what homosexual men do to one another. And when you contemplate what people do, you think of yourself doing it. And they don't like that." For many heterosexual men, two women having sex is titillating—Joe raises no scruples about his wife's lesbian sister—but the idea of two men making love is revolting because they equate the masculine expression of intimacy, sensuality, and tenderness with weakness.[36]

Joe perpetuates the toxic ideal that homosexual males are not considered "real men" because of their same-sex desires and rejection of hegemonic masculinity. To him, gay men are feckless and abominable creatures to be feared for their sexual and gender fluidity. "I hate how they try to be macho and faggot at the same time," he says. As Joe's involvement in Andrew's trial gains notoriety, his insistence on upholding his heterosexual manhood intensifies; he takes care to assert that he finds homosexuality sickening and verbally threatens a gay man who hits on him with derogatory slurs. *Philadelphia* also explores the roots of Joe's homophobia so that spectators might reflect on their own, similar indoctrination. Joe tells Andrew that he was brought up to believe that "queers are weird, queers are funny, dress like their mother, afraid to fight, danger to little kids, all they want to do is get into your pants."

While Joe is indifferent to Andrew's suffering because of his dismal view of homosexuality, Andrew searches for some semblance of an interpersonal relationship with him. In the "Streets of Philadelphia," Andrew's only hope in a world bereft of benevolence is that his "brother" Joe will accept him before he is consumed by his disease. Springsteen's harrowing descriptions of Andrew as "bruised and battered" and "wastin' away" so much that he barely recognizes his own face implies various AIDS symptoms. The loss of an immune system instigates assorted maladies, such as Kaposi's Sarcoma (darkened lesions of the skin), severe bruising, fluid in the lungs, immense fatigue, shortness of breath, and pneumonia, as well as rapid weight loss. Hanks lost twenty-six pounds for the role in order to embody Andrew's emaciation—the "wastin' away" and shedding of clothes that no longer fit him. Carl Fullerton and Alan D'Angerio's makeup work (for which they received an Academy Award nomination) gave Hanks the dark eye circles, pallid complexion, and clamminess of his character's steady degradation. Throughout the film, Andrew grows "increasingly wearied and depleted as he vainly fights to restore his humanity in the unforgiving and cruel courtroom—one representative of a microcosm of American society," and we read this emotional and physical weight in the sublime Hanks' withering body.[37]

The second verse of "Streets of Philadelphia" shifts the focus from Andrew's deteriorating physical condition to his inner torment and overwhelming isolation. Andrew tromps through the streets until his legs feel like stone, an interminable thousand-mile journey symbolic of his inability to find political sympathy or social acceptance. "Each mile represents a crucial part of the labor he has invested into finding a loving community," Nathan Smith argues.[38] During the onset of the AIDS epidemic in the late 1980s and early 1990s, victims were ostracized on national, communal, and familial levels. They received little public acknowledgment or legislative intervention. Even clergy members would rebuff them, either out of fear or through faith-based repudiation. Although Andrew is lucky to have a doting and accepting family,[39] he is rejected by all of his legal peers until Joe reluctantly takes the case. And even though Joe takes on Andrew as his client, he does not fully support him or his cause.

While Andrew walks down the winding avenues, the ghostly voices of "friends vanished and gone" surround him, referring to the mass deaths of AIDS victims. By 1999, nearly 120,000 Americans had died of AIDS, and one year after *Philadelphia*'s release AIDS was the leading cause of death for all Americans aged 25–44.[40] Springsteen's line about those who have departed may also allude to friends who abandon those with AIDS. In the next lyric, Andrew confesses that at night he listens to the sound of his blood coursing through his veins "as black and whispering as the rain." The sound of his corporeal deterioration humiliates and overwhelms him. His rotten and disease-ridden blood does not have the red color of life but the black mark of death, and "like the rain, it mixes with the unclean, trash-littered and publicly soiled pavement, but contrarily, will not evaporate the next morning."[41]

The final line of the first verse in "Streets of Philadelphia" presents Joe Miller (and, consequently, the audience) with "a momentous choice: to accept the dying man in an act of grace, or abandon him."[42] Will Joe succumb to his bigotry and leave Andrew alone and "wastin' away on the streets of Philadelphia"? Two scenes in *Philadelphia* place Joe at this critical crossroads. Roger Ebert describes the moment when Joe witnesses Andrew's confrontation with his waning mortality as one where he "undergoes a conversion of the soul. What he sees, finally, is a man who loves life and does not want to leave it," a man no different from himself—regardless of who he chooses to sleep with.[43] This moment comes when Joe drills Andrew on questions for the upcoming trial. Andrew slyly notes that he may not be alive to see the outcome and turns his stereo on to his favorite opera aria, "La Mamma Morta" from *Andrea Chénier*, sung by the famed Maria Callas. Joe checks his watch in exasperation—the last thing he wants to do is listen to a musical genre he considers too effeminate for any straight man to willingly consume.

Andrew closes his eyes and tilts his head, wrapped in unbridled ecstasy as the dazzling solo floods the room. The apartment's natural lighting melts into a deep red highlighted with flickering yellow, as if Andrew now occupies the opera stage. It is not the red of hell, nor of the blood that his disease wears thin, but a perfervid red of vivacity and fortitude. Demme uses canted angles high above Andrew's head to evoke the song's celestial aesthetic. Andrew basks in its salvific power—for a moment he feels understood and heard.

He begins to translate each line for Joe. The aria recounts Madeline di Coigny's mother's persecution and murder by raging mob during the French Revolution. "The place that cradled me is burning, I am alone," Andrew interprets, painting a devastating picture of the speaker's childhood home being ravaged by fire. This lyric brings to mind Demme's note on the DVD commentary that pure hatred of the LGBTQ community can cause "people to burn down each other's houses."[44] Several scenes in *Philadelphia* display the mass throngs of protesters outside of Andrew's trial, resembling the raging rabble that bedevils Madeline's mother. Andrew identifies with the same scorn, maltreatment, and profound loneliness she faces. They are both figures who are cruelly scorned by society. He continues his translation: "I bring sorrow to those who love me. It was during this sorrow that love came to me," a lyric that expresses his guilt over making his loved ones mourn his early death. "Live still"—Andrew repeats Callas' emboldened supplication with a clenched fist, taking her words to heart and vowing to live life to the fullest for as long as he possibly can. The moving aria functions as a cathartic profession of Andrew's anguish. He confronts his arresting fear of his impending death and questions whether the afterlife awaits him.

The opera's final line imagines God descending from heaven "to make of the earth a heaven," as Andrew explains. In "Streets of Philadelphia," God has abandoned his mortal denizens. There are no angels waiting to greet Andrew, no possibility of holy grace—only the humane virtues of companionship and empathy he requests from his peer Joe. Will Joe accept Andrew's entreaty and embrace him? "It was during that sorrow that love came to me!" Andrew shouts during the piercing soprano solo, an expression of his hope that Joe will comfort him during this significant moment in which he has laid bare his soul.

During this tormented scene, Demme periodically cuts to a slow dolly-in of Joe's transfixed and misty-eyed reaction. Witnessing this disturbingly private moment of self-reflection and unvarnished agony, he can no longer keep the reality of Andrew's dire illness at bay. Once believing Andrew got what he deserved by contracting this disease, Joe now begrudgingly acknowledges that his client is a person with tangible feelings and that his sexuality has no bearing on the fact that his young life will be cruelly stolen.

After Maria Callas' rousing high note concludes, the red hue swiftly snaps back to a sobering natural light and the camera simultaneously drops from its theatrical position at the top of Andrew's head to fix him in the frame's center. This nimble motion from a dramatic and ethereal close-up to a plain mid-shot thrusts Andrew back to reality and out from under the song's spell. For Joe, this vulnerable display of emotions is too much to bear, and he rushes out the door. Although he is deeply affected by Andrew's unfurled emotions, he does not accept the subtextual plea to console him—effectively leaving Andrew alone on the streets of Philadelphia. In the original draft of the script, Joe went back inside to hug Andrew, but Nyswaner and Demme felt this act was too melodramatic. Instead, they waited until the film's climax for a more intimate physical gesture to signify Joe's true acceptance of Andrew.

With a shaved head, crackling white lips, and dark purple circles ringing his eyes, Andrew lies on his hospital bed, feeling himself gradually "fading away," as Springsteen sings. After Joe arrives to announce that he won the case, Andrew weakly pats the bed, inviting Joe to sit beside him, and he reluctantly acquiesces. In a barely audible and hoarse voice, Andrew commends Joe on his excellent work. After Joe finally acknowledges him as a peer, saying, "It was great working with you, counselor," Andrew sluggishly reaches for the oxygen mask by his throat. Hesitant at first, Joe assists him by gently holding the sides of his face and placing the mask over his mouth. This is the film's version of Springsteen's "faithless kiss" in "Streets of Philadelphia": a benevolent gesture that marks Joe's solicitude and genuine embrace of Andrew for who he is. Most important, it is their first skin-to-skin contact since Joe wiped off Andrew's handshake.

"When there are walls between people and there is a lack of acceptance, you can reach for that particular kind of communion: 'Receive me, brother' is the lyric in the last verse. That's all anybody's looking for—basically some sort of acceptance and to not be left alone," Springsteen explained to *The Advocate*.[45] *Philadelphia* centers on Andrew's longing for Joe, his former colleagues, and all those involved in the trial to "receive him," to overcome bigotry and truly care for him. Joe's refusal to touch Andrew was an outward marker of the hate he held in his heart, and the empathetic display of touching him on his deathbed to provide him with the last few breaths of his life signifies Joe's changing attitude. Demme and Nyswaner's removal of the post-opera hug solidifies the textual significance of this small act of compassion. Joe was faithless because he did not believe in rights for the LGBTQ community and castigated Andrew for his sexuality—an indelible aspect of his humanity. By getting to know Andrew as a person, Joe learned to reject his myopic anxieties about his client's sexual preference. Although Joe does not completely yield his prejudices, his action designates a significant turn toward a more positive perception of queer men and women—a newfound perspective that Demme hoped his spectators would reflect.

Brothers and Lovers: Springsteen's Queer Musical and Performative Aesthetic

In a December 2015 talk show appearance on *The Tonight Show with Jimmy Fallon*, Springsteen joked that he played a lot of his early gigs for predominantly male audiences "due to the homosexual undercurrents in my music."[46] While said in jest, Springsteen addressed an oft-discussed observation that decidedly queer images and content pervade his writing and concert performances. There seems to be a "strong distance between Springsteen's famously 'All-American,' hypermasculine image" (which Demme hoped to capitalize on in *Philadelphia*) "and his sustained artistic commitment to performing a queer aesthetic," as Rosalie Zdzienicka Fanshel argues.[47] This queer aesthetic is an extension of Springsteen's "progressive patriotism that insists that the promise of the American Dream should be available to everyone," men and women of all backgrounds, races, gender identities, and sexual orientations.[48] As a champion for social justice, Springsteen's artistic vision of love and community included members of the LGBTQ community long before "Streets of Philadelphia."

Springsteen's love proclamation "Tougher Than the Rest" is primarily about a heterosexual couple, with the male narrator speaking to a woman and referencing her ideal boyfriends: a "handsome Dan," "good-lookin' Joe," and "sweet-talkin' Romeo." However, in between Springsteen's ogling of a flame-haired Patti Scialfa, the music video includes gay and lesbian couples in the black-and-white boardwalk photo booth–esque vignettes of lovers smiling, cuddling, and kissing.[49] By inserting queer sweethearts in such a down-to-earth and nonchalant manner, Springsteen normalizes their unions and embraces them as a fundamental part of the all-American tapestry. Regardless of the song's heterosexual male subjectivity, Springsteen uses the music video format to situate "Tougher Than the Rest" as a universal love song for men and women of all sexual orientations. The 1988 music video is one of the most notable and explicit inclusions of the LGBTQ community in his work.

Characters of all gender and sexual identities populate the eclectic countercultural landscapes of Springsteen's early 1970s albums: the "wolfman fairies dressed in drag" of "Lost in the Flood"; the high-heeled boys of "4th of July, Asbury Park (Sandy)"; and the "golden-heeled fairies" of "Incident on 57th Street," in which barefoot boys bid each other goodbye with intimate, quasi-romantic kisses. These homoerotic images were influenced by Springsteen's early collisions with the gay community at his local haunt Asbury Park, which had numerous gay bars and clubs, and New York City's Greenwich Village, where he played at Café Wha? and the Gaslight Café. Springsteen told *The Advocate* that these colorful environments nurtured his accepting attitudes toward the LGBTQ community. "I was open-minded, and I wasn't naturally intolerant," he elaborated.[50] Springsteen did not "feel a part of those homophobic ideas" that pervaded his insular hometown of Freehold, New Jersey, which he deemed a brutal and "ugly part of the American character."[51]

"Mary Queen of Arkansas" from *Greetings from Asbury Park, N.J.* presents Springsteen's most problematic queer representation. Springsteen confirmed during his appearance with Joe Grushecky and the Houserockers at a "Soldiers and Sailors" benefit on May 22, 2014, that this song is about a man in love with a transvestite, an offensive and outdated term for those who identify as transgender. Mary bewitches, frightens, and mortifies Springsteen's lonely acrobat. Her white skin fools him into believing she is something she's not—a woman.[52] Springsteen's description of her "soft hulk" connotes her gendered dualities: the softness of a woman's skin and the hulk of a man's hardened body. Mary is a liminal figure, neither man enough for him to hate nor woman enough for him to kiss. Within this lyric, Springsteen does not consider Mary a woman, despite her identification as female, but rather something odd and half-formed. The song's carnival aesthetic adds an erotic exoticism to Mary's transgender identity.

Springsteen's music "returns again and again to themes of deep love between men, love that frequently occupies the liminal space between brother and lover."[53] His male characters often harbor a profound—and almost primal—affinity for their male friends, whom they address in various terms of endearment that as "often as not ha[ve] direct—or at least highly suggestive—eroticism attached," as Fanshel argues.[54] The euphoric "No Surrender" centers on a pair of blood brothers, one of whom the wistful schoolboy frequently addresses as his "baby," bound by a steadfast vow to make their rock and roll fantasies come true. The bare acoustic *Live/1975–85* version includes an alternate verse in which Springsteen's devoted idealist ogles his blood brother's winsome smile and soothing voice and desires to sleep with him by the riverside while they share their innermost romantic dreams. "This Hard Land" incorporates similar pastoral images in the troubadour's yearning to sleep with his friend Frank in the fields beside the river. He requests one kiss from his brother before they embark on a lengthy cross-country journey together. Although the physical actions in this song may belong to a platonic friendship, there is an electric passion within the lyrics and Springsteen's voice that suggests the pair share a deeper ardor. Springsteen is not afraid to describe intimate male relationships defined by a desire for close physical affection. Furthermore, "This Hard Land" subverts the western genre by placing arguably queer characters within the white male heterosexual space of the American frontier.

The *Born in the U.S.A.* outtakes "Unsatisfied Heart" and "Fugitive's Dream" are elegiac depictions of homosexual repression in their similar narratives of a character who encounters a mysterious stranger from his past. The urging keyboards of "Unsatisfied Heart" evoke the overwhelming dread that gnaws at George in the middle of the night after he allows the man into his home with the promise that he will keep his ominous secret. A desperate paranoia seizes him as the elusive visitor reignites his suppressed same-sex desires; he feels himself "changing deep inside," drawing further and further away from his idyllic suburban life in a "house of gold" with "two beautiful children and a kind and loving wife." A liberating dream where he stands "high in the green hills" on the edge of his quiet town wrapped in the arms of his former lover plagues him nightly before he awakens next to his sleeping wife, left without the satisfaction he pines for. These themes of homosexual suppression are more overt in "Fugitive's Dream" during a verse when George rises from his dreamless slumber and travels to his visitor's bed. After he adoringly gazes at the man's sleeping face and fondly touches his cheek, a chill rattles his bones and he hurriedly flees. The return of this cryptic nomad kindles the voltaic sexual desires that have lay dormant in George for far too long. He struggles to understand why he feels these newfound attractions, and their metamorphic power forces him to walk the streets as "a stranger to myself," leaving his placid suburban life behind.

Some critics read the honeyed "My Lover Man" as Springsteen's most explicitly gay song since it uses first-person narration to describe a roller-coaster romance with a man, but there is more evidence to support the argument that it is one of the rare Springsteen works told from a woman's perspective. The booklet accompanying the *Tracks* box set calls it a "full-blown relationship song told from the other side," or the female side of a heterosexual relationship.[55] The protagonist shrewdly observes that the lover man has only returned to revive their relationship because his life with another woman "turned to black." However, Springsteen could still be writing from the male perspective about a bisexual or closeted partner.

Another aspect of Springsteen's queer musical sensibility is the numerous characters with gender-neutral names, such as Ricky, Bobby Jean, Terry, Sandy, and Frankie. The most hotly debated character in Springsteenian lore is Terry from "Backstreets" (off the *Born to Run* album). The name "Terry" has appeared multiple times in Springsteen's canon as both male and female. In "The Promise," Terry is a failed male rock and roll singer, but in "Zero and Blind Terry," Terry is a girl whose overprotective father prevents her from dating a gang member. "Backstreets" never refers to Terry with any pronouns, leading fans and critics to question whether Springsteen is describing a hetero or homosexual relationship. Fanshel favors the latter reading; if they are not gay lovers, "what makes their lives together so forbidden that they must hide on the backstreets?"[56] Why else must they sleep in abandoned beach houses and run for their lives? Why must they be forced to confess that they are together? Furthermore, the park they are stranded in may allude to Central Park, a popular spot for gay cruising during *Born to Run*'s release in the 1970s. More than "forever friends," these desperate lovers slow dance under the moon at Stockton's Wing beach, the soft sand coursing beneath their toes. After they make love, Terry lies on the man's chest in the sweltering summer twilight like an angel in the dark. Both Terry and the narrator share a common aspiration to emulate their male-coded cinematic heroes. However, the "Sad Eyes" and "Drive All Night" interlude during concert performances ruptures a queer reading of "Backstreets," as Springsteen castigates Terry as a lying and cheating little girl. Nevertheless, Springsteen's willingness to obscure gender and sexual identity in the canonical version of his song demonstrates his commitment to inclusivity and a sexually malleable star image.

Springsteen's concert performances are more queerly subversive than his lyrics—namely, in the passionate kisses he shares with saxophonist Clarence Clemons at the end of jubilant songs such as "Born to Run," "Thunder Road," and "Rosalita (Come Out Tonight)." These fanfares of escapist fantasies directed toward Mary, Wendy, and Rosie climax in a victorious musical crescendo embodied in Springsteen's ecstatic journey across the stage to meet Clarence's expectant lips, thereby transferring the woman of his lyrical text onto the hefty male body of Clemons. Their fervent smooch transforms Clemons into the one "whose velvet rims *he* wants to wrap his legs around, who he *really* wants to climb into his car as he 'pulls out of here to win.'"[57] When not kissing, they often lie on top of one another and rub their disparate bodies together. John Lombardi recounts his observation of this arrangement during the *Tunnel of Love* tour in his *Esquire* article "St. Boss": "Clarence and Bruce no longer do their famous 'soul kiss,' but at one point Clemons literally backs Springsteen up, humping dryly, and Bruce slides sensually down Clarence's brawny chest to his belly, his head finally lolling on the Big Man's crotch. The fans go into paroxysms over this display of racial/sexual 'harmony,' but before anyone can get any funny ideas, Bruce is over to stage left, being belly-bumped by Patti. Erotically and politically, he works both sides of the street."[58]

Physical attention is paid not only to Clemons but also to his blood brother Steve Van Zandt, whom Springsteen intimately shares the microphone with, staring affectionately and intensely into his eyes as their lips nearly touch. The musicians "seem to have no need to search further to find the 'special one' that the lyrics indicate," Fanshel argues.[59] Through his willingness to be corporally intimate with his fellow bandmates, Springsteen boldly subverts his hypermasculine and staunchly heterosexual star image as perceived by his predominantly straight white male, blue-collar audience, many of whom occupy the pockets of America that uphold insidious homophobic ideologies. The Springsteen/Clemons kiss in particular personifies Springsteen's all-inclusive vision of America, which he advocates throughout his musical canon. This valiant gesture crosses racial, gender, and sexual boundaries to emphasize our common humanity and equality—the cardinal dogma of Springsteen's patriotism. He uses both his heteroflexible concert performance acts and his homoerotic lyrics to critique the political paradigms and conservative credos that prevent the United States from being truly united. Springsteen is an American icon willing to bend the contours of his heterosexuality, and he welcomes the LGBTQ community into his depiction of his country.

Decades after participating in *Philadelphia*, Springsteen has continued to use his position as a popular culture icon to advocate for the LGBTQ community. In December 2009, Springsteen published a statement on his website in support of passing a same-sex marriage bill in his home state of New Jersey:

> I've long believed in and have always spoken out for the rights of same-sex couples and fully agree with Governor Corzine when he writes that, "The marriage-equality issue should be recognized for what it truly is—a civil-rights issue that must be approved to assure that every citizen is treated equally under the law." I couldn't agree more with that statement and urge those who support equal treatment for our gay and lesbian brothers and sisters to let their voices be heard now.[60]

In 2012, he lent his support to an advertising campaign for gay marriage called "The Four 2012," noting once again, "I couldn't agree more with that statement and urge those who support equal treatment for our gay and lesbian brothers and sisters to let their voices be heard now."[61] On April 10, 2016, he cancelled his concert in Greensboro, North Carolina, over the passing of the HB2 law, which prevented those who identify as transgender from using their chosen restroom facilities. He released a statement on the home page of his website deeming the law "an attempt by people who cannot stand the progress our country has made in recognizing the human rights of all our citizens to overturn that progress."[62] Springsteen's cancellation was made in order to "fight against prejudice and bigotry" and oppose those "who continue to push us backwards instead of forwards."[63] This act of protest singlehandedly sparked a wave of other event cancellations throughout the year in Greensboro. Springsteen not only promotes social justice in his music but also frequently engages in political action to bring his ideals of an egalitarian America to life.[64]

When most people think of Springsteen, his image as the sweaty and herculean bandana-clad blue-collar worker of *Born in the U.S.A.* frequently comes to mind, a simplistic effigy of rigid white hypermasculinity and heterosexuality. Demme had this image in mind when he asked Springsteen to compose a song for *Philadelphia*, but Springsteen is so much more than that myopic 1980s star persona. Although "Streets of Philadelphia" more explicitly confirmed his support of the LGBTQ community, close inspection of his musical and performative landscape reveals a decidedly queer aesthetic. Demme's film parallels what Springsteen considers the fundamental tenets of his music: "tolerance and acceptance."[65] "If my work was about anything, it was about the search for identity, for personal recognition, for acceptance, for communion, and for a big country," Springsteen declared in *The Advocate*, and he has firmly clarified that the LGBTQ community is unequivocally a part of that vision.[66] Across his canon, "same-sex desires are so thoroughly and consistently interspersed that he effectively moves queer from a position of 'other' to one of 'normal,'" as a quotidian part of the American experience.[67]

Both Demme and Springsteen use Andrew Beckett's story to, as Springsteen stated in his Academy Award acceptance speech, "take the edge off of fear … [and] recognize each other through our veil of difference."[68] They gently assuage homophobic audiences' trepidation by delving deeply into a gay man's universal emotions. While the effect of popularizing *Philadelphia* perpetuated some problematic aspects of queer cinematic representation, the movie was nevertheless a trailblazer. Demme's film was one of the first to bring queer lives to mainstream cinema and raised significant awareness and empathy for AIDS victims. *Philadelphia* was also the perfect widespread platform for Springsteen to use in making his enduring and wholehearted support of LGBTQ people known. Both *Philadelphia* and "Streets of Philadelphia" provided 1990s audiences with a sensitive, authentic, and identifiable portrait of the pain, isolation, and marginalization that those suffering with AIDS grappled with, particularly those who were queer. Demme and Springsteen's benevolent portraits of Philadelphia continue to encourage America to live up to its promise of brotherly love and receive those in the LGBTQ community with open arms.

Dead Man Walking

Directed by Tim Robbins, *Dead Man Walking* (1995) is based on the memoir of Sister Helen Prejean, a Roman Catholic nun who served as a spiritual advisor for death row inmates. In the film, she counsels Matthew Poncelet at the Louisiana State Penitentiary. Springsteen received a Best Original Song Academy Award nomination for "Dead Man Walkin." Working from the footage and script Robbins provided him, Springsteen penned a first-person narrative of Matthew on the eve of his execution for the film's end credits. Robbins personally appointed Springsteen to write song not only because they were friends but also because "he seemed like the natural choice."[1] Springsteen was the "natural choice" for the *Dead Man Walking* soundtrack because his empathetic exploration of the outlaw aligns with the humanist and liberal thematic framework of *Dead Man Walking*. As a sharecropper's son who murders two teenagers, Matthew embodies the low-class criminal characters who populate several of Springsteen's albums, particularly *Nebraska*. Like Robbins, Springsteen confronts his audience with realistic, complex, and non-didactic depictions of societal miscreants and the American justice system. Furthermore, he shares Robbins' anti–death penalty views, frequently promoting organizations such as People of Faith Against the Death Penalty at his concerts.

Apart from his connections to Matthew, Springsteen's brand of Catholicism parallels Sister Helen's progressive secularism. Springsteen grew up literally "in the shadow of the steeple" on 87 Randolph Street, "spitting distance" from his hometown church and parochial school St. Rose of Lima in Freehold, New Jersey.[2] Coming of age unremittingly "surrounded by God" went on to shape and strongly influence his songwriting. Springsteen says religion provided him with "an epic canvas and it gave you a sense of revelation, retribution, perdition, bliss, ecstasy.... I think I've been trying to write my way out of it ever since."[3] His slant on religion has metamorphosed over the years, gradually maturing from a critical agnosticism to salvific enlightenment. Catholicism is the dominant through-line of Springsteen's oeuvre, its beatific iconography coloring the language and thematic concerns of the majority of his songs. His participation in *Dead Man Walking* incites consideration of the theological themes found in his work and its intertextual relationship with the character of Sister Helen.

Sister Helen's challenge in *Dead Man Walking* is to sway the racist and volatile apostate Matthew to confess his sins and accept Jesus in his heart so that he may be granted eternal life—no easy task. She must care for him with the kind of unconditional love a mother has for a child, or Jesus had for his flock, despite his despicable actions and acrimonious demeanor. She must see beyond the horrific crimes and sins Matthew has committed and overcome her judgment of him in order to find his inner goodness and love him regardless of his faults, as Jesus Christ does. A member of the Aryan Brotherhood, Matthew's deep-seated racism and sexism make it difficult for Sister Helen to follow in Jesus' benevolent footsteps. Matthew tells Sister Helen that he hates "coloreds" because, unlike him, they are lazy, suck up tax dollars with welfare, and portray themselves as victims. "I ain't whining. I ain't sitting on a porch going 'slavery, slavery,'" Matthew glibly brags.

During one of Sister Helen's visits, Matthew spits out, "Nigger on the gurney before me. I hope they clean it before me." In a local news television interview, he declares his admiration for Adolf Hitler's leadership abilities: "He got things done…. Hitler might have gone overboard on the killing, but he was on the right track." This statement mortifies Sister Helen because she is publicly known as his spiritual advisor, and she chastises Matthew for portraying himself as "some crazed animal, Nazi, racist mad dog who deserves to die. You are a fool. You are making it so easy for them to kill you." These bigoted attitudes bespeak Matthew's lack of education and insular familial upbringing in the Deep South. He turns his internal rage outward onto those who are marginalized by society more than he is. Nevertheless, Sister Helen wants to believe that beneath Matthew's grotesque bigotry there is a capacity for righteousness.

Matthew echoes Springsteen's white supremacist characters in "The Klansman" and "Galveston Bay." A *Born in the U.S.A.* outtake, "The Klansman" is one of Springsteen's most audacious songs because he sings from the perspective of a young Ku Klux Klan recruit. The boy's father dreams of the apocalyptic war between races that will leave the Klansmen victorious and cleanse the country of its vile people of color. The mesmeric synthesizer chords belie the dark lyrics and evoke how easily the Klan's incensed and prejudiced rhetoric can sway young minds. The boy's repeated phrase of "look away" suggests that he disdains the Klan's ethnocentric ideologies and will not be tempted to inherit his Pa's sacred robes, but Springsteen leaves his ultimate stance rather vague. In "Galveston Bay" from *The Ghost of Tom Joad*, a Vietnam veteran and fishing boat captain named Billy Sutter partners with his local Texan Klan to purge their harbor community of Vietnamese refugees. Championing an "America for Americans," Billy Sutter cannot fathom how the foreign enemy he was once charged with vanquishing is able to peacefully inhabit his country.

Both Sister Helen and Springsteen understand sin "as the process by which innocent individuals, confronted with difficult circumstances, lose touch with their better selves."[4] They consider the myriad factors—economic, social, and familial—that contribute to a person's immoral exploits and behaviors. One of Springsteen's most poignant lines in "Dead Man Walkin'" professes that in between our dreams and our actions lies the world we live in. Springsteen understands that desperate circumstances often force us to commit grave malefactions that betray our lofty aspirations for the future, our dreams of transcending our current lot in life, and these actions do not define our entire existence. The world does not adhere to simplistic Manichean divisions, but rather lies in a dubious grey zone. Springsteen rejects a rigid demarcation of men and women into categories of merely good and bad and embraces the kaleidoscopic complexities of our human nature. *Dead Man Walking* testifies to Springsteen's conviction by asserting that there is more to Matthew than his malfeasance, just as there is more to Sister Helen than her faith. They are not defined by a sole aspect of their selfhood or limited to a singular moral standpoint.

"Dead Man Walkin'" locates Matthew on the night before he is to be killed. After he fails to get parole, Matthew learns that he will be put to death in just a few short days. He will "rise in the morning" knowing that his fate has already been decided for him as the nonpareil "dead man walking." Springsteen incorporates Matthew's caustic macabre humor ("I'm on a greased rail to the death house") in his description of riding the pale horse, the apocalyptic bringer of death. He sonically evokes the claustrophobic terror of one's execution drawing nearer and nearer in what David Thurmaier calls a syncopated rhythm that "invokes the march to the death chamber in its repetition and insistence," and in the rich drums, "one may even hear the syncopation as walking with shackles and chains."[5] Robbins visually represents this sense of trepidation in recurring intercuts to the foreboding clock, each tick inching dangerously closer to Matthew's final second. Through an oppressive mise-en-scène with claustrophobic close-ups of Matthew's anxious face and the ominous clock looming overhead, Robbins conveys the surreal, inexplicable horror of knowing that "your death is determined by a date and time." "Waking up in the morning knowing this day will be your last is not something that a lot of human beings go through [because] death usually comes by surprise," Robbins notes on the DVD commentary, and his methodical pacing intensifies this terrifying concept.[6] Robbins wanted his spectators to realize that "in any other context outside of prison and capital punishment arena," it would be considered psychopathic torture to "take a person and lock them in a room and tell them that they're gonna kill them."[7] For the director, the death penalty is nothing less than premeditated murder at the hands of the government. By making the site of action the night before Matthew's execution and using a dilatory rhythm with a light acoustic guitar, Springsteen forces his listeners to embody Matthew's purgatorial wait for the death knell—the eerie, petrifying ritual that Robbins cannot fathom is a sanctioned American practice.

Whereas Springsteen's version of Matthew insists there is no need for anyone to listen to a soon-to-be-dead man's story, in the film it is imperative that Matthew tell his tale before his death so that he may enter the kingdom of heaven. "Dead Man Walkin'" also differs from the film in that the song's Matthew tells Sister Helen that he does not need forgiveness because his sins are the only thing he has of value in this world—one of the saddest lines Springsteen has ever written. The mission of Robbins' Sister Helen is to get Matthew to truly ask for forgiveness for killing Hope Percy and Walter Delacroix. Only he will not admit to committing any sin—he maintains that his friend Carl Vitello was the true culprit and he was merely an unwitting accessory. Moreover, he falsely assumes that since Jesus died on the cross for humankind's sins, he does not have to worry about going to hell for anything he has done. Helen forcefully reminds him that redemption is not a "free admission ticket"—it must be earned.

Matthew's hardened masculine bravado erodes as his final hour nears. When he returns from his final phone call with his family, he is uncharacteristically quiet and deeply uncomfortable. He admits to Sister Helen that he told his mother he could have stopped Carl from killing Walter and Hope, but he was too chicken because his friend "was older and tough as hell." A lengthy pause follows as Sister Helen waits with bated breath, her wide eyes transfixed on Matthew's restless body, waiting to hear the admission of guilt she has been longing for. Matthew's fitful gaze finally focuses, and he quietly confesses to killing Percy. Sister Helen exhales a deep sigh of relief and then asks whether he was the one to rape Hope. "Yes ma'am," Matthew replies, his brow furrowed and face twisted in agony and shame. He stares at Sister Helen like a wounded child while tears pour down his cheeks. Here actor Sean Penn exquisitely conveys Matthew's profound remorse.

Matthew then makes another confession: the night before his execution, he got down on his knees and prayed for the kids he murdered as an act of true penance. This image brings to mind the tranquil final lines of Springsteen's "Dead Man Walkin'," underscored by the ethereal keyboards and orotund drums, as Matthew watches the clouds languidly roll across the summer sky from the window of his prison cell before falling into a dream-filled

Dead Man Walking

slumber, ready to greet the dawning of his last day. Springsteen illustrates the peace that overcomes Penn's Matthew after he atones for his sins and offers regret for the souls he so cruelly stole from Earth. Now that Matthew has shown true remorse, Sister Helen can truly declare him a son of God. Dumbstruck, Matthew cannot believe that someone like him will be able to enter the kingdom of heaven. Sister Helen teaches him that Jesus Christ accepts everyone, saints *and* sinners (as Springsteen sings in "Land of Hope and Dreams"), if they genuinely repent of their sins.

"Dead man walking!" the prison guards shout as they roughly drag Matthew from his cell. Before he is brought into the execution chamber where he is put on display for the victims' families and other eager audience members watching from behind a curtain like some sadistic pageant, Sister Helen says, "I want the last thing you see in this world to be a face of love. So you look at me when they do this thing. I'll be the face of love for you." Robbins uses slow motion to emphasize Matthew's excruciating trudge to his grave followed by a close-up pan across the humiliating slippers and diaper he is forced to wear, a signification of how inhumane and infantilizing this procedure is. Sister Helen stands behind him with an unyielding hand on his shoulder—an important gesture because it marks the first time they have touched. Robbins specifically avoided any physical interaction between Sister Helen and Matthew throughout the film, often separating them by a glass partition that resembled a confessional, so that this moment would hold more dramatic weight and emotional resonance.

The majority of Sister Helen and Matthew's interactions occur within dialogue-heavy shot/reverse shot scenes. Robbins employed a distinct visual technique to suggest their growing intimacy: after each meeting, the physical barrier between them, such as a win-

As their relationship intensifies, director Tim Robbins uses increasingly tighter close-ups to obscure the glass partition that separates Sister Helen Prejean (Susan Sarandon) and Matthew Poncelet (Sean Penn) (www.moviestillsdb.com).

dowpane or grate, would diminish in increasingly tighter close-ups. "He'll be less obscure as the movie progresses and more and more layers will be melted away visually and emotionally," Robbins explains on the DVD commentary.[8] As Matthew begins to open up, he reveals more about his childhood. Sister Helen learns that his father died when he was fourteen and was never a good influence to begin with, once giving him whiskey at the age of twelve. In "Dead Man Walkin'," Springsteen juxtaposes the innocent and garden-variety details of Matthew's past—he was born and christened in St. James Parish, he used to have a job and a girl—against those of his crime so that audiences may see beyond his vice and grasp his innate humanity.[9] He was once a child and hard-working man like most, but economic squalor drew him toward delinquency.

In a stark montage of callous close-ups, the guards methodically strap Matthew onto the gurney and inject the needle into his veins. One of them rolls back a curtain, presenting the macabre sideshow for the audience sitting behind the windowpane, with the victims' parents perched at the helm. Matthew's chair rises upright so he can speak his last words, revealing a Christ-like image with his arms outstretched in a crucifixion pose. The visual conflation of a criminal such as Matthew and Jesus Christ indicates humanity's liminality: we all have the capacity for both good and evil. Between violent, juddering breaths, Matthew pleads for the Percys' and Delacroixes' forgiveness and selflessly hopes his death gives them relief. He also makes a statement on the death penalty that recapitulates the film's thesis: "I just want to say, I think killing is wrong no matter who does it. Whether it's me or y'all or the government." These are not the words of the wildly irate man Sister Helen met at the beginning of the film; she has accomplished her mission in placating Matthew and getting him to sincerely seek absolution.

The machinery whirs and grinds as a severely quivering Matthew lies horizontally for the lethal injection process to begin. He turns away from the sterile close-ups of the life-draining mechanics that surround him to face Sister Helen, and they exchange "I love you" as she affectionately reaches her arm out toward him. Robbins specifically chose to portray lethal injection because the graphic realities of the electric chair would only cause audiences to argue that this form of execution was barbaric and lethal injection was the more humane option. Robbins' goal was to present all methods of capital punishment as savage. "It is just as brutal, putting poison into someone's veins as it is to shock them or to shoot them or to put gas in their lungs," he argues.[10] In the scene of Matthew's trial, his lawyer points out that lethal injection merely conceals the "Armageddon" that ravages the inmate's internal organs as they writhe, twist, and contort. He may lie in a gentle repose, but inside his body is a horror show. No matter which method is used, justice is not served and the prisoner's blood is still on America's hands.

Robbins challenges spectators to connect Matthew's death with that of the victims by interweaving the scene of his execution with a flashback of his monstrous actions. Can they feel compassion and shed tears for Matthew despite what he's done? Throughout the film, Robbins had interspersed subjective black-and-white shots of Sister Helen's imagining of Matthew's crime: ominous close-ups of the gun lowering toward Walter's head, Matthew unsheathing the knife and plunging it into the teenager's off-screen body, Hope's bare legs sprawled in the gnarled grass covered in splattered blood, her dead hand clutching the weeds in a final attempt to escape and her skirt caked in mud. Now Robbins uses color to signify the truth of what happened.

Springsteen's song draws from the harrowing sequence of Walter and Hope's deaths inside the deep forest. Robbins intercuts Matthew's craven, expiring face on the gurney with him unbuckling his pants in glee and bending down to rape Hope, his mouth twisted in an evil grin and eyes as black as those of a ravenous shark. His savage action caused her vagina to become "all tore up" and her beloved "Class of '88" pin deeply embedded in her skin during the brutal stabbing that followed, Hope's mother tells Sister Helen. After he places his boot onto Walter's lacerated back and shoots him, Matthew, framed in slow motion, steps back in wide-eyed disbelief and runs his fingers through his hair. This image impeccably matches Springsteen's description of the "fear up inside" Matthew churning along with the drugs (downs and acid) and alcohol he consumed to keep up with his haywire friend. Within this small gesture, Penn deftly conveys Matthew's incertitude. He stands in trepidation before his victims' "blood and tears," as Springsteen intones. The "Dead Man Walkin'" music video connects this verse with Robbins' haunting visuals by overlaying Matthew's visible unease during the forest murder scene onto a close-up shot of Springsteen, looking eerily like Penn with his slicked-back hair and goatee, singing into a microphone against a pitch-black background.

The next shot in the film is a bird's-eye view of Matthew lying on the cross-like execution table, his blank eyes directed toward heaven, followed by a graphic shot of the mangled bodies of his victims in the middle of the forest to suggest that "in the end, another person is dead."[11] By juxtaposing the "specifics of the execution, the graphic nature of it, the horrifying premeditation of it" and the events of Walter and Hope's deaths, Robbins provokes spectatorial contemplation of "not who deserves to die, but who deserves to kill" and critiques America's "eye for an eye" brand of justice.[12]

"There's no justification for violence, for taking another human life," no matter who the life belongs to, Robbins argues in *Dead Man Walking*.[13] He rejects society's simplistic demarcation of its people into rigid good versus evil classifications, which works for the death penalty because "we'd much rather execute monsters than human beings."[14] Midway through the film, Sister Helen cautions Matthew that the media and parole board are "gonna be thinkin' of the crime, and you as a monster." During the hearing, the prosecutor castigates Matthew as a heartless killer who deserves to die for the "calculated, disgusting, and cruel murders" he committed. Afterward, Hope Percy's father launches into a vehement tirade that voices what the spectator may already be thinking:

> This is not a person. This is an animal. No, I take that back, animals don't rape and murder their own kind. Matthew Poncelet is God's mistake. And you want to hold the poor murderer's hand? You wanna be there to comfort him when he dies? There wasn't anybody in the woods that night to comfort Hope when those two animals pushed her face down into the wet grass.

When Sister Helen discovers that Matthew has a daughter with a woman he crassly calls "a stupid bitch," whom he has not seen for many years due to his previous incarceration, a black-and-white image of Hope Percy's naked body lying in the field punctures her subconscious. How can she fawn over Matthew's daughter when he took someone else's out of the world? Sister Helen consistently struggles with her religion's tension between punishing those who commit evil and granting them forgiveness. She tries not to perceive Matthew with the same disdain as the parole board or the victims' families, giving him a fair chance of being heard and attempting to empathize with him during their sessions as another person with hopes, dreams, fears, and regrets just like everyone else.

Sister Helen visits Matthew's family to get a sense of his upbringing, to see whether it was nature or nurture that led him down the wrong path. Raised along with three brothers in a narrow and dilapidated trailer, Matthew shares the lower-class socioeconomic background of innumerable death row inmates and the pestilential characters that populate Springsteen's canon. In between puffs of smoke, Matthew's mother says that the government once asked whether she had death insurance. "What a laugh—I ain't even got food money," she quips. In the beginning of the film, Sister Helen asks Matthew directly if he was brought up poor, to which he bluntly replies, "Ain't nobody with money on death row." Many scholars argue that the death penalty is a form of eugenics that targets "the poorest, most powerless, most marginalized people in society."[15] Andrew Cohen explains that "virtually all of the people selected for execution are poor," with an undisputed bias toward African American men, a fact Matthew himself points out in the film.[16]

Over Easter dinner, Sister Helen's parents and siblings argue that Matthew's troubled adolescence with a destitute single mother should not excuse an adulthood of rape and murder. Their ostentatious environment, with its lavish dining room table, candelabras, flower arrangements, fine china, and red velvet curtains, could not be any more different from the Poncelets'. Her parents caution their empathetic daughter, who constantly took in stray animals as a child, against being manipulated by him, but she feels drawn to counsel Matthew because she wants "to follow the example of Jesus, who said that every person is worth more than their worst act."

Dead Man Walking sensitively balances various perspectives on the controversial issue of the death penalty—the criminal himself, the victims' families, the prison guards, the clergy, and government officials. Without favoring one point of view over another, Robbins deftly explores the various thoughts and experiences of those in Matthew's orbit, offering the spectator a fair and balanced consideration of each side of the story. Robbins' film is a deeply felt and poignant work that uses Springsteen's introspective and humanist end credits song to undergird its empathetic intentions.

Vigilante Men: Springsteen's Criminals

Without dishonoring the victims and their families, Robbins presents Matthew as a complex individual with nebulous impulses in the same vein as Springsteen's scrofulous protagonists. By delving into their hearts and minds through subjective narratives, Springsteen offers clemency and keen emotional insight that rescues his recalcitrant characters from being one dimensional. Matthew resembles the low-class murderers sentenced to capital and lifetime punishment in "Nebraska" and "Johnny 99" from Springsteen's tenebrous *Nebraska* album.

"Nebraska" invokes the poetic solemnity of Terrence Malick's baleful neo-noir *Badlands*, the true account of Charlie Starkweather and Caril Fugate's week-long killing spree in the Midwest during the 1950s that claimed ten innocent lives. In a muted, southern-twanged voice, Starkweather asserts his low-class status by addressing authority figures as "mister" and "sir," just as Matthew calls Sister Helen "ma'am." But his gentleness is a mere façade. Springsteen-as-Starkweather's guileless recollection of his slaughter—boastfully killing "everything in my path"—combined with the caterwauling harmonica, uncanny reverb, and apathetic, susurrant vocal style, endows "Nebraska" with a gnawing terror. Unlike Matthew, Starkweather shows no remorse—to him, the slayings were mere tomfoolery. He eschews any sense of responsibility and attributes his actions to a haphazard "meanness in this world," a nihilistic view that evil is elemental and an intrinsic part of human nature. Starkweather receives his guilty verdict, being deemed "unfit to live" and sentenced to the electric chair, with a chilling aloofness, the opposite of Matthew, who collapses from anxiety on his way to the execution table and undergoes a spiritual awakening in the process. In "Nebraska," Springsteen graphically describes the execution details: the leather straps pull across his chest, and the switch readies to snap his "poor head back." Starkweather's final wish is to have his "pretty baby" and partner in crime Caril Fugate sitting on his lap while his body chars from the tidal wave of electricity. Matthew chooses Sister Helen to accompany him in his final moments, a personification of his newfound piety, as opposed to Starkweather's earthly libidinous desires.

In the beginning of *Dead Man Walking*, Matthew is an apoplectic young man in grave danger of letting his malevolence overcome him. However, through Sister Helen and the grace of God, Matthew is able to transcend the kind of bitter nihilism that ensnares Starkweather. The warmth of God's heavenly kingdom does not await Starkweather as it does Matthew, for Starkweather's soul will be hurled "into that great void"—a dismal, vacuous image of a condemned man's eternal damnation. It is very easy to read Starkweather as a purely insidious individual or a mindless killer, but Springsteen manages to convey through the somber musicality the disaffection and loneliness that submerges him and instigates his heinous misdeeds. Through this plainspoken and minatory ballad, Springsteen portrays with frank sensitivity Starkweather's "heartlessness of a life that exploded in malice against all social connections and deeper relationships. His was the utter callousness that results when a person turns his back on all those forces that hold life together and provide it with some vestige of meaning."[17] Although the cursory lyrics present his brutish perspective, in Springsteen's voice we hear an acute gloom that situates Starkweather as more than just a cruel savage.

"Johnny 99" launches with a falsetto cry that is as lonesome as a wandering coyote in the dark New Jersey timberlands. This ear-piercing wail portends the protagonist's fractured psyche. Left without a job after the Mahwah auto plant shuts down and without a home following a foreclosure, the title character Ralph loads up on "Tanqueray and wine," shoots a night clerk, and is arrested, tried, and sentenced in the span of two stanzas.[18] He inebriates himself in order to forget his pain and winds up taking someone's life without intending to. This "startling economy of narrative space ... bespeaks the suffocating socioeconomic forces acting upon Ralph's life" that cause him to lash out in barbarity.[19] The frantic pace of Springsteen's guitar matches Ralph's psychological tailspin in the ghetto, the place where "when you hit a red light you don't stop" and where he is caught "wavin' his gun around," threatening to take even more lives. Like Matthew, Ralph is assigned a public defender because of his lower class, and he faces an ignoble judge nicknamed Mean John Brown, who refuses to sympathize with his devastating situation, the massive "debts no honest man could pay."

Mean John Brown condemns Ralph with a sentence of "ninety-eight and a year," thus christening him with the sobriquet "Johnny 99." Just as Mrs. Poncelet pleads for the life of her beloved son before the parole board with a childhood photograph, Ralph's mother stands in the courtroom and begs the judge, "Don't take my boy this way." These mothers try to get the authority figures to envision their young men as the little boys they once were before they turned into the monstrous men now on trial. But Ralph knows the odious judge will not be swayed by a mother's cries. Echoing Starkweather, Ralph believes that he is better off dead and asks the guards to shave his head and put him "on that execution line" instead. The sharp bark at the song's fadeout is foreboding, leaving the listener with the sense that the chaos and misery that drove Ralph to his breaking point still endure. Although he concedes his guilt, Ralph acknowledges that it was "devastating poverty, existential emptiness, and societal neglect" that put the gun in his hand, grueling forces that listeners can readily identify with.[20]

"James Lincoln Deere," a caliginous outtake from the *Nebraska* album, similarly explores how poverty generates crime. Springsteen sings in a melancholic tenor from the title character's first-person perspective. James explains that he was just an everyday young kid, "no better or worse than you," when he committed his crime. As a newly married twenty-two-year-old, James scrimps and saves to provide for his bride Terry, but soon factory shutdowns leave him unemployed. After fruitlessly searching for a "bigger job," James finds himself on the curb of his affluent brother-in-law Sill's house, mulling over whether to partner with him. Sill makes his living stealing farm equipment in Wiggonville, the profits of which he frequently tempts James with by flashing wads of cash in front of him. James strives to remain on the straight and narrow, all too aware of the dangerous ramifications if he chooses to join Sill. However, now he is desperate and can find no other way to feed his wife and child.

On a squally night, James accompanies Sill to a Stop & Shop robbery. An arresting terror flashes in the young grocery store clerk's eyes when James squares the pistol in his face and tells the boy to remember his name—a cruel method of asserting dominance and reclaiming control over his downward-spiraling life. James does not value the clerk's life any more than he does allowing his family to starve, so he swiftly shoots him before making his escape. Now James passes the days in prison behind "double-paned Richfield glass," his wife and child growing older with each visit. The icy, industrial fortress of Richfield is James' new home, where he will pay "for the wrongs I done." We hear in Springsteen's tearful vocals and the lachrymose tempo that James harbors a profound remorse for killing an honest man and truly understands that he must atone by doing hard time. "James Lincoln Deere" is one of Springsteen's most tragic songs, made more so by his tremulous vocals. James was only a young man trying to fulfill his role as a husband and father by providing for his family, but economic collapse caused him to succumb to the temptations of delinquency that he avoided for so long.

Springsteen uses his *Nebraska* album to represent the struggles of hardscrabble individuals suffering from hard-pressing external circumstances that force them to transgress. Charlie Starkweather, Johnny 99, and James Lincoln Deere are downtrodden young men whose socioeconomic standing provokes their devastating and deadly actions. Springsteen intimately studies their psychological and emotional interiority so that his listeners may understand the demons that haunt them and how they got to such a lowly place. "I wanted to let the listener hear the characters think, to get inside their heads, so you could hear and feel their thoughts, their choices," Springsteen once explained.[21] Robbins saw in Springsteen a musical artist with the ability to depict felons as more than monsters and willing to critique the American criminal justice system and its unfair treatment of the lower class.

Springsteen Sanctified: Religious Transformations from Greetings *to* Springsteen on Broadway

Robbins selected Springsteen to compose a song for *Dead Man Walking* not only because of his thoughtful depiction of criminals but also due to his identification with Sister Helen's progressive religious ideals. For both Sister Helen and Springsteen, "religion functions not so much as a set of doctrines or rituals, but as a way of thinking, feeling, and living in the world" where the Bible is not meant to be taken as literal truth.[22] One of the main reasons Matthew appreciates Sister Helen is because she doesn't "preach that hellfire and brimstone crap." Sister Helen's plainclothes attire and refusal to wear a habit externally signifies her free-spirited interpretation of Catholic dogma.

Throughout *Dead Man Walking*, Sister Helen finds herself at a spiritual crossroads: she believes Matthew is in dire need of redemption and that she is doing the right thing by getting him to receive the sacraments before he dies, but she constantly meets with objections from her family, fellow nuns, prison workers, and others. Even radio preachers seem to disapprove of her decision to be Matthew's spiritual advisor: "Ye advocates of killers and child molesters, ye opponents of execution. Ye cannot walk upon the high ground. Ye do not have the moral authority to walk there. Ye traverse with scum, and scum is where—" Sister Helen flicks off the radio before he can finish.

Sister Helen is dismayed that the prison's priest supports Matthew's capital punishment and uses the Bible to support his convictions, particularly the Old Testament commandment "Thou shall not kill" and "Let every person be subordinate to the higher authorities.", A guard argues that the death penalty fulfills the "eye for an eye" adage: "If anyone sheds the blood of man, by man shall his blood be shed." Sister Helen counters that, by that logic, we must strictly adhere to the Bible's other commands, such as "death as a punishment for adultery, prostitution, homosexuality, treason upon sacred ground, profaning the Sabbath, and contempt of parents." The evangelical protesters outside of the prison gates share the guards' bloodlust; their signs read "Hang Him High," "Revenge Is Sweet," "Die Scum of the Earth," and "A Life for a Life." Sister Helen prefers the peaceful credo, "He who lives by the sword shall die by the sword," meaning that violence only begets violence, no matter who it is directed toward. She rejects the view of the Bible as a dogmatic, infallible document and values the virtues of the New Testament, grace and reconciliation, rather than God's vengeful and choleric rhetoric from the Old Testament. Robbins explains that "people like Sister Helen are more in spirit of what Jesus Christ represents.... Could you see Jesus Christ pulling the switch, becoming actively involved in an execution?"[23]

Matthew asks Sister Helen why she became a nun, sacrificing the earthly pleasures of a husband and family for the divine. She explains that she wanted to give the kind of love and support she had growing up back to those who were less fortunate and, above all, seemed to be drawn to the vocation by some unknown force. Springsteen's relationship with faith is far more complicated. Like many 1950s-era Catholic schoolchildren, Springsteen feared and detested the tyrannical clergy—the nuns at school who shoved him in a garbage can, locked him into a closet, and allowed another classmate to slap him across the face, and the priest who knocked him down for misunderstanding directions while serving as an altar boy. Their apocalyptic rhetoric of eternal damnation frightened him and felt as tangible and "real as the gas station next door to you."[24] There was no escape from the church's oppression because Springsteen lived "a football's toss away" from the school, convent, and priest's rectory. His elderly relatives adhered to a strict old-world Catholicism, with his grandmother Alice sensing the presence of Satan in lightning and thunder. With its gloomy, dark lighting and mystical-sounding Latin language, Mass had an intimidating and unknowable quality that "held you in the palm of its darkness" and left an immense impression on Springsteen as a young boy.[25] The constant overwhelming presence of the menacing Catholic Church wearied him, and he sought freedom in a public high school and agnosticism. "Over the years as a St. Rose student I had felt enough of Catholicism's corporal and emotional strain. On my eighth-grade graduation day, I walked away from it all, finished, telling myself, 'Never again.' I was free, free, free at last … and I believed it … for quite a while," he says in his memoir.[26]

Yet, despite his aversion to St Rose's "none-too-subtle form of brainwashing," the church "was the world where I found the beginnings of my song … there existed the poetry, danger, and darkness that reflected my imagination and my inner self," Springsteen says.[27] It was a spellbinding world "filled with the unknown bliss of resurrection, eternity and the unending fires of perdition, of exciting, sexually tinged torture, immaculate conceptions and miracles. A world where men turn into gods and gods into devils."[28] The monotonous intonation of prayers, resounding church organs, endless parades of blushing brides and gleaming oak caskets, crying newly baptized babies, the sweet smell of incense, and ornate, flower-bedded gravestones that surrounded him as a child living next door to St. Rose of Lima had a marked impact on his musical artistry. Religious iconography pervades nearly every song in Springsteen's unique canon, from the devils disguised as Jesus appearing through the steam of New York City's potholes to Mary's crosses in "Thunder Road" to Moses' banishment from the chosen land in "The Price You Pay." Although the nature of its inclusion continually changes, Catholicism is a consistent thread that runs throughout Springsteen's work.

Springsteen's early songs are informed by his teenage disdain of parochial school education, as he condemns and satirizes the Catholic Church in a way that often borders on blasphemy. From his early band Steel Mill, Springsteen's hard rocker "Resurrection" rails against the sisters who enforce severe beliefs on him that he is not permitted to question. Backed against vocals that evoke a choir of twisted angels, Springsteen's Devil-affiliated nonbeliever resents being dragged to church every Sunday and Friday and forced onto his knees with a bowed head to seek an absolution he cares little for, especially since his mother already screams that he is going to burn in hell someday. The end of the second verse has a zippy rhythm to emphasize the ridiculousness of being given a "special old price of three Hail Marys" to automatically cleanse one's soul. If it is that easy to be forgiven, why bother asking?

"If I Was the Priest" is a zealous piano ballad that reimagines religious icons as Wild West characters: Jesus is the town sheriff, the Holy Ghost hosts a burlesque show, and the Virgin Mary is a junkie and boozer who runs the Holy Grail Saloon, serving Mass on Sunday and prostituting herself on Monday. Elsewhere, Springsteen lusts after the golden-haired title character of "Sister Theresa." He implores the docile nun to let a man of the flesh into her bedroom every night instead of the divine. Opposing her mulish and truculent master Jesus Christ, he promises a sexual rather than spiritual ecstasy that will put a smile on her face. In the meandering ramble "Mary Louise Watson," performed with Steel Mill, the title character is an imperious, formerly corpulent shrew who forces her boyfriend to confess his sins at Mass every morning, a nettlesome place he has not been to since being yanked there by the nuns at Catholic school every Friday. This frequent churchgoing causes him to have strange dreams of dining with angels and the Lord himself, ogling the beguiling Virgin Mary (who is a vision in blue), and being seduced by the Devil disguised as a nubile Egyptian princess "with the biggest diamond you've ever seen … right between her thighs." "Lost in the Flood" is one of Springsteen's most scathing religious critiques. He paints a dark portrait of a godless, morally bankrupt world colonized by defiled, pregnant nuns and suicidal saints, symbols of the church's frequent hypocrisy and feigned moral righteousness. Jimmy the Saint, "Bronx's best apostle," races hot rods in Jersey on Sundays instead of going to church and ogles a lusty "storefront incarnation" of the Virgin Mary named Maria before the explosion of a vicious gang war. Inspired by Springsteen's despotic Catholic school education, these sacrilegious songs are full of venom and boast a firm anti-religious stance, often lampooning sacred theological idols by regarding them in a sexual manner.

Some of Springsteen's later music amalgamates a tongue-in-cheek lasciviousness or jocularity with religious iconography. "Pink Cadillac" surmises that Adam was not merely tempted with an apple but also with Eve's pink Cadillac (a euphemism for her female anatomy). Springsteen's satirical concert monologue preceding this ribald roadhouse ditty asserts that sex was the gateway out of the immaculate Garden of Eden, which in Springsteen's world is located ten miles south of Jersey City on the New Jersey turnpike. Instead of that utopian space, Springsteen favors life on earth, with McDonald's, air conditioning, and the joys of sex. "When it comes to no sex, I prefer the state of guilt that I constantly live in," he declares.[29] A 1990 outtake released on *Tracks*, "Part Man, Part Monkey," rejects creationism. The narrator considers his animalistic lust for women and depravity as evidence of Darwin's evolutionary theory that we descended from monkeys instead of the first man, from the "muck and mire" rather than God's "breath of holy fire." The corner steeple's church bells ring while the speaker sits in on a barstool, having easily given into his temptations. His drifting and unsatisfied ways assert humanity's savage bestiality and fly in the face of soul-sucking preachers' rhetoric about the piousness of man.

Not all of Springsteen's religious songs are satirical censures. There is a notable metamorphosis in Springsteen's later work, from *Tunnel of Love* onward, that moves beyond pictorial theological allusions to a poetic piety that lionizes the awesome power of God's light, holy blessings, mercy, will, command, and so on in countless songs such as "Cautious Man," "Across the Border," and "Life Itself." In the heady "Living Proof," Springsteen extols God for rewarding him with the birth of his beautiful son, his entrance into the world a purifying light at the end of the dark psychological tunnel Springsteen crawled into "to burn out every trace of who I'd been" and the living proof of God's mercy in a fouled and confusing world. "I Wish I Were Blind" revels in the beauty of the world God sculpted with his benevolent hands: the summer twilight skies, cottonwood blossoming in the springtime, twittering bluebirds, the shining hair of his paramour. The gritty song "Devils & Dust" is an unreserved study of an Iraq War veteran haunted by the horrors witnessed on his tour of duty. The protagonist's faith has been tested by the brutality of war, by those he has maimed and the friends he has seen killed, and he strives not to lose his belief in God. He aspires to harness the "love that God wills" and "faith that He commands" before fear fills him with the wickedness of the Devil and withers his soul into crumbling ash. Although "Devils & Dust" is bleaker than the aforementioned songs, it features a character who sincerely aims to live in God's benevolent image. Throughout his oeuvre, Springsteen's subjects humbly and sincerely praise the Holy Trinity for their earthly benedictions of love and family and beseech them to provide the strength, faith, and hope needed to overcome tragedy. There is an authentic ardor in these religious allusions that markedly differs from Springsteen's earlier songs, a beatific vision that imparts a serious and devout reverence for spirituality not previously seen in his work. As the presence of God begins to make its way back into Springsteen's own life, it manifests in his music and lyrics in a genuine, reverent manner.

There are songs from *Wrecking Ball* (2012) that are soulful reformulations of Gospel stories into somber accounts of man's disillusion with religion. "Rocky Ground" is a modern hip-hop church hymn featuring multiple biblical references and phrases. Recalling the Noah's Ark narrative in the Book of Genesis, Springsteen's languid dirge opens with a bleak portrait of a land flooded by rain for the past forty days and nights, leaving God's flock abandoned in the stormy seas. As Judgment Day looms, the mighty shepherd's lost children search for higher ground in the prosperous land of Canaan. They dread betraying their savior like the money changers in the temple from the Book of John, but Michelle Moore's rap interlude admits that their faith has indeed faltered. The disciples struggle in vain to do their best and raise their children right in the face of austerity, but God does not answer their prayers and they have completely abandoned their beliefs. The title of Springsteen's urban psalm refers to the Parable of the Sower found in the Book of Matthew, which attests that the seeds planted in rocky ground resemble people with faltering convictions who renounce their fealty to God during difficult times. Springsteen's community stands on rocky ground as their hope for the future and belief in their ability to overcome hardships with God's aid withers. In a similar vein, with deep, booming drums that evoke the inside of the "great black cave," jagged guitar twang, and harsh, eerie vocals, "Swallowed Up (Belly of the Whale)" transforms the story of Jonah into a metaphor for a broken spirit and crisis of faith. Once cloaked in God's mercy, Springsteen's sailor was able to conquer the formidable seas and trusted that the righteous would prevail, but now his belief in God has been swallowed up just as he lies in the belly of a great beast and gazes upon the bones of other perfidious seamen. These somber elegies profess how strenuous maintaining faith can be during trying times—no matter how ardent one's beliefs are. Although many of his songs are messianic rhapsodies, Springsteen does not shy away from depicting the complexities of faith.

The religious transformations in Springsteen's canon reflect his realization that "once you're a Catholic, you're always a Catholic."[30] For better or worse, his education at St. Rose of Lima seeped into his creative mind and shaped the contours of his music. The birth of his children and rewards of familial life provoked a personal return to a deeply felt and genuine spirituality that he had forsaken in his early adulthood. "I stopped kidding myself. I don't often participate in my religion, but I know somewhere … deep inside … I'm still on the team," Springsteen reveals in his memoir.[31] Cementing Springsteen's theological evolution is his recitation of the Lord's Prayer and benediction—"May God bless you, your family, and all those you love"—at the conclusion of his Broadway show. These are not the words of the snarky twenty-something who composed mordant religious satires but of a wise older man who has reshaped the ideologies he learned as a child to fit within his personal progressive outlook. Springsteen's Catholicism adheres to a belief that there is beauty in all of our ugly transgressions and shortcomings. He writes in his memoir, "The way I see it, we ate the apple and Adam, Eve, the rebel Jesus in all his glory and Satan are all part of God's plan to make men and women out of us, to give us the precious gifts of earth, dirt, sweat, blood, sex, sin, goodness, freedom, captivity, love, fear, life and death … our humanity and a world of our own."[32] Springsteen has little concern for life everlasting—only life in the here and now on the earth's soil. Like Sister Helen, Springsteen does not cleave to the Old Testament view of God. He describes having a "personal" relationship with Jesus Christ but no longer believing "in his godly power. I believe deeply in his love, his ability to save … but not to damn … enough of that."[33]

In *Dead Man Walking*, after Matthew starts reading the Bible, he admits that he admires Jesus for being a "turn-the-other-cheek" kind of guy, and Sister Helen reminds him that Jesus was also a rebel of his time. Knowing that Matthew despises indolence, she explains that Jesus was a dangerous man who "changed the world with His love … [for] the people nobody cared about: the prostitutes, the beggars, the poor." The train that welcomes *all*—saints, sinners, whores, gamblers, thieves, fools, kings—in Springsteen's gospel revival

"Land of Hope and Dreams" personifies Jesus Christ's genuine ideology of acceptance. "They finally had somebody who respected them, loved them, made them realize their own worth." Sister Helen continues: "They had dignity and became powerful. The guys on the top got real nervous. So they had to kill Jesus." Sister Helen and Springsteen share a view of Jesus Christ as a redeemer for all, even the worst of sinners.

"Jesus Was an Only Son" from Springsteen's *Devils & Dust* invokes Martin Scorsese's *The Last Temptation of Christ* in its frank exploration of the war between Jesus' mortal and divine halves. The balmy ballad details Jesus' quotidian Nazarene adolescence and Mary's maternal need to protect her child. Springsteen's Jesus is like any other boy who reads books by his mother's side and gets tucked into bed at night while she prays for him to have sweet dreams. When he grows up, Jesus begs God in Gethsemane to let him survive the crucifixion as he imagines the earthly life he will never live. Springsteen elaborates on this image in his introduction to the song on the VH1 *Storytellers* special: "If you're Jesus, you gotta be thinking 'Gee, the weather is pretty nice in Galilee this time of year … there was that little bar. I could manage the place, Mary Magdalene could tend bar and we could have some kids, do the preaching on the weekend.' I always thought it was the humanness of the choice that He made that was what made it mean something." Springsteen boldly presents the diurnal life of the valorized Mary and Jesus, capturing their internal selfhood in order to shrink the gap between man and deity. What matters to Springsteen is not that biblical characters are revered as faultless paragons, but rather that they are seen as human beings with their own variegated intricacies.

In Catholicism, Springsteen "found a land of great and harsh beauty, of fantastic stories, of unimaginable punishment, and infinite reward. It was a glorious and pathetic place I was either shaped for or fit right into. It has walked alongside me as a waking dream my whole life."[34] Springsteen molded that enchanting world into an engaging thematic canvas that he could paint his prosaic characters on while they navigated the harsh truths and pleasures of life. "Jesus Was an Only Son" manifests Springsteen's intriguing liminality between the humane and the divine throughout his canon. In Springsteen's mind, mankind is "crookedly blessed in God's mercy," meaning that humans are not immaculate, our sins are an inevitable and necessary part of human existence, but we will always find comfort in the loving embrace of God's magnanimous arms.[35] Eden collapsed and led us to the marvelous world of ecstasy and anguish, yearning and revulsion, tranquility and rage, where we are perfectly flawed. There may be darkness on the edge of our towns, but there is beauty in that darkness. Throughout his canon, Springsteen subverts the traditional fire-and-brimstone biblical interpretation and opts instead for Sister Helen's brand of faith, one without a condemnatory rhetoric that understands humanity's transgressions and emphasizes grace.

A champion for social justice with a progressive spirituality, Springsteen is the ideal artist to contextualize the moral, political, and theological concerns of *Dead Man Walking*. Throughout his oeuvre, he captures the inner emotional and psychological life of those whom society most ostracizes and fears to reveal how such feelings can lie within all of us. Robbins' goal with *Dead Man Walking* was to help victims and those affected by crimes to move past fury and toward "reconciliation and recognition of unconditional love" without resorting to capital punishment.[36] "I think that whatever divinity we can lay claim to is hidden in the core of our humanity and, when we let our compassion go, we let go of whatever little claim we have to the divine," Springsteen says during his VH1 *Storytellers* monologue for "Jesus Was an Only Son." Compassion is the driving force of *Dead Man Walking*, as spectators are asked to identify with all sides of the capital punishment narrative: the criminal, the victims, the prison workers, the clergy, and more. Sister Helen believes that acceptance, love, and forgiveness are the true messages of her Lord and Savior and that abiding by those virtues will bring her closer to her faith. In the same way that Springsteen asks his audience to empathize with the worst of miscreants, Sister Helen strives to live in the vein of Jesus Christ by understanding Matthew as an imperfect human being, acknowledging what he has done without condemning him as a heartless, cruel monster, and ultimately forgiving him. For Robbins and Springsteen, living in God's image means caring for one another despite our deepest flaws and gravest sins.

No Looking Back

After spending years listening to Springsteen, paragon of independent filmmaking Edward Burns went on to direct, write, and star in a *Darkness on the Edge of Town*–esque film. Inspired by Springsteen's raw, grease-soaked realism, *No Looking Back* (1998) is a significant departure from Burns' usual male ensemble-driven romantic comedies with a Woody Allen comic style. The son of a police officer in a close-knit Irish Catholic family, Burns wanted to authentically capture his own Long Island working-class experience, which was, in many ways, similar to Springsteen's. Opposing the predominantly masculine focus of Burns' past work and Springsteen's music, *No Looking Back* is a female-centric drama about Claudia, who still toils as a waitress at her hometown greasy spoon diner years after her former high school sweetheart Charlie left for California. Charlie's return reignites her dormant disquietude, and she regrets having rejected his proposal to head west. Now, however, her codependence on her depressive mother, wayfaring sister, and doting fiancé keeps her from making any escape on her own.

Claudia embodies Springsteen's prosaic *Darkness on the Edge of Town* subjects, who are stuck "in Asbury Park, driving the circuit, going nowhere down Kingsley street … worn down by inertia, the realities of classism, and the grind of a low-skill job," people who want more from their lives but struggle to find the means to obtain it.[1] At the 2018 Tribeca Film Festival, Burns specifically cited the *Darkness on the Edge of Town* outtake "Iceman" and its portrait of a "small town girl stuck in a rut" as inspiration for his melancholy examination of a beach town in the off season.[2] Springsteen uses husky, Elvis-like vocals in his dark tale of a preacher's daughter living in a sleepy, oppressive town without the "guts to budge," an environment that Burns reflects in his dour cinematography and muted landscapes.

The film's dismal blue-collar setting is reminiscent of Springsteen's *Darkness* album while several of his other songs appear as both diegetic source music and non-diegetic score—mostly from *Tunnel of Love* to draw out the film's romance genre conventions. But the most intriguing aspect of the intertextual relationship between *No Looking Back* and Springsteen is that through the character of Claudia, Burns imagines what would have happened to the proverbial Wendy and Mary of "Born to Run" and "Thunder Road" had they not accepted the dashing hot rodder's proposal to abandon their death trap of a town for the splendorous promised land. Would these characters have regrets as adults? And what would happen if the man who was born to run crawled back to his hometown? Would Mary/Wendy take a second chance to "pull out of here to win" once and for all? By telling the stories of his friends who "hit their thirties and started to put their adolescent dreams aside," Burns envisages the afterlife of the idealistic *Born to Run* characters as they enter the adult world of *Darkness on the Edge of Town*, a space where they abandon their "adolescent definitions of love and freedom," as Springsteen writes in his memoir.[3]

The squalid exterior visuals of *No Looking Back*'s opening montage—ramshackle Texaco stations, scrubby bars, skeletons of deserted cars, "weather-beaten houses surrounded by chain fences… and murky sunsets fading over a deserted boardwalk"—are symbolic of the town's ennui and resemble Springsteen's Asbury Park and northern New Jersey.[4] *No Looking Back* was filmed in Rockaway Beach, New York, because shooting in Asbury (as Burns originally intended) was too costly. A humble blue-collar town populated by people "who work hard but still struggle to make ends meet, and who want more from life than what they currently have," it is the kind of place that prompts Charlie's character to sardonically retort when asked if he missed home, "Is there something here to miss?"[5] Claudia's insipid, dead-end nightmare of a town leaves her, like Springsteen's characters, proverbially "stuck on a tilt-a-whirl, trapped in a life that keeps [her] spinning and spinning in the tedium of mere existence."[6] Sullen grey clouds perpetually blanket the wind-scoured town as a meteorological manifestation of Claudia's despondent stasis. There seem to be no cars, clothes, or appliances from past the year 1982, as if her somnolent town has been frozen in time and she never left high school. Burns also incorporates a recurrent visual motif embodying the idea that "nothing changes" (more in line with his original title for the film *Long Time, Nothing New*), wherein Claudia drags her empty garbage cans to the garage every night after work.[7]

The majority of Springsteen's working-class characters are prosaic figures; they do not possess any exceptional talent upon which to hinge their small-town flight (a notable exception being the Springsteen proxy singer of "Rosalita (Come Out Tonight)," with his record company advance). Likewise, Burns presents the everyday lives of his friends "who knew they wanted more in their life but didn't have special skills."[8] Burns contemplated giving Claudia "some sort of creative skill such as painting or writing" that would motivate a move to New York City, but he felt this attribute would belie his film's quotidian blue-collar milieu.[9] He elaborates in the *No Looking Back* DVD commentary, "Sometimes the dream can be just getting in your car and busting out of your hometown. You don't have to have a purpose or some special gift or some hidden talent or know exactly where you're going, but the fact that you have the balls to get in your car and go is sometimes enough of the accomplishment."[10] The *New York Times* critic Stephen Holden argues that "Ms. Holly is simply too refined and glamorous to make Claudia's crisis seem credible. You have the feeling that if she strolled into any modeling agency in Manhattan, she would instantly be spotted as a potential covergirl."[11] Burns counters this insipid critique by noting that there were gorgeous girls who still lived in his quiet hometown and their looks had no bearing on their lack of achievement. Burns emulates Springsteen by presenting naturalistic small-town characters who know they want more but have "no way to escape the drudgery of their day-to-day working-class life."[12]

With her luminescent blue eyes and golden blonde hair, Lauren Holly exquisitely fulfills the role of "the best-looking girl in your town," as Burns says, who everyone assumed "would go on to bigger, better things" but nevertheless remained in her disconsolate hometown—similar to the gorgeous ex-cheerleader who used to turn "all the boy's heads" in Springsteen's "Glory Days."[13] Charlie initially embodies the male subjects of "Thunder Road" and "Born to Run," as he abandons his hardscrabble seaside town for the west—his place in the sun. But just as *Darkness on the Edge of Town* transforms the winners of *Born to Run* into losers, former high school "big shot" Charlie (shades of "Glory Days" in him as well) returns "with his tail between his legs" after realizing that "life outside is not much different" from his hometown, as Burns explains on the DVD commentary.[14] It is here that

Charlie (Edward Burns) confronts his ex-girlfriend Claudia (Lauren Holly) at the local diner where she works (www.photofestnyc.com).

Burns dismantles the male preoccupation with the salvific promises of the car and open road. The image of Charlie's beloved Buick with the tires removed and sheathed in a worn tapestry literalizes this ideal and serves as a visual metaphor for his splintered nomadic dreams.

Claudia and Charlie's exchange at the diner, the first time she has seen him in years, reveals their tumultuous past. In a series of shot/reverse shots, we learn that Claudia disdains Charlie because he has "a habit of running away when things get a little ugly," a reference to his departure for California while she was recovering in the hospital after aborting his child. But Charlie does not want to dwell on the past. Instead, he expresses concern over her subservient vocation: "I've known you your whole life, and I can't see how you're happy." After Claudia insists that she will not be working at the diner for the rest of her life, Charlie points to an elderly waitress in the background and jokes, "She said the same thing. Another couple of months in this town, and your hair will turn blue." Charlie cannot fathom that the girl he used to call "Cloudia" because she had her head in the clouds, with dreams of "getting out of here and seeing some of the world," has ended up here. In this scene, Burns transmutes the "Thunder Road" and "Born to Run" subtext by shifting the male narrator's naive idealism and dreams of transcendence onto the Mary/Wendy role.

The gradual erosion of Claudia's youthful and somewhat dereistic visions mirrors Springsteen's *Darkness* characters. Claudia's line—"I was 18 years old and I grew up. We were just kids and that's why it seemed so romantic, but it doesn't seem so romantic now, does it?"—adroitly captures the seismic shift in Springsteen's music from sanguine romanticism to post–*Born to Run* disenchantment with the adult world. Returning from his failed journey out west to reclaim the woman who should have been by his side, Charlie proposes that they rekindle their romance and chase down their dreams once more. He still believes that the open road will provide them with "the manna of the future and the capacity for remaking the past" and leaving town is their "single, last-ditch opportunity for salvation" and personal resurrection.[15]

Despite Claudia's misgivings about Charlie, who (per Burns) was a jerk all throughout their high school relationship, she eventually succumbs to his seduction. The former flames share a moment of soft eroticism in her home when Claudia's fiancé Michael is away. The sparks flying between them seem to bounce off the white plaster of her kitchen sink as Charlie kisses her neck. "I'm not gonna feel like this again," she protests in vain, even though she has secretly been longing for their reunion. Days later, Charlie visits Claudia inside the local laundromat. In between their kittenish banter and smiles, Springsteen's "One Step Up" faintly emits from a nearby boombox. The mesmeric rhythm of Springsteen's fractured love song sets a romantic mood that brings Charlie and Claudia closer together, but the lyrics about doubt and infidelity backed by a gently repetitive acoustic guitar portend the strife that their relationship faces, especially with Michael. The sudden materialization of Springsteen's vocals stops Claudia in her tracks, and an incredulous smile spreads across her face. Turning up the volume with a mischievous grin, Charlie turns to Claudia and says, "If I remember correctly, you kind of like this song, don't you?" "You know I like all his stuff," she replies. Although Claudia rejects Charlie's proposal to re-create their prom night with a dance, her coquettish response hints at her growing re-attraction.

Charlie exits the laundromat with one final gibe: "I told you you'd be cleaning his dirty underwear, didn't I?" Claudia's grin plummets into a grimace, and she flicks Michael's underwear to the side, ashamed that her life has come to this. The meditative "One Step Up" becomes non-diegetic score when the laundromat scene transfers to a wide shot of Claudia in the diner. Using the song as Claudia's emotional signifier transcends the lyrics' male subjectivity and enables the spectator to identify with her misery. Beneath the harsh fluorescent light at closing time, Claudia mops the diner floor to the rhythm of Springsteen's timorous ballad. The tedium of her banal occupation wearies her; she, too, performs "the same thing night on night." Claudia identifies with the narrator's confession that when he gazes into the mirror, he does not see the person he "wanted to be" and has fallen "off track" from his ideal self; she never imagined she would be working at her hometown diner in her thirties. The scene then cuts to Claudia's trek home from the late shift in the pouring rain, an atmospheric symbol of her internal melancholy. The camera draws closer and closer to Claudia's face through the window of her car while she sits at a red light until it nearly fills the frame, as if Springsteen compels Claudia to abandon her "same old story, same old act" and take that crucial step toward a prosperous future.

Burns' use of a *Tunnel of Love* song—an album famously about the dissolution of Springsteen's first marriage—foreshadows the domestic squabble that follows. The "One Step Up" sequence fades into a shot of Michael and Claudia walking across an abandoned baseball field, bundled in their coats to stave off the bitter wind and gloomy mist of rain.[16] The couple tries to settle on their plans for the night, but the pickings are slim; Michael is content to watch the game at the local bar, but Claudia wants to leave the familiar surroundings and visit a "nice restaurant" in Manhattan. "We haven't left this town to do anything in over a year. It'd be nice to see some difference faces, some different streets," she argues despite Michael's protestation that they cannot afford such a luxurious excursion. Michael's suggestion that they visit his family aggravates Claudia because every time they go to his home, she must field interrogations from his mother and sisters about their impending marriage while he watches sports with his brothers. Burns' camera circles feverishly around the couple as they argue to convey their increasing agitation.

Springsteen's wife Patti Scialfa makes an appearance on the soundtrack with "Romeo" from her album *23rd St. Lullaby* (2004), a wispy love song about a former lover that expresses Claudia's increasing desire for Charlie. Scialfa's tenuous vocals accentuate the montage's languid temporality; one day bleeds into the next as Claudia mechanically pours coffee for her patrons, goes home, and returns to the diner the next day. The amorous lyrics insist that Charlie is invariably on her mind. Finally fed up with the monotony, Claudia ruptures her nightly ritual of bringing in the garbage cans by leaving them on the sidewalk. In the next shot, she is back in the diner, which seems stuck in a permanent lull with little to no customers. Claudia sits on a counter stool filing her nails and turns to see the elderly waitress performing the same action, a terrifying facsimile of her future if she remains in her hometown. The sight goads Claudia to meet with Charlie to form getaway plans.

Before they meet, Claudia concedes to her sister that she is not "happy with Michael anymore" and never truly moved on from her relationship with Charlie. The reliable Michael embodies her immutable blue-collar existence, while Charlie represents an exhilarating, unpredictable future. Since Claudia longs for "a different life than the one I'm living so much," she decides to go on a date with Charlie. "I don't want to wake up ten years from now and ask 'what if?'" she declares.

As non-diegetic score overlaying a montage of Claudia and Charlie's preparations for their much-anticipated rendezvous, Springsteen's hypnotic "I'm on Fire"—a song of torrid anticipatory torture with bedroom-whisper vocals, throbbing bass line, and scintillating images of rumpled, soaking wet sheets and sleepless nights—immerses the sequence with a sense of tantalizing prurience. Springsteen's song breathes heavily with a frightening intensity and conveys Claudia and Charlie's "all-consuming desire and the absolute *need* for physical and emotional communion" after many years apart.[17]

Aside from getting Claudia and Charlie in the mood, as it were, "I'm on Fire" emotionally signifies their illicit longing because Claudia is still engaged to Michael. Springsteen taps into the song's forbidden love theme in the music video, where he performs as a garage mechanic tormented by his concupiscence for a married, moneyed client with a Ford Thunderbird. Director John Sayles keeps her face out of the frame to signify her elusive allure. In *No Looking Back*, dressed in a rumpled T-shirt and jeans, Charlie washes his greasy hands in a rusted sink after a hard day of work at Busby's garage, mirroring Springsteen in the music video. Burns pans up to Charlie's reflection in the mirror as he smooths his hair back with a steely gaze, ready for the night.

Burns follows an overhead shot of Claudia in the claustrophobic employee bathroom preparing for the date—a confined space that signifies her oppressive labor—with a mollifying wide shot of her exiting the diner's back door, free at last. Charlie waits in his resurrected Buick, the icon of his teenage "Thunder Road" and "Born to Run" dreams, and then drives off screen past an abandoned post-industrial edifice to relive their teenage years. The sequence ends with a backward tracking shot driven by the night's latent ecstasy, centering Charlie's torso in the frame as he brings two glistening bottles of beer back to his corner booth with Claudia. There is an adolescent giddiness in their debate over travel plans. Desiring a disparate landscape, they reject the familiar beaches of Gainesville, Florida, and stormy skies of Seattle, Washington, settling instead on the west. Springsteen often invokes the American west in his work as a place of renewal where people go to set things right, and it is within this mythological space that Charlie and Claudia intend to set their second chance. À la "Born to Run" and "Thunder Road," they seek their place in the sun—"someplace warm," as Charlie says—where they should have gone together nearly a decade ago.

Springsteen's dreamy waltz "Valentine's Day" softly emerges as diegetic source music from the bar's jukebox. It opens with the familiar scene of a driver rushing down a spooky, darkened highway, but this time Springsteen subverts the lone wolf masculinity found in his road narratives because his male subject turns away from the Rudyard Kipling credo of "he travels fastest who travels alone" and the manifold potential of the open road for the security of a stable home where his lover waits. No longer born to run, the narrator aches for the comfortable bliss of domesticity. Charlie identifies with Springsteen's besotted protagonist because he is finally ready to settle down with Claudia—a woman he has known since childhood and cares for deeply. Indeed, it is his line "I told you we were meant for one another, didn't I?" that cues "Valentine's Day." Yet there is a twinge of doubt that courses through ballad's lovesick narrator: he stands on the precipice of wandering alone so far down his beloved highway that he can never return. Charlie, by contrast, wishes to re-create his escapist fantasies with Claudia accompanying him in the passenger seat. The profound connection Claudia and Charlie once shared, one that never quite vanished, drives the "Valentine's Day" sequence and is manifest in the moonstruck lyrics and serene keyboards.

The lyrics about the narrator's friend who recently became a father—a transformative and beatific experience for him—expose the unspoken tensions that lie between Charlie and Claudia regarding their unborn child. "Valentine's Day" impels the subtextual theme of parentage to govern the rest of the scene. Springsteen's lyrics prompt Claudia to ask Charlie, "Do you ever think about what our lives would be like if we'd had the baby?" Charlie tries to reassure her that they would have been miserable, but Claudia points out that they are not happy now either. She then makes a devastating confession: there were complications after her abortion, and she can no longer have children. This revelation brings to mind an earlier scene in which Claudia dejectedly listened to her friend's enthusiastic talk about her sonogram. In light of this confession, the spectator now understands Claudia's distanciated and somber reaction. Claudia is left behind as her friends move on to the next stage in their lives; preoccupied with the love and care a child requires, they have a distraction from their mundane existence in this crestfallen town. Burns languorously pulls the camera from a mid-shot to a close-up of the couple's faces to signify Claudia's news fortifying their bond. "Valentine's Day" increases in volume to complement this absorbing camera motion and compel Claudia to accept Charlie's proposal to dance.

Springsteen's song synchronizes their waltz, each dulcet lyric articulating Claudia and Charlie's subconscious thoughts and informing their gestures. Just as Claudia turns to face Charlie, Springsteen sings that the only thing that frightens him is the idea of losing his lover. The saccharine synthesizer rises while Burns' static camera fixes on Claudia and Charlie circling one another in a tender slow dance. "So hold me close," Springsteen commands just as Claudia inches toward Charlie, ruffles the back of his hair, places her cheek upon his until there is no space between them, and then gently lays her head on his shoulder. The couple is "born anew" by this second chance to be together. In the last lines, Springsteen's narrator pleads for his girl to "say you're forever mine." For Claudia and Charlie, no matter what their romantic status is, their unborn child will always unite them; they are forever entwined.

"Valentine's Day" transfers to non-diegetic score on a fade out from their dance in the bar to an exterior of a motel parking lot. Springsteen's gentle instrumental coda of wedding bell–esque chimes underscores an image of Claudia standing in front of a bathroom mirror and preparing to spend the night with Charlie. The camera maintains a careful distance from the lovers as they share a timid, yet passionate, kiss. Their darkened silhouettes against the angelic white curtains, coupled with Springsteen's melodic serenade, imbue this sequence with a honeyed grace. A jump cut triggered by the screech of Michael's tires sharply ruptures this idyllic moment as he searches for Claudia at their local bar when she does not return home from her shift.

The doubled sensuousness and romanticism of "I'm on Fire" and "Valentine's Day," which Burns places within five minutes of each other, does not come to a satisfying visual—or literal—climax. The consummation that the couple had so meticulously prepared themselves for does not go as expected. After Michael's scene, Burns cuts to a shot of a forlorn Claudia smoking in her nightgown with Charlie sitting on the side of the bed with his back toward her, lost in perturbed thought. "They thought this encounter would be like when they were eighteen. They both realized it wasn't going to solve anything," Burns explains.[18] Their failed copulation disproves Charlie's notion that he can recapture his youth and "Thunder Road" and "Born to Run" dreams after entering adulthood. By the end of *No Looking Back*, both Charlie and Claudia "discover that you can't relive your past."[19] Patti Scialfa's sultry "Rumble Doll" from her album *Rumble Doll* (1993) slices through the uncomfortable post-coital silence as they leave the motel. Like Claudia, Scialfa's narrator contemplates her feminine identity and sense of self-worth; she feels as if she is nothing more than an object, a toy to be easily tossed aside by the men in her life, as the title suggests.

The song fades when Claudia returns to Michael and reveals her infidelity. Lauren Holly's delivery of Claudia's profound remorse in this scene is exquisite. By the time Claudia leaves Michael and reaches her childhood home, it is dawn. For the first time in months, Claudia's mother emerges from the confines of her room and saunters onto the porch to comfort her heartbroken daughter. "Ever since you were a little girl, you were always much more like your father than you were like me," she says, explaining that Claudia's father was unlike "everybody around here" because of his nomadic wanderlust. Claudia shares his same dreaminess and desire for a life outside of their small town. "It's okay to take care of yourself," Claudia's mother stresses, subtly beseeching her daughter to take advantage of her newfound singledom.

The next day, Claudia seeks out Charlie at Busby's garage. Despite their ineffectual night at the motel, Charlie reminds her that they should leave town as early as next week, but Claudia informs him that she will not be along for the ride. Charlie demands, "You gonna marry Michael after all?" but Claudia insists that her change of plans has nothing to do with another man and is not her malicious "idea of payback." Echoing her mother's maxim, she tactfully declares that she needs to figure things out on her own, and for once she is "just taking care of [her]self." Before Claudia exits the shop, Charlie gently says, "I hope you find what you're looking for." For the first time, Claudia seems entirely certain of her course and gives him a determined nod.

No Looking Back's final sequence opens with a montage of a tranquil morning at the boardwalk town. For the first time in the film, the grey clouds part for a golden sunrise, symbolic of Claudia's joyous departure. Burns cuts to a shot of Claudia walking from the front porch of her childhood home to her car with a suitcase in hand, prepared for her journey, transfiguring the "Thunder Road" space of the porch from a site of the male gaze to one of female dominance and independence. In the next shot, Claudia's car slows down in front of Busby's garage, hoping for one last glance of Charlie, but he does not emerge. *No Looking Back* ends with a wide shot of Claudia's car ascending over the hill of a highway bridge—the mystifying two lanes that will transport her from the world she's known to that elusive anywhere filled with endless possibilities—and then reaching a fork in the road. Which direction will lead to her new life? Without hesitation, Claudia speeds off screen to the left. Scialfa's unreleased "I'm a Big Girl Now" operates as non-diegetic score for the final sequence. This song crystallizes Claudia's arc from girlish codependency and fear to autonomy and freedom. There are textual clues within the film suggesting that after her high school relationship with Charlie, she immediately settled down with Michael; therefore, she has never been on her own as a single woman before. Like Scialfa's narrator, Claudia acknowledges that she and her lover were not meant to be and embraces her newfound emancipation.

Burns subverts the masculine subjectivity of the "Thunder Road" and "Born to Run" narratives by placing his Wendy/Mary proxy Claudia at the wheel. In doing so, Burns reconfigures the automobile, "a prime American symbol of male escapism (disguised as freedom)," into a feminist object.[20] Whereas the male subjects of Springsteen's iconic road songs want to claim Mary and Wendy as their prized objects in order to achieve their wildest dreams and find their own piece of heaven, Burns insists that Charlie cannot rescue Claudia. She is meant to stand on her own, not as a passenger but as the one to pull out of town to win in that coveted front seat. It is in the final shot of Claudia driving into the distance that the meaning of the film's title becomes clear. For Claudia, there will be no looking back at her diminutive hometown, no returning to the boys she has already known, only looking forward on her own toward an unpredictable future. She tastes the cherished liberation of the open road, free to chase her dreams and have her head in the clouds again.

Little Dollies and Queens: Bruce Springsteen's Women

According to Gareth Palmer, Springsteen's corpus straddles "a rhetoric that expresses support for women as individuals with rights, and very narrow, stereotypical representations."[21] Scholarship surrounding Springsteen's portrayal of women remains divisive, ranging from harshly critical to feminist praise. For Pamela Moss, Springsteen's women are "objects of disdain, sex, and obsession" delineated by puerile pet names such as "little girl," "little dolly," or "pretty little miss," their presence serving merely to "deliver men from one emotional state to another, continually assisting the generation of his subjectivity."[22] By contrast, Samuele F. S. Pardini views Springsteen's female characters as kaleidoscopic in nature: "mature, complex, sexual, relational, graceful, and independent."[23] I adhere to Palmer's notion that "it is difficult to see a clear development as simplistic representations in songs dot all of Springsteen's albums."[24] Despite Springsteen's willingness to critique hegemonic masculinity and promote romantic partnerships based on equality, as well as his own personal maturation past Eisenhower-era ideals of female submission, oftentimes his depiction of women submits to a dominating male gaze.[25]

Rebecca Bohanan divides Springsteen's women into the disparate categories of a pure, virtuous *deus ex machina* or damaged goods for the male subject to heroically rescue.[26] They are "either idealized as symbols of moral perfection, or … likened to objects and thought of as possessions."[27] In the case of "Thunder Road" and "Born to Run," it is both. Springsteen's narrators adulate Mary and Wendy as angelic bearers of salvation from their hardscrabble lives, proving to them that love is indeed real. The names of these women are emblematic of Springsteen's idolatry: Mary refers to the Catholic figure of the Virgin Mary, the preeminent symbol of immaculate goodness, and Wendy alludes to *Peter Pan*'s Wendy Darling, positioning her as a conduit that affords Springsteen's tramp safe passage to manhood. Lisa Zitelli argues that this "kind of idealization is another version of objectification, albeit on the other side of the spectrum."[28] At the same time, Mary and Wendy are plagued by an overwhelming woe that only Springsteen's rebels without a cause can assuage. They vow to save and protect the girls by whisking them away from their dead-end towns and bringing their "dreams and visions" to life—but only if they "climb in back" or sit in the front seat. Springsteen's men are the captains of this journey, leading the women toward the promised land on their own terms. "Iceman," Burns' inspiration for *No Looking Back*, also fits within this paradigm. The titular iceman reveres the lily-white preacher's daughter and seeks to liberate her from the draconian shadows of her father's church with his old, dirty Ford blazing on the midnight road to the Devil's door. Rather than wait for the promises of the afterlife, Springsteen's tombstone-eyed racer encourages his miserably cloistered girl to live wantonly in the here and now. In *No Looking Back*, although Charlie cares deeply for Claudia as a person, she is also a symbol of his youth and the promise of a better life. She fulfills his savior fantasies because he vows to finally take her away from the drudgery of their hometown as he should have done all those years ago.

After Mary and Wendy choose to stay behind and do not accept the hot rodder's proposal to journey toward the sun, Springsteen relegates them to working-class drudgery from which only he can unfetter them. These working-class female characters most resemble Claudia. Although "Springsteen has been successful at capturing the inner life, turmoil, heartache, ennui and regret that make up the working-class male experience, that is not always the case with his working-class women," Lisa Delmonico contends.[29] Filtered through his male gaze and virtually voiceless, these women stand in contrast to the valiant, persevering men of songs such as "Badlands" or "The Promised Land," who are afforded an ascension from the dead ends and bad scenes of their impoverished towns. Such male protagonists are "continually allowed to *react* to their circumstances in a way his women are not."[30] Instead, the female characters lie in wait for Springsteen to save them, their penurious existence seemingly inescapable.

"Party Lights" and "Point Blank" have interchangeable lyrics in which the women have given up on their quest for Romeo and spend their nights counting welfare checks. In "Party Lights," the young and exhausted single mother's only reprieve from her soul-sucking job is when the male narrator takes her for a night out, but such a brief rendezvous cannot quell her desire to see the party lights of her rollicking youth once again. Penury leaves the female subject of "Point Blank" a hollow, depressed shell who feels as if she is dying every waking hour. Springsteen's narrator pines for her from afar in the hopes that their eventual reunion will bring her despondent soul back to life. Shades of both of these characters can be seen in Claudia as she reminisces about her past with Charlie and looks with dismay at her torpid existence, struggling to make ends meet as a waitress.

Springsteen frequently features waitress characters like Claudia, an occupation that fits within his significant musical motifs of "women as servile (forced, for financial reasons, to be friendly to male clientele), and woman as waiting."[31] In "Open All Night," Wanda waits for her boyfriend to arrive home from his night shift and the subsequent two-hour drive across the New Jersey turnpike. The song is told from the male narrator's perspective while he impatiently traverses the "spooky old highway" toward Wanda, the beacon guiding him home. While driving, he wistfully recalls meeting her when she worked at Bob's Big Boy on Route 60, a memory purely of corporeal pleasure where she sat on his lap and batted her "big brown eyes" at him. "Daddy's coming on home," he promises her, a pet name that positions him as a domineering figure who must safeguard and govern his little girl. How Wanda feels about the narrator, we are never sure; she merely stands high on a "scrap metal hill" as a symbol of domestic comfort.

"I'll Work for Your Love" from *Magic* features another waitress character whom the male narrator ogles but also reveres as a celestial figure. Springsteen equates the woman's physical features with the Christological symbols of an angelic halo and crown of thorns. After he commands Theresa to pour him a drink, the diner patron gapes at her captivating beauty, which both enchants and terrifies him in its power to either soothe or destroy. The minute detail of Theresa's gestures—combing her hair and smoothing her blouse—elevates him into a divine ecstasy. Any insight into Theresa's inner life or perspective is overshadowed by the song's flamboyant religious motifs of rosaries, the Book of Revelation, and drops of Jesus Christ's blood.

On *Working on a Dream*, "Queen of the Supermarket" romanticizes the banal space of the supermarket as one of rapturous eroticism. Soft chimes introduce the male narrator's refrigerated house of worship, where at its pulpit stands his queen: the girl at the checkout counter who waits for him each day in the "aisle number two." Surrounded by sweeping violins, he observes her in all her beauty, bagging the groceries with bored, vacant eyes, and longs to rescue her from her insipid kingdom and give her the life that a true royal deserves. The song ends with the monotonous drone of the checkout register to signal that he has not gained the courage to tell her that he loves her, leaving her confined to the tedium of her profession. "Queen of the Supermarket" mirrors Charlie's desire to liberate Claudia from her listless work at the local diner, but Charlie cares for Claudia's authentic self more than Springsteen's protagonist, who exalts his "queen" only for her exterior appearance.

Although Claudia disdains her mundane occupation, she also fears what will happen to her after she marries Michael. She refuses to set a wedding date and wear an engagement ring because she is "not ready to become a goddamn housewife! What would I do for the rest of my life?" Claudia dreads turning into the weary post–*Born to Run* women of Springsteen's somber marital portraits "Racing in the Street" and "Stolen Car." In "Racing in the Street," Springsteen repurposes the "Thunder Road" space of the porch, where an older, wrinkled Mary now sits interminably waiting for her husband, who distracts himself from the existential void and working-class grind with hot rod racing, the formative pleasure of his youth. Left with broken dreams and the eyes of someone "who hates for just being born," Mary speaks with a heavy sigh and cries herself to sleep every night. The housewife of "Stolen Car" mourns her eroded relationship when she reads the romantic letters her estranged husband wrote her when they were young and madly in love; they make "her feel one hundred years old" because the impetuous passions and intimacy they once shared have been gone for so long. Springsteen empathizes with these broken ladies and gives us some insight into their subjectivity, but these heart-rending songs also align with his vision of women as noble burdens, someone the male protagonist valiantly loves in spite of being regrettably bound to them. They are "the albatross around the man's neck—something to emphasize the hero's perseverance."[32] Claudia does not want to resemble these types of female figures, who spend the rest of their lives in their hometown with an extinguished flame for their former loves.

"Car Wash" demonstrates Springsteen's periodic inclination to step outside of his male gaze and craft a well-rounded female character. He boldly rejects the hypermasculinity of some of his other work by writing from the perspective of a woman.[33] Catherine LeFevre is the speaker in "Car Wash," an exuberant tale of a single mother who toils at Sunset and Vine's Astrowash for "a dollar and a dime." Whereas most of Springsteen's working-class women are "unable to muster the energy required to move out" of their position, Catherine has the specific dream of becoming a famous singer, opposing the goal of his male protagonists, who merely want to escape from their current situation.[34] Backed by a driving rockabilly beat, she refuses to give up her ambition for a life outside of subservience in the same way that Claudia takes control of her destiny by the end of *No Looking Back*.

Both Burns and Springsteen are artists known for their male-oriented narratives, but they occasionally transcend their male gaze to depict the auspices of womanhood. In *No Looking Back*, Burns uses Springsteen's relationship album *Tunnel of Love* as both non-diegetic score and diegetic source music to frame his wistful love story. Centered on fractured love lives, these delicate songs about the pleasures and struggles of courtship perfectly encapsulate the knotty romance of Burns' seaside subjects. Burns disrupts his narrative's "Thunder Road" and "Born to Run" subtext by placing Mary and Wendy in the driver's seat, the space typically occupied by Springsteen's male protagonists. In doing so, he negotiates with Springsteen's depiction of women across his oeuvre and how they relate to Claudia. Unlike Springsteen, Burns enables his working-class female protagonist to have more of a voice and transcend the circumstances that threaten to bury her alive. By focusing on Claudia's quest for autonomy and independence, he subverts Springsteen's occasional tendency to position women as mere hood ornaments.

The Sopranos

The Sopranos (1999–2007) was a revolutionary tour de force that changed the face of television. Maurice Yacowar lauds the series as a Shakespearean "work of art for the ages."[1] Ellen Willis deems it the "richest and most compelling piece of television—no, of popular culture—that I've encountered in the past twenty years."[2] Creator David Chase's magnum opus has the texture of epic fiction, which Franco Ricci describes as a "sprawling story reminiscent in its style of encyclopedic nineteenth-century narratives and thoroughly engaged with the events, circumstances, and attitudes of the times, the culturally defining Big American Novels of the 1960s, the art house cinema of the 1970s, and the sociocultural malaise of the end of the millenium."[3] *The Sopranos* went on to become the most financially successful cable series in television history and the recipient of 60 major award wins and 231 nominations.[4] Most significantly, it birthed the Third Golden Age of Television, giving rise to an approach to crafting television shows that counters the medium's dominant structure and form with elongated serialized storytelling and a cinematic visual aesthetic.[5]

The Sopranos is about a New Jersey mobster named Tony Soprano who meets with a therapist weekly to work on his struggles with depression and anxiety resulting from the strains of his professional and familial life ("If one family doesn't kill him … the other family will," as the first season's tagline states). The enormity of the series' thematic breadth is astonishing, for it contemplates a myriad of cultural, philosophical, and existential ideals. It is "a meditation on the nature of morality, the possibility of redemption, and the legacy of Freud" as well as the hypocrisies of Catholicism, the erosion of the American Dream, and the post–twentieth century crisis of masculinity—themes that frequently appear in Springsteen's music.[6] These themes are "naturally oppositional: public law and order versus lawlessness and private code, speech versus silence, strength versus weakness, family versus business, them versus us, masculine versus feminine," and such juxtapositional tensions are the driving force of Tony's conflicts.[7] Furthermore, like Springsteen, "creator Chase has an abiding sympathy for workaday people and deploys their simple, direct language and actions to summon up truths about family, trust, and honor."[8]

Despite being a definitive New Jersey icon, Springsteen is used only once on the show's soundtrack, with "State Trooper" from *Nebraska* serving as non-diegetic score in the Season One finale "I Dream of Jeannie Cusamano." Springsteen is also referenced in the series' text twice: in the first-season finale, an FBI agent tells Tony Soprano, "There's something we want you to hear," and he cheekily replies, "The Springsteen box set? I already got it"; and in Season Five's "Long Term Parking," Christopher quotes "Born to Run" when he attributes his lateness to a jammed highway "with broken heroes on a last-chance power drive." An extratextual source, *The Sopranos: A Family History*, also references Springsteen. This book is a fictional chronicle of the Soprano family's past and Tony's childhood, with several passages "written by" friends and neighbors. One of Tony's college roommates recalls the future mobster's musical tastes: "He had a lot of records. Journey. Deep Purple. 'Hooked on a Feeling.' But not Springsteen. You'd think it'd be natural for a Jersey guy to like Springsteen, but Tony didn't. Fuckin' depressing, he would say."[9] Lance Strate argues that Tony dislikes Springsteen because his gritty, hard-nosed songs "force an identification with exactly the type of people who tend to be Tony's victims, an identification that has already driven him to seek psychoanalytic services at Dr. Melfi's Montclair office," as well as a recognition of his own internal demons.[10]

The most significant intertextual link between *The Sopranos* and Springsteen is co-star Steven Van Zandt, Springsteen's guitarist and longtime friend. Van Zandt plays Silvio, Tony's level-headed and empathetic right-hand man who occasionally provides comic relief with his Al Pacino impressions. The musician-turned-actor was actually Chase's first choice for Tony Soprano, inspired by Van Zandt's E Street Band stage wardrobe, which featured an old-fashioned mobster-esque pork pie hat. Van Zandt's quirkiness fit within Chase's original vision of the show as a *Simpsons*-style comedy. "It would have been a gangster show, but some of the more tortured aspects of Tony would probably have gone away. With Steven, it would have been a little broad. We would have played it more for laughs," Chase clarifies.[11] To portray Silvio, Van Zandt drew upon his experiences playing with the E Street Band and his relationship with Springsteen. "We had that gangster kind of Jersey thing going on…. Like the Rat Pack translated through some bizarre rock n' roll prism. Bruce was like Sinatra. I was the fun Dean Martin character. And Clarence was Sammy Davis on steroids," he says.[12] He also notes in an interview with Frank DiGiacomo:

> My relationship with Bruce was the same relationship that Silvio had with Tony Soprano. Silvio was not afraid of Tony. Bruce and I grew up together, so I'm never going to be afraid of him. You want a buffer in between the leader and the day-to-day problems that a band has. [Longtime Springsteen tour director] George Travis fulfills that role for Bruce now, but in the old days, I was that guy. I was a very good *consigliere*.[13]

After *The Sopranos*, Van Zandt went on to become his own boss in the Netflix series *Lilyhammer* (2012–2014), about a reformed Mafioso who retreats to Norway. In the series finale, Springsteen makes a cameo appearance as Giuseppe "The Undertaker" Tagliano, the older brother of Van Zandt's character, marking his first performance in a fictional role (since he played himself in *High Fidelity*). Springsteen's song "Loose Ends"—an outtake from *The River* album in which Van Zandt played a large part in as co-producer—overlays the series finale end credits and serves as the episode's title. Van Zandt's wife, Maureen Van Zandt, also appears in both shows, playing Silvio's wife Gabriella in *The Sopranos*.

Soundtracking The Sopranos

Drawing from his formative influences of Jean Luc-Godard, Stanley Kubrick, and Federico Fellini, David Chase approached each episode of *The Sopranos* as if it were its own mini-movie. In the tradition of cinema, *The Sopranos* is rife with popular culture references—cinematic, artistic, televisual, and musical—combining in what Franco Ricci calls "a dance of creative communion."[14] It is this variety of intertextual allusions, as well as Chase's scrupulous attention to visual and aural detail, that places the series in this "hallowed aura of art house cinema."[15] Working with producer Martin Bruestle, music editor Kathryn Dayak, and occasionally Van Zandt, Chase's executive decision to forgo traditional music scoring and rely exclusively on a popular prerecorded soundtrack both heightens the role that music plays in *The Sopranos* and contributes to the series' overall cinematic aesthetic. This integral role of soundtrack music calls for an examination of how Springsteen influences the televisual text, particularly the song "State Trooper."

Chase's infatuation with how soundtrack can manipulate the film form began at an early age. He recalls being a teenager and putting "Peppermint Twist" on the record player while the television was on with the sound off. "You would notice strange synchronicities, like the rhythm of the cutting of the TV show would miraculously fall in with the rhythm of the song. And the chance juxtaposition of, say, Joey Dee and wheat harvesters rolling across the plains was very funny. It blew out the idea of score," he told Allen Rucker.[16] Chase elucidates this artistic choice to reject traditional orchestral score in *The Sopranos* during an interview with director Peter Bogdanovich:

> Music has always been intrinsic to me with movies. It's television, but I consider it movies. But … as a writer I've always been inspired by music. I listen to music while I'm trying to think of ideas and I just like it. So even from the beginning I said [that] we really need to have a good music budget. And originally people said, "Why, I don't get it, what do you mean music budget?" And, now I think they see it. It creates a tremendous mood and it also creates a sense of contemporaneity. I think that's the word, whatever the word is, contemporaneousness.[17]

For Dayak, compositional score was too "over-the-top and manipulative … As in: 'Here's a cue that's sad, so we'd like for you to feel sad.' Sometimes there's much more impact in not trying to tell people how to feel."[18] Instead, a soundtrack drawn from popular music would serve as the fundamental means of relaying unspoken information about a character and their circumstances, with the lyrics expressing the narrative's overarching themes and the song's rhythm dictating the action, structure, and temporality of a sequence. Dayak, Chase, and Bruestle also acknowledged that popular music offers an inordinate assortment of options in terms of arrangement and selection: "Does the instrumental bridge fall over the dialogue? Or, maybe we tag the end of the scene with four words from a chorus that are very meaningful. Because besides the choice of the song, it really makes a difference in how the song is prepared, and how it's placed."[19] This careful consideration of how soundtrack informs the film body demonstrates why music analysis is so integral to understanding *The Sopranos*.

While there are many scenes in *The Sopranos* structured by either non-diegetic score or diegetic source music, the majority of songs occur within the time-space of the end credit sequence. According to Annette Davison, this space "involves a significant affective and reflective moment in which music plays a vital role."[20] Unlike the repeated introductory theme "Woke Up This Morning" by Alabama 3, the end credits of *The Sopranos* feature a different song each episode, encouraging spectators to "focus on the specificity of the episode, namely how does the song relate to what I've just experienced?"[21] It is within this time-space that Springsteen's "State Trooper" from *Nebraska* appears in the Season One finale, and it is worth reading how not only how this song is used in the end credits but also how each of its lyrics articulates Tony's inner thoughts and the series' subtextual thematic concerns with New Jersey's cultural geography, Tony's psychology, and the overall ideals of morality and justice throughout the first season.

The Storm

Lightning flashes and thunder roars while Tony squints through the blinding sheets of rain behind the wheel of his off-road Chevy Suburban. His wife Carmela and his children beg him to abandon this treacherous odyssey to a neighbor's house and find somewhere else to eat. Taking a detour past a fallen tree, Tony and his family find a momentary respite from the raging storm in the familiar warmth of Artie Bucco's restaurant, Nuovo Vesuvio. The restaurant has lost power in the storm and must be lit by candles, adding a sense of tranquility to an episode fraught with tension and anxiety. Just a few scenes earlier, Tony attempted to smother his mother with a pillow after learning she orchestrated his assassination attempt. Illuminated by the small shafts of candlelight, Tony's two families surround him. He sits at the table with his wife and children while his protégé Christopher flirts with Adriana at the bar and his underlings Silvio and Paulie sit nearby. The candlelight brings an old-world quality to the mise-en-scène that is representative of Tony's longing for the past.

The scene is inspired by Edward Hopper's *Nighthawks*, a painting of an all-night diner lit by fluorescents. Chase opposes the dominant critical reading of the artwork as a portrayal of urban loneliness "[b]ecause it's in the light. In the middle of all this darkness, they're in the light. And they're talking to each other. There's a little community in there. If you were walking along that street at night, and you saw that place, you'd want to go in."[22] Like the diner, Vesuvio is a space of comfort, one where Tony's personal and professional lives can harmoniously coexist. After Artie brings out his delicious food, Tony raises his wine glass in a toast: "To my family. Someday soon you're gonna have families of your own. And if you're lucky, you'll remember the little moments. Like this. That were good." For a moment, it seems as if all is well for Tony: he has made a safe passage through the storm, he is now the boss of the family, and his assassination has been thwarted, earning him a new lease on life. However, after clinking their glasses and downing their drinks, a crash from the outdoor gale sounds and lightning blazes, propelling the methodical guitar introduction to Springsteen's "State Trooper." This hummed melodic line synchronizes with the fade to black; it is a pumping, reverberant bass chug that "evokes the sound of tires ricocheting off of the grooves in the highway, bringing to life Springsteen's vision of a lonely outlaw driving along the New Jersey turnpike in the hopes that the law—and perhaps his own past—does not catch up with him."[23] With its brooding atmosphere, intense repetition, and taut pace, the eerily tense "State Trooper" disrupts the serene scene at Vesuvio and imbues it with a juxtapositional gloom and paranoia.

Chase's careful structure and selection of soundtrack songs indicates that "State Trooper" was chosen to speak for Tony, his survival and arc throughout the entire season. Springsteen's use of first-person narration easily attaches the lyrics to Tony's subjectivity. By placing the song specifically within the space of the first season's end credits, Chase uses "State Trooper" to anticipate and foreshadow what will happen in the next season. Tony is unaware that he will be on the run for the rest of the series, just like Springsteen's hunted highwayman. His repeated plea in a dark, vacant voice—"please don't stop me"—becomes Tony's motto because "he doesn't want to be stopped by any number of things: by the government agents tailing him, by the middle-class constraints of his wife and kids, by the fractious behavior of the Mob cronies who are his dearest friends and worst betrayers."[24] Springsteen's otherworldly howl at the end of the song concludes the end credits and the first season, a sinister shriek that belies the final scene's tranquility and foretells Tony's wild future.

A dangerous force propels the nighttime journey of Springsteen's character. As he makes his way through the twilight, akin to Tony driving his Suburban through the storm, he begins to lose his patience with the innocuous talk show stations on the radio. In his mind, their inane chatter rises to a deafening and babbling blur. At first, it seems that Tony

Soprano's experience vastly differs from that of the unnerved driver: Tony has reached a destination, a home-like space that surrounds him with those he loves, while Springsteen's outlaw is left speeding down the highway in desperation—removed from any sense of community, family, or security. Yet while Tony may appear to be content in the glowing light of Vesuvio, the dark lyrics and spooky rhythms of "State Trooper" articulate his disturbed state of mind. The use of the melancholic "State Trooper" in the end credits indicates that Tony has not found peace and the sangfroid he displays in the restaurant is a merely a chimera. The storm outside rages on, and though Tony finds momentary respite, its mighty force will soon break down the door.

The City by the Sea

The opening lines of "State Trooper" immediately place the listener within the driver's seat on a cold, wet night in the "wee, wee hours," cruising the New Jersey turnpike and passing by a churning black river at the foot of glowing refineries. These geographical images circle viewers back to the main *Sopranos* title sequence, thus serving as the perfect bookend to the first season. "State Trooper" is a fitting song for *The Sopranos* because it explicitly references the series' iconic locale of New Jersey. The series has been described as Chase's paean to New Jersey, bringing the idiosyncrasies and minutiae of the state to the forefront of cultural consciousness even more than Springsteen himself. "I do believe that New Jersey is to Chase what a part of Italy was to Fellini," says Frank DeCaro.[25] Ellen Willis asserts that *The Sopranos* "does for northern New Jersey what *film noir* did for Los Angeles, with soundtrack to match."[26] DeCaro and Willis insist that Chase's richly detailed New Jersey in *The Sopranos* is more than a mere locale; it defines the mood of the mise-en-scène and serves as a microcosm of the series' overarching thematic concerns, including the American Dream and classicism. Despite resistance from studio executives, Chase insisted on shooting in New Jersey in order to maintain a gritty realism that would oppose the artificiality of studio-shot shows. Contributing to this authentic milieu were the numerous cast and crew members who were raised or lived in the state, such as Chase in Clifton and North Caldwell (the latter the site of the Sopranos' private residence); the location manager Mark Karmine in Jersey City, Wayne, and Montclair; and James Gandolfini in Park Ridge.

The Sopranos' opening credits montage situates the action within the distinctive New Jersey space. Similar to Springsteen's "State Trooper" narrator, Tony drives on the turnpike from New York City to New Jersey, "from the familiar crime-film setting into this show's unique territory."[27] One of the shots pans up to the giant New Jersey Turnpike sign, a direct invocation of the very first lines of "State Trooper." After dutifully paying his toll (here Tony uncharacteristically obeys the law, unlike the subject of "State Trooper," who does not carry his license and registration), Tony passes through the Lincoln Tunnel, entering a congested sphere fraught with tension. Gliding past post-industrial edifices not unlike Springsteen's refineries, Tony continues along the road. He surveys his Springsteenian blue-collar kingdom of smokestacks, bridges, water towers, trains, a cemetery, Pizzaland, the spires of a church, rows of cramped uniformed bungalows, and the far-off Statue of Liberty. The most significant place he glimpses in this montage is Satriale's Pork Store, "where so much of his business is conducted—meetings, butchering, cold storage—and the site of his most shaping, (that is, traumatic) boyhood experience. This shot disturbs the comfort of that montage; it connotes Tony's psychological vulnerability. That's where Tony saw his father chop off the debtor's finger and where his own panic attacks began."[28]

Finally, "Tony takes us from the wasteland to the pocket of luxury that wasteland supports": his North Caldwell mansion, with all its new-money flash.[29] While Springsteen's narrator descends deeper into darkness after he flees the state trooper's gaze, the light at the end of Tony's passage through the tunnel illuminates him with a false sense of quietude. Although it leads Tony toward the comforts of suburbia, his home is a site of turmoil. Tony may arrive at his destination by the scene's end, but the ensuing episodes certify that he is trapped in the same purgatorial state as the outlaw of "State Trooper" as he struggles to balance his various responsibilities.

There is one New Jersey filming location in *The Sopranos* that explicitly connects to Springsteen: Asbury Park in the Season Two finale "Funhouse." Asbury Park was a musical mecca during Springsteen's reign in the 1970s. The boardwalk was lined with an array of nighttime hotspots ripe for up-and-coming musicians to traverse the post–British Invasion rock and roll scene, spaces for Springsteen in which he cultivated his eminence as bar band king. It was here that Van Zandt performed with Springsteen in early incarnations of what would become the E Street Band, and he also partnered with the Asbury Jukes headed by Southside Johnny, the "Grandfather of the New Jersey Sound," who has a cameo appearance in the *Sopranos* Season Six episode "Chasing It." (Nils Lofgren, a later E Street Band member who did not grow up in New Jersey, also appears on the soundtrack with "Black Boots" in Season Three's "Second Opinion.")

Springsteen famously borrowed from the title and postcard image for his debut album *Greetings from Asbury Park, N.J* because he wanted to explicitly assert his position as a New Jersey musician, a unique idiosyncrasy that would set him apart from the New York persona his bosses at Columbia Records were pushing. Springsteen has continued to draw upon his Garden State youth throughout his oeuvre, carving out a space for himself in popular culture as a quintessentially New Jersey icon. Songs that specifically reference Asbury Park include "Something in the Night" ("riding down Kingsley"), "4th of July, Asbury Park (Sandy)" (the title itself, "boys from the Casino"), "Born to Run" ("beyond the Palace"), and "Blinded by the Light" (the Zanzibar amusements). Springsteen frequently films his music videos in Asbury Park, including "Lonesome Day" and "Tunnel of Love." The mise-en-scènes of these videos have striking similarities to the Asbury Park sequence in *The Sopranos*. Like Tony, Springsteen walks along an empty, dilapidated boardwalk in its off season. The "Tunnel of Love" video captures the dark ride and distorted funhouse atmosphere of Tony's nightmares, with Springsteen shrouded in shadow while leaning against the tatterdemalion walls of the abandoned Casino and black-and-white Lynchian cutaways to carnival freaks.

"Funhouse" ostensibly gets its title from the Palace Amusements, Asbury's famed indoor amusement park built in the late 1800s with bumper cars, a Ferris wheel, a carousel, and a dark ride called "Ghost Town." Despite its historical significance, the building was torn down in 2004 after being out of operation since 1988, thus marking *The Sopranos* as one of the site's last filmic documents before its demolition. Chase structures the episode around Tony's three dreams that take place around the boardwalk in Asbury Park and signify his guilt about his obligation to murder Pussy. The episode's carnival-esque soundscape, fish-eye lens visuals, and canted angles personify the surreality of Tony's hallucinatory state while he suffers from food poisoning. His illness provokes his subconscious Freudian anxieties. The deserted boardwalk, ramshackle buildings blanketed in snow, and gusty grey skies imbue the scenes with a brooding, desolate quality. The images of the Jersey shoreline tie into Pussy's watery grave and appearance as a fish.[30]

In the first delirium, Tony walks along the isolated boardwalk in a daze. The wind whistles and seagulls cry while he glances behind him to survey the Convention Hall building. Inside is the Paramount Theatre, where Springsteen saw artists such as Janis Joplin, the Who, and the Doors in late 1960s and 1970s and later went on to perform himself. Today, an emblazoned sign that sits on top welcomes visitors with a line borrowed from Springsteen's album: "Greetings from Asbury Park, New Jersey." Later in the sequence, Tony peers into the caliginous hall through a pair of beachside viewfinders and observes his doppelgänger murdering Paulie, emblematic of his fear that the rest of his crew will turn against him and he will have to execute his sovereign responsibility to slaughter another one of his friends.

Then Tony passes Madame Marie's Temple of Knowledge, one of the key icons in Springsteen's oeuvre, notably included on his quixotic farewell ballad for the seashore town, "4th of July, Asbury Park (Sandy)." Suddenly, Tony finds himself stuck walking in place, his legs stepping without making any movement forward. The boardwalk planks vociferously squeal and creak with each futile tread. These visual and sonic special effects convey Tony's fugue state and are symbolic of his immobilizing paranoia that he is being hunted. "Somebody's looking for me," he repeats throughout the sequence. Tony's dream suggests that no matter how far he runs, his enemies will still catch up with him. The fortune teller iconography denotes the knowledge of the future that Tony yearns to acquire: he wants to know his fate after he ascends through the perilous gangster world.

In another part of his dream, Tony steps from the left into the frame, his face aligning in a mid-shot with the mural of the grinning clown Tillie on the side of the Palace Amusements building—two famous Springsteen icons. Springsteen has been photographed with the Tillie image in several publicity photos, and he references the Palace Amusements in "Born to Run" and "Tunnel of Love." The farceur Tillie connects to Tony's therapy confession that as a mobster he feels like "the sad clown: laughing on the outside, crying on the inside." There are, as the title of the first episode of Season Five indicates, two Tonys—the tempestuous, hypermasculine, and charismatic Mafioso he is and the vulnerable, mollified family man he longs to be—and they wage a psychological battle within his subconscious. It is this performance of self and trouble balancing the competing expectations of both families that unravels him. The infelicity he buries beneath his herculean exterior comes to the surface in the form of his panic attacks.

The episode's closing image of the ocean waves that swallow Pussy's body harkens back to these seaside shots of an abandoned Asbury Park. Once brimming with bar band music and entertainment, the city by the sea became a derelict wasteland after the 1960s race riots. It was no longer a destination for vacationing nuclear families but a crumbling haven for countercultural figures such as bikers, hippies, rockers, and the LGBTQ community. As time wore on, planks in the boardwalk curled and rotted, landmarks such as the Empress Hotel were boarded up, and the once-proud Asbury Park Convention Hall became a mausoleum to more prosperous times.[31] By the early 1980s, it was a "seedy, run-down seaside town, languishing in the afterglow of its earlier heyday, when it was the jewel in the crown of the Jersey Shore," and remained that way for decades.[32] Today, the jewel shines again with new shops, tourist attractions, and completely refurbished buildings—and it seems to be growing brighter, especially as financiers plan invest more than one billion dollars in residential and commercial developments in the coming years.[33]

The *Sopranos* Asbury Park sequence captures the town's ramshackle state before its latest resurgence in the eerie, lugubrious atmosphere of blank storefronts, broken windows, and decaying façades. Ron Bernard argues that the deterioration of Springsteen's Asbury Park "ties in to the *angst* that Tony voiced in the Pilot—the feeling that he has come in at the end of something. Our best days are behind us."[34] Tony's apocalyptic vision of the future manifests in brooding nightmares in which he shoots his best friend Paulie in the chest and douses himself with gasoline and lights himself on fire after being diagnosed with cancer like his boss Jackie Aprile. The waning seaside surroundings of Asbury Park reflect the end of Tony's sanity as the paranoia and violence of mafia life consume him. Bernard also argues that as "the poet of a tough, blue-collar, workhorse ethic that New Jersey personified and the country admired," Springsteen embodies the robust working-class masculinity of Tony's father, which he spends the rest of his adult life fatuously attempting to recapture.[35] The glory days of Johnny Boy Soprano's reign are long over; now informers and rats infest the once-loyal crew. Tony strives to recapture those days, but the upstanding morals of allegiance that once defined his circle have deteriorated, and he never knows who he can trust. The more Tony tries to emulate his father and the days of yore, the more his psychological well-being shatters like a funhouse mirror. Asbury Park in this woebegone episode serves as a microcosm of his anxieties—its bedraggled mien indicative of the existential anxiety and uncertainty that Tony bemoans.

Two Tonys

In "State Trooper," Springsteen's roadrunner bounds along the New Jersey highway without his license and registration, praying that he can make it to his baby without the state trooper stopping him along the way. Despite these anxieties, the narrator has a clear conscience, unconcerned with whatever misdeed has put him on the run from the law. His lack of contrition stands in opposition to the mighty guilt that weighs upon Tony Soprano—the series' raison d'être. Tony's devotion to two families with vastly opposing moral codes tears his soul apart and incites his anguish. The mafia's criminal obligations defy his aspirations for a quotidian nuclear family. The fifth and ninth episodes of the first season, "College" and "Boca," deftly explore the emotional and psychological tug of war between the two Tonys, his fractured halves and incongruous desires.

"College" marks the moment when Tony reveals his truly monstrous half for the first time, the Frankenstein—or "golem," as his Jewish business partner Shlomo calls him—that lurks inside. On a college tour with his daughter Meadow, Tony spots Fabian Petrulio, a former member of the DiMeo family relocated by the Witness Protection Program after he became a rat for the FBI. During Tony's reign as boss, there is a fear that other members will become government witnesses to avoid a thirty-five-year drug sentence. There is an overwhelming sense of paranoia and terror hovering over the gang that parallels the anxious mental state of Springsteen's "State Trooper" narrator.

Tony spends most of the episode debating whether he should kill Petrulio himself, even though Christopher is more than willing to volunteer for the job. Torn between his fatherly and mafia duties, he eventually decides that this opportunity for vengeance is too good to pass up and savagely murders Petrulio with a wire. Director Allen Coulter shoots the cruel death scene from a low angle so that the spectator is in line with Petrulio's bulging eyes and tomato-red face. Coulter intercuts gruesome close-ups of the wire digging into

Petrulio's throat and his spilled blood with shots of Tony hovering above him at the top of the frame, assaulting the spectator with his hulking power. "What remains shocking in 'College' isn't the death itself," Brett Martin argues, but rather "Tony's unmitigated relish in doing the deed."[36]

Coulter emphasizes Tony's vulnerability after he kills Petrulio by cutting to a bird's-eye-view shot of him watching a flock of ducks fly into the distance. The camera pulls away from him, mimicking the birds in their flight by moving farther from his figure, making it smaller. This is a callback to the ducks that departed from Tony's pool in the first episode and caused his panic attack. Dr. Melfi theorized that the mallards symbolized his desire for a normal, acceptable family life. "I'm afraid I'm going to lose my family like the ducks. That's what I'm full of dread about. It's always with me," Tony reckoned during the therapy session. They fly away from Tony once again in "College" to remind him that he has let bloodlust overcome his familial duties.

After the killing, Tony meets Meadow at Bowdoin College. Sitting on the hardwood seat behind an intricate and ornate pale yellow wallpaper, Tony glances up at a statue of a Nathaniel Hawthorne quote: "No man can wear one face to himself and another to the multitude, without finally getting bewildered as to which one may be true." Coulter shoots the large-font edifice from a sideways angle so that it seems to scream at Tony. This quote echoes Springsteen's "Two Faces"—a *Jekyll and Hyde* tale of a man mystified by his darker half, which forces him to doubt and sabotage his relationships—and clearly refers to the two Tonys: his good and evil sides, his brutality versus his vulnerability. Out of the genuine love he has for his wife, daughter, and son, Tony strives to keep his status as a formidable Mafioso from bleeding into his everyday family life; he does not want them to be affected by the dangers of his profession. However, "College" illustrates the liminality between Tony's métier and his domestic duties when Meadow begins to suspect her father is more than just a waste management consultant.

In "Boca," Tony tries to atone for his sins and assuage his guilty conscience by doing something good for once. When he and his crew learn that Meadow's soccer coach slept with one of his students and indirectly caused her suicide attempt, they aim to execute him. Tony's friend Artie Bucco beseeches him not to put a hit out on the coach and to let the police handle the situation, but Tony furiously counters that the judicial system is inherently flawed and will not provide the physical sentence that the coach's deplorable acts deserve: "They'll arrest him, right? He'll get out in two fuckin' years, move to Saskatchewan. Then you know what he'll do? He'll teach girls' soccer, and he'll start all over again. You don't think I wanna rip him apart like a fuckin' chicken?" Dr. Melfi wonders why her patient believes he must bear the weight of justice on his shoulders, asking, "Why do you think you, Anthony Soprano, always has to set things right?" Tony spits in reply, "You'd call the cops, who'd get some judge, who'd give him psychiatric counseling. So maybe he could talk about his unhappy childhood and we could have sympathy for the fuck, cause he's the real victim here, right?" What Dr. Melfi fails to grasp is that Tony sees this situation as his chance to honorably provide for his family. Now that the kind of depravity he witnesses and enacts in his criminal gangland has infected his darling daughter's world, he wants to use his position of power to vanquish what he considers genuine evil. In his eyes, true justice would be to end the life of this child molester, to make him suffer as much as his victims, rather than allow him to roam free in prison. This deed would act as penance for all Tony's past wrongdoings. However, Tony ultimately allows the police to arrest the soccer coach after he realizes that this act of vigilante justice and need to "set things right" was selfish and would only serve to make him feel better, not the real victim. The episode closes with Tony returning home drunk and weeping "I didn't hurt nobody" before crashing onto the floor. Meadow watches from the balcony, admiring the first time her father did not have a brutish response to trouble. Instead of succumbing to the darker impulses of his mobster nature, he behaves like a model citizen and allows the law to handle the situation. Tony comes to understand that murdering an abuser would not be an act of righteousness, but rather another notch on his homicidal belt that would not relieve him of his guilt.

Out of the Past

The despondent driver of "State Trooper" states in the second verse that his only possession has been bothering him his whole life, an inborn encumbrance that will plague him until his death. When reading the song as Tony's emotional signifier, we must consider what has been bothering him for *his* whole life: namely, his mother and father. At first, the character of Livia Soprano "seems peggable as a better-done-than-usual caricature of the overbearing ethnic mother but [she] is gradually revealed as a monstrous Medea."[37] Beneath her little old lady exterior, she is a "borderline narcissist lacking empathy and remorse" with the extraordinary ability to manipulate and guilt everyone around her.[38] Observing his mother's shrewd, exploitative ruthlessness, Tony remarks that she "would've been a real gangster." It is Tony's complex and abusive relationship with his mother that sends him to therapy in the first place. Carmela particularly recognizes Livia's looming sway over Tony's subconscious and well-being: "You know your power, you use like a pro.... You are bigger than life."

Tony's description of Livia as a "black poison cloud" perfectly articulates her perpetually melodramatic and dolorous demeanor. Her favorite subjects include how much she wants to die ("I pray the Lord takes me now") and infanticide, often regaling listeners with news stories of mothers throwing their babies out of skyscraper windows. Such behavior is not the result of Livia's aging, nor a symptom of dementia, but simply how she has always been. Tony tells Dr. Melfi that as a child he never received support or affection from her. Moreover, his only fond familial memory is an act of clownish violence when his entire family laughed at his father after he fell down the stairs. Although Tony made the right decision to move his mother into a nursing home after she caused a fire in her house and ran a car over her friend, Livia feels this is unforgivable evidence that she has been abandoned by her family—blindly ignoring Carmela's generous offer to let her move into the North Caldwell mansion. Livia retaliates by seeking to arrange her son's murder.

In "I Dream of Jeannie Cusamano," Tony wrestles with the realization that his mother orchestrated the attempt on his life as revenge for divulging their family secrets in therapy and sending her to the Green Grove nursing home despite her avowed protestations. Tony storms into the home, casually grabbing a pillow to suffocate his mother with before a worker informs him that she has suffered a stroke. As the hospital workers wheel her away on a gurney, Tony leans over her, places his face so uncomfortably close that they touch noses, and moves his hand from her cheek to her throat. With simmering rage, he reveals to her that he heard the FBI tapes and knows of her foiled murder plan. "I'm gonna live a nice, long, happy life, which is more than I can say for you," he seethes in a caustic whisper before screaming, "I tried to do the right thing by you, and you try to have me whacked?!" Livia Soprano's wolfish grin in response sends Tony reeling into an explosive fury.

The seventh episode in Season One, "Down Neck," reveals the thorny circumstances of Tony's childhood through a series of flashbacks that echo the "black bedtime stories" on Springsteen's *Nebraska* album, the unknowing meditations on his childhood and its mysteries punctuated by the dreamy glockenspiel.[39] Young Springsteen yearns to escape the squalid streets of his hometown and recalls the shame hidden in his mother's minute gesture of twisting her wedding band as her factory worker husband haggles in vain with the used car salesman in "Used Cars." Elsewhere, he and his sister peer through the gates at the unattainable opulence of the "Mansion on the Hill" that rises above their industrial wasteland. In *The Sopranos*, the song "White Rabbit" ushers in Tony's memories, cued by his consumption of Prozac and zonked gaze into his bathroom mirror. Not only does Jefferson Airplane's psychedelic rocker signify Tony's drug-addled state, but the wailing guitars and lead singer's high-octane voice, as well as the surreal *Alice in Wonderland* iconography, embody the chaos of Tony's adolescence. He is the proverbial Alice, lost in a disordered world of murder and madness. Tony's childhood gaze constructs the mise-en-scène of his reminiscences, such as the way the sun sparkles over the quiet streets and glistens off the Cadillac fenders. The placidity of Tony's exterior suburban landscape belies the tensions and anxieties found inside of his home.

Tony's reverie also focuses on his father roaming the streets as the capo of the original Soprano crew. We discover that the patriarch is "a narcissistic sociopath and impulsive hooligan prone to very unscrupulous acts of anti-social violence."[40] Hiding behind a tree, young Tony witnesses his father nearly beat a man to death. In the third episode of Season Three, "Fortunate Son," Tony recalls his first panic attack after he watched his father chop off the local butcher's pinky finger. At home, an eight-year-old Tony begs his mother for an electric organ, only to be met with her contempt and exasperation; stamping her foot as if she were a child, she commands him to stop complaining. "I said enough! You won't give me a moment's peace!" she bellows. Then she threatens filicide when she grabs a fork and screams, "You're driving me crazy! I could stick this fork in your eye!" The shot is an assaulting and terrifying close-up from young Tony's point of view; Livia hovers above him, the fork's sharp points ominously glistening and dangerously facing the screen at eye level. Tony also remembers overhearing his mother threaten to murder him and his siblings: "I'd rather smother them with a pillow than take them to Nevada." However, Tony dismisses—and even laughs off—these moments as evidence of Livia's high-strung histrionics. "You know every night to her's a night at the opera," he jokes to Dr. Melfi.

"Down Neck" aligns with Springsteen's desire to have the blood in his *Nebraska* songs "feel destined and fateful"[41] as it explores the ideas of heredity and the effects of one's personal history on the future. Tony's adolescent memories underscore his dreams of success for his own children, his hope that they will obtain a college education and position in legitimate society. He fights to keep the criminal underworld from infringing on his home life because he does not want Anthony Jr. and Meadow to have the same tumultuous childhood that he did or share in his psychic wounds. The Soprano family's ties to the mafia will end with Tony, for he refuses to expose his sensitive son to the violence and depravity of the gangster arena, which he acknowledges in therapy as the fulcrum of his depression and anxiety. The formidable mafia boss' son will not be bound to the same dangerous fate as his father.

Tony frequently laments the path his forebears laid out for him: "You know I had to put food on the table. My father was in it. My uncle was in it. Maybe I was too lazy to think for myself. To consider myself a rebel. Maybe being a rebel in my family would have been selling patio furniture." This constant reference to being a patio furniture salesman is symbolic of his yearning for a simple, noble life as the "Good Tony," following a quiet profession in which he helps (rather than harming) others.

The Sopranos and "State Trooper" each reflect upon life's burdens. Both Tony and the narrator of Springsteen's ballad wrestle with miseries that have been eating away at them for their entire lives. Springsteen never names what is hounding his highwayman—it is more of a ubiquitous blue-collar nihilism—but Tony was clearly shaped by a cruel and vicious upbringing and does everything in his power not to pass that burden along to his own children.

Into the Abyss

The persistent, deep bass line of "State Trooper" evokes the nagging cacophony of the talk show stations that blare in the narrator's ears. A jealous lonesomeness dogs him, and he mocks the state trooper's pretty wife and family, envying their suburban comfort and the trooper's status as an upstanding citizen—a resentment that Tony readily identifies with. The vacuous darkness of the New Jersey twilight engulfs Springsteen's outlaw as he drives into the distance, representative of his existential void and all-consuming despair. He begs for deliverance from this harrowing "nowhere." "To be 'nowhere' for Springsteen—both in a geographic and in a spiritual sense—is the most terrifying state of all," Frank Fury contends.[42] Springsteen's sense of "nowhere" is the penetrating desolation of mental illness.

Samuel J. Levine reads "State Trooper" as more of an urgent plea for help than a song, and its placement within the first-season finale of *The Sopranos* articulates Tony's own prayer for relief from his depression and anxiety.[43] It is fitting that such a sepulchral dirge was composed during a time when Springsteen was suffering from severe depression and suicidal thoughts.[44] Springsteen titles the chapter in his memoir that covers these struggles "Deliver Me from Nowhere," after the "State Trooper" lyric, thereby cementing the doleful ballad's intrinsic connection to his psychological problems. Shortly after releasing *Nebraska*, Springsteen suffered a nervous breakdown during a cross-country road trip and subsequently, at the urging of Jon Landau, underwent psychotherapy. Like Tony, Springsteen's depression stemmed from an anxious childhood and home life, particularly the volcanic rage of his volatile father. However, Springsteen was fortunate enough to have the love of his kindhearted mother to nurture the artistic gifts that distracted him from the ugliness and dread of his unstable adolescent environment.

There are two inciting events in Season One that aggravate Tony Soprano's depression: the knowledge that his mother tried to kill him and his obligation to murder his friend Pussy for being a rat. In the eleventh and twelfth episodes of the first season, "Nobody Knows Anything" and "Isabella," Tony is deeply distraught over Pussy's mysterious disappearance, knowing that it likely indicates his guilt. Although Tony is already on Prozac, he is prescribed lithium after he expresses to Dr. Melfi a debilitating sense of doom, a feeling that a safe is about to fall on his head, which leaves him bedridden. At one point he sits in the shower with his eyes rolling back in his head, framed in canted angles to signify the drugs' hypnotic power and his numb interiority. At dinner, he emerges downstairs in his bathrobe, prompting Livia Soprano to callously remark that he reminds her of Cakey, a relative of hers who got a lobotomy. "The children don't have a father anymore, he just comes down in his bathrobe at 7 p.m.," she whines.

Glassy-eyed, unshaved, and wearing crumpled clothing, Tony nihilistically echoes his mother's condemnation to Dr. Melfi: "I'm fucking King Midas in reverse here. Everything I touch turns to shit. I'm not a husband to my wife, I'm not a father to my kids, I'm not a friend to my friends, I'm nothing." Tony feels dead inside, as if both he and the world at large are "all a big fucking nothing." It is the first time in the series that Tony seems to be truly suicidal. The montages of Tony lying in bed consumed with the despairing futility of life and worried about his illness' effect on his family reflect Springsteen's writing on his own experiences with depression: "I spent good portions of the day with the covers up to my nose waiting for it to stop.... The fire in me had gone out and I felt dark and hollow inside. Bad thoughts had a heyday. If I can't work, how will I provide for my family? Will I be bedridden? Who the fuck am I?"[45] Springsteen eventually turned to the psychotropic drug Klonopin for relief.

"For the first time, I felt I understood what drives people toward the abyss," Springsteen writes on his soul-crushing bout of agitation during his sixties.[46] He uses the term "abyss," a black and bottomless chasm, as a metaphor for the isolation and hopelessness of his mental illness. For Springsteen, figures in popular culture such as Gary Cooper are presented as faultless effigies with a dogged masculinity and lack of this abyss:

> We have our mythic hero, Gary Cooper, who is capable of pure action, where it's either all or nothing, and he looks like he's walking over the abyss of anxiety, and he won't fail. Whereas the moviegoer, the person watching the movie, is not capable of that. There's no real abyss under Gary Cooper, but there is one under the guy watching the film! Bringing people out over that abyss, helping them and myself to realize where we all "are" … that's what I'm interested in doing with my own work.[47]

Tony is one of those moviegoers who idolize the cowboy icon's inscrutable and virile construction of manhood. He laments to Dr. Melfi the current societal repudiation of the self-assured stoicism that defined his 1950s upbringing: "What happened to Gary Cooper? The strong, silent type. That was an American. He wasn't in touch with his feelings. He just did what he had to do." Tony is seduced by cinema's mythological ideal that men must maintain a phlegmatic strength and cannot confront their "abyss," or the inner demons that torment them, because that would signify weakness. This belief causes Tony to dangerously stifle his internal emotions. What also exacerbates Tony's mental anguish is the fact that he cannot publicly go into a residential treatment center because a mafia leader cannot have any flaws that would affect his calculated decision-making and iron-fisted rule. Therefore, for the sake of his survival, Tony must embody the "strong, silent type" of Cooper. Yet the more he tries to conceal his psychological afflictions, the more he is sent into a tailspin that, like "State Trooper," causes him to descend further into madness. The final line of "State Trooper"—"Hi ho, silver-o"—is a reference to *The Lone Ranger* (1956) that indicates the driver also wishes to embody the burly masculinity of the classic Hollywood cowboy.

Eventually a lithium-induced fugue dream of a gorgeous, robust Italian woman and a botched attempt on his life briefly lifts Tony out of his melancholia. The end credits choice of Cream's resplendent "I Feel Free" literalizes Tony's freedom from depression. However, in the Season One finale, Tony's discovery that his mother was behind his assassination attempt plunges him back into those same feelings of worthlessness, a self-esteem that is virtually nonexistent, he tells Dr. Melfi. The "State Trooper" and *Nebraska* album intertext undergird Tony's struggle with mental illness during his daunting reign as a mafia boss. He attempts to model himself after the robust and abyss-less Gary Cooper, but this only plunges him into further psychological anguish. Like the "State Trooper" narrator, Tony yearns to be the kind of upright man society values, but he is ultimately pulled into the darkness of his psyche and criminal netherworld—his spiritual and physical "nowhere." Both *The Sopranos* and Springsteen explore the foreboding abyss that unmoors their characters from sanity.

Life Goes On

The series finale of *The Sopranos* left most fans scratching their heads and checking to see whether their cable boxes had accidentally cut off. In the final scene, Tony, Carmela, and A.J. share onion rings in a diner—a quintessentially New Jersey locale—and Meadow struggles to parallel park her car outside while Journey's "Don't Stop Believin'" blares from the diner jukebox. Carmela and Tony's banal conversation about their children's future—Anthony Jr.'s internship and Meadow's careful family planning with birth control—functions as a passing of the narrative baton; Tony's story has ended, and the legacies of his children, who have successfully assimilated into legitimate society, are his only concern now. During this conversation, Chase repeatedly cuts to other diner patrons sharing their meals: a grandfather with a group of Boy Scouts, a teenage couple, and a mysterious man in a Members Only jacket who keeps stealing glances at Tony—the subject of countless critical and fandom debates. The finale's cryptic concluding shot left spectators wondering whether the man in the jacket murdered Tony. While Journey wails its electric power anthem, Tony glances up after the front door dings, glancing at either Meadow or a hit man. We never know which, for Chase abruptly cuts to a silent black, interrupting Journey mid-song and concealing the identity of whoever lies in the reverse shot. He holds on the darkness for a few seconds before the end credits roll. Many critics interpreted the brusque cut and linger on black as a subjective shot signifying Tony's sudden death, foreshadowed in the quote "I guess you never hear it coming when it's your turn" from the sixth season's first episode, "Members Only."

More than a decade later, Chase is still questioned about Tony's fate and the meaning of his denouement, but he never offers a concrete answer. He told Brett Martin, "I don't know if it means this, but a lot of it had to do with people huddled against the cold. It was a repeat of that scene [in the season one finale]: there's a storm outside and they're in a place where there's food, and light, and warmth, and human companionship."[48] The parallels between the finales of the first and last seasons are made explicit in A.J.'s reference to Tony's toast at Vesuvio: "Focus on the good times. Isn't that what you said one time? Try and remember the times that were good?" Despite the turmoil of Tony's life during the past six seasons, his apprehension that he will lose his family is temporarily allayed—as it was on the night of the storm all those years ago—and he basks in the comfort of their presence and the placidity of the moment. Tony focuses on what is good: being able to share a meal with those he loves.

"The music is very important to me in terms of the timing of the scene, the rhythm of the scene. The song dictates part of the pace. And having certain lyrics of the song, and certain instrumental flourishes happen in certain places, dictates what the cuts will be," Chase elaborates regarding his soundtrack sequences. The final scene of the series was carefully constructed and timed to fit a specific portion of Journey's "Don't Stop Believin'."[49] Chase subverts Journey's climactic and thrilling temporal rhythm with an ironic cut—ceasing all sights and sounds in the middle of the song's title line, which mirrors Springsteen's "don't stop me" line from "State Trooper." If the series finale is meant to echo the Season One finale, then the final shot with that accompanying lyric leaves Tony in a purgatorial state akin to the paranoid driver of "State Trooper." As a Mafioso, he will never stop looking over his shoulder, and as a father, husband, and man, he will always battle his inner demons.

Despite their disparate musical tones, "State Trooper" and "Don't Stop Believin'" present protagonists who both will themselves not to stop. They are figures of perpetual motion—whether by train or by car, they ride on into the night, on and on into the ineluctable darkness that swallows them whole along with Tony. Journey's stentorian paean insists that life will continue to go on for not only Tony and his family but also Dr. Melfi, his crew, and America itself. Chase elucidates the meaning of this soundtrack selection: "Life ends and death comes…. There are attachments we make in life, even though it's all going to come to an end, that are worth so much, and we're so lucky to have been able to experience them. Life is short. Either it ends here for Tony or some other time. But in spite of that, it's really worth it. So don't stop believing."[50] The series leaves Tony in a New Jersey diner as it had in Vesuvio during the Season One finale: surrounded by the comfort of his family but also with the knowledge that his harried journey toward self-actualization still continues. Chase uses the soundtrack as an integral device to express the themes and inner life of Tony Soprano's titanic being. Chase's regard and careful selection of songs cements the significance of Springsteen's inclusion. "State Trooper" not only crafts a razor-sharp season finale but also superbly voices the series' thematic concerns with moral and psychological identity and the titular New Jersey setting.

High Fidelity

Based on Nick Hornby's 1995 British novel, *High Fidelity* (2000) is an American romantic comedy and Generation X bildungsroman that focuses on Rob Gordon, the owner of a declining record shop and an "overgrown adolescent who's too narcissistic and self-indulgent to be easily liked, but too willing to admit his more unpleasant qualities to be wholly unsympathetic."[1] One of these unpleasant qualities is his sexist treatment of women and benighted understanding of their subjectivity. Rob's fetishistic consumption and encyclopedic knowledge of pop and rock music mobilizes his vainglorious ego, misogyny, and middle-age immaturity. His elitist demarcation between cheesy and credible music sustains his fanatical categorization of songs, genres, and artists as well as his stringent curation of mix tapes. Rob looks down on anyone who does not share his precise musical tastes. He even goes so far as to tell his girlfriend at the time that enjoying both Art Garfunkel and Marvin Gaye "is like saying you support the Israelis and the Palestinians."

Rob's phallic-narcissism structures the mise-en-scène through the subjective filmic devices of breaking the fourth wall (utilized by director Stephen Frears to evoke the novel's use of first-person narration), flashbacks, fantasy sequences, and dramatized representations of "what really happened."[2] Rob also arranges the pop/rock score that appeals to his white, male demographic, which not only articulates his emotional state of being but also incites his misogynism. Since Rob's infatuation with music circumscribes his entire identity, he continues rock and roll's sexist tradition of penis worship by subjugating and objectifying the women in his life. Tom Brown considers Rob's dogmatic dominion over the mise-en-scène a form of visual chauvinism that forces the spectator to submit to Rob's way of ordering the world, particularly the female characters.[3] His myopic subjectivity constructs them as mere archetypal projections of his insecurities and sophomoric masculinity.

At one point Rob listens to Springsteen's "The River," a song that articulates the narrative concerns of commitment and adult relationships. More significantly, the musician also appears on screen in a brief cameo role. Springsteen's performance-as-self invites extratextual readings of his autobiographical circumstances in congruence with the male midlife crisis narrative of *High Fidelity*. Both the evolution of Springsteen's musical canon and the constructed life narrative in his memoir *Born to Run* mirror Rob's arc; these men eventually renounce their egotism and practice of rock and roll's patriarchal hierarchy—its infantile masculinity that sublimates women's autonomy and selfhood—for a male/female partnership based on equality. As a pop culture mélage, *High Fidelity* embodies Springsteen's thematic concerns of lost youth, masculinity, and rock and roll.

Good Luck and Goodbye

Rob's recent breakup with Laura launches him into a reflective "what-does-it-all-mean thing," a specific brand of midlife crisis that, according to his ex-girlfriend Charlie, all unmarried men go through when they reach the age of thirty-five. He questions what went wrong during his past romantic relationships—more specifically, his "Top Five Breakups," the ones that wounded him the most. That Rob meticulously constructs lists of women with the same dogmatic fervor as music indicates his objectification of them. The first on Rob's list is Alison Ashmore, his middle school sweetheart (for six whole hours), whom he unceremoniously caught kissing his schoolmate Kevin Bannister on the playground.

Since Rob's to-camera monologues are "the expression of his 'private' thoughts," the spectator understands the degree to which Rob derides women as vindictive ciphers.[4] He says to his audience, "It would be nice to think that since I was fourteen, times have changed—relationships have become more sophisticated, females less cruel, skins thicker, instincts more developed. But there seems to be an element of that afternoon in everything that's happened to me since. All my romantic stories are a scrambled version of that first one." Alison's infidelity, which foreshadows all of Rob's subsequent girlfriends leaving him for another man, fixes Rob into a pattern of self-victimization wherein he perceives himself as eternally "doomed to be left … doomed to be rejected," and this belief fuels his scorned misogyny. When he calls Alison, he ends up speaking to her mother, who informs him that she moved after marrying her first boyfriend Kevin. At first, Rob arrogantly argues that "technically" he was her first boyfriend. "Technically, number one. Me," he conceitedly repeats until he realizes that Kevin and Alison's union was "fate … destiny … beyond my control," thereby pacifying his wounded ego.

This news emboldens Rob to reunite with his other ex-girlfriends, "just to see 'em and talk to 'em. You know, like a Bruce Springsteen song," he tells the spectator while he lies on his bed in a bird's-eye-view shot. Frears then cuts to a shot of Springsteen in a studio picking at his famous Telecaster before he slyly looks into the camera and advises Rob, "You call, you ask 'em how they are, and you see if they've forgiven you." In this daydream, Springsteen's words address Rob, not the audience, and echo the thoughts Rob also narrates into the camera. This moment could thus be seen as an example of an "'axial shot-reverse-shot' … as it presents a discussion between Rob and Springsteen rather than a moment of direct address *per se*."[5] In other words, Rob selfishly does not afford his spectators the privilege of being spoken to by his idol.

Springsteen's cameo scene "visualizes Rob's solipsistic view of the world as he is shown to imagine a dialogue that is really only a monologue."[6] Since Springsteen's rhetoric is merely a product of Rob's imagination, it extends Rob's self-absorbed chauvinism. "They'd feel good, maybe, but *you'd* feel better," Springsteen affirms. Rob has little regard for how his ex-girlfriends will fare after his visit; what is most important is that *he* will "feel clean and calm." "That's what you're looking for. You wanna get ready to start again, that'd be good for you," Rob vainly avows to himself through the vessel of Springsteen. It is telling that in Rob's egotistical fantasy, only he is worthy of the venerable rock god's attention and the pair get along as well as lifelong buddies.

John Cusack, who plays Rob and serves as a co-producer and writer for the film, originally wanted Bob Dylan for this cameo, but the inclusion of Springsteen hews more closely to Hornby's novel, and there are extratextual elements of Springsteen's star image that imbue this sequence with a greater thematic weight. First, Springsteen's nickname "The

Boss" connotes knowledge and authority, cementing him as a paradigm of formidable white masculinity. This imagery readily appeals to male Springsteen fans who, like Rob, laud him as their ideal and potential selves. Yet, despite his authoritarian nickname and unattainable superstardom, Springsteen's humble star image has always been that of an American Everyman, the guy next door. His intimate, anecdotal lyrics often evoke the kind of private exchanges heard in a roadside bar between friends. He has always stressed the significance of his profound and lifelong emotional connection with fans, which he considers, outside of his family, "the most important relationship in my life."[7] Springsteen's cameo capitalizes on the strength of this kind of audience identification. His articulate wisdom regarding the common man's plight, along with his virile masculinity, differs from Dylan's enigmatic and androgynous star image. There is far more believability in the idea of Springsteen doling out romantic advice to his fan/friend than Dylan.

Springsteen's approval of Rob's mission to revisit his exes—"You'd give that big final 'good luck and goodbye' to your all-time Top Five and just move on down the road"— echoes the lyrics of "Bobby Jean" from *Born in the U.S.A.*[8] While some critics read this song as a lament on male friendship inspired by Springsteen's farewell to guitarist Steven Van Zandt when he left the band during the *Born in the U.S.A.* tour, Rob views it through the lens of a heterosexual romance. In a scene similar to Rob's interaction with Mrs. Ashmore, the narrator of "Bobby Jean" attempts to visit his girlfriend only to be told by her mother that she has left town. This news devastates the narrator, and he wishes he had one last chance, not to stop her from embarking on her journey, but rather to satisfactorily conclude their relationship, as Rob hopes to do with his Top Five.

Bobby Jean and the narrator were both outsider figures bound by their similar tastes in clothes and music. Rob regards similar pop culture tastes as the benchmark of a solid romantic relationship: "What really matters is what you like, not what you *are* like. Books, records, films, these things matter. Call me shallow, it's the fucking truth." During one of his dates, Rob tells the audience that it's going well simply because they "hate the same actors." In "Bobby Jean," Springsteen's male subject hopes that Bobby Jean will hear his song on the airwaves during her far-off travels. These lines situate music itself as transcending time and space, as "inextricably bound up with our memories and our psychological states of being."[9] No matter how many years pass, Bobby Jean could listen to Springsteen's song and fondly recall her blissful bygone romance.

Music functions in this same way in *High Fidelity*—that is, as an emotional and temporal language experienced autobiographically. Cusack explains on the DVD bonus features that the simple act of turning on a certain song can "get me right where I need to go," propelling him "into a certain mindset," just as it does for Rob.[10] With dominion over the film's soundtrack, Rob consistently selects songs that indicate his mood, particularly miserable ones about heartbreak blues. During the flashback scenes, the songs mirror the time period and evoke the particular ex-girlfriend's personality. One of Rob's favorite pastimes is the "subtle art" of constructing mixtapes, difficult because you are, as he notes to the camera, "using someone else's poetry to express how you feel." Rob explains that the methodical arrangement of songs must aptly guide the listener on the appropriate sensorial journey: "You gotta kick it off with a killer to grab attention. Then you gotta take it up a notch, but you don't want to blow your wad. So then you gotta cool it off a notch. There are a lot of rules."

He also indulges in his musical compulsion with his friends and co-workers at the record store. "The bald, neurasthenic Dick and the portly, monomaniacal Barry ... sit around the store all day," discussing music "as if they were monks debating sacred texts of medieval catechism"[11] and curating Top Five lists such as "Top Five: Side Ones, Track Ones," "Top Five Musical Crimes Perpetrated by Stevie Wonder in the 80s and 90s," and even "Top Five Songs about Death: A Laura's Dad Tribute List." The record shop is a quintessential eternal-adolescent setting, a space where the boys frantically fret over the minutiae of pop culture while their real lives slowly slip away. A self-proclaimed "prisoner of rock and roll" ever since he first laid eyes on Elvis' wiggling hips and Ed Sullivan uttered the words "Ladies and gentlemen … the Beatles!" Springsteen shares an obsessive devotion to music. A glimpse into his iTunes playlist from an October 4, 2017, *Variety* article indicates that Springsteen, like Rob, has a wide-ranging appreciation of multifarious musical genres, eras, and artists.[12]

For the narrator of "Bobby Jean," Bobby Jean is a "nostalgic conduit to his past, to his youth, even to the existential fabric of his own mortality."[13] All the women of *High Fidelity* function in this manner, as signposts along Rob's collective memory that (he believes) have shaped him into a miserable and emasculated failure. Every failed relationship marches Rob closer and closer to dying alone. Spurred by his early midlife crisis, Rob embarks on his mission to meet with his exes so that he may relieve the burden they inflict on his psyche. Only then, he believes, will he be able to garner the kind of hypermasculine success he desires—a relationship with the girl of his dreams and a prosperous profession outside of his record shop—before it is too late and he is an old man.

Springsteen was thirty-five years old when he released the *Born in the U.S.A.* album in 1984, the same age as Rob in *High Fidelity*, and it marked a time when he began to ruminate on his impending adult commitments. "Glory Days" explicitly tackles the idea of lost youth. The narrator is a former high school baseball star who constantly reminisces about his successful past, a period that his current life has never measured up to. Once his days were filled with the rapturous applause of his school peers; now he cheers for the Major League Baseball players on television and fantasizes about playing against them while he practices at the local batting park. Springsteen introduced "Glory Days" at the Parc de la Courneuve venue in Paris, France, on June 29, 1985, as a song about "growing old." Now that Springsteen was thirty-five, he told the audience, "every minute of my life I can hear that big clock ticking away."[14] Thirty-five seemed to be a terrifying age for Springsteen, particularly because, as he grimly noted in a 1978 interview, "rock and roll is like all sports in that when you're thirty-five you're considered an old man."[15] This age also marked his first serious contemplation of marriage. "My psychological/biological clock must have been ticking," Springsteen surmises in his memoir, leading to his rapid engagement and ill-fated marriage to Julianne Phillips.[16]

In the comedic monologue preceding "Glory Days" at Parc de la Courneuve, Springsteen imitates that ominous clock, mocking himself by slowly counting from thirty up to his current age of thirty-five. After much stuttering and trepidation, he reaches thirty-five with a horrified grimace. Then Springsteen and Clarence Clemons put their hands on their hearts and, overcome by their feigned seniority, fall backward onto the ground. At this point, a crew member costumed as the elderly Father Time—complete with a giant sculpted head, a blue wizard robe and nightcap, and flowing white beard and hair—hands them canes. The two subsequently perform as irate curmudgeons struggling to stand, hunched over with their hands on their backs and hands cupped to their ears while mock shouting. All of these extratextual elements lie within the small reference made to "Bobby Jean" in Springsteen's dialogue. The song coalesces the overarching the themes of *High Fidelity*—the loss of youth, love, and the veneration of rock and roll. Springsteen is the perfect contemporary pop culture icon to materialize these themes in *High Fidelity* and Rob's characterization.

"The River" and Rob's Top Five

One example of Rob purposefully selecting diegetic music to underpin his emotional state of being is his inclusion of the melancholic title song from *The River*. Rob drops the record onto his turntable immediately after a horrible day of work and the news that his ex-girlfriend Laura will come to the apartment that night to pick up her things. Surrounded by her boxes filled with the objects of their once-shared intimacies, Rob slumps onto the couch and uses Springsteen's lament about love succumbing to harsh realities in order to wallow in his pain. Here the soundtrack functions as an extension of Rob's narcissism; in his mind, his breakup with Laura is on par with the suffering of Springsteen's young and impoverished construction worker who struggles to provide for his pregnant wife. "The River" aggrandizes the reality of Rob's situation as he, too, tries to ward off sexual and romantic memories that "haunt [him] like a curse."

The song plays beneath a flashback sequence of Rob's split from a Top Five girlfriend named Sarah Kendrew. What we see is his histrionic reimagining of past events directly influenced by the song that emits from his turntable. The exaggerated qualities of the mise-en-scène clarify Rob's imperious gaze. He embellishes the configuration of his memories in order for the spectator to empathize with him. Tom Brown points out that Rob's "dark, mainly black clothes, leather jacket and bandana, and Sarah's hooded jacket over

In this flashback sequence with his former girlfriend Sarah (Lili Taylor), Rob (John Cusack) wears a leather jacket and bandana reminiscent of Springsteen's 1980s stage wardrobe (www.photofestnyc.com).

checked shirt situate them firmly within the depressed white working-class milieu of the Springsteen song."[17] Springsteen wore a similar outfit on the album covers of *Born to Run* and *Darkness on the Edge of Town*, his black leather jacket and plain T-shirt referencing the iconic image of the independent male rebel embodied in Marlon Brando's character from *The Wild One* or James Dean in *Rebel Without a Cause*. Rob wishes he could embody Springsteen's virile masculinity in the tradition of past rebellious cinematic icons.

Rob ironically restages the waterside imagery of "The River" through his walk with Sarah past the crashing Chicago coastline while Springsteen sings of the titular river that has run dry. These melodramatic images are "ironic in their romanticism and in the comic literalism of the match between music and visuals," Brown explains.[18] Springsteen's wailing harmonica and anguished vocals about a devastating teenage pregnancy and life imprisonment in blue-collar labor facetiously underpins Sarah's trivial complaint of a "painful and draining" breakup with her ex. In one of the film's funniest moments, the somber Sarah and Rob firmly agree that they want to be on their own before immediately embracing in a passionate kiss, their entwined shadows cast against a theatrical and picturesque backdrop of the glistening sun illuminating the waterfront's breaking waves. The water in *High Fidelity* is also baptismal, symbolizing the idea that their union has the ability to wash away the pain of their recent breakups. But like the tragic lovers of "The River," Rob and Sarah do not have a happy ending—his "partner in rejection" ends up rejecting him.

One of the ways rock and roll music informs Rob's chauvinism is on the issue of consent—namely, the notion that men cannot be refused sexually and can persuade women into satisfying them. A significant aspect of Rob's narcissistic sexism is his control or repression of his girlfriends' sexualities. As is par for the course in rock and roll, Rob demarcates women within limited Madonna/whore constructs, as objects that exist solely to give him—and no one else—pleasure. As an example, Rob recalls his sexual frustrations with his high school girlfriend Penny; she was too much of a "nice girl" to let him touch her breasts, despite other boys telling him that she "would give it up" easily. He would try to touch Penny between her legs, but naturally she resisted that as well. Rob's blatant disregard for consent is highly troubling, especially when he confesses to his audience via voiceover, "It was as if breasts were little pieces of property that had been unlawfully annexed by the opposite sex. They were rightfully ours, and we wanted them back." Rob subsumes the toxic ideologies of rape culture, particularly the idea that women's bodies are men's property, thus excusing sexual assault or abuse. Much to his indignation, Penny chooses to have sex with Chris Thompson instead, "after something like three dates." This line speaks to Rob's misogynistic belief that women have no physical autonomy and are obligated to have sex with him under his conditions only.

Springsteen's songs "Fire" and "You Can Look (But You Better Not Touch)" continue the rock and roll tradition of patriarchal sexual relationships. In "Fire," the male narrator attempts to seduce his girlfriend in the car with romantic croons on the radio. Despite his attempts to pull her closer and get inside her bedroom, she insists that she "don't like it" and would rather be alone. But Springsteen insists that she is a fraud and cannot disguise her desire because their kisses scorch with an inexorable carnality that they "cannot deny," underscored by the blistering bass line. Springsteen's male subject does not regard the woman's verbal aversion as a definitive refusal, and his prioritization of only her physical response has undertones of assault. "You Can Look (But You Better Not Touch)" describes the male frustration of being denied female physical contact. In this song, Springsteen's copulation with Dirty Annie at a drive-in "lover's rendezvous" is interrupted by a meddlesome policeman. During a Copenhagen concert on July 25, 1988, Springsteen introduced the song with a comic monologue recalling his time as a seventeen-year-old driving his girlfriend to a "nice little dark place to park."[19] Engine off and "the radio down low," Springsteen slid over to her side of the seat and "started whispering some sweet things in her ear" as his hand slowly slid up her thigh.[20] Yet his affectionate words were hollow—simply a means to a very specific end. Just when Springsteen "got my hand a little bit closer" (dragging out that last word to build anticipation and demonstrate his overwhelming desire), she abruptly said, "Son, don't you touch that thing."[21]

Rob's reunion with Penny reveals the degree of his self-absorption. We learn that Penny did want to sleep with Rob, but she felt that she was too young. His post-breakup admission that she was too "tight" shattered her sense of self-worth, contributing to her rape by Chris Thompson—not the consensual sex he boasted to Rob about. This traumatic ordeal affected her throughout college, and only recently was she able to have sex again. After Penny divulges her painful past, tells Rob to "fuck off," and exits the restaurant, he deliriously whirls around to face the camera and exclaims, "God, she's right. I broke up with her. I rejected her! That's another one I don't have to worry about. I should've done this years ago!" Although Rob's ignorance and apathy are played for laughs, we realize that he cares nothing for the psychological scars he has inflicted upon Penny. Brown argues that in this scene, "[w]hat is potentially unpleasant about Rob's self-obsession and limited understanding is carried off by Cusack's skills as a performer and (even harder to pin down) his 'charisma'—were this not the case, Rob would be too loathsome for us to bear such 'direct' access."[22]

It would be easy to write off Rob's conflicts with Penny as a teenage misunderstanding, but he commits this kind of sexual tyranny well into adulthood. When Laura leaves him to live with their former upstairs neighbor, a haughty hippie named Ian, Rob cannot stop imagining their entwined bodies engaged in a salacious sexual encounter. Zany close-ups and soft-core Barry White music accompany Rob's hyperbolic nightmare. Laura's sweat glistens as she tangles with Ian in tantric, exotic sexual positions, complete with sultry red velvet curtains billowing behind them. Rob envisions Ian pulling down her lacy black thong to reveal a heart-shaped tattoo inscribed with his name on her upper thigh. "You are as abandoned and noisy as any character in a porn film, Laura. You are Ian's plaything, responding to his touch with shrieks of orgasmic delight. No woman in the history of the world is having better sex than the sex you are having with Ian … in my head," Rob narrates.

The first thing Rob asks Laura when she returns to the apartment to get her things is whether sex with Ian is better than with him. He has no qualms about sleeping with someone else post-breakup; yet he hypocritically demonizes Laura for doing the same thing. The cuckolding he frequently experiences seems to shape his anxieties about sexual performance. Furthermore, in a post-second-wave feminism society, he feels pressured to provide the female orgasm.[23] Rob's sense of fractured masculinity is tied to his lack of prowess in the bedroom and how it measures up against other men. If he can claim ownership over a woman's body and prohibit her from having sexual experiences with any other man, he will have no competition and thus emerge victorious.

Most of Rob's sexual anxieties and sense of powerlessness and inadequacy stems from his college relationship with Charlie Nicholson. With her silky jet-black hair, sultry eyes, and impressive artistic abilities, Charlie is a perfect, idealized abstraction whose love is mystical. Rob describes her as "too pretty, too smart, too witty, too much." There is a metaphysical quality to her allure; Rob thinks "she should be living on Neptune. She's an extraterrestrial, a ghost, a myth. Not a person in a phone book." Charlie embodies the impervious and enigmatic female figures in Springsteen's canon. She is the girl with the "killer graces" and midnight sun eyes from "She's the One," as well as the tempestuous Candy of "Candy's Room," with her secret, shining worlds; she is Cynthia, "the finest thing" in town whom every single man desires, though no one knows precisely where she resides, as if she manifests from the ether to satiate the fantasies of bored blue-collar laborers; she is Marie, a strange girl with an unyielding grip on the narrator like a sharp-clawed falcon after she lures him in with her coy purr and then brashly slashes him with a knife. These women are unattainable, immaculate, and often noxious objects of the male gaze.

Rob felt Charlie was far out of his league—"Why would a girl—no, a woman—like Charlie go out with me? I felt like a fraud"—and this made him doubt his abilities as a lover and envious of any man who befriended her. It turned out that Rob's suspicions were not unfounded, because Charlie left him for another artist. Their breakup taught Rob to "punch your own weight," or, in other words, only date women on the "same level" both physically and professionally. Rob adheres to this credo when he begins seeing Laura. At first, Rob relates to her rocker chick aesthetic—her short, dyed pink hair and proclivity for leather jackets (akin to Bobby Jean, she likes the same music and wears the same clothes as Rob)—but Laura soon abandons that style and stops going to clubs with him after she joins a high-profile corporate law firm. Laura's upward mobility in the face of his own mediocrity and stagnation (his non-occupation at a failing record shop) shames and emasculates him.

Fairy Tales and Storybook Endings

There is a greater extratextual significance to the inclusion of *The River* in *High Fidelity*, one that points toward the impetus of Springsteen's entire oeuvre. As a double album that oscillates between disparate moods, *The River* straddles the patriarchal ideals of Springsteen's early music and a romantic fragility that fractures the male ego. At first, Springsteen returns to his usual milieu of late-night hot rodding alongside countless girls "with pet names such as: baby, little baby, girl, little girl, pretty little girly, pretty little miss, little honey, little sugar."[24] The male subjects of Springsteen's bar band rockers "Cadillac Ranch," "Ramrod," "Sherry Darling," and "Crush on You" ogle tight-jeaned girlies, dollies, beachside babes, and a bewitching knockout who puts Sheena the Jungle and Venus de Milo to shame. Critics such as Gareth Palmer point toward these songs as evidence of Springsteen's overall misogyny, arguing that he positions women as "objects to possess, drive, control, or take pleasure in."[25] However, Lisa Zitelli makes a sound counterpoint: "[M]ost critics who have written about Springsteen and gender have categorized women in his lyrics as trophies or objects whom the male may swoop in to rescue and redeem. But this interpretation fails to realize that it is the male in Springsteen's work who is in need of being rescued."[26] Indeed, when closely examining his corpus (particularly the latter half), we find that Springsteen sketches a sad portrait of patriarchy with men who work to combat their misogyny and ugliest behaviors in order to participate in a romantic relationship predicated on true equality.

Entering his thirties marked a significant shift in Springsteen's post–*Darkness* writing about masculinity and relationships. As he explains in his memoir *Born to Run*, *The River* was his first album "where love, marriage and family would cautiously move to center stage," symbolized on the album's back cover of bride and groom cardboard cutouts.[27] "The Ties That Bind" brings Springsteen's contemplation of commitment to the forefront. His narrator consoles a brokenhearted girl weeping on the street, assuring her that there is no value in a "cheap romance." The deep, personal ties that bind us to one another make life truly worth living, even if they expose your emotional vulnerabilities and crack your tough and cool outer shell. "Two Hearts" shares a similar, if not simplistic, thesis that two hearts are far better than one. Springsteen soothes yet another brokenhearted girl crying on the street by avowing that loneliness does not provide "peace of mind" and cynicism will erode your spirit and turn your heart to stone. Springsteen's male subject admits that he once fell into the patriarchal trap of "playing tough guy scenes," trying to embody the strong, silent type of the pop culture pantheon. Springsteen suggests that the borders we construct to delineate gender are nothing more than the product of "childish dreams" that limit the inherent complexity of human nature. He maintains that the only true way to "become a man and grow up" is to reject these limitations. "Two Hearts" and "The Ties That Bind" pivot from male savior narratives to critiques of mighty and aloof masculinity.

Delmonico argues that "Springsteen's compulsion to serve as Prince Charming or savior is operating on high mode" in his song "I Wanna Marry You."[28] For Palmer, this song perpetuates Springsteen's depiction of women as "hopeless figures in need of men to protect them via marriage, thus perpetuating the male/female divide of patriarchy."[29] Springsteen's narrator spies a single mother pushing a baby carriage across the street and dreams of providing for her as a husband and father figure; Danny Federici's wedding march–style organ undergirds his quixotic reveries. However, the aforementioned analyses ignore the fact that Springsteen acknowledges the infantility of his romantic illusions. He rejects the role of male savior through his insistence that he will not "clip [her] wings" or encumber her autonomy and that true love is not a fairy tale; he is not a knight in shining armor come to rescue her, and she is not his docile, helpless princess held captive in a tower. Most important, he does not have the power to make all of her "dreams come true." He can, however, "help them along" as they work together in an equal partnership.

"Could it be that with *The River*, Bruce Springsteen finally has come to understand that the uncommitted life is not worth living?" Jeffrey Symynkywicz ponders.[30] The above-mentioned examples point toward an unequivocal affirmation and articulate Springsteen's personal longing at the time to settle down. His work during the late 1980s and 1990s continued this exploration of adult romantic relationships as he tamed his rocker image and narrowed his focus onto the trials of domesticity after his own experiences with marriage. These latter songs sustain the argument that traditional masculine gender roles are damaging and must be dismantled in order to find true happiness.

Unlike any record he had made before, *Tunnel of Love* was exclusively about love and marriage, with each song defined by the themes of romance and fidelity. This newfound diegesis had much to do with Springsteen's marriage to actress and model Julianne Phillips on May 13, 1985. But the album's sincere scrutiny of the perils of commitment and the characters' paralyzing anxieties concerning their vows seemed to suggest that its songwriter had some ambivalence about married life and was now experiencing firsthand the complexities of adulthood he had initially explored on *The River*. However, not every song on *Tunnel of Love* plumbs the depths of matrimonial despair; the sweet "Valentine's Day" and "All That Heaven Will Allow" glorify coupled bliss.

Springsteen explains that with *Tunnel of Love*, he "wanted to make a record about what I felt, about really letting another person in your life and trying to be a part of someone else's life. That's a frightening thing, something that's always filled with shadows and doubts and also wonderful things and beautiful things."[31] In the album's title song, he equates the concept of love with a nebulous fairground and carnival rides where internal monsters and temptations lurk behind every corner and make it "easy for two people to lose each other." Both partners must be obstinate enough to make it to the other side of that dark ride unscathed. In his menagerie of valentines navigating mystifying sexual and romantic territories, of men torn between being faithful and their old roving ways, and of jilted lovers praying at night on their knees for the fortitude to see their vows through, Springsteen views an authentic relationship as something that wears away one's façade and emotional guards to expose one's fragilities.

Tunnel of Love explores the "different types of emotional experiences of any relationship where you are really engaging with that other person and not involved in a narcissistic romantic fantasy or intoxication," according to Springsteen.[32] His song "Tougher Than the Rest" refutes glorified visions of manliness. Women may desire men who embody traditional hypermasculinity—"a handsome Dan," "good-lookin' Joe," or "a sweet-talkin' Romeo"—but these are shallow constructions of manhood, ones that prioritize surface textures as opposed to what composes a man's inner being. Most significantly, this ballad subverts our cultural perceptions of masculine strength because, for Springsteen's narrator, trust, acceptance, and sacrifice—values of equality that dismantle patriarchal structures—are what enable him to achieve a total sense of manhood. The title signifies not physical toughness but emotional fortitude.

After the *Tunnel of Love* release and tour, Springsteen divorced Julianne Phillips, dissolved the E Street Band, relocated to California, and married and had children with his backup singer Patti Scialfa. Due to this whirlwind series of life events, it was not until March 31, 1992, that he simultaneously released *Human Touch* and *Lucky Town*. These albums express "how someone bred on rock and roll dreams comes to terms with the knowledge that he has aged"[33] (a midlife crisis that Rob readily identifies with). David Burke describes *Human Touch* and *Lucky Town* as "the work of a man who has grown up with rock 'n' roll, but has seen it replaced as the Holy Grail by marriage and fatherhood."[34] Springsteen returns to the romantic themes found on *Tunnel of Love* with characters who make peace with their personal hang-ups and find fulfillment in the venerable position of "family man."

On "Human Touch" and "Better Days," sad men who cannot stand living in their own skin display their mature relationships with a lover who is more of a friend, someone they can candidly talk to about their dilemmas rather than a voiceless vessel for their sexual gratification. They are equal partners with a mutual dialogue of respect. In the dreamy "With Every Wish," Bobby is reborn after being dragged by a fish into a lake. He renounces his deep-seated jealousy and "mean and cruel" behaviors toward his beloved Doreen because of the other men in town who desire her. Springsteen's silky tenor and the soft chimes in "Book of Dreams" create a picturesque tableau of a star-lit backyard wedding where the groom is forgiven for the sins of his past. The scars of that execrable time remain, but the searing pain slips away at his lover's gentle touch. His book of dreams is open to a new chapter in which he is free to begin again as an ameliorated man alongside the woman he cherishes. "If I Should Fall Behind" is Springsteen's most beautiful love song, circumscribed by a couple's steadfast promise to stand squarely beside one another no matter what hardships derail their steps forward into the future. Their oath values the shared hard work it takes to make true love last in such a wearisome world.

"Man's Job," "Gloria's Eyes," and "Real Man" on *Human Touch* lyrically subvert rock and roll's patriarchal masculinity within their turgid sound. In "Man's Job," the toys men fetishize, such as cars, guitars, or extensive vinyl collections, imply immaturity and therefore an inability to be involved in a successful adult relationship. The narrator admits that he is no swaggering hero, but he does have the nerve to reveal his foibles to the woman he loves. Rather than promoting an infallible machismo, his frankness is a true marker of masculinity. "Real Man" makes the same contention. The narrator rejects cinematic and televisual images of hypermasculinity (Rambo wielding his phallic machine gun, a suave private eye, etc.). He mocks the primitiveness of aggressive masculinity, joking that it is easy to "beat on your chest … [like] any monkey can," but what truly takes guts and makes one a real man, Springsteen argues, is an embrace of feminine virtues: sensitivity, candor, and tenderness. Springsteen's real man admits that he is not a fighter with "nerves of steel," and true toughness comes not from a mask of virility but an unreserved declaration of profound love. The male subject of "Gloria's Eyes" performs as a "prince charming" and "king on a white horse" and objectifies Gloria as a "little dolly on the shelf." However, Gloria is wiser now and sees through his tricks; she reproves his playacting and whispering of sweet nothings, with her sharp eyes cutting him down to size and reducing him to a mere court fool. He realizes that Gloria is no pliant lady-in-waiting and he cannot inhabit these patriarchal roles if he wants to be with her.

Working on a Dream is written from the perspective of an artist who has been happily married for nearly thirty years. Springsteen's personal contentment colors the slices of tranquil middle-age domesticity found on this album. His poetic songs consistently glorify love's celestial power as lasting not only the rest of one's mortal life but also into the hereafter and beyond. He returns to beatific visions of love repeatedly throughout the record in songs such as "My Lucky Day," "What Love Can Do," "This Life," and "Life Itself." However, *Working on a Dream* met a lukewarm reception from critics and audiences. Its lush textures and bright, giddy optimism seemed to alienate listeners; a thoroughly angst-free Springsteen was an unusual sound. It seemed that Springsteen no longer had to work to find the dream he was looking for—he had already found it in his marriage to Scialfa.

Springsteen's perception of masculinity and romantic relationships has evolved over time and informed the arc of his music. Both his life and his art reach a similar conclusion: an authentic relationship can only be achieved when one dismantles traditional gender hierarchy and conceptions of masculinity. He has discovered that "[t]rue partnership, a veritable, equitable transaction, does not allow for the objectification of the partner. To succeed in a partnership, the two partners must share a multidimensional view of each other: strengths and weaknesses, fears and hopes, joy and sadness."[35] Springsteen eventually consecrates domesticity as perhaps the only thing truly worth living for—a far cry from the sex, drugs, and rock and roll ethos of traditional rock music.

Despite being a few generations apart, there are considerable parallels between Rob's character trajectory in *High Fidelity* and Springsteen's personal life. Through decades of therapy, Springsteen learned how to renounce the "family-patented misogyny" he inherited from his father so that he could reap the benefits of his "beautiful reward"—namely, marriage and children.[36] As a young man, his father taught him that family life was stifling and weakened men, transmitting the distorted idea that "the beautiful things in your life, the love itself you struggled to win, to create, will turn and possess you, robbing you of your imagined long-fought-for-freedoms." According to this view, "you always withhold something, you do not lower your mask," resulting in a "psychological bullying that is meant to frighten and communicate that the dark thing in you is barely restrained."[37]

The author of the candid and often captious biography *Bruce*, Peter Ames Carlin, discusses Springsteen's formerly sexist, old-world Italian views of women as a young man, when he would hotly command his girlfriends to cook, clean, and do his laundry.[38] Springsteen often took the emotional turbulence that roiled inside of him out on his women in vitriolic ways. In his memoir, Springsteen reveals with disarming candor the psychological demons that complicated his past romantic relationships. He grappled with an "inner yearning for isolation, for the world on your terms or not at all," which manifested itself in "a misogyny grown from the fear of all the dangerous, beautiful, strong women" he cared for.[39] This is the self-indulgent Rob to a tee. Springsteen's ex-girlfriend Joyce Hyser affirmed to Carlin that Springsteen's mercurial modus operandi in those days was "When I want to see you, you need to be here, and when I don't, you need to be gone."[40]

Springsteen confesses to a rebellious pride in his "emotionally violent behavior, always cowardly and aimed at the women in my life"—namely, intimidation, boiling rage, and an erratic tendency to drive at breakneck speed in order to terrify his passengers.[41] Carlin describes an apoplectic spar between Springsteen and his ex-girlfriend Pam Bracken after he confessed to cheating on her: She "reacted so heatedly to Bruce's news that their argument escalated into a screaming match that ended when Bruce slapped her hard, across the face. Hurt and outraged, Bracken tore open the front door and took off down the street. She soon had Bruce running at her heels, wailing that he was sorry and had smacked her only because he feared she might become 'hysterical.'"[42] There is also the notorious squabble that took place at No Nukes, a string of concerts hosted by the Musicians United for Safe Energy activist group. During one of the performances on September 23, 1979, Springsteen was frightened by the prospect of turning thirty and irritated by the birthday cake he received on stage. He was also vexed by the presence of his ex-girlfriend, rock and roll photographer Lynn Goldsmith, in the audience and demanded that she be removed. Goldsmith recalls the incident in her book *Photodiary*:

> Bruce was pointing at me from the stage, wiggling his finger for me to come to him. I shook my head no and smiled because I was scared. I knew the look in his eye when he was angry. I grabbed my camera bag and tried to head toward the back of the hall. Bruce jumped from the stage and chased me. He twisted my arm behind my back. I thought he was going to break it. I pleaded for him to let me go. He twisted harder.[43]

Springsteen eventually pulled her up and spat into the microphone, "This is my ex-girlfriend," and then threw the degraded photographer off stage. Rob is not prone to such rough conduct, but he does share in Springsteen's past narcissistic and selfish tendency to force women to submit to his wants and needs without ever considering theirs.

As a young man, Springsteen "grew very uncomfortable, very fast, with domestic life" and abandoned his relationships before they lasted too long because he had "no intimate knowledge of men who were at ease with family life. I didn't trust myself to bear the burden of, the responsibility for, other lives, for that all-encompassing love."[44] He sought consolation in making records and touring the country with his merry E Street Band of lost boys, shielded from the adult world lurking just around the corner, just as Rob does with his vinyls and record shop buddies. Rob's fear of vulnerability and distrust of others also leads him to develop shallow, short-term relationships. He avoids intimacy and constantly lies about his past, emotions, and inner thoughts so that women never discover his inadequacies. What frustrates him toward the end of the film is that he, like young Springsteen, remains emotionally untethered from the women in his life: "What am I gonna do now? Just keep jumping from rock to rock for the rest of my life until there aren't any rocks left? Should I bolt every time I get that feeling in my gut when I meet someone new?" Rob admits to his audience that he "never really committed to Laura. Most of the time I always had one foot out the door, and that prevented me from doing a lot of things, like thinking about my future, and I guess it made more sense to commit to nothing. Keep my options open." Springsteen similarly describes himself as a commitmentphobe with "one foot out the door (someplace, at my worst, I always twistedly thought I wanted to be)."[45] His relationships continually fell into a two-year pattern that his mother mocked him for: "Two years inside of any relationship and it would all simply stop. As soon as I got close to exploring my frailties, I was gone. You were gone."[46] Rob's mother admonishes him for a similar relationship cycle: "You meet someone; you move in, she goes! You meet someone; you move in, she goes!" Springsteen explains that it was not the girls themselves that he disliked, but rather "what they triggered, the emotional exposure, the implications of a life of commitments and family burdens."[47] It is here that Rob's experiences differ: whereas Springsteen pulled the pin on his relationships, the women of Rob's Top Five became fed up with his laziness, self-delusion, insecurity, and vanity and left him for another man.

It was not until Springsteen met Scialfa that he was able to bear the emotional exposure that comes with a genuine, loyal relationship and understand that familyhood was a sign of strength. "I'd let Patti know me like I'd never done with anyone else. This frightened me. I believed a lot of me wasn't so nice to know," he admits in his memoir.[48] Springsteen's marriage to Scialfa taught him that life without his misanthropic proclivities was worth living and that he was worthy of being loved in spite of his psychological hardships and flaws. "It was knowledge that I was searching for, and she came into my life and just provided me with an enormous amount of vision and love and security that I never had previously," he stated in an interview.[49] Perhaps Laura, whom Rob proposes to at the end of the film, will provide the same for him.

Life Trumps Art

Rob is a critic and professional appreciator of music who collects, categorizes, and manipulates women as if they were part of his treasured vinyl collection. Above all, he idolizes the "unrealistic, often outdated, models of behavior that work only on the silver screen or in comic books and that continue to bombard and delude young men."[50] Donald L. Deardorff II encourages men like Rob to "persevere through romanticized, idealized versions of manhood to see life as it truly is: confusing, dirty, and hard but worth the struggle."[51] As previously discussed, Springsteen's men often model themselves on male figures within the pop cultural zeitgeist, particularly the determinism and inscrutability of celluloid male heroes such as James Dean or Marlon Brando (see "The Promise" and "Backstreets"). "I'm a Rocker" from *The River* references various paragons of masculinity: James Bond, Batman, and Columbo. However, there are two outtakes from *The River*, "Be True" and "Mary Lou," that strongly correlate with Rob's personal conflicts.

These songs, with overlapping lyrics and premises, critique Hollywood's idealized versions of masculinity, femininity, and love. Mary Lou desires the patriarchal fantasy of a leading man, imagining her cinematic paramours leaping out of the screen and coming home with her, an image that brings to mind Mia Farrow in Woody Allen's *Purple Rose of Cairo* (1985). The narrator warns Mary Lou against these adolescent, ivory tower falsehoods, telling her that their cursory pleasures are not as fulfilling as real-world relationships. Even though life outside the movie theater palace is complex because it does not adhere to a preordained script (Mary Lou is afraid to "shake up" her "neat little world"), it is rewarding nevertheless. Springsteen encourages Mary Lou "not to buy into the Hol-

Rob (John Cusack) surrounded by his beloved record collection (www.everettcollection.com).

lywood doctrine of leading men rescuing damsels in distress that ends up undermining the potential for individuality of both genders."[52] The celluloid figures she reveres are mere caricatures that perpetuate dreams of romance "that can never come true" and misguided gender expectations, leaving her to weep in the theater alone as the end credits roll. Springsteen's narrator understands Mary Lou's predicament; he, too, suffers from the strictures of patriarchy and understands "the hurt too much dreaming can do." The movies that he has seen too much of inform his belief that he must conceal his frailties in order to live up to an inflated machismo.

Just like Mary Lou, Rob takes his relationship cues from pop culture effigies and expects the women in his life to live up to fantasies of perfection and servitude. Hornby symbolizes this neurosis through the object of Laura's underwear. Initially Rob hates the sight of her masculine, plain cotton underwear scattered around the house because it ruptures his chimerical visions of women as vampish objects meant purely for his own sexual pleasure. "I used to dream I'd be surrounded by exotic women's underwear forever and ever. Now I know they just save their best pairs for the nights they know they're gonna sleep with somebody," he seethes to the camera. By the end of *High Fidelity*, however, Rob has abandoned his female fantasies. He tells Laura, "You have great lingerie, but you also have the cotton underwear that's been washed a thousand times, and it's hanging on the thing, and they have it too. It's just…. I don't have to see it because it's not in the fantasy. Do you understand? I'm tired of the fantasy because it doesn't really exist." Rob learns to forego these patriarchal notions of romance and regard women as individuals with their own thoughts, bodies, and desires. One of the ways he demonstrates his enlightenment is by creating a mixtape "full of stuff *she'd* like. Full of stuff that'd make *her* happy." For the first time, Rob's real-life relationship means more to him than his musical elitism, and he puts Laura's wishes first.

Throughout *High Fidelity*, Rob fears change and attempts to control his life as if it were the notes in a song or the lines of a script, ignoring Laura's advice: "You have to allow things to happen to people, most of all to yourself." This line brings to mind one of the most poignant quotes from Springsteen's *The Ties That Bind* documentary for the *River* box set: "A creative life, an imagined life, is not a life. It's merely something you've created, it's merely a story. A story is not a life. A story is just a story." Both Rob and Springsteen bury themselves in their musical compulsions, but as they grow older and enter their mid-thirties, that mode of escapism no longer works. The *Human Touch* outtake "Trouble in Paradise" articulates the lessons of *High Fidelity* in a couple's realization that a relationship does not always have the romantic ease of a "storybook story," nor does it stick to a preordained script like "an old black and white movie." The leading players of a relationship are not heroes without a vice, but rather deeply flawed individuals. A solid partnership weathers the unpredictable complications that life begets and embraces each partner's flaws.

The misogynistic impulses of the Boss' early songs inform Rob's imagined conversation with him. But if Rob had taken the time to truly listen to other tracks on *The River*, or to Springsteen's relationship albums from the late 1980s and 1990s, he would have heard a musician who consciously dismantles the harmful gender hierarchy of rock and roll music. Springsteen's brief and humorous cameo appearance has great intertextual thematic significance for *High Fidelity*, particularly because his autobiographical narrative mirrors Rob's character arc in his movement away from a Peter Pan complex and deep-rooted misogyny. While both eventually break free from popular culture's infantile, narcissistic perception of masculinity, it is ultimately Springsteen who gains a deeper sense of self-knowledge, demonstrated by his willingness to deconstruct and critique his toxic masculinity in his work. In his memoir, Springsteen deeply atones for having hurt women in the past with his callous behavior and flashes of rage, whereas Rob, though he certainly makes room in his life for Laura, never completely repents of, or even acknowledges, his incredibly vile and sexist behaviors.

"Purified by the fires of demythologization,"[53] Rob and Springsteen emerge as self-assured men ready to live in the real world, a world made beautiful by its complexities and value of women as equals. When Springsteen closes one of his most forthright memoir chapters, "Downtime," with "at the end of the day, life trumps art ... always,"[54] he speaks to people like Rob or Mary Lou—those who are so enamored with the mythic constructions they see on screen or listen to in music that they model their lives on such supposed sublimity. Both Springsteen and Rob Gordon of *High Fidelity* discover that society's construction of gender is a barrier that must be overcome in order to find true happiness. They learn that equal gender relations and a genuine interpersonal connection outside of their egocentric world is worth pursuing. By the end of *High Fidelity* and the latter half of Springsteen's musical canon and life, relationships with women no longer represent an oppressive ball and chain, but rather the chance to find true happiness and a greater sense of self.

Prozac Nation

Springsteen has the unique ability to make the specific circumstances of his seashore disenchantment universal. His songs are "like hearing your own life music, even if you never lived in New Jersey or made love under the boardwalk in Asbury Park."[1] For Elizabeth Wurtzel, author of the bestselling memoir–turned–film *Prozac Nation*, Springsteen's humanist lyrics about the hangdog everyman seemed to understand and empathize with her depression. She found solace from her mental illness; addictions to drugs, alcohol, and self-mutilation; and the trauma of her parents' divorce in his blue-collar poetics. "That's how it was—I'd listen to Bruce, and if I sat there calm and quiet long enough, I'd stop feeling myself disappear," she writes.[2] *Prozac Nation* is Wurtzel's self-proclaimed love letter to Springsteen, and she also dedicated her second memoir (*More, Now, Again*) to him.[3]

Springsteen became Wurtzel's idol after she attended his infamous 1978 No Nukes concert at Madison Square Garden when she was twelve years old. Her devotion to Springsteen was so intense that she attended Harvard University merely because he mentioned it in "Blinded by the Light," and she frequently reviewed his albums for the *Harvard Crimson*. An introverted child who often spent time reading and writing alone, in *Prozac Nation* Wurtzel recalls her joy at finding Springsteen's simultaneous *Time* and *Newsweek* covers from October 1975 at the New York Public Library. She also recounts haranguing her fellow summer camp bunkers about Springsteen's genius, but once they became interested in him, she yelled "that they're all a bunch of unoriginal copycats and Bruce belongs to me alone."[4]

The film version of *Prozac Nation* (2001) directed by Erik Skjoldbjærg does not incorporate most of the moving Springsteen passages from Wurtzel's book, but it does use his *Darkness on the Edge of Town* outtake "The Promise" twice as diegetic source music and makes other visual and textual allusions to Wurtzel's ardor for the rock star. A *Tunnel of Love* poster proudly adorns her bedroom wall, and she leafs through LPs of *Darkness on the Edge of Town* and *The River*, as well as a 12-inch "Dancing in the Dark" single, while moving into her dorm.[5] In the recurring motif of voiceover narration, Elizabeth begrudgingly informs the audience that, in an effort not to isolate herself, she will befriend someone at Harvard even if they are not a Springsteen fan.[6]

Despite the inclusion of "The Promise" on the soundtrack and several references to the New Jersey icon, Skjoldbjærg's *Prozac Nation* could have magnified Elizabeth's emotional identification and connection with Springsteen; this is an integral aspect of the memoir that would have strengthened his film. The parallels between Wurtzel's and Springsteen's tumultuous upbringings, paternal conflicts, and struggles with mental illness—in spite of their class differences—account for his profound insight into Wurtzel's plight. Springsteen's searing depiction of his lifelong struggle with depression in his memoir *Born to Run* cements his affinity with Wurtzel and often echoes her own written experience with psychological problems. Although the "Promise" scene is an arresting Springsteen moment, on the whole *Prozac Nation* neglects to elaborate on his intertextual relationship with Wurtzel and fails to affirm the significance of his music to her.

Full of Promise

The soundtrack appearance of "The Promise" is drawn from Wurtzel's reference in her memoir: "One night, very late, [Mrs. Wurtzel] walked into my bedroom to find me lying face down on my shag carpet with a set of big, bulbous earphones on, listening to a live bootleg of the somber Springsteen tune 'The Promise,' and bawling because everything about the desolation of the song seemed so terribly true."[7] Skjoldbjærg exchanges the private space of Elizabeth's bedroom for the public space of her elementary school locker room. The camera scans past a departing group of giggling Catholic schoolgirls to find a young, uniform-clad Elizabeth sheltered in a corner with a cassette player plastered against her ear. Springsteen's song softly hums in the background as she rolls down her knee socks, cuts herself with a razor, and watches the blood languorously run down her leg. Self-harm is a common symptom of depression, especially for young girls, as it provides a sense of control and relief from their emotional problems. (Wurtzel notes in her second memoir *More, Now, Again* that "For You" was the song that she would listen to in the girls' gym locker room while performing this self-destructive act, imagining herself as the broken girl on the beach.) "The Promise" is included in the film a second time as diegetic source music when Elizabeth is a college student and the precipitous return of her long-absent father triggers her mental breakdown. She listens to the melancholy ballad while writing an article about Springsteen, high on the dangerous combination of alcohol, cocaine, and ecstasy.

Skjoldbjærg structures "The Promise" as an elegy for Elizabeth's relationship with her deadbeat father. After the song's first appearance in the locker room scene, Elizabeth reveals via voiceover that her dad suddenly vanished from her life when she was twelve—"No numbers, no letters, just gone." She penned a heartfelt letter about him in *Seventeen Magazine* that culminated in a fabricated happy ending in which he returned. The second inclusion of the *Darkness* dirge precedes their authentic reunion, which sends Elizabeth into a self-destructive tailspin. Skjoldbjærg's organization of the soundtrack invites the spectator to conclude that Elizabeth's acts of self-harm are a method of coping with her father's abandonment.

Ignoring the protestations of her roommate, Elizabeth stays up writing her article until four in the morning while listening to Springsteen's dirge loudly on her record player for inspiration. Skjoldbjærg warps the scene's temporality, visuals, and soundscape so that the spectator can identify with Elizabeth's drug-addled mania. Repeated close-up shots rapidly and seamlessly fade into one another, showing Elizabeth chewing on her nails, a mountain of crumpled paper balls steadily rising with her abandoned ideas, and a bulletin board veiled by scribbled notes and incomprehensible sketches. A dolly zoom pulls into Elizabeth's blank face when her roommate informs her that she has been working for four days straight, but this news does not deter her. Overhead shots of Elizabeth's hand feverishly writing notes onto a yellow legal pad and Springsteen's record spinning on the turntable follow, the pace increasing to hyperspeed. Elizabeth then faces the camera in a close-up, her body fixed and centered in the frame while the background wildly rotates in a 360-degree shot before quickly dissolving into the previous overhead images of her writing intercut with the Springsteen record. The camera embodies the record player's movement as the shots whirl in a dizzying circle. Skjoldbjærg uses these abstract, gyroscopic visuals to convey Elizabeth's unbalanced mental state.

Sonic distortions also function as an expression of her delirious condition. Springsteen's voice in "The Promise" transmogrifies into an eerie echo, as if she is listening to the song underwater. His guttural, Orbisonian intonation of "Thunder Road," combined with Elizabeth's high-pitched whispering, pen scratching, odd fluttering, and wind-like noises, creates an unsettling, phantasmic soundscape. Elizabeth's voiceover narration reading her Springsteen article evolves into a frantic whisper, rising in pitch as the words crash and tumble into one another until they sound like a gallimaufry of insects. Although the text of Elizabeth's article is not taken from Wurtzel's real-life writing on Springsteen, it is nevertheless an eloquent description of his artistry and what he means to her:

> Springsteen's like this garage-mechanic poet. You can feel the sweat in his voice, the grime in his guitar. When he sings, I see steamy streets, lovers groping hands, busted fenders, the dirt under his nails, and the clairvoyance in his eyes. His words twist and grind and hammer out a story for the brain, but his guitar and voice go straight for your heart. Music bellows from his insides, and out comes the struggles of the world. He feels with knowledge that goes back through the ages to a single chord in our brains. He has the power of pure emotion. Emotions so intense the body literally must do something.

Springsteen's extraordinary ability to transmute humanity's diurnal tribulations into urgent, visceral poetics shakes Elizabeth to the core. This facund monologue is one of the few examples in which *Prozac Nation* successfully conveys Elizabeth's profound bond with Springsteen. However, although the sound design's special effects and Elizabeth's sharp hisses convey her emotional unrest, they muffle her beautiful prose.

Elizabeth desperately clings to writing as her only reason to live and a method of escape from the demons in her head. The "Promise" scene demonstrates how she pushes herself to write for days on end beyond the limits of sanity. In the same way, young Springsteen feverishly poured himself into his songwriting and the catharsis of his barnstorming marathon concerts to keep his psychological pain at bay. "I think music was the way that I medicated myself in the beginning. It was the first thing that centered me and chased away the blues.... I found that the experience of playing cleared my mind and give me a brief moment of respite from the things that tended to disturb me.... I found out that exhaustion was my friend. Because if I got myself tired enough, I was simply too tired to be depressed," Springsteen explained during his book tour.[8] Both Springsteen and Wurtzel eventually learned that their manic obsession with their craft could be a dangerous form of self-harm—a wonderful emotional outlet, but not their personal savior.

Wurtzel describes "The Promise" as filled with an "angst and alienation and anger that could make Kurt Cobain look like Mr. Rogers."[9] It is a bitter portrait of a man who has been trampled by life and worn down by the dissolution of his dreams. This dark sequel to "Thunder Road" eulogizes the narrator's fantasy of roaring down the highway in a souped-up hot rod like his cinematic idols. The nomadic fancies flickering on the drive-in screen offer him temporary solace from his despondent working-class existence. Yet his pain is so great that he feels he bears the weight of other broken spirits who have lost what they once held dear. After selling his beloved car that he toiled over with his bare hands and confessing secrets he swore to keep, it becomes difficult for him to believe that his hopes and dreams will come true. Elizabeth similarly abandons her lifelong wish for her father to finally return and take care of her. The only lines of "The Promise" not warped by Skjoldbjærg's sound effects articulate Elizabeth's miserable impression of her father as a reprehensible liar. His broken promises that he will move back in, visit, pay for her therapy, or even make a simple phone call deaden her soul and freeze her heart, just like Springsteen's forlorn narrator.

Springsteen repeatedly keens "Thunder Road" in honor of the majestic highway that once held the escapist promise of a glorious and carefree life. The highway transforms from a mythical passage of aspiration into something that has been lost and can never be regained. For Elizabeth, "Thunder Road" represents what she never had to begin with: a tranquil life without depression and a loving nuclear family.

Since only a snippet of "The Promise" plays in the film, we do not hear the final line of the song that Wurtzel references in her memoir. Springsteen's crushing lament that he is going to "take it all then throw it all away"—one of the most haunting lines he has ever written—articulates the severity of her depression, which causes her to carelessly squander any sense of joy, opportunity, or promise that her privileged future holds. Mrs. Wurtzel mourns her daughter, who is "full of promise"—an Ivy League student who writes for *Rolling Stone* magazine before she is twenty-one—but weighed down by her mental maladies and substance addiction. As one of Springsteen's most tragic songs, "The Promise" rips your heart out and stomps on it. Every thud of Max Weinberg's forceful drums sounds like a punch pulverizing the narrator. Springsteen's voice is as sharp as the gravel that spurts out on the dirt road as his tires rush by in the rain. There is an operatic misery in Springsteen's anguished moans of "Thunder Road," his wailing the sound of his surrender after fighting "the fight that no man can ever win."

Springsteen situates "The Promise" in his familiar blue-collar milieu, which plays a part in Wurtzel's emotional response to the song and relationship with him. The film adaptation fails to explore how their stark class differences mobilize Wurtzel's fascination with Springsteen's work. In her memoir, Wurtzel admits that she was ashamed of her depression because she had such an affluent lifestyle and wished she could inhabit the grimy, ramshackle environments of Springsteen's canon:

> I try to convince my mother that we should move out there, that she should work in a factory or as a waitress in a roadside diner or as a secretary at a storefront insurance office. I want so badly to have my life circumstances match the oppressiveness I feel internally. It all starts to seem ridiculous: After all, Springsteen songs are about getting the hell *out* of the New Jersey grind, and here I am trying to convince my mom that we ought to get *into* it. I'm figuring, if I can just become poor white trash, if I can just get in touch with the blue collar blues, then there'll be a reason why I feel this way. I will be a fucked-up Marxian worker person, alienated from the fruits of my labor. My misery will begin to make sense.[10]

Wurtzel's beloved "spokesman of the rumpled, working-class suburbs" and his stories of "hiding in the back streets or riding the Tilt-A-Whirl or the sound of a calliope on the Jersey Shore" belie her bourgeoisie Upper West Side upbringing, a backdrop unworthy of her suffering.[11] "Nothing about my life seemed worthy of art or literature or even of just plain life. It seemed too stupid, too girlish, too middle-class. All that was left for me to do was shut down and enter the world of Bruce Springsteen," she continues.[12] Wurtzel wanted her mother "to do anything so that my uninspired, embarrassing white-girl blues could be like the fire and energy and rage that made Bruce run."[13] Wurtzel longed to identify with the working class in order to validate her depression.

The aforementioned quotes were included in a May 14, 2000, draft of the *Prozac Nation* film script during a scene in which Elizabeth's friend Noah reads an excerpt from her latest article, but they were later omitted and replaced with Skjoldbjærg's own "busted fenders" monologue. The film adaptation would have been far more nuanced had it kept the Wurtzel excerpt and considered the relationship between class and mental illness that she examines in her memoir through the figure of Springsteen; such an exploration would have added greater thematic significance to the inclusion of "The Promise."

Inheriting the Sins

Wurtzel and Springsteen had similar traumatic childhoods and fraught paternal relationships that serve as their personal and artistic idée fixe. They both inherited a predisposition to mental illness and substance abuse from their fathers. Springsteen avoided drinking alcohol and participating in the countercultural drug scene of his 1970s youth because he worried that it would hinder his creative abilities, damage his already unstable psyche, and turn him into his father. To this day, he has never touched drugs. Conversely, Wurtzel succumbed to her father's vices and dabbled in cocaine, heroin, and snorting Ritalin. One of the few memories Wurtzel has of her father is when he was so high on tranquilizers during *The Last Waltz* (1978) that she had to sit through the film three times before he came to.

As a child, Wurtzel frequently witnessed her parents' tempestuous sparring. In the film adaptation, she sits in the background of both sides of an ear-shattering, apoplectic telephone argument between her mother and father, where they howl about their piercing hatred for one another. This temporal disruption and physical impossibility conveys how their never-ending feud is a damaging emotional tug of war that frays Elizabeth's mental stability. Springsteen witnessed a similar altercation between his parents when he was a young boy. One night when he was about ten years old, Springsteen had to hit his father with a baseball bat in order to stop him from hollering at his mother at the top of his lungs inches away from her face.[14]

Skjoldbjærg frequently obscures Elizabeth's father in the frame to signify his prolonged absence from Elizabeth's life. To Elizabeth, he is nothing more than an apathetic enigma, a stranger who makes random promises that he never fulfills and leaves just as soon as he arrives. The spectator's first glimpse of Mr. Wurtzel is from Elizabeth's point of view of him flirting with a Harvard co-ed in the distance. Inside Elizabeth's dorm, he displays a frigid and stilted demeanor when he callously reveals his refusal to pay for her therapy. There is no life behind his eyes, as if he is looking through his daughter and not at her. Skjoldbjærg's camera cannot keep up with Mr. Wurtzel when he circles Elizabeth, slipping out of the frame as easily as he does his daughter's life.

To make up for her husband's abandonment, Mrs. Wurtzel smothers Elizabeth with an all-consuming love and attention. She forces her gifted daughter to partake in a plethora of extracurricular activities ("plays, spelling bees, studying, writing, museums, concerts, and even more writing") in order to secure a more promising future than the one she had as a failed housewife. But Mrs. Wurtzel's compulsive devotion backfires, molding Elizabeth into a maniacal overachiever and perfectionist. "You brought me back to life, and you became everything for me. I was so wrapped up in you…. And I wanted so much for you in your life. And I couldn't see that it wasn't good for you," Elizabeth's mother admits toward the end of the film, finally recognizing the incredible pressure she put on her daughter. "You wanted me to be everything, and I can't be," Elizabeth cries in reply.

Adele Springsteen encouraged her son's feverish obsession with music because she wanted him to have a better future than her disconsolate factory worker husband. Music could offer her timid and nearly friendless son a creative escape from the dread of his father's violent outrages and some much-needed confidence. For Springsteen, music became the only thing that made his young life worth living. "I lived half of my first thirteen years in a trance," he recalls, bruised by his father's vehemence and his own bashfulness.[15] "The first day I can remember looking into a mirror and being able to stand what I saw was the day I had a guitar in my hand," Springsteen divulges.[16] With an ardent rigor, young Springsteen poured his heart and soul into the sixty-dollar Kent guitar his mother borrowed money to purchase, practicing for nearly eight hours a day.

Just as Elizabeth revived Mrs. Wurtzel from her post-divorce melancholia, Springsteen's birth restored his grandmother to a life of purpose.[17] "She seized on me with a vengeance.... I was lord, king and messiah all rolled into one. Because I was the first grandchild, my grandmother latched on to me to replace my dead aunt Virginia," he explains in his memoir.[18] Contrary to Elizabeth's regimented extracurriculars, Springsteen's grandmother Alice allowed her toddler grandson to rove "in a terrible freedom for a young boy," where he could eat whatever he wanted, watch television until three in the morning, and sleep until three in the afternoon.[19] Her worshipful indulgence warped young Springsteen's sense of boundaries and entitlement; he believed the world was his castle and everyone in it his lowly subjects, an attitude that vexed the authoritative nuns at his Catholic school.

Douglas Springsteen resented his mother's affinity for his son, who reflected too much of his own authentic self, the same "gentleness, timidity, shyness and a dreamy insecurity" that he kept concealed beneath his rage because it harshly contrasted with the tough, taciturn masculine ethos of his 1950s-era upbringing.[20] "These were all the things I wore on the outside and the reflection of these qualities in his boy repelled him. It made him angry. It was 'soft.' And he hated 'soft,'" Springsteen explains in *Born to Run*.[21] Douglas was like a ticking time bomb—his timid son never knew when his father was going to explode in a savage fury. His volatile nature riddled Springsteen with an overwhelming anxiety that caused him to blink hundreds of times per minute and chew on his knuckles until they were covered in hard, brown, marble-sized calluses.[22] Douglas' misanthropic loathing sometimes channeled into physical abuse, such as the time when he gave his son boxing lessons and the punches landed "just a little too hard."[23] From then on, they "slipped into the dark nether land beyond father and son" that would take decades to emerge from.[24]

Although Douglas was physically present in his son's life—often sourly nursing a six pack in the darkened kitchen after a grueling day at one of his many blue-collar jobs—he was an impenetrable emotional void, much like Mr. Wurtzel. According to Springsteen, his father uttered fewer than one thousand words during the entirety of his adolescence and never said "I love you"—not even on his deathbed.[25] Beneath his irascible surface lay an ocean of woe, grief for the dreams he could never articulate and his inability to escape his small-town working-class drudgery. "I'd watch my father, how he'd come home from work and just sit in the kitchen all night like there was something dying inside him, or like he'd never had a chance to live," Springsteen recalled in one of his on-stage monologues during the 1980s.[26] These famed confessionals were his way of forming a dialogue with his father that he did not have off stage. During one of the most poignant moments in *Springsteen on Broadway*, lifted from his autobiography, Springsteen describes a dream in which he sits beside his father and watches the "man on fire onstage," his brawny doppelgänger performing a concert, and then leans over and whispers, "Look, Dad, look ... that guy onstage ... that's you ... that's how I see you."[27] As Springsteen explained to Terry Gross, "I think I created my particular stage persona out of my dad's life. And perhaps I even built it to suit him to some degree. I was looking for—when I was looking for a voice to mix with my voice, I put on my father's work clothes, and as I say in the book, and I went to work, whether it was the result of wanting to emulate him so I felt closer or whether it was—I wanted—as I say in the book, I wanted to be the reasonable voice of revenge for what I'd seen his life come to," a life that was paralyzed by mental illness and lack of opportunity.[28]

The elder Springsteen suffered from paranoid delusions, suspecting that one of his friends was a Russian spy, that his wife was committing adultery, and that love songs on the radio were governmental ploys to make people marry and pay taxes. These manic fantasies worsened with age. One of his worst episodes occurred in a McDonald's where he shouted and cursed at the voices in his head, making the patron across the way think he was instigating a fight. Springsteen and his mother eventually coaxed Douglas to seek professional help, and he was diagnosed and medicated for paranoid schizophrenia. The entire Irish side of Springsteen's family—his father, agoraphobic cousins, men with trichotillomania, and hysterical, superstitious aunts—passed down various mental illnesses from generation to generation. Springsteen always feared that his own depression would worsen to a frightening degree: "You don't know the illness' parameters. Can I get sick enough to where I become a lot more like my father than I thought I might?"[29]

Wurtzel's and Springsteen's childhood traumas affected their personal and romantic adult relationships in different ways. The "ultimate security, full license and … horrible unforgettable boundary-less love" of Springsteen's grandmother, merged with his father's alienation and silent ferocity, both ruined Springsteen and made him the man he is today.[30] "Ruined, in that for the rest of my life I would struggle to create boundaries for myself that would allow me a life of some normalcy in my relationships. It made me in the sense that it would set me off on a life-long pursuit of a 'singular' place of my own, giving me a hunger that drove me, hell-bent, in my music," he says.[31] Fearing the pain, risks, and consequences of romantic intimacy, Springsteen kept his partners at a careful emotional and psychological distance. The transient life of a rock star, the sight of new faces and new towns every single night, perfectly suited his fear of commitment. However, in *Prozac Nation*, instead of running from love, Elizabeth has a wolfish desire for it, craving devout affection and attentiveness from all of her friends and lovers. She blames her severe codependency issues on her father's desertion—"I don't have to be Freud to know I have a fear of rejection. And I know where it comes from. I know it's from my dad," she tells her therapist—but still naively believes that her lovers will have the magical ability to rescue her from her depression. Endowing her boyfriends with this salvific power causes Elizabeth to emotionally disintegrate whenever she is separated from them, even for a short time. Any small indiscretion they commit becomes clear evidence that they are going to leave her. As such, Rafe's eventual breakup with her sends Elizabeth into a severe crisis.

In an interview with the *New Yorker*, Springsteen noted that the wounds of childhood "stay with you, and you turn them into a language and a purpose."[32] Springsteen's and Wurtzel's creative work is a mode of catharsis that enables them to "rework, repossess and rebirth the conflicting voices of [their] childhood, to turn them into something alive, powerful and seeking light."[33] Their stories and songs help make sense of their troubled paternal relationships. Wurtzel uses her *Seventeen Magazine* article about the joyous return of her father as wish fulfillment, as a way to envisage a dream she "held onto for way too long." Throughout his early music, Springsteen paints his father "as an archetype of the neglecting, domineering parent. It was an *East of Eden* recasting of our relationship, a way of 'universalizing' my childhood experience. Our story is much more complicated," he explains.[34] Their strains have since become the pith of Springsteen's canon.

The vitriolic "Adam Raised a Cain" draws upon the biblical myth of Cain and Abel and John Steinbeck's *East of Eden* to tell the story of the Springsteens. The scorching introductory guitar licks, combined with Springsteen's ferocious and scratchy wails, thrust the listener into a father-and-son battle. They are bound by the "same hot blood" that courses through their fiery veins and the weighty chains of their oppressive, complex love/hate relationship. The son inherits the same dilemmas, doubts, and fears that plague his hard-working father, who is devoured by a pained range. Wandering the hallways "looking for something to blame," he uses his son as a scapegoat to unleash his unrelenting fury, unfairly forcing his boy to pay for the sins of his past.

In "Independence Day," the prodigal son can no longer endure his father's oppressive wrath, and he bids him farewell on a quest for, as the title suggests, independence. They are already "too much of the same kind," and he does not want to become a morose and embittered reflection of his father, anchored to the same miserable town and monotonous factory job. Returning home years later in "My Father's House," the son attempts to rekindle their squandered relationship, but he discovers that his father moved long ago. The house that once "got the best of us" in "Independence Day" now symbolizes a long-lost past and vanquished future, and the sins the father and son fostered in "Adam Raised a Cain" still "lie unatoned."

It was not until the late 1980s and 1990s that Springsteen mollified his vexed viewpoint of his father. "Walk Like a Man" from *Tunnel of Love* is Springsteen's love song to Douglas and an "acknowledgement that despite the acrimony of their earlier years he still wants to emulate him."[35] Now middle aged, Springsteen's narrator understands that his troubled father was robbed of a fulfilling life, that he had his "best steps stolen away"—an allusion to Douglas' severe mental illness and entrapment in blue-collar menial labor.

Springsteen did not suffer the fate as his character in "My Father's House." Luckily, he was able to reconcile with his father before Douglas passed away. Prior to the birth of Springsteen's first son Evan, his father visited his home and quietly apologized for his past mistreatment: "'Bruce, you've been very good to us,' he said, 'and I wasn't very good to you.' That was it. It was all that I needed, all that was necessary."[36] This anecdote is the pith of Netflix's *Springsteen on Broadway* recording, in which Springsteen is so overcome with emotion that he must fight to hold back his tears. Wurtzel's father offered no such atonement. She told *The Telegraph* after his passing, "To be honest, his death hasn't really affected me because I hardly knew him.... He was a stranger to me, which is sad ... if I'd wanted to speak to him I would have. I tried many times but it just wasn't possible. And it wasn't that I was angry at him—I had forgiven him—but he had a personality that was impossible to get through to."[37] In the end, her *Seventeen Magazine* article serves as the happy ending she always wanted but could never have. Elizabeth Wurtzel readily identified with Springsteen's tempestuous fatherly relationship, and it is one of the many reasons why his music so profoundly affected her.

The Black Wave

On a *Late Night with Jimmy Fallon* appearance in 2012, Springsteen sardonically responded to Fallon's gushing about his wild four-hour concerts by commenting that "manic depression will get you anywhere you want to go."[38] That same year, Springsteen revealed in David Remnick's extensive *New Yorker* profile "We Are Alive" that he had been in therapy and on medication for depression for the past thirty years. Yet another reason why Wurtzel identifies with Springsteen's work so strongly is because he also suffers from mental illness. Springsteen's memoir *Born to Run* delves into his psychological problems with a surprising frankness, from its origins in childhood to his maniacal obsession with music to his distant, neurotic relationships with women.

Springsteen openly describes the crushing moment when he first realized that he needed professional help. During a cross-country road trip in the early 1980s with his friend Matt Delia, the sight of an embracing couple beneath the twinkling lights of a county fair triggered a daunting nervous breakdown because it reminded him of his own internal loneliness and lack of an authentic romantic relationship. He writes of the encounter:

> [A]ll I can think of is that I want to be amongst them, of them, and I know I can't. I can only watch. That's what I do. I watch … and I record. I do not engage, and if and when I do, my terms are so stringent, they suck the lifeblood and possibility out of any good thing, any real thing, I might have. It's here, in this little river town, that my life as an observer, an actor staying cautiously and safely out of the emotional fray, away from the consequences, the normal messiness of living and loving, reveals its cost to me. At thirty-two, in the middle of the USA, on this night, I've just exceeded the once-surefire soul-and-mind-numbing power of my rock 'n' roll meds.[39]

Plummeting to an emotional nadir, Springsteen begged Delia to turn back around shortly after they sped out of town, consumed by an inexplicable need to root himself somewhere before he drifted into ether.[40] A surge of anxiety deeper than he'd ever known engulfed Springsteen and caused him to crumble into tears: "The defenses I built to withstand the stress of my childhood, to save what I had of myself, outlived their usefulness, and I've become an abuser of their once lifesaving powers. I relied on them to wrongly isolate myself, seal my alienation, cut me off from life, control others and contain my emotions to a damaging degree."[41] Shortly after reaching his California destination, Springsteen called his confidant Jon Landau, who recommended that he enter therapy.

Decades later, in his sixties, Springsteen suffered a severe bout of agitated depression that left him "so profoundly uncomfortable in my own skin that I just wanted OUT. It feels dangerous and brings plenty of unwanted thoughts."[42] Michael Hainey observed in his *Esquire* article "Beneath the Surface of Bruce Springsteen" that Springsteen's writing on his depressive episodes was that "of a man desperate to escape profound pain," and he bluntly inquired whether the musician had ever attempted to take his own life, which Springsteen curtly denied.[43] Hainey followed up by asking, "But have you ever contemplated suicide?" and Springsteen confessed that it was during this agitated depression that he "felt bad enough to say, 'I don't know if I can live like this.' It was like … I once got into some sort of box where I couldn't figure my way out and where the feelings were so overwhelmingly uncomfortable."[44] Springsteen makes it clear throughout his memoir that he understands the depths of psychological despair, which he terms an "abyss," a chasm where dangerous thoughts push you toward the edge of your sanity and force you to contemplate or imagine your death. "You get a look into the abyss, you get a bit of a view into it where you know that's as far as you want to go," Springsteen says of his depressive spells.[45]

Wurtzel, however, is far more explicit in her descriptions of suicidal impulses. One of her chapter titles plainly states, "I Hate Myself and I Want to Die." Wurtzel recounts her intense and perpetual desire to end her life all throughout her memoir, imagining every method possible, whether by hanging, drowning, or slitting her wrists in the tub before one last spin of *Darkness on the Edge of Town*.[46] The film re-creates her attempt in her therapist's bathroom, but it changes her method of swallowing pills for the more dramatic approach of smashing the mirror and cutting her arms with the broken glass.

There are several moments within the *Prozac Nation* film adaptation directly lifted from the book that parallel Springsteen's memoir, particularly the language used to chronicle the difficult experiences of living with mental illness. Wurtzel describes depression as "some kind of black wave" that drowns her, while Springsteen pictures it as a "big black sea" or "oil spill [that] spews over the beautiful turquoise-green gulf of my carefully planned and controlled existence. Its black sludge is threatening to smother every last living part of me."[47] Elizabeth's poignant final line, borrowed from Ernest Hemingway's *The Sun Also Rises*, says depression hits "gradually, then suddenly.... You wake up one morning afraid that you're going to live," echoing Springsteen's statement, "The blues don't jump right on you. They come creeping."[48]

During a candid BBC interview with Will Gompertz, Springsteen stated that depression feels like hitting a wall and being unable to get back on your feet after you've fallen: "You hit a wall where you simply don't know what to do with the next day. You're very uncomfortable in your skin, you're very unsatisfied with where you are. You're completely at loose ends. And you don't know how to continue constructing your life, you just don't know how to step any further."[49] This overpowering feeling of vacant misery transforms Springsteen and Wurtzel into immovable objects that cannot be wrested from the cocooned havens of their beds. The inability to get out of bed is one of the most debilitating symptoms of depression. In the film, Mrs. Wurtzel travels to Harvard to check on Elizabeth after she has a nervous breakdown. The sight of her daughter with dark circles rimming her glazed eyes while burrowed under the covers in her grubby single dorm room (given to her for "mental instability") leaves the concerned mother aghast. Elizabeth lies motionless on her bed, surrounded by wine bottles, piles of books, papers scrawled with indecipherable chicken scratch, empty pizza boxes, and dirty clothes. After her mother opens the shutters to illuminate the dingy and stale space, Elizabeth immediately shuts her eyes tight. "If I could just get out of bed in the morning, everything would be okay," Elizabeth wishes in her voiceover narration. Worst of all, this overwhelming fatigue extinguishes her ability to write, the one thing that gave her life fulfillment and purpose.

Springsteen had a similar experience during the depressive flare-up in his sixties after the *High Hopes* tour. Springsteen soberly recalls, "All I wanted was the bed, the bed, the bed and unconsciousness.... Reading, or even watching television, felt beyond my ability. All my favorite things—listening to music, watching some film noir, caused an unbearable anxiety in me because they were undoable. Once I was cut off from all my favorite things, the things that tell me who I am, I felt myself dangerously slipping away. I became a stranger in a borrowed and disagreeable body and mind."[50] Like Elizabeth, Springsteen found himself so incapacitated by his illness that he was unable to function in the world of the living.

"In New Jersey, in my crowd, the psychiatric profession might as well not have existed," Springsteen states in *Born to Run*.[51] Springsteen's manager and mentor Jon Landau was the only person he knew who saw an analyst and encouraged him to do so once he faced the precipice of that glooming abyss. Opposing the repressive attitudes of Springsteen's 1950s small-town environment, Wurtzel's elite Manhattanite upbringing lauded the benefits of psychoanalysis—she had her first therapy session at the age of eleven. Both talk therapy and psychotropic medication helped lift Wurtzel and Springsteen out of their unbearably black moods. Their memoirs are forthright explorations of the benefits and complexities of using pharmaceuticals to treat depression. For Springsteen, drugs such as Klonopin gave him "a life I would not have been able to maintain without them. They work. I return to Earth, home and my family. The worst of my destructive behavior curtails itself and my humanity returns."[52] But he also notes that they "interact with your body chemistry in different ways over time and often need to be tweaked."[53] Wurtzel was one of the first people put on Fluoxetine, or Prozac, shortly after its FDA approval. Although Prozac gives her the breathing space to "gain some perspective and not spin out of control," Elizabeth initially feels the pills mask *all* of her emotions, not just the toxic ones, taming her tempestuous nature so that she is unrecognizably docile and demure. She eventually learns that taking medication is a delicate balancing act that alters throughout the years and takes time to adjust.

Springsteen describes depression and treatment with medication as a nebulous, lifelong journey: "In all psychological wars, it's never over, there's just this day, this time, and a hesitant belief in your own ability to change. It is *not* an arena where the unsure should go looking for absolutes and there are no permanent victories. It is about a *living* change, filled with the insecurities, the chaos, of our own personalities, and is always one step up, two steps back."[54] The cryptic final scene of *Prozac Nation* brings this passage to life, opening with a blurred image of Elizabeth walking down the street that comes into focus as soon as she gets closer to the camera and then hazes again after she walks out of the frame. These obscured visuals signify the indeterminate ebb and flow of mental illness, conveying the understanding that Elizabeth will continually have to work to maintain her well-being. Psychotropic medication and psychoanalysis helped Wurtzel and Springsteen confront their tumultuous childhoods and rebuild their sense of self-worth. Their stories teach us that living with mental illness may be a constant battle, but there are moments of clarity and small, everyday triumphs.

Disappearing into Nothing: Depression in Springsteen's Music

Wurtzel imagines that *Darkness on the Edge of Town* would be the perfect overture to her suicide because it is an album filled with downtrodden characters wading in the depths of their emotional despair. Throughout the record, Springsteen employs multiple visual and textual allusions to depression and suicide. He composed these bleak songs during the fallout from his bitter, nearly yearlong lawsuit against former manager Mike Appel, one of the most dismal periods of his career because he lost control of the one thing that gave him a reason to live: music. Appel took advantage of Springsteen's naiveté by forcing him to sign an unfair contract that would cede his publishing rights and a large portion of his earned profits. After Springsteen sued Appel, Appel filed a motion that prevented Springsteen from entering a recording studio with his newfound producer and comrade Landau. For someone whose work and artistic success meant absolutely everything to him, this was a scathing betrayal. During this three-year gap between any album releases, Springsteen feared the public would lose interest and he would become a one-hit wonder. "After he stabbed me in the fucking eye. I don't own [anything]. I don't own any of that stuff. Man, that is my blood in that thing. That is mine. I lived every fucking line of that song. Do you understand that? I lived every fucking line of that," Springsteen cried in court over the loss of songs he had so lovingly and painstakingly crafted.[55] "He broke his fucking word. Somebody stabs me in the fucking heart, I learn to stab them back in the heart," Springsteen venomously seethed about Appel during his deposition.[56] The taut cynicism, acerbic language, and gloominess of "The Promise" and other *Darkness on the Edge of Town* songs poignantly capture the perfidy surrounding his fraught relationship with Appel. However, Springsteen's own struggles with mental illness strongly influenced the record as well.

"Something in the Night" pictures a midnight rider cruising down Kingsley Street in Asbury Park. He uses the radio's clamor to drown out the demons that caterwaul in his mind, embodied in Springsteen's guttural wails that open the song. Black, nihilistic thoughts about the futility of life and visions of the entire human race as depraved thieves run around his head. His soul is left burned and blind now that the things he once loved lie "crushed and dying in the dirt." The street loop of Asbury Park's Circuit symbolizes his never-ending search for something in his miserable circumstances to make sense. In an earlier version of the song, the midnight rider cannot live with his abject thoughts, so he picks up a female hitchhiker to distract himself. The girl hangs her head out the window and lets out a blood-curdling scream—a gut-wrenching cry in supplication of either death or redemption. She begs the driver to push his machine to hypersonic speeds so that the whole world will disappear out of sight and they will perish from the momentum. The wife in "Racing in the Street" is a haunting and hollow figure completely devoured by depression and a hatred for living, as she does nothing but sit on the porch and wait for her drag-racing husband to return. The life of Springsteen's strung-out, exhausted "Streets of Fire" loser hangs by a thread; he wants to let go and allow the cold walls that surround him to tumble down and plunge him into the sweet release of death, an overpowering desire that Springsteen conveys through the elongation of his words. Fed up with the weak lies he tells to conceal his pain and the frigid ignorance of the strangers who surround him, he tears through the blazing streets, transforming his body into a cinder.

Skjoldbjærg's film adaptation of *Prozac Nation* excludes the other songs in Springsteen's canon that Wurtzel references in her memoir because they relate to her depression. The impassioned concert performance version of "For You" from *Hammersmith Odeon London '75* profoundly resonated with Wurtzel as a young girl. Having listened to the "cryptic lines about a girl's fading presence, about 'barroom eyes shine vacancy,' about someone whose grip on life is so vague that to see her you have to look hard," Wurtzel identifies with Springsteen's wounded waif because she is also disconnected from the world and her life is like "one long emergency," constantly teetering on the edge of committing suicide.[57] She, too, wears her mental illness like a medal or trophy, believing that it is the only thing that defines her.

Wurtzel references the Cheshire Cat–like smile of Springsteen's tragic heroine that flickers across her face to conceal the hopelessness of her waning existence: "That's me, I say to Paris. I'm the girl who is lost in space, the girl who is disappearing always, forever fading away and receding farther and farther into the background. Just like the Cheshire cat, someday I will suddenly leave, but the artificial warmth of my smile, that phony clownish curve, the kind you see on miserably sad people and villains in Disney movies, will remain behind as an ironic remnant."[58] "For You" provokes Wurtzel's romanticized inclination to attempt suicide in order to see who—if anyone—truly cares about her and to prove that her depression is real.

Wurtzel particularly envies her idol's devotion to his damaged paramour:

> I'd be just like the girl in the song except for one thing. One thing. And that's that he says she's all he ever wanted. He loves her so much. The whole song is about how he's come to take her to the hospital, to rescue her from suicide. I start, as if on cue, to cry. I am so caught up in the idea that nobody would actually try to save me if I were to slit my wrists or hang myself from one of the rafters in the bunk. I can't believe anyone might care enough to try to keep me alive.[59]

She continues, monologuing about the heartrending ballad to her summer camp bunkmate: "How nice it must be to have someone so in love with you they'd sing about the day you died ... if anyone ever loved me enough to write such a beautiful song about me, you know I wouldn't kill myself.... I have to think the girl in 'For You' is totally crazy because she decided to die when there was so much love for her right here on earth."[60] Wurtzel wishes she had someone like Springsteen to save her.

Initially, Wurtzel's self-effacing college boyfriend Rafe fulfills her male rescue fantasies. "Rafe didn't seem to realize he'd just been appointed to save my life," Elizabeth states in the film's voiceover. Rafe becomes the one whose ambulance she can crawl into, the soldier who can break through the indestructible windows and ram through the immotile doors of her illness. But she soon discovers that Rafe is not the superheroic Springsteen of her romanticized "For You" reveries; he does not have the power to prevent her emotional breakdowns and suicidal impulses. The inclusion of the "For You" passage in the film adaptation would have added greater depth to Wurtzel's unhealthy romantic attachments. Instead, Skjoldbjærg presents Elizabeth as a shrill, paranoid, jilted lover obsessed with keeping Rafe by her side at any cost. Akin to Springsteen's sad "For You" girl, she clings to Rafe like a leech, calling him more than ten times a day over Christmas break and traveling to his home despite his insistence that she not do so. Skjoldbjærg never lets us probe Elizabeth's internal architecture enough to understand the roots of her all-consuming infatuation with Rafe.

Wurtzel reads "For You" slightly differently in *More, Now, Again*, her second memoir about the throes of her Ritalin addiction. Springsteen's line offering everything he has if only the girl would ask connects to Wurtzel's friends, who are weary of continuously helping her when she does not truly want to recover: "When I was young and depressed, I never had a sense that anyone cared. That's no longer my complaint. It's just that, indeed, they cannot reach me, because nothing they can do for me will equal the annihilating and totalizing cold comfort that I get from drugs.... I used to wish somebody wanted to give it all to me—I used to ask all the time. Now, with Ritalin, I just wish they'd leave me alone." She comes to the sober realization that even though Springsteen is madly in love with his damsel in distress, "everything he does doesn't prevent her from wanting to be dead.... He can't reach her. Just as it is now—nobody can reach me."[61] Love and physical affection are not enough—she must truly want to get better on her own.

Wurtzel uses the poignant final line of "Brilliant Disguise," about a man asking for God's mercy because he "doubts what he's sure of," as a chapter epigraph. Springsteen's driving, synth-laden ballad probes the liminal space between our authentic and performative selves in the story of a distrusting couple inhabiting the roles of "loving woman" and "faithful man." The self-doubting groomsman is frustrated by the masks he and his bride both wear to conceal their incompatibility. In the film, Elizabeth confesses that she wears a brilliant disguise of her own by faking happiness around her friends; her effervescence and wild antics merely camouflage her internal anguish. Just as Springsteen's lonely pilgrim suspects that his wife is secretly betraying him—finding trinkets under her pillow and spying a suspected lover beneath their willow tree—Elizabeth's lack of self-esteem and her attachment disorder cause her to doubt Rafe's fidelity. She becomes the "ultimate nightmare girlfriend," harshly accusing Rafe of sleeping with any woman he briefly glances at and constantly needing to be near him. Her uncertainty also mirrors Springsteen's Bellevue-bound "For You" girl because she lets the blue walls of her depression obscure the reality that Rafe is a good, loyal boyfriend.

Another song from the *Tunnel of Love* album, "Two Faces," "glimpses the mind of a manic depressive—one minute 'sunny and wild,' the next prey to 'dark clouds.'"[62] Two opposing selves lie within the narrator: one who laughs, another who cries; one who says hello, the other goodbye. The dark half of Springsteen's bifurcated speaker forces him to do unfathomable things that sabotage his romantic relationship. At night he prays for this shadow man to leave him, but he knows this is not possible—a somber recognition that his malady is everlasting. The lightly strummed "Two Faces" relates to Elizabeth's therapist confession that she unwittingly does horrible things to her loved ones. "I hate myself for it, but I just can't stop," she cries. Like Springsteen's tortured protagonist with a split psyche, Wurtzel cannot tell the two faces she wears apart—where her true self begins and where the depression ends. "I was so scared to give up depression, fearing that somehow the worst part of me was actually all of me," she writes in *Prozac Nation*.[63]

Wurtzel would also listen to "Stolen Car" from *The River* while crying profusely because it "captured the essence of depression with perhaps even more precision than all of Sylvia Plath's poems combined."[64] Springsteen's despondent driver laments his disintegrated marriage but also faces "an existential emptiness much more encompassing than the breakup blues."[65] As he barrels down Eldridge Avenue, his self-reassurances that everything will be all right are bested by a paralyzing fear that the darkness of his misery will consume him like the pitch-black night he drives into. Springsteen punctuates the car thief's disquietude with the ominous sound of deep, rumbling drums. His hope fades, along with his sense of belonging and purpose, to the sound of soft piano tinkles and a wailing organ—a cinematic fadeout as the thief drives further into his emotional nadir.

"This Depression" from *Wrecking Ball* contains the most explicit references to Springsteen's decades-long struggle with mental illness. In this song, he brilliantly crafts a dismal, dissonant listening experience to convey to his listeners the austerity of living with depression. The hollow drums' languid pace embodies the drudgery of his daily life—the same sluggish malaise that confined Springsteen to his bed for days on end—and the screeching cacophony of white noise from the moaning guitars evokes the monstrous thoughts that threaten his sanity. In the lyrics, Springsteen confesses that he has never been this down, lost, or low before; he is weak, utterly bereft of hope, and his faith has been shaken. The jagged, unpleasant melody and emotionally vulnerable lyrics make "This Depression" one of Springsteen's boldest works.

In an article for *The Guardian*, Wurtzel explains that what she admires most about Springsteen is his ability to express "how difficult it is to be good when being bad is so much a part of you."[66] His protagonists "don't merely mess up: they travel across rivers, drive down lonesome highways, cross rusty old bridges to make a mistake that they know they are about to make, they push against the pull."[67] Through his menagerie of prosaic characters, from hardened criminals to browbeaten waitresses to aimless midnight riders, Springsteen "feels for everybody—the good and the bad, the ugly and the gorgeous—and most especially for the person out there who happens to be listening to, or reading, the words."[68] Listening to Springsteen helped Wurtzel not to feel ashamed of her darkest moments and worst transgressions under the influence of her mental illness and drug addiction. *Prozac Nation* details her ugliest actions: giving her roommate's boyfriend an "accidental blowjob," getting plastered at her birthday party in front of her grandparents, mocking her mother's praise for her *Rolling Stone* article, ungratefully sneering at the pear tarts that Mrs. Wurtzel had lovingly baked for her, screaming at her mother on the top of her lungs. The film revels in Wurtzel's badness through its unflinching portrayal of her hypocrisy, egotism, and cruelty.

One of the main critiques of the *Prozac Nation* film was that Elizabeth was too narcissistic, tiresomely vexing, and unsympathetic, emphasized by her cold and flat voiceover and Skjoldbjærg's distanciated mise-en-scène. However, producer Paul Miller felt that the character's solipsistic characterization was in line with Wurtzel's wry, self-aware prose: "It's not a Hollywood version of depression at all … the character that Christina [Ricci] plays is not very pleasant a lot of the time. It's a self-flagellating perspective truthful look at depression, and depression isn't always pretty.… People who are depressed are not sympathetic. They can be narcissistic, they can be mean, and that's just the truth."[69] Christina Ricci's performance as Elizabeth is a "shrill, sometimes hysterical spectacle of self-hurt" that captures the indulgent histrionics of Wurtzel's writing.[70] She nakedly displays Elizabeth's "need to cause others pain and how her behavior challenges the people around her to keep their sanity."[71]

Like Springsteen's characters, Elizabeth pushes against the pull of those who care about her and want nothing more than for her to be happy. She regrets the awful things she does and how she hurts the people who love her. "I'm so sorry, Mama. I dream about all the things I wish I'd said. The opposite of what came out of my mouth. I wish I'd said, 'Mom, please forgive me. Please help me. I know I have no right to behave this way,'" she bewails in her voiceover. There is some unknowable force inside Springsteen's workaday folk that pushes them toward self-destruction, a capricious chaos that reigns in their souls into which Wurtzel likewise taps.

"Choose your idols with care"

On December 10, 2017, Wurtzel posted a photo on Instagram of her and Springsteen backstage after a performance of his Broadway show. Wurtzel wrote, "I am #lucky that I admired #brucespringsteen because I learned excellence from him. I learned #discipline and I learned that you do it for yourself and you do it to connect. I learned #redemption. Choose your #idols with care. You become what you love."[72] As the small but significant "The Promise" scenes indicate, Wurtzel shares Springsteen's intense devotion to the craft of writing. She respects him as a fellow artist who similarly used his work to make sense of his psyche's grimmest regions and connect to others who felt the same. Both writers candidly detail their struggles with mental illness to raise awareness of its devastating power and encourage others not to feel ashamed for seeking treatment. At her very worst, Wurtzel abhorred herself and believed she was worthless and better off dead. However, Springsteen's music and lyrics taught her that no matter how iniquitous her past, she was deserving of forgiveness and salvation. No matter what wrongdoings Springsteen's dramatis personae commit, he does not deny them compassion, knowing that their transgressions come from a universal desire to find amity in a world where darkness slinks on the edge of town, threatening to consume them whole. He deeply cares for them and empathizes with their struggles. With a tender benevolence, Springsteen continually grants his afflicted protagonists mercy and aids their climb up the arduous hill to the other side where their long-lost sense of self-worth awaits.

Since Springsteen is one of the most influential figures in Wurtzel's life, he should have been a stronger intertextual presence in the film adaptation. Not only is he her hero, but his work and life story also relate to the issues of depression, class, love, and family that Wurtzel explores throughout her memoir. Expanding on these connections would have enriched the film adaptation. While Skjoldbjærg structures the beginnings of Elizabeth's self-harm habit during private school and her nervous breakdown in college around the diegetic use of Springsteen's music, the director does not portray their bond as well as the memoir. One of the film adaptation's greatest flaws is that it does not include enough flashbacks of Wurtzel's childhood. The "For You" summer camp scene from the book and her teenage longing to live in the bland working-class environment of Springsteen's blues could have enriched Skjoldbjærg's depiction of Elizabeth's mental illness. However, this analysis does not dismiss the "Promise" sequences, which are instrumental in identifying Elizabeth's thorny history with her father and the severity of her mental illness and drug addiction. These scenes are searing expressions of how Springsteen's music was able to console her during the most devastating moments in her life.

"When I was in the worst way with my depression, I found solace in the music of Bruce Springsteen," Wurtzel writes in the *Prozac Nation* epilogue.[73] Behind Springsteen's bleakest lyrics was a volatile upbringing and fervent dedication to his vocation that resonated with the darkest parts of Wurtzel's soul. Springsteen's own experiences with depression offered insight into her own harrowing abyss. No matter how much the black wave of depression threatened to anchor Wurtzel down to the bottom of despair, Springsteen's music was always there, whispering softly in her ear, guiding her to the surface.

Reign Over Me

Written and directed by Mike Binder, *Reign Over Me* (2007) depicts an emotionally wounded widower named Charlie Fineman who lost his entire family—his wife, three young daughters, and pet dog—in the September 11, 2001, terrorist attacks. Charlie aligns with the characters of post–9/11 cinema who are "stuck in a syndrome of grief and anger that overpowers them for months or even years after the traumatic event."[1] After 9/11, Charlie excommunicated the few friends and family he had left in order to suppress memories of his past. A rekindled friendship with his former college roommate, Alan Johnson, offers Charlie the chance to heal and Alan some reprieve from his midlife crisis. Charlie takes to Alan simply because Alan knows nothing about his wife and children, and Charlie figures that he will not ask him many questions. But, much to his chagrin, Alan makes it his mission to heal his bereaved friend by helping him confront the traumatic memories of that day.

Post–9/11 popular culture attempts to "contextualize the uncontextualizeable," as Springsteen puts it,[2] or make some sense of the great tragedy, often through polarizing and didactic narratives that avoid complex interrogation of sociopolitical issues and include stereotypical portrayals of Muslims. Limited to a simplistic good versus evil, us versus them rhetoric, the majority of post–9/11 American cinema detaches itself "from disconcerting questions of politics, history, and casualty" and "perpetuate[s] the myth that the United States had excluded itself from international events prior to 9/11 and was forced to enter into the geopolitical world against its will."[3] *Reign Over Me* fits within the cycle of post–9/11 films that place the experience of the catastrophe within a "liberal therapeutic framework" that serves to "sequester the experience of 9/11 squarely in the realm of the personal and in doing so turn away from more ... critical views of the attacks."[4] Such films operate as humanist narratives that focus on domestic "tales of loss, heroism and redemption" and remove "any discussion of why the attacks may have been perpetrated in the first place."[5] *Reign Over Me* fulfills this paradigm through its coy references to September 11 and its focus on Charlie's personal recovery and mental health issues.

Reign Over Me uses two Springsteen songs from *The River* diegetically. Charlie employs his 1980s music as a mode of escapism "into an earlier, more quiescent time in his life ... before 9/11."[6] Throughout the film, Charlie is rarely seen without headphones wrapped around his neck or in his ears; this constant consumption of music is an obsessive-compulsive symptom of his post-traumatic stress disorder that enables him to retreat into the past and forget the nightmare of his current life and the painful memories of his lost loved ones. There is also an extradiegetic intertextual relationship between Springsteen's 2002 album *The Rising* and *Reign Over Me*. Critics dubbed Springsteen the "Poet Laureate of 9/11" after the release of *The Rising*, a record described by *Uncut* as "a brave and beautiful album of humanity, hurt, and hope from the songwriter best qualified to speak to and for his country," a towering achievement that poignantly captured the post–9/11 zeitgeist.[7] Including Springsteen within a 9/11 text, even without directly referencing *The Rising*, invokes his intrinsic connection to this event.

Residing in Monmouth County, merely an hour from the World Trade Center buildings, many of Springsteen's neighbors were either victims of the attack or family members left behind. His local newspaper was bursting with obituaries, many of whom were described as loyal Springsteen fans, and he would often call their relatives to offer his condolences.[8] He also spoke with many blue-collar rescue workers about their experiences: the firemen who bravely ascended the towers and Sandy Hook ship captains who brought back survivors with "their decks inch-deep in ash."[9] Days after the tragedy, a man drove past him shouting, "Bruce, we need you now," and although the prolific musician felt "the physical and psychic horrors were beyond music and art's ability to communicate, explain, heal or even comment upon," Springsteen considered it his duty to help heal his broken nation through the only language he understood: music.[10] In *The Rising*, Springsteen gingerly journeys through the devastating attacks and aftermath before offering hope for the future. His simple, tender tales oscillate between small domestic scenes of bereaved widows and expansive vistas of mourning nations on both sides of the catastrophe.[11] The post–9/11 texts of *The Rising* and *Reign Over Me* frequently intersect in their depictions of grieving characters enduring post–9/11 traumas but diverge in Springsteen's critique of Islamophobia.

Two Worlds

In *Reign Over Me*, an older woman who persistently attempts to speak with Charlie outside of his apartment turns out to be Mrs. Templeman, the mother of his deceased wife. She offers to buy Alan a meal in exchange for a discussion about Charlie's mental health, explaining that after the September 11 attacks, Charlie stopped speaking to his in-laws and pretended he no longer remembered his wife and children. The only other human contact Charlie has had is with his landlady and his accountant, Bryan Sugarman, who handles the massive government payout and insurance policy Charlie received after losing his family. The pair enable Charlie's isolationism and assist in keeping his in-laws away from him. Staring solemnly at her food, Mrs. Templeman ruefully jests, "I was gonna do nothing but travel and spoil my granddaughters. Then those monsters flew over here from across the world and rearranged my dance card." This line emphasizes the binary framework of post–9/11 American cinema, the "stark divide between good and evil, with America uncritically on the side of the former," that constructs the genre's ham-fisted moralism.[12]

Such films "privilege American subjectivity, humanity and moral authority at the expense of the Other, perpetuating the idea that suffering is a First World privilege by both marginalising and even excluding non–westerners from the cinema screen."[13] When Middle Eastern characters are included on screen in post–9/11 films, they are almost always reduced to disposable, violent stereotypes "lacking humanity and agency in their own way. These Others become the subject of a controlling and objectifying imperial gaze, viewed through the symbolic and literal lens of the West."[14] The diegesis of *Reign Over Me*—an American man who mourns the tragic loss of his innocent family—leaves little room for Middle Eastern perspectives and serves only to demonize them. The film submits to this vexed Western gaze that renders the Muslim community virtually faceless and voiceless. Mrs. Templeman's curt line swiftly abstracts all Middle Eastern men and women as monstrous, "motivated only by a desire to take innocent American lives,"[15] reaffirmed by their only on-screen appearance—namely, burning American flags in news footage.

Kurt Loder attests that the small miracle of Springsteen's musical accomplishment in *The Rising* "is that at no point does he give vent to the anger felt by so many Americans" toward the Muslim community.[16] Instead, Springsteen includes empathetic stories from their point of view and encourages mutual understanding, a bold artistic decision that flies in the face of any jingoistic readings of the album.[17] Springsteen challenges the divisive post–9/11 zeitgeist by humanizing Middle Eastern men and women and critiquing the United States' hunger for revenge within "Lonesome Day," "Empty Sky," "Worlds Apart," and "Paradise." Although many of those who dared to challenge the post–9/11 good versus evil rhetoric were "vociferously criticised by the mainstream media and condemned as unpatriotic,"[18] Springsteen was praised for his brazen and nuanced depictions of both sides coping with Islamic terrorism.

In the propulsive "Lonesome Day," Springsteen uses biblical language to relate the political tensions between America and the Middle East.[19] He symbolizes his country's collective desire for vengeance as a spoiled, hard-to-swallow fruit from the once splendid Garden of Eden that leaves a bitter taste on your tongue, one that doesn't "easily slip away." The Devil disguises himself as a viper in the grass, slithering up to lonely humans and tempting them to lash out against the betrayal and deceit of the great tragedy. A vicious tempest of hellfire brews on the horizon, but Springsteen beckons "Let kingdom come," calling upon the virtues of goodness and grace to find his way through. With a stony twang, Springsteen warns us not to succumb to our rancor, insisting that these incensed feelings will pass and we will see through the agony of our lonesome days. We can contend with the loss of our loved ones without succumbing to violence. His repeated assurances that "It's all right" offer an invigorating promise for a better tomorrow and soothe America's bereavement. Soozie Tyrell's strident violin, the hammering drums, and scratchy layers of guitars propel the song's sanguine ethos.[20]

"Empty Sky" describes another survivor with a revenge fixation. Standing before a tree of both evil and good on the "plains of Jordan," he is torn between longing for a kiss from his deceased lover and seeking vengeance against the terrorists. He resists the urge to obtain an "eye for an eye" from those who have caused blood to flow from the sky and spill onto the ground where the spirits of his slain loved ones cry out. Springsteen's narrator is left bereft in a world where all that he holds dear has vanished, and he fights with all the strength he has to resist seeking retribution. The sharp guitar riffs splinter like chainsawed wood, and the piercing, doleful harmonica solo holds the enormous weight of the grief that encumbers Springsteen's disconsolate protagonist.

Tribal drums and ethnic chanting from Pakistani Qawwali singer Asif Ali Khan and his group haunt the background of "Worlds Apart" to craft a multiethnic soundscape like nothing ever heard in Springsteen's canon.[21] In his memoir, Springsteen explains that he wanted to include "Eastern voices, the presence of Allah … [to] find a place where worlds collide and meet."[22] "Worlds Apart" is a love story between an American soldier and a Muslim woman that springs from a "dry and troubled country." Following an erotic introductory verse of covetous lips and tongues, the couple prays that the world will embrace their relationship despite the enormous number of casualties in the war between their respective territories. They fantasize about building a bridge from the blood of their fallen countrymen that spans across and joins their disparate worlds, a metaphor for uniting the oppositional sides of the tragedy.

Opening with lachrymose strings, "Paradise" amalgamates two cross-country first-person narratives of a teenage suicide bomber who contemplates his or her last moments on earth and a navy wife who longs for her husband lost in the attack on the Pentagon. Springsteen's flat singing style adds an otherworldly detachment to the bleak lyrics and is emblematic of his subjects' melancholia.[23] The first verse features a grim juxtapositional image of a bomb's plastic wires and an innocent child's schoolbag. Wandering the congested marketplace in a daze, the suicide bomber's grieving family member yearns for the sweet release of paradise that waits beyond the grave. On the other side of the world, the Virginian widow finds refuge only in dreams of the sensorial pleasures of her lover's body. "Paradise" concludes with both characters meeting as they swim "deep into the waters between worlds" to confront their lost loves.[24] "They're searching for the peacefulness that people feel comes with death and passing on, or with an imagined version of paradise that you'll attain, and they get close enough and they just see emptiness," Springsteen explained to *Uncut*.[25] The facsimiles of their loved ones at the bottom of the river stare back at them with a frosty vacuousness and the breath of the eternal void upon their lips. A choir's uncanny, spectral vocals accompany their ascension to the surface—abandoning the gelid, empty site of their attempted suicide for the warmth of the sparkling sun and an earthly existence. "Paradise" attests to our shared humanity by erasing the differences between Americans and Muslims through characters united in the same grieving process. Charlie from *Reign Over Me* can relate to their despair and contemplation of the afterlife.

Through the aforementioned songs, Springsteen "suggests that differences between us and them are negligible in the extreme and movement toward vengeance will only perpetuate violence and suffering for everyone."[26] He insists that in order for us to heal, there can be no room for hate. Springsteen's masterpiece *The Rising* valiantly grants "courage and hope to the victims without demonizing the perpetrators."[27] By humanizing his Muslim characters and incorporating their voices and viewpoints, Springsteen refutes the binary ideologies of post–9/11 popular culture. In Springsteen's eyes, seeking revenge is worthless and vilifying others based on their religion or ethnicity only enables us to stand "worlds apart" from one another.

Music Heals Broken Hearts

Reign Over Me opens with a shot of the sunrise jutting through the New York City skyline and then pans down to a bird's-eye view of Charlie riding a motorized scooter while wearing headphones as a sonic barricade from any thoughts or regard for the world around him. These empyrean images immediately confront the spectator with the site of the catastrophe and the film's post–9/11 milieu. In post–9/11 texts, the sky is a signifier of absence: the space where the soaring towers once reigned and deceased loved ones now reside. "The destruction of the World Trade Center left an emptiness, a gaping absence, on the Manhattan skyline and in the cultural consciousness. When the towers fell, they took with them a sense of security that now seems … as unrecoverable as any attempt to build on the site seems unthinkable," Roxanne Harde elaborates.[28] Spectators look down upon Charlie in this heavenward visual as if they were his departed family in the afterlife silently keeping vigil over their grieving father and husband. Similar atmospheric images consistently appear on Springsteen's *The Rising*, in which "characters look up to the sky or cry out to their loved ones, but an answer is never forthcoming."[29] In the aptly titled "Empty Sky," Springsteen parallels a bed's "empty impression ... there you used to be" with the vacant Manhattan horizon, the place where the speaker's beloved lost their life. *Reign Over Me* similarly focuses on New York City years after the tragedy. Binder imbues the exterior shots of the city with a reflective solemnity that quietly mourns the disaster's lost souls.

In the film's opening, Alan calls out to his old friend and roommate on the street, but Charlie ignores him. After recounting the chance sighting to his family at dinner, Alan's daughter asks whether Charlie is "the one from dental school whose family was on the plane?" This is the first of several vague references to September 11 in the film. Charlie eventually meets with Alan because he represents "a long time ago ... a whole other life" before the death of his wife and daughters, which Alan takes specific care never to mention. For Alan, spending time with Charlie is a welcome reprieve from his clingy wife and adult responsibilities. At first, however, he can barely recognize his old roommate, not with his bedraggled exterior, languid and disjointed way of speaking—often on bizarre, fantastical subjects such as inhabiting another dimension or the world of his favorite video game *Shadow of the Colossus*—and outré behaviors.

Charlie exhibits how "disaster obliterates ... our relation to the world" and how trauma is a "disruptive experience that disarticulates the self and creates holes in existence."[30] The tragedy has broken his psyche and compromised his ability to function as a normal human being. Charlie squirrels himself away within his apartment walls, rarely emerging and never without the safety of his headphones that keep the din of the outside world at bay. When Alan accidentally mentions Charlie's wife and daughters, he is met with a volcanic rage. Furiously pacing back and forth, Charlie shouts, "I don't have a family!" and accuses Alan of being a government specialist sent to monitor him. Later, Charlie confesses that he often sees his dead wife and family dog on the street: "I see her in someone else's face, clearer than any pictures. I look at a German Shepard, I see our goddamn poodle." Eventually, Charlie is diagnosed with post-traumatic stress disorder, which, according to several studies, affected as many as 7.5 percent of New Yorkers after 9/11.[31] As a method of coping, Charlie operates under the delusion that his family never existed and comforts himself with popular culture relics of the past, like Springsteen's music, in order to get out of bed in the morning.

Charlie's apartment is just as strange as his behavior. Several of the rooms appear to be in the midst of a remodeling project: empty, half painted, or filled with sheet-covered furniture that looks like sad ghosts. One of the few furnished rooms features an elaborate drum set, a row of sleek, high-quality guitars, and a shrine of more than 5,500 vinyl albums—the nostalgic icons of Charlie's pre–9/11 existence. In the center of the living room sits a giant television screen and couch, where he hypnotically plays *Shadow of the Colossus*. One evening, Charlie flaunts his new Pretenders record to Alan and basks in its vintage pheromones. "It smells like the late 70s," he says. "More like the early 80s," Alan replies, prompting him to remember when Charlie "used to jam to that Bruce Springsteen album ... what was the name of that album?" Charlie questionably repeats "Bruce Springsteen?" as if hearing the name for the very first time. "*The River*!" Alan answers himself before admitting that it was not his favorite record. Charlie echoes the album's title with the same unfocused daze, as if the toll of forcing himself to forget his familial memories has erased all others in the process. Charlie claims that he does not remember, despite Alan's comment that he "always wanted to jam to *The River*" back when they were in dental school. "Maybe if you smelled it, it'd all come rushing back," he jokingly suggests. As the subsequent scene indicates, Charlie takes Alan's advice and gives *The River* another listen.

The next time Alan visits Charlie's apartment, he hears music thumping through the half-painted walls. "Is that *The River*? You know, I gotta get you enrolled in a music appreciation class," he jokes. "Oh, right! Yeah, tell that to Clarence Clemons," Charlie retorts, having clearly reacquainted himself with Springsteen's music. After Alan enters the band room, Charlie forces him to remove the priggish clothes of his mundane occupation and provides him with a guitar. Charlie then sits behind the drums, declaring it "psychedelic time" and counting down to initiate a "Burrows Hall–style jam," a re-creation of their past dental school music sessions. Charlie turns the stereo knob to full volume, filling the room with the vivacious sounds of Springsteen's Friday night romp "Out in the Street."

Binder's nimble camera weaves between Charlie and Alan as they synchronize their drums and guitars to the diegetic soundtrack. Jump cuts of them enthusiastically trading off instruments and singing along visually meld with the song's buoyant, celebratory up-tempo. Its euphoric uplift temporarily assuages Charlie's pain. Whereas Springsteen's dockworker finds liberation from his despair in public spaces, Charlie typically retreats into the inner sanctum of his apartment to avoid the world at large; when he must be out in the street, he needs his music to safeguard him from any human interaction. Now, the utter joy of Springsteen's music and playing it with Alan opens him up and lets him feel something other than acute misery—something as renewing as when Springsteen's blue-collar protagonist steps out of the ennui of his labor and onto the galvanizing streets. Charlie and Alan end the jam session by bowing and bidding farewell to their imaginary audience. "Good night, New Jersey!" Alan calls out, a bit carried away with the Springsteen fantasy.

Although *The Rising* is a somber reflection on tragedy and loss, Springsteen adds

Charlie (Adam Sandler) enthusiastically plays "Out in the Street" from *The River* on the drums (www.everettcollection.com).

frothy pop tunes as a "conscious part of establishing balance."[32] The effervescent "Waitin' on a Sunny Day" (written in the style of Smokey Robinson), the mellow beachside bop "Let's Be Friends (Skin to Skin)," and the boardwalk-style jamboree "Mary's Place" inject the poetic album with unabashed joy. "Mary's Place" positions rock and roll music as a euphoric force "in the face of overwhelming absence," paralleling the "Out in the Street" scene in *Reign Over Me*.[33] The narrator mourns the loss of a loved one whom he keeps a picture of in a locket beside his heart.[34] Enveloped in a daydream of holding her in his arms, surrounded by her loving grace, he loses himself in the dancing crowd that gathers at Mary's place. Within the album's specific post–9/11 milieu, he is a widower like Charlie.

Max Weinberg's exuberant drums crack as soon as Springsteen invokes the chorus, inviting the listener to join in Mary's party. This ebullient celebration is a response to the narrator's broken heart, a moment of respite from his grief and reentry into the world of the living. The simmering solemnity of the "ambiguous question that concludes the chorus" bespeaks his concerns about moving forward.[35] When is "this thing" going to get started? How can one live while brokenhearted? Roxanne Harde proposes that the thing that needs to get started is life after loss.[36] Yet how can one overcome such a traumatic event? According to Springsteen, a lost soul finds temporary sanctuary in "familiar faces, the sound of laughter, and the permanently renewable resource of music."[37]

The narrator of "Mary's Place" surrounds himself with the fellowship of a raucous gathering, bringing the furniture onto the front porch to cavort with his friends in the living room. After dropping the needle onto his lover's favorite record, he prays for the strength to endure. From the turntable come the familiar rock and roll sounds of a band that counts down to midnight, a floor that rumbles with the stomping feet of avid listeners, and a singer who performs until dawn. In between each of these lines, a choir softly beckons the narrator to turn up the music while the singer eagerly waits for the shout of the crowd. Each time Springsteen repeats this lyric, it ascends in both volume and fervor. The verse ends with an ecstatic plea to "turn it up," over and over and over again, until the E Street Band bursts in a firework of orgiastic elation culminating in Clarence Clemons' rapturous saxophone solo. This effusion of unbridled ecstasy is the sound of the narrator's dark heart rising to greet the new day.

Springsteen's continual repetition of the key phrase "turn it up" grants music a salvatory power. The record's sonorousness has the ability to wash away the narrator's pain. Binder's "Out in the Street" sequence in *Reign Over Me* channels "Mary's Place" as an exultant celebration of friendship and music's ability to palliate despair. The corporeal pleasures of engaging with rock and roll music—dancing and playing music with friends—give Charlie and the bereaved widower of Springsteen's song a momentary reprieve from their suffering. Yet what is a redemptive tonic for the narrator of "Mary's Place" can sometimes be toxic for Charlie as he slowly loses his sanity the more he immerses himself in his fantasy world. All of Charlie's modes of escapism—video games, comedy films, rock and roll—operate as self-defense mechanisms that insulate himself "from the awful reality of his family's traumatic deaths."[38] Springsteen ends "Mary's Place" with another repetition of "Let it rain" to assure us that we can withstand the gales of life and safely emerge in the sun. He exhorts listeners not to wallow in their misery and grief but to revel in what life still has to offer: the pleasures of music, friendship, and laughter. "Let it rain," Springsteen beckons, welcoming the tempests of life with the knowledge that there is the hope of a bright new day once the clouds part. However, Charlie cannot cope with the downpour of tragedy that submerges him. The only way he manages to live while brokenhearted is by suppressing his sorrow.

Alan eventually schedules an appointment for Charlie with his psychologist friend Dr. Oakhurst. It takes a great amount of coaxing for Charlie to even enter her office. Once he does, he slumps on the couch and completely shuts himself off with his trusty shields of an iPod and bulbous headphones. He insists that he is okay and does not need therapy; then he instantly throws up his hands and declares, "I can't do this," and begs for the session to be over. But Charlie still returns each week because he cannot quell his internal desire to seek help. "I have these things that I don't like to think about," he softly admits during the next session, one step closer to disclosing the reality of his family. However, this vulnerability is too much for Charlie to handle, and he puts his headphones on and leaves. During the third session, Charlie once again tells Dr. Oakhurst, "I don't wanna talk about those things…. I don't remember," and she gently states that "there is no point in you coming here every week if we eventually don't discuss your life and discuss your family." Dr. Oakhurst calmly urges Charlie to face his fears, to cease the toxic denial of his past and divulge the truth—namely, that he suffered the terrible loss of his beautiful wife and daughters. Immediately after this line, Binder cuts to a shot of Charlie withdrawing from reality by increasing the volume on his iPod for Springsteen's heartrending "Drive All Night" from *The River*.

Charlie eventually decides that he should tell Alan his story. "Drive All Night" faintly emits from Charlie's headphones to underscore his agonizing monologue—the film's emotional crux. The raw, throaty vocals, languid melody, and moony saxophone solo transmit Charlie's hopeless longing to be with his family again and his ardent love for them. He relates to the male subject's pious devotion to his lover, a woman for whom he would embark on the mundane task of purchasing shoes in the middle of the night. Adam Sandler delivers one of his finest performances in Charlie's recollection of his wife Doreen, three

During his therapy session with Dr. Oakhurst (Liv Tyler), Charlie (Adam Sandler) refuses to engage, instead listening to "Drive All Night" from *The River* on his iPod (www.moviestillsdb.com).

young daughters, and dog named Spider.[39] He proves that his memory was not wiped but suppressed because he can recall every Lilliputian detail about his family: their long, silky hair, the way they would wake him up by harmonizing Beatles songs, and one daughter's aspiration to be a gymnast despite her klutziness. Another daughter had a burn-like scar—an eerie premonition of her terrible fate.

Through a stream of tears, Charlie reveals the events of that harrowing day. His wife and children were visiting their aunt in Boston and brought their poodle along because they didn't trust Charlie to remember to feed her. Charlie was going to meet them in Los Angeles for a wedding but would not be able to take his girls to Disneyland like they wanted. While inside a taxi on his way to the John F. Kennedy airport, he heard about the hijacked plane from Boston on the radio. Once inside the airport, he beheld the calamitous crash into the Twin Towers on television. "I saw it and I felt it at the same time. I thought about Gina's birthmark and I felt them burning," Charlie whimpers to Alan. The carnage is so horrific that it transcends the boundaries of the screen and forges an embodied experience in Charlie as a spectator. In his memoir *Born to Run*, Springsteen similarly describes witnessing the attacks for the first time and having a paralyzing corporeal experience: "I sat, like the rest of the country, transfixed by a television screen, where the unimaginable was occurring, feeling like anything, truly anything, could or might happen next. We were untethered and skimming across deadly and absolutely unpredictable waters as I saw the towers fall, such an impossible and confounding event that the newsman on the scene could not conceive of what he was witnessing."[40] Springsteen then drove out to the Rumson Sea-Bright Bridge, where the towers crumbled only fifteen miles away, the torrents of thin, grey smoke appearing "like the smudged edge of a hard blue sheet folding and resting upon the autumn Atlantic."[41]

Charlie's monologue echoes "Into the Fire," a twangy spiritual from the perspective of a bereaved lover and one of the many heroes who sacrificed their lives to save others during the catastrophe (inspired by Springsteen's phone conversation with Stacey Farrelly, the wife of a fallen Manhattan fireman). The elemental opening lines backed by the mournful hurdy-gurdy viscerally depict the horrors of that fateful morning: the falling sky streaked with spilled blood and a firefighter's lumbering and valiant climb into the blinding soot and fire of the collapsing towers. The narrator's husband is just one of countless others, like Charlie's wife and daughters, who "disappeared into the dust" that day. Left behind on earth, the widow clings to a metaphysical yearning for her lover's touch and kiss before he makes his final ascension to heaven in the darkness of his smoky grave. Springsteen's high-pitched keening articulates this intense desire to see and feel the warmth of a departed loved one's body once more. In the gospel chorus, Springsteen repeats the simple nouns of "strength," "hope," "faith," and "love," imploring America to seek comfort in those virtues "so that they may rise again from the ashes of that dreadful day in September."[42] Within these two post–9/11 texts, "Into the Fire" and *Reign Over Me*, survivors are left to grapple with the grisly realities of their loved ones' untimely deaths and hopelessly pine for them.

Springsteen's soulful ballad "Drive All Night" transitions from barely discernible diegetic source to non-diegetic score after Charlie exits Dr. Oakhurst's office. Its impassioned yearning constructs a moving montage that connects Alan and Charlie with the mourning city at large. Exterior twilight shots of the bustling metropolis accompany the somber lyrics of "fallen angels" and crying, defeated strangers engaging in "dances of the dead." Reading these lines through a post–9/11 lens situates the angels as those lost in the tragedy and the strangers as the millions who lament them. Springsteen urges Charlie not to join in the "dances of the dead"—the isolated rituals of overwhelming grief—by wallowing in his pain and succumbing to mental ruin. Too worried about his friend, Alan cannot sleep beside his estranged wife. At the same time, Charlie watches a late-night news report on New York City's rising terror alert status. Images of concerned NYPD officers investigating a subway car fill the screen, followed by the news anchor's statement that this incident is "just another long chapter in the ongoing war on terror," suggesting that no matter how much time has passed, Charlie will always face reminders of that terrible day. Springsteen's line beseeching his sweetheart to dry her eyes and go to bed ironically accompanies this shot, as if directing the request to the bleary-eyed Charlie. The ballad continues over a bird's-eye shot of Charlie not driving but walking into the night, wearing his trusty headphone companions. Whereas Springsteen's narrator will do anything not to lose his lover, including the simple and generous act of purchasing shoes in the middle of the night, Charlie has already lost his. He would give anything to be able to, as Springsteen wails, sleep again in his wife's arms or taste her "tender charms." "Drive All Night" imbues the montage with a romantic woe that crystallizes Charlie's pain, and he deeply identifies with Springsteen's aching profession of love. The ballad's overall melancholic mood bespeaks the collective sense of loss that permeates New York City.

Elegiac and gut wrenching, "Drive All Night" serves as the catalyst for Charlie's emotional breakdown and attempted suicide. After picking up a bottle of alcohol from a corner kiosk, Charlie returns to his empty apartment and tries to escape in the television's hypnotic glow. He switches from dire footage of Middle Eastern men burning the American flag to the salve of a Fred Astaire and Ginger Rogers musical. The quixotic simplicity of this black-and-white cinema classic brings to mind the love Charlie has for his wife that he can no longer give. Binder centers Charlie in the middle of the frame, mesmerized by the soothing strings and lithe vocals, and then slowly zooms into his tear-filled face.

While Charlie searches for a gun throughout his darkened, drab apartment, the mise-en-scène oscillates between the past and the present. His body exiting the side of the frame operates as a wipe transition that unveils his blissful, sun-dappled memories of his family. We see his wife brushing her teeth in the bathroom, the photographs of their contented life adorning the walls, and his giggling daughters running up to his clean-shaven past self wearing a suit. Their laughter echoes as Charlie wanders through the now-empty halls. These nostalgic vignettes recall Springsteen's "most precious, intimate portrait of … loss" and one of the finest songs ever written about the grieving process: "You're Missing."[43] In this song, Springsteen poignantly captures how death brings the most minute of details of a loved one and the things they've left behind into sharp, devastating focus. A haunting and lachrymose meditation on mourning with deep, aching cellos that juxtaposes presence with loss, "You're Missing" pictures a widower like Charlie wandering through his home, observing all the objects that the deceased left behind: the shirts, shoes, and jackets she wore, the coffee cup she drank from, and the paper she read. Everything is still there, but when the sun rises each day, she is still missing. These objects all seem to be lying in wait for her return, just as Charlie keeps the remodeling project unfinished.

Beginning Again

"[H]ow do I begin again?" Springsteen cries out in his exquisite benediction for a devastated New York City titled "My City of Ruins."[44] This question concerns Charlie Fineman in *Reign Over Me* and the scores of other Americans who had to contend with an enormous tragedy that cruelly stole the lives of their families, friends, and neighbors. As an affecting tale of loss, *Reign Over Me* channels the theme of grief that Springsteen tackles in nearly every song on *The Rising* through widowed characters who, like Charlie, are consumed by a deep-seated longing to see, hear, and touch their lost loves once more. Every song is written from the perspective of someone who has lost their closest companion and must face life without them. Through reverent songs that sound more like prayers, Springsteen salutes the courage of those whose lives were cruelly stolen on September 11, 2001, and those who continue to struggle in the aftermath. He unflinchingly captures the impenetrable despair and embittered fury that shrouded his country in the wake of that devastating catastrophe without resorting to jingoism or promulgating a thirst for revenge. *The Rising* is Springsteen's requiem for a brokenhearted America, with poignant themes of death, mourning, and resurrection. He uses sparse language persistently peppered with the simple nouns "love," "faith," and "hope" to emphasize the enduring virtues that Americans can rely on in such troubled times. *The Rising* has since become the nonpareil of post–9/11 popular culture. The gospel proclamation "Rise up!" at the end of "My City of Ruins" articulates the album's cardinal theme of ascension, of rising above tragedy. Through beatific images of holy light and blessed grace, Springsteen offers Americans the comfort of knowing that even in their despair, there is still hope and a "dream of life."

Reign Over Me does not necessarily end with this sense of uplift. While Charlie does manage to move out of the apartment he clung to because of his wife's incomplete remodeling project, he still numbs himself with video games and other entertainment goods. There are hints that he may begin a new relationship with another woman, but their connection is superficial and purely sexual. Charlie is not healed by the film's end; his wounds cut too deep and may never truly close. However, he has family and friends to assist him in building his coping skills. In this way, Binder departs from the majority of post–9/11 cinema, which attempts to neatly package and resolve grief.[45] "Without your sweet kiss, my soul is lost," one of the many bereaved characters populating Springsteen's post–9/11 album weeps in "My City of Ruins." Charlie is, as Alan remarks, "completely lost" without his wife and children. How can he, alongside the entire nation, begin again and contend with so much loss? Both *Reign Over Me* and *The Rising* refuse "to offer pat answers or convenient closures when none were or are possible"[46] in light of such a calamitous event, instead offering the idea that simplistic human pleasures such as spending time with loved ones or singing along to a favorite song may be the only way to temporarily assuage the profound pain of cultural traumas such as September 11, 2001.

The Wrestler

A New Jersey performer enraptured by the intoxicating allure of a cheering crowd and so consumed by his own stage persona that he is willing to sacrifice both body and soul at the altar of his barnstorming theatrics for his zealous worshipers. This is both Robin Ramzinski (or Randy "The Ram" Robinson) of Darren Aronofsky's *The Wrestler* (2008) and Bruce "The Boss" Springsteen. Performing in the self-reflexive title role, boxer-cum-actor Mickey Rourke hand picked Springsteen to compose the end-credits song for Aronofsky's bleak drama, supplicating him with "a very long, heartfelt letter" and a copy of the script.[1] With its aching vocals and elegiac piano and strings intro, Springsteen's ballad "The Wrestler" soulfully captures the desolate inner life of Rourke's lonely wrestler and Aronofsky's kitchen-sink realist mise-en-scène. Given to Aronofsky for no charge in order to aid his low-budget, no-frills indie, "The Wrestler" went on to win the Golden Globe Award for Best Original Song but was shockingly denied an Academy Award nomination. The music video for the song features Springsteen performing as his own version of Randy inside a threadbare New Jersey gym lined with tattered event posters on the wall; in between shots of him weightlifting in a thin black undershirt and grasping the ropes as if his life depended on it, wrapped in a bulky leather jacket, he stares into the camera in a haunting close-up, entreating the spectator to heed his pained words.

The nostalgic opening montage of *The Wrestler* succinctly journeys through Randy's undoing. Aronofsky's camera glides past a collage of posters, photos, and boisterous news headlines from Randy's illustrious past. He wears a beaming smile and holds trophies after infamous victories against legendary opponents. These images are accompanied by the sounds of the adulating crowd and fervid sports announcers. His defeat of Ayatollah will "forever go down in wrestling history," one proclaims. This is the time Randy fruitlessly longs to return to. Far removed from the hallowed halls of Madison Square Garden, Randy now performs in half-empty gymnasiums for less than two hundred dollars. The diegesis begins with a shot of Randy sitting in the corner of a suburban elementary school, infantilized and humiliated by the children's toys that surround him. Aronofsky's abrupt cut from Randy's glory days to his present lowly state stuns the spectator, and the distant proximity from Randy's hunched figure gives the sense that the camera is too embarrassed to be near him. But Randy withstands these vacant, pathetic spaces—just as a young Springsteen performed in a ShopRite parking lot, mobile-home park, and the Marlboro Psychiatric Hospital—because wrestling, like Springsteen's music, is the only thing he truly loves and gives him the will to live; he will take the chance to perform no matter where it happens to be.

Wrestling is Randy's way of escaping from the dismal realities of his existence—his squalorous mobile home, dull supermarket job, economic disparity, and, most significantly, estrangement from his daughter. The brutal attacks of his opponents serve as punishment for his sins and the mess he has made of his life. Similarly, Springsteen performs exhaustive musical marathons in order to distract himself from his loneliness and depression. In many ways, Springsteen's manic concert performances, legendary in both their excess and their length—his longest being more than four hours—mirror Randy's crazed wrestling acrobatics.[2] The theatrics of both a concert and a wrestling match revolve around a fabled ringmaster to whom fans look to provide a thrilling and transcendental experience. The Ram and the Boss use their whole bodies to provide this for their ardent audiences. There is a religious subtext to Randy's corporeal mea culpa that Aronofsky frequently touches upon which intertextually invokes Springsteen's Catholic musical aesthetic and standing as not merely a rock act but also a religion, one that is glorified by the messianic devotion of his legions of disciples.

The Wrestler inhabits Springsteen's gritty working-class New Jersey milieu, shot on location over the span of forty days throughout the state in Elizabeth, Hasbrouck Heights, Garfield, Linden, Rahway, Roselle Park, Dover, Bayonne, and the pre-revival Asbury Park boardwalk, in spaces such as a two-bit bar, a grimy trailer park, a strip club, a cramped thrift shop, and a fluorescent-washed deli counter. A drab, grey winter sky looms over these post-industrial landscapes, an external signifier of Randy's isolation and despair. Each frame aches with the same blue-collar verisimilitude as Springsteen's music. Aronofsky shot in a proactive documentary style, foregoing storyboards for impromptu moments as they naturally unfolded. This visual realism contrasts with the histrionics of Randy's stage performances and reveals the liminal space between his public persona and his private self, his daily existence and his art, which can also be placed in the context of Springsteen's own star image. Whereas Randy fizzles out after his 1980s prestige, Springsteen transcends his bombastic Rambo-esque persona of the 1984 *Born in the U.S.A.* phenomenon—released the same summer of Randy's most iconic fight, the one his faded stardom is inexplicably tied to—and endures for decades to become one of the most definitive cultural icons of this century.[3] Randy is stuck in the past of his paltry legacy, a mere shadow and parody of his former glorious self, while Springsteen rises to such eminence that he is able to reshape, and even lampoon, his star identity. Springsteen not only creates a stunning portrait of an artist in his affective song "The Wrestler" but also connects to the themes of performance, celebrity, religion, and corporeality found in Aronofsky's film.

Bruises and Broken Bones

With frenzied eyes and fists pumping in the air, Randy's fans gather to witness their idol work his magic on stage: the swift obliteration of his enemies. While there are obvious differences between music and wrestling—one involves the use of words and music to touch a listener's soul and the other a voyeuristic, sadistic wish to watch bodies beaten to bloody pulps—the audience's ecstasy in the wrestling arena is similar to that of a Springsteen concert; however, while Randy's admirers call upon him to shed his blood, Springsteen's fans want to see him bare his soul and feel a little of his human touch. Indeed, there is a sense of personal and physical communion between the Boss and his disciples that the Ram does not experience in his fans' quest for his bodily torment. Springsteen devotees covet the simple graze of a hand during a song, the grope of his muscular body during the "Hungry Heart" crowd surf, or the honor of being chosen to fill Courtney Cox's dancing shoes in "Dancing in the Dark." They have a reciprocal relationship with their rock god's stage performance enacted in various rituals such as finishing off the chorus to "Badlands," responding to the beck and calls of "Out in the Street," and raising their hands in unison to "Tenth Avenue Freeze-Out." Within the concert setting, Springsteen fans are able to fully inhabit the songs that profoundly affect their emotions, speak to their innermost thoughts, and shape their sense of the world. They share a deep-seated kinship with Springsteen and his music that harshly juxtaposes the voyeuristic superficiality of wrestling.

Both Randy and Springsteen provide "pleasure to others through endurance of pain."[4] Springsteen's pain stems from a masochistic obsession to perfect his craft, a "furious fire" within him "that just … don't … quit … burning."[5] This fixation began as a child, when he would practice the guitar for eight to ten hours a day, and continued into his laborious recording processes, recursively going over and over the same song into the early hours of the morning with no food or rest, aiming for his sounds to reach the seraphic perfection heard in his head. One of the most famous incidents is the "Stick!" story from the *Darkness on the Edge of Town* recordings: Springsteen frustratingly intoned "Stick … stick!" at Max Weinberg for nearly a full day, trying to have him mask the sound of the stick hitting the snare drum. But this indomitable compulsion to excel mostly manifests in his live performances. Springsteen is famous for his marathon concert extravaganzas, lasting nearly three or four hours, which are epic displays of fidelity and authenticity that have earned him the reputation of being one of the greatest live performers of all time.

Jay Cocks describes Springsteen's James Brown–esque onstage presence as one with the wild "energy of a pinball rebounding off invisible flippers, coming down the alley past traps and penalties dead center for extra points and the top score."[6] Springsteen has retained this rampant freneticism throughout his entire career—from his emergence as "a glorified gutter rat from a dying New Jersey resort town"[7] to his contemporary standing as the ultimate American father figure. For nearly four hours (without a break!), Springsteen will twist around microphone stands as if they were stripper poles, leap on top of Roy Bittan's piano in a single bound (or play it with his head or feet—anything but his hands), promenade across the stage at superheroic speeds, boogie with his bandmates, tote toddlers for "Waiting on a Sunny Day" sing-alongs, crowd surf his rapturous audience, and even pose mid-song for selfies. Once, during his March 9, 2012, performance at the Apollo Theater, he climbed and performed high up on the rafters.[8] All the while, he shredded his guitar with the unparalleled lightning-quick slickness that garnered his reputation as the "Fastest Guitar in Asbury Park" during the early 1970s. After these wearying shows, Springsteen can be seen slumped on a chair and dousing himself with ice water to cool off. He performs with such rigorous mania so that his audience can partake in "an extreme experience" that leaves them exiting the arena "with your hands hurting, your feet hurting, your back hurting, your voice sore, and your sexual organs stimulated!"[9] Springsteen wants his audience to physically feel the same euphoric bliss that he does.

Springsteen's setlists are sonic odysseys that probe every gamut of the emotional kaleidoscope, from galvanic power anthems to the gut-wrenching grief of tenebrific ballads. He bares his soul in lengthy personal monologues that are either startlingly candid or delightfully corny. Springsteen's vulnerable sincerity nurtures a deeply authentic interpersonal relationship with his fans that defies the inscrutability of other rock stars. His concerts with the E Street Band are qualified by an effusion of joy that he believes "makes us somewhat unique. Rock bands try to project a lot of different things: intensity, mystery, sexuality, cool. Not a lot of rock bands concentrate on joy, and I got that from my relatives on the Italian side."[10] At the core of his performances lies his incandescent dedication to and profound bond with his fans. He continues, "I come out on stage to deliver to you the greatest band in the world. I still have great pride in what I do. I still believe in its power. I believe in my ability to transfer its power to you."[11] Springsteen pours his entire body, heart, and soul into making each performance the absolute greatest it can be because "you only have one chance. Some guy bought his ticket, and there's a promise made between musician and audience…. It's at the heart of everything."[12]

Springsteen modeled his stage theatrics and persona on the hard-working blue-collar ethos of his father, envisioning himself as a repairman of souls and his artistic craft as his own form of manual labor. "So I, who'd never done a week's worth of manual labor in my life (hail, hail rock 'n' roll!), put on a factory worker's clothes, my father's clothes, and went to work," Springsteen writes in his memoir, envisioning his onstage self as a manifestation of his father's working-class brawn.[13] He and the E Street Band's "shared history of scuffling around the bars of the Jersey Shore created a mythology built on a blue-collar, lunch-bucket ethic" that was connected to Douglas Springsteen's unflagging virility.[14] Springsteen's enthusiastic performances with the E Street Band "can be read as celebrations and validations of heavy, physical unambiguously 'masculine' work" like that of his father.[15] The exhausting intensity with which they play also "has its counterpart in the heavy physical work that the songs' characters perform."[16]

The Wrestler "celebrates a character whose defining trait is his masochism—his ability to endure, and even take pleasure in, absurd amounts of physical pain."[17] Aronofsky enables the spectator to inhabit Randy's suffering by placing the camera disturbingly close to his wounded flesh: the sharp objects that penetrate his skin—the twangs of a fork in his forehead, the staples gunned into his chest, the barbed wire that punctures his side—as well as their removal and the blood that oozes forth. This bleeding "functions as proof that he is still tough, that he can still absorb pain and exceed his physical limits."[18] Randy revels in the savage acts his fans beckon him to perform. He craves their smiles "when the blood, it hits the floor" (as Springsteen sings), the only semblance of affection Randy receives from any singular person in his life. "Can you ask for anything more?" Springsteen-as-Randy ponders. With no family, friends, or home to call his own, there is nothing more for Randy than the hyperviolent world of wrestling. Thus Randy will gladly suffer for that elusive, intoxicating rush of glorification that Randy never receives in daily life. Springsteen can relate to Randy's deep infatuation with performing on stage and fan adoration, telling Jay Cocks in the legendary "Rock's New Sensation" *Time* 1975 cover story, "It's the stage thing, that rush and moment that you live for. It never lasts, but that's what you live for."[19] Springsteen also pushes his body to its physical limits in order to please his fans and achieve that elusive rush, but not to such a violent degree. Unlike Randy, Springsteen eventually learned that there is more to life than his art that makes it worth living.

It is nearly impossible to select a singular example from Springsteen's decades of performing that best demonstrates the feverish glory of his concerts, nor is it easy to put the empyrean experience into words, but the encore in 1979's *No Nukes: The Muse Concerts for a Non-Nuclear Future* comes to mind. His performance of Gary U.S. Bonds' "Quarter to Three" is infused with the infectious, demonic joy that he is known for. Springsteen frantically bops to the bubblegum beat, his shoulders moving up and down at a jackrabbit pace before slamming his guitar at his side to every smack of Weinberg's drums. With his shirt unbuttoned and sweaty chest on display, Springsteen commands the band with a virtuoso finesse—every arm movement and hip thrust perfectly in sync with Weinberg's supersonic drumming. "That's all I can stand! I can't stand no more!" he shouts into the microphone before feigning a near heart attack and collapsing onto the floor.[20] In other concerts, crew members costumed as doctors whisk Springsteen away on a stretcher. Garry Tallent and Clarence Clemons then assist him back on his feet. "I'm thirty years old, my heart's starting to go on me!" an exasperated Springsteen spits out. After imploring the audience to beg him for more, he immediately launches into his blistering repeat of the raucous chorus. For the song's finale, he climbs to the top of the riser and plays behind the drums for the back of the audience, circles around and flails center stage, and then tinkles Roy Bittan's piano with his foot. "Quarter to Three" culminates with his triumphant scream into the microphone: "I'm just a prisoner of rock and roll!" Springsteen's imprisonment is both a blessing and a curse: his devout obsession with rock and roll may have made him one of the greatest showmen in history, but it came at the price of loneliness; akin to Randy, Springsteen's consumption of his craft caused him to neglect his personal relationships.

During the 1980s, Springsteen's wiry body popped to sinewy life, catapulting his proletariat characters to superheroic proportions. His rippling biceps of the *Born in the U.S.A.* era did not quite reach the Ram's size, but they were nonetheless impressive. Springsteen explains that this was his way of continuing to sculpt himself in his father's image: "My father was built big, so there was some element of 'O.K., I'm 34. I'm a man now.' I remember my father at that age. There was the idea of creating a man's body to a certain degree. I suppose I was measuring that after my dad. And also, perhaps, in some way, trying to please him."[21] Like Randy, Springsteen enjoyed the mind-numbing repetitiveness of exercise: "It was perfectly Sisyphean for my personality—lifting something heavy up and putting it down in the same spot for no particularly good reason. I've always felt a lot in common with Sisyphus. I'm always rolling that rock, man."[22] Springsteen's reference to the Greek figure of Sisyphus, doomed to the monotony of physical labor for all eternity, is an apt analogy for both his and Randy's internal conflict. The wrestler and musician use their art forms to masochistically burn themselves out and keep the dismal reality of life at bay. In a profile for the *New Yorker*, Springsteen confessed that he once used life on the road and his four-hour concerts as a drug to relieve the "pure fear and self-loathing and self-hatred" that roiled inside him.[23] "For years, music and travel have been my faithful companions and surefire medication. As Sisyphus can count on the rock, *I* can always count on the road, the music and the miles for whatever ails me," Springsteen writes in his autobiography.[24]

His father's verbal abuse and terrifying schizophrenic episodes that resulted in volcanic rages, as well as his grandmother's "emotionally incestuous" infatuation with him during childhood,[25] caused Springsteen to avoid emotional intimacy, "the normal messiness of living and loving," as an adult in his personal and romantic relationships.[26] Feeling distanciated from the world at large—always on the "outside looking in," as he sings—Springsteen would pour himself into his work, whether it was creating music in the studio or playing it on stage. Life on the stage liberated Springsteen from his disquietude, providing him with a sense of positive self-image and control away from the storm of his chaotic upbringing and destructive impulses. In this way, Springsteen related to Randy's crippling isolation and self-abnegation relieved by the warm glow of the spotlight.

Springsteen told David Remnick that his barnstorming concerts allow him to abandon his self and forget his crippling isolation and self-loathing: "You are free of yourself for those hours; all the voices in your head are *gone*. Just *gone*. There's no room for them. There's one voice, the voice you're speaking in."[27] Wrestling literalizes the artists' obsession with self-obliteration. Every punch and stab Randy endures serves as punishment for his sins, dulling his senses so that he can forget his heartache. Randy has absolutely no one in his life, save for Cassidy, a stripper from his favorite dive bar whom he occasionally purchases lap dances from. He yields to the truculent whims of strangers because they are the only ones who "love" him. The abandonment of the self on stage is Randy's only salvation. Springsteen and Randy earn their audiences' adulation with their blood, sweat, and tears, substituting it for their lack of stability and emotional connection to others in their daily lives.

The Wrestler also functions as a social critique "of the contemporary fascination with public appearance, the role of the body as a predominant marker of our identity, and the consequences of bodily decay affecting the psyche."[28] Randy's profession "contradicts the natural aging process, leading to a twisted reality and Randy's inability to cope with it,"[29] which Springsteen brilliantly expresses in the wrestler's comparison of himself to abject, broken bodies and objects such as a one-legged dog, an empty scarecrow, and a one-armed man. It is the weathering of his body, the slow degradation of his once herculean glory, that so bitterly separates Randy from the rest of society and plunges him into a deep depression. Like the one-legged man who tries in vain "to dance his way free," Randy mocks himself in his attempt to hustle an unstoppable force. A sad scarecrow filled with tatters of dust and wheat, there is an emptiness inside of Randy after he acknowledges that his race against time is fatuous. Randy spends the majority of the film attempting to revive his youth by dying his hair and tanning. Since his body is no longer young, strong, and healthy, he must consume painkillers, steroids, and other drugs in order to maintain it. The combination of these pharmaceuticals and the physical aggravation of his vocation causes his heart attack midway through the film. Yet Randy presses on, continuing to wrestle because he cannot resign himself to the idea that his body, his only means of work and self-satisfaction, is failing him. By the film's end, Randy has pushed himself into literal obliteration.

At seventy, Springsteen is no stranger to these ideas. During the *High Hopes* tour and afterward, he could no longer do backbends or knee slides or climb onto the piano. That same year, he had surgery for damaged discs in his neck, which prevented him from being able to play his guitar properly, a procedure that also involved rearranging his vocal chords. However, it was Clarence Clemons who most keenly felt the ramifications of the earth-shattering concerts on his body, requiring hip and knee replacements and back surgery. During the *Wrecking Ball* tour, he was driven around arena tunnels in golf carts and sat on a stool when not playing his saxophone solos. In David Remnick's *New Yorker* piece "We Are Alive," Clemons said, "I deserve a God-damned Academy Award," adding that "he felt like Mickey Rourke's character in *The Wrestler*," in the sense that "he was portraying a powerful figure onstage even as he was falling apart physically."[30] Springsteen continues this correlation of Clemons to *The Wrestler* in his autobiography, declaring that "if it'd been up to him [Clemons], he would have died there [on stage]."[31]

Fortunately, Springsteen does not suffer from Randy's delusions about his age and body entropy, recognizing that the stage can lure one into thinking he or she is immortal: "Playing a show brings a tremendous amount of euphoria … and the danger of it is, there's always that moment, comes every night, where you think, 'Hey, man, I'm gonna live forever!' You're feeling all your power. And then you come offstage, and the main thing you realize is 'Well, *that's* over.' Mortality sets back in."[32] This sense of loss found within the on/offstage dichotomy permeates Springsteen's song. With "The Wrestler," Springsteen was able to translate his own experiences and ideas about being a performer (particularly the juxtapositions between rapture and despair) and the toll it takes on one's physical and mental psyche. The final frame confines Randy within such a euphoric moment, his infamous "Ram Jam" move, for all eternity so that he may never confront his mortality again.

The Empty Funhouse

After Randy suffers his heart attack, he decides to retire from wrestling and assimilate into civilian life by obtaining steady employment at an Acme deli counter. But can he endure the dismal realities of his blue-collar job and an existence outside the rapturous fantasy of the wrestling world? Aronofsky portrays this transition with a behind-the-shoulder shot of Randy walking toward the back kitchen surrounded by the sounds of non-diegetic cheering, which abruptly halts when he enters the plastic-curtained door, signifying his emergence onto a different kind of stage and his subsumption into the dull role of counter clerk. Since he can no longer wrestle and is forced to take this prosaic job, Randy mourns the treasured sound of applause that he will never hear again. The only way Randy is able to cope with the grocery store grind is through a performance of a different sort: he flirts with customers and tosses meats like footballs as if he were the supermarket's court jester.

Randy uses his newfound freedom to kindle his relationship with Cassidy, the only stable presence in his life. She encourages Randy to reunite with his estranged daughter Stephanie, whom he abandoned as a child because the role of father was incompatible with his transient wrestling career. Although Springsteen's exhilarating life on the road allowed him to suppress his loneliness, he secretly longed for the stability that a nuclear family and home would provide, which he eventually obtained with his wife Patti Scialfa and their children, Evan, Jessica, and Sam, after working hard in therapy. In this way, Springsteen became what Randy Robinson could have been, or wishes he could be: both legend and patriarch.

On the advice of Cassidy, Randy visits Stephanie bearing gifts. Although Stephanie is still angry over her father's longtime absence, he eventually convinces her to visit "our old favorite place," which Stephanie, having not seen her father since she was a child, does not remember. It turns out to be the Asbury Park boardwalk, a famed Springsteen site.[33] Like their relationship, it is broken seemingly beyond repair and haunted by the echoes of a sunny past; gone are the roar of carnival rides and children's laughter as they frolicked along the beach. Walking along the rotted planks of the abandoned boardwalk, Randy wistfully recalls how Stephanie loved the funhouse and the Monster Motel inside the Palace Amusements building, with the "spooky-ass skeleton" that would "pop out of a coffin." "You'd get really scared and cry and wanna run out. And then you'd beg to go back in again … you wouldn't go in unless you could sit on my foot and wrap your arms around my leg. And we'd walk all the way through like that," Randy reminisces. Stephanie chides that she "always was a glutton for punishment," an ironic suggestion that she has inherited her father's flagellatory obsession. Stephanie's beloved funhouse has since been demolished—just like her love and childhood adoration of Randy. Once he was her protector, but he wounded her, and now she regards him with a venomous disdain.

The father and daughter make their way through the gusty winter haze toward Convention Hall, a significant Springsteen locale, where he often held concerts and rehearsals inside the Paramount Theatre. As they sit on a concrete edifice overlooking the squally ocean waves, Randy apologizes to Stephanie: "I'm the one who was supposed to take care of everything. I'm the one who was supposed to make everything okay for everybody. But it just didn't work out like that. And I left. I left you." With a lonely tear rolling down his cheek, Mickey Rourke masterfully conveys Randy's profound remorse during this heart-rending monologue. Randy also reveals that he tried to pretend that his daughter did not exist so that he could fully immerse himself in the hedonistic and violent labyrinth of his celebrity. He could not stay in the place that should have been his home, with his daughter

An empty, off-season Asbury Park serves as the backdrop for Randy (Mickey Rourke) and Stephanie's (Evan Rachel Wood) long-awaited but short-lived reunion (www.moviestillsdb.com).

and her mother, because he was drawn to the allure of the ring, as Springsteen sings in his tenebrous tone poem.

Springsteen's mournful "The Wrestler" bespeaks Randy's inner thoughts as a man forgotten by his family and the world due to his inability to stand the things that nurtured him and gave him a life. With a worn, gravelly voice, Springsteen embodies Randy's damaged soul and self-destructive regret after driving away the comfort of his loved ones. Springsteen sees Randy as a character who found his identity in the damage that had been done to him and used the bodily torment of wrestling as punishment for repudiating his family. "You find your identity in your wounds, places where you've been beat up, and you turn them into a medal. And it's a very dangerous thing to do," Springsteen said in a behind-the-scenes feature on the "Wrestler" music video.[34] "We all wear the things we've survived with some honor. But the honor is in … also transcending them. So this is somebody in search of that honor. He's living in search of that honor," Springsteen elaborated on his interpretation of the song and Rourke's character.[35] By the film's end, it becomes clear that Randy's quest for such honor is fruitless, as he fails to reunite with his daughter, be with Cassidy, or live a normal life; he finally escapes the pain by stepping into the warm embrace of the spotlight for all eternity.

For Randy, the wrestling ring is an easily definable and controllable space; agreements are made regarding who will win or lose, and the roles of good and evil, hero and villain, are clearly demarcated. Randy governs the reactions of his audience through the moves he selects and the amount of pain he withstands. His corporeal torture has the dual function of pleasing his fans and allowing him to atone for his sins. Randy cannot place his faith in the unpredictable changes of the real world, the messy emotions of those he continually disappoints. The "broken bones and bruises" he displays are the only aspects of his life he can depend on. While visiting Asbury Park with Stephanie, Randy admits that he is just "an old, broken-down piece of meat," comparing himself to an abject object, just as in Springsteen's song. "And I'm alone. And I deserve to be all alone. I just don't want you to hate me," he implores his daughter. This is as close as Randy gets to divulging his inner feelings; for that, we have Springsteen's end-credits ballad to serve as his final monologue.

Randy and Stephanie make their final stop at the deserted Casino that exudes an old-fashioned carnival charm that contrasts with the rough post-industrial scenery in the rest of the film. Springsteen shot several music videos in this space, including "Tunnel of Love," which alludes to the dark funhouse rides that Stephanie loved. Despite the graffiti on the walls and the littered ground, the intricate windows, soft serene lighting, spaciousness of the frame, and nostalgic score craft a bittersweet mise-en-scène. The pair dance around the Casino while the camera dizzily circles around them. This beautiful moment is the only time Randy feels true happiness in the film. With their dance, Randy engages in a tender physical exchange that opposes the brutalizing pain of his profession and the soulless sexual gratification of one-night stands he frequently participates in.

Yet the overall frigid setting of Asbury Park and its derelict boardwalk seems to anticipate how Stephanie will forever freeze her father out after he betrays her. The heyday of Asbury Park has vanished, along with their second chance to be a family. Shortly after their reunion, Randy succumbs to his usual vices of drugs, drinking, and sex. Following a cocaine-fueled one-night stand that has him roleplaying as a fireman—another indication that Randy must always be performing a role and can never be his true self—he forgets to meet Stephanie for dinner, solidifying her view of him as a failure and perpetually absent father, thus rendering their movement toward reconciliation completely undone. He successfully drives away the things that have comforted him, as Springsteen sings. Randy's blossoming romantic relationship with Cassidy also dissipates when she begins to fear the ramifications of dating one of her clients and starts turning Randy away from the club. Without the promise of these relationships, Randy sees no more reason to forsake his one true love—namely, wrestling; it is the only thing he truly has left to live (and die) for. This idea becomes clear when a deli counter customer recognizes him as "the wrestler from the 80s ... except older." After this excruciating exchange, Randy "has had it with his emasculating job and decides that he would rather die on his feet in the ring than live on his knees in the supermarket."[36] He quits in grand theatrical fashion by launching his hand into the deli slicer, running through the aisles, and smashing the cereal boxes smeared with blood on the floor. Randy may be nothing more than the ghost of his former 1980s alter ego "The Ram," or a "one-trick pony," but the sport is all he has left in his life. He happily returns to the hermetic make-believe world of wrestling to bask in the awe of strangers.

Randy's brief reconciliation with his daughter recalls Springsteen's evocative ballad "The Hitter" from *Devils & Dust*. The song is about a former boxer who returns to his estranged mother's home to rest his worn-out body before heading off in search of another fight. The hitter shares the wrestler's inborn hunger for violence, which trumps all other familial or personal relationships, acknowledging that "the fight was my home and blood was my trade." During his match against the reigning champion Jack Thompson, the boxer's bloodlust possesses him and he pounds his opponent's "bloody body into the floor" long after the bell rings, the frantic fury of his punches loosening the leather of his glove until there is nothing but flesh hitting hard bone. "The Hitter" can be read as an early incarnation of "The Wrestler," as both characters feel more at home wandering to different fighting rings across the country and have addictions to physical torment that ravage their bodies and alienate them from their loved ones.

"This is where I belong"

Randy relives his triumphant past in a rematch against Ayatollah, his legendary opponent of the 1980s. Cassidy, who has unknowingly followed Randy to Wilmington, attempts to stop him backstage with the promise that they can pursue a romantic relationship. She worriedly reminds him of his defective heart, but it matters little to Randy, who has become all too aware of the incongruity between his on- and offstage life: "The only place I get hurt is out there. The world don't give a shit about me." The only pain Randy can withstand is physical, not emotional. So he enters the arena, abandoning Cassidy in the dressing room for the welcoming and familiar embrace of the dazzling strobe lights and fans' raucous chants of "U.S.A.! U.S.A.!" A vivid American flag is draped behind him. This Americana iconography evokes Springsteen's *Born in the U.S.A.* era and overall star image as the country's working-class hero. The announcer introduces Randy as "a true American … the people's hero," aligning him with a similar star image to Springsteen. The long hair, heavy makeup, and flamboyant neon spandex that Randy wears for wrestling parallels the homoerotic camp aesthetic of Springsteen's stage costume during the mid–1980s: the leather vests, comfortable worn-in jeans, and *Deer Hunter*–esque bandana, his own version of a mechanic's cloth. Springsteen wrote of this aesthetic in his autobiography: "Looking back on these photos now, I look simply … gay. I probably would have fit right in down on Christopher Street in any one of the leather bars."[37] The ordinariness of Springsteen's typical jeans and T-shirt stage wardrobe mobilizes his authentic, all-American, "one of us" persona, humbling him from his rock star affluence.

Once on stage, Randy borrows the referee's microphone and launches into an emotional monologue that reframes his life story as triumphant: despite his loss of hearing, his mangled face ("I ain't as pretty as I used to be," he says[38]), and being told he would never wrestle again, he has risen like a phoenix from the ashes to perform for his brethren. "I'm the Ram," he declares, renouncing his mortal self for his godly alter ego. Rejecting the cruel outside world that regards him as nothing but a washed-up loser, he basks in the praise and applause of his fans. "You people here are the ones who are worth bringing it for, because you're my family," Randy tearfully admits. He spurns Stephanie, his own flesh and blood, for the affection of strangers. Stephanie and Cassidy's removal from Randy's life situates his fans as the only ones who can provide him with a sense of self-worth.

During the fight, Randy begins to hear the high-pitched, whiny buzzing that signifies his palpitating heart. Although he severely wobbles and Ayatollah tries to get him to end the match, Randy heeds the audience's call to conduct his infamous "Ram Jam" maneuver—the zenith of his routines, the moment that everyone is waiting for. Randy's greatest trick requires him to stand on the ring's top rope and leap onto his opponent. Aronofsky first frames Randy's stance in a gorgeous wide shot, taking in the joyous crowd, old-fashioned beauty of the theater, and stage lights' shine before cutting to closer shots of Randy's front, then his bulging back, as he raises his arms in a Christological stance, ready to offer his body on the altar of his art and transcend earthly life in the glory of one last spectacular performance.[39] Springsteen also assumes this crucifixion pose during his concerts, as seen in the *Live in New York City* film or "Leap of Faith" music video.

Aronofsky imbues *The Wrestler* with a religious intertext that aligns with Springsteen's Catholic musical aesthetic. Randy's nickname "The Ram" refers to the biblical story of Abraham, who sacrificed a ram instead of his son Isaac as God commanded. Randy submits to his fate as the sacrificial ram through the final act of his famed "Ram Jam." In an earlier scene, Randy flouts his scars and permanent wounds to Cassidy: "Well, it hurts when I breathe, but you hear the roar of the crowd, you just motor through, you know?" For Randy, the adoration of strangers outweighs the pain of his wounds. His scars remind Cassidy of Mel Gibson's torture porn *The Passion of the Christ* (2004). She repeats a Bible verse from the film—"He was pierced for our transgressions. He was crushed for our iniquities. The punishment that brought us peace was upon him and by his wounds we were healed"—and recalls with wide-eyed wonder that the Romans threw "everything at him, whips, arrows, rocks. They beat the living fuck out of him the whole two hours, and he just takes it." Randy admires this strength and murmurs, "Tough guy." Here the spectator is meant to connect Randy's bodily torment during wrestling matches—when he is beaten with staples, ladders, glass, barbed wire, and more—to that of Jesus Christ's passion. Both Randy and Jesus endure intense physical pain before they sacrifice their lives for their worshipers.

The Catholic church service is another form of theater that is fundamentally no different from that of a wrestling match or a Springsteen concert. The physical configuration of a church parallels the traditional drama stage: the pews are the space for the audience, facing the altar/stage, where costumed figures perform carefully scripted words buttressed by poetry, music, and physical actions. Audience participation in the ritualized drama and song leads to catharsis—a purging of spiritual, physical, and psychic ills that burden them as human beings. In the same vein, wrestling is a mode of entertainment that absolves spectators' troubles within its good versus evil narrative. Fans delight when they see a villain suffer and a hero triumph; in turn, they forget their own troubles and are relieved from the mundanity of daily life. Concertgoers are likewise acutely affected by Springsteen's ability to vocalize their innermost feelings and troubles through his lyrics. His songs touch the inner recesses of their souls, healing their loneliness and disconnection from humanity in a beatific communal experience.

Springsteen discussed the reciprocal relationship between church and theater on his *Late Show with Stephen Colbert* appearance in 2017. Colbert suggested that Springsteen's short-lived tenure as an altar boy could be considered his first stage experience. The talk show host proposed that Springsteen's cathartic musical experiences are a form of transubstantiation in which "you and the audience become another thing."[40] In the Catholic sense, transubstantiation is the consecration of the bread and wine into the body and blood of Christ; for Springsteen, this concept means that he is capable of connecting men and women to something beyond the mortal coil through the sheer power of his music. "That's a little bit of what my job is every night. My job is to come out there and assist you and for us together to create this sense of whatever you want to call it; it is cathartic, and hopefully on a good night when we're at our very, very best there's a little transcendence," he told Colbert.[41] Springsteen's concerts are often described by fans as "religious experiences," or, as David Garrett Izzo states, "not just a bunch of songs but a transcendental celebration of mystical significance that unifies the stage and the audience."[42] Springsteen believes there is something spiritual in the communion of thousands through the mesmeric enchantment of music. There is an imperceptible mystical quality to the art of music and its ability to emotionally influence audiences. Springsteen mobilizes the religious intertext of his concerts during the Reunion Tour, in which he inhabits the persona of a preacher ready to baptize his followers in the holy waters of rock and roll. Both Springsteen and Randy regard their artistic talents with a monk-like sanctity, viewing it as their vocation rather than a mere profession, and they commit to delivering their audiences absolute perfection.

Springsteen's extraordinary ability not to turn water into wine but to turn everyday experiences into the sublime has caused him to be "adored and venerated beyond rock star status, as would be spiritual master, a pop philosopher, a revolutionary, a head of state, or a saint."[43] Although Springsteen is quick to point out his frailties and is no stranger to scandal (most notably his affair with Scialfa and divorce of his first wife, Julianne Phillips), many fans have made him their flawless hero and role model because he champions the underdog, supports and promotes charities for the disenfranchised, and performs the miracle of transforming—or even saving—their lives through his music. Springsteen bristles at this idea of his supposed perfection, this image of him as "Saint Boss," during his introduction to "Brilliant Disguise," a song about the dissonance between one's public and private selves, during his *VH1 Storytellers* performance. He recalls one time outside a strip club when an angry fan confronted him in the parking lot—"Bruce, you aren't supposed to be here!"—and he mystically replied, "I'm not. I am simply an errant figment of one of Bruce's many selves. I drift in the ether over the highways and byways of the Garden State, often touching down in image-incongruous but fun places. Bruce does not even know I am missing. He is at home right now, doing good deeds!"

"Local Hero" from *Lucky Town* examines the tension between Springsteen's superheroic, do-gooder stage self and the man he sees in the bathroom mirror every morning.[44] He relates to the local hero's "dilemma of never being able to live up to his heroic reputation and, ironically, being resented by many people because of his status."[45] The local hero's adulators sanctify him as king and then pope before hanging him, a reference to the societal infatuation with toppling stars after they're made. Randy experiences this process firsthand after his glory days in the 1980s abruptly end and he is left penniless, virtually homeless, and forgotten. Randy would love to be seen as a local hero instead of the local trailer park's sad old man who entertains the neighborhood kids with dated, pixelated video games based on his reign as the Ram.

Springsteen on Broadway demythologizes Bruce Springsteen as he is known to his fans and popular culture. Immediately in the self-deprecating opening monologue, he caustically reminds his audience that he "comes from a boardwalk town tinged with fraud" and is merely a charlatan who performs a magic trick: he has never worked an honest job in his life—"Standing before you is a man who has become wildly and absurdly successful writing about something of which he has had absolutely no personal experience," he says—and despite writing odes about racing in the streets and fleeing New Jersey, he never learned to drive until he was in his twenties and currently lives ten minutes from his hometown. He simply made it all up. That's how good he is. The voice he has sung in for nearly five decades is not his own but that of his disconsolate factory worker father. Springsteen performs these monologues with a sardonic irony and mordant wit that gleefully cuts through his legendary persona. Yet no admission of deceit can abjure the truth of Springsteen's magic: his extraordinary ability to transform his homespun experiences into beautiful music that touches people's hearts and souls.

Springsteen fans often approach their idol from the perspective of first-person authenticity "where Springsteen-the-performer is understood as identical to, or collapsed onto, our best sense of Springsteen-the-person."[46] Just as he responded to the enthusiastic admirer who shouted, "I love you," during the 1990 Christic performance by saying, "But you don't really know me," or replied with a curt, deadpan, "No," to the *VH1 Storytellers* audience member who asked, "I feel like I know you. Do I?" we get the sense from *Springsteen on Broadway* and his well-crafted *Born to Run* that there is a gap between his star image and the man behind the curtain. Springsteen often speaks of his vigorous and formidable onstage self in the third person within the dichotomies of "the guy with the guitar" and "the guy without the guitar."[47] He told Terry Gross that "people see you on stage and [think] yeah, I'd want to be that guy. I want to be that guy myself very often … there's a big difference between what you see on stage and then my general daily … existence."[48] In other words, "The Boss" is Bruce Springsteen's idealized self just as Randy "The Ram" is Robin Ramzinski's—the person he wants to live (and die) as. For both of them, the man on stage is a flawless abstraction, one built on crowd-pleasing myths.

Randy and Springsteen's triumphant stage personas offer them respite from their quotidian existence and psychological problems. However, Springsteen maintains a healthy balance between his two identities, whereas Randy would do anything to inhabit his former celebrity image. During the 1990s, Springsteen had spent more than a decade in therapy and began to understand that he could no longer play with such intense ferocity in order to burn himself out and shut himself away from the rest of the world. "Now I see that two of the best days of my life were the day I picked up the guitar and the day I learned how to put it down," he told *Rolling Stone*.[49] Although he still uses his concerts to relieve his depression, it is no longer with the same self-destructive urgency as when he was young. Randy, however, refuses to leave the ring or hang up his tights—to the point of suicide.

Springsteen's unreleased outtake "Jesse" contemplates the polarities of on- and offstage life using religious motifs. The title character is a bandleader who dazzles the crowd, donning crosses around his neck and sporting nails in his hands—living up to his Jesus-esque name. The "old soul feeling" of his "old Chicago blues" and his willingness to reveal his insides deliver audiences from their daily troubles and raise them to a state of joyous ecstasy. Like Randy, Jesse is enraptured by the narcotic rush of performing and disdains the mundane nature of his domestic responsibilities. The dual roles of rocker and patriarch crucify Jesse as he strives to please both his musical and his suburban families. He soon discovers that his treasured life on the road is not compatible with providing for his slobbering baby and miserable wife. Under the spotlight, Jesse and Randy transform into revered Christ-like figures; they bask in a "self-adoring haze" of fan adulation that extinguishes as soon as they step off the stage into the real world.

In the final scene of *The Wrestler*, Randy dives off the ropes, catapulting his body out of the frame and off screen into his nirvana. Aronofsky hovers on the empty ropes and the raucous cheers before abruptly cutting to black. The sound of applause that continues over the darkness immortalizes Randy within his sacred performance space, his one true home, as not Robin but "The Ram"—the person he always wanted to be. The audience's roar softly fades out into Springsteen's song and overlays a pitch-black screen for a few beats, a conscious directorial choice that enables the non-diegetic spectator to reflect on Randy's fate and Springsteen's poignant memorial for him. Through the voice of Springsteen and use of first-person narration, Randy is able to leave his final words to the spectator. He eulogizes himself as someone who is broken beyond repair and continually forsaken by the world, a hollow figure who always leaves with less than he had before. The various doors he stands before are representative of his interminable quest for human connection. In Aronofsky's refusal to show the aftermath of Randy's leap to his death, Randy becomes the "true wrestling immortal" that he was purported to be in the film's opening flashback montage. Springsteen's "The Wrestler" ensures that Randy's story will live on in every person who is beaten down and broken but struggles to rise above the turmoil.

Magic Trick

"DNA, natural ability, study of craft, development of and devotion to an aesthetic philosophy, naked desire for … fame? … love? … admiration? … attention? … women? … sex? … and oh, yeah … a buck," Springsteen opens both his autobiography and his Broadway show.[50] These are the things that draw him and other performers such as Randy Robinson to that ever elusive stage. In his soul-stirring end credits ballad, Springsteen incorporates his identification with Randy's complex relationship to stardom. Although their careers are markedly different—Randy lives in the shadow of his former 1980s self, while Springsteen endures as one of the greatest artists of our time—both share a dedication to their heavily physical crafts.

However, Randy cannot let go of this obsession. Because his offstage life is so fraught with pain and isolation, Randy lives for nothing but the moment that Springsteen describes in his autobiography: when you emerge on stage and "come face-to-face with eighty thousand (or eighty) screaming rock 'n' roll fans who are waiting for you to do your magic trick. Waiting for you to pull something out of your hat, out of thin air, out of this world, something that before the faithful were gathered here today was just a song-fueled rumor."[51] Springsteen elaborates on the meaning of his magic trick to Stephen Colbert: "You're there to manifest something. Before you go in there it's an empty space, an empty building. The audience is going to come, you're going to show up, and together you're going to manifest something that's very, very real, that's very tangible, but you're going to pull it out of thin air. It wasn't there before you showed up. It didn't exist. It's real magic."[52] Randy would rather remain in this exalted fantasy world than endure his dour, solitary existence. The magic he creates onstage through his physical sacrifice is far more tangible and authentic than his prosaic life of wandering the streets of northern New Jersey like a ghost with little to no genuine human contact. Therefore, Randy decides to go out in a blaze of glory by having his final moment on earth be his greatest magic trick. It is bittersweet poetic justice that he ends his life and career by defeating his greatest opponent with his most famous move.

The Wrestler is a devastatingly raw tour de force. Aside from Springsteen's blue-collar, Catholic New Jersey aesthetic, he was the perfect choice to craft a song for this haunting film because he understands the emotional and psychological complexities of being a performer. It is Springsteen's emotional identification with Randy—the tension between his disparate on- and offstage lives, his obsessive devotion to his art—that makes his end-credits song "The Wrestler" so powerful. Aronofsky crafts a heart-wrenching portrait of a beleaguered "one-trick pony" eclipsed by the shadow of his fame. If only the Ram could have balanced the roles of superstar and mortal as well as the Boss.

Show Me a Hero

The six-part HBO miniseries *Show Me a Hero* (2015), based on Lisa Belkin's nonfiction book of the same name, explores a civil rights mandate to build two hundred scattered units of low-income housing in predominantly white neighborhoods that tears apart the municipal government and city of Yonkers, New York, during the 1980s. At the heart of this acrimonious battle lies Nick Wasicsko, a young and highly ambitious politician who tries to face the ignorant bigotry of his constituents with grace, but the cutthroat Yonkers political world threatens his belief in justice and pushes him to an emotional nadir from which there is no recovery. Creator and writer David Simon, director Paul Haggis, and co-writer William Zorzi wanted to find a musical identity for Nick, a soundtrack to "function as a kind of emotional shorthand … [and to] speak when people are too busy to really talk."[1] During post-production they had already decided to include Springsteen in the introductory and final montages, but after toying with other musical artists, HBO executive Kary Antholis suggested they use Bruce Springsteen as the miniseries' defining sonic throughline. "We went back and in talking to David he said yes, let's make this his music. We just made him a Springsteen guy. It really, suddenly, brought the whole piece to life," Paul Haggis told *IndieWire*.[2] Indeed, it is difficult to imagine *Show Me a Hero* without Springsteen's twelve songs.

According to Nick Wasicsko's wife Nay, her husband was a big classic rock fan who liked and frequently listened to Springsteen, especially his *Born in the U.S.A.* hits such as "Dancing in the Dark" and "Glory Days," which they would listen to on the radio or from her own personal mixtapes.[3] Nay had suggested some of Nick's other favorite musicians, such as Led Zeppelin, the Doors, and Aerosmith, for the soundtrack, but the showrunners insisted on Springsteen, who Nay understood would "make more of a connection to understand who Nick really was."[4] Appearing as both non-diegetic score and diegetic source music, Springsteen situates the series' late 1980s and early 1990s milieu, embodies former cop and Carvel factory worker Nick's all-American blue-collar northeastern masculinity, and structures his lapsarian narrative. His songs articulate Nick's interiority and incite spectatorial emotional affinity for his character. Additionally, Springsteen's extratextual canonical concerns with race, community, and American democracy align with the liberal heart and spirit of *Show Me a Hero*.

Everybody Wants a Home

Show Me a Hero opens with Springsteen's "Gave It a Name," an atmospheric outtake from *Human Touch* included on the *Tracks* album. By juxtaposing images of placid suburbia with the grimy projects, the opening montage demarcates the borders between two (seemingly) disparate milieus. We see a young black man walking home to the towering projects while sirens wail, a stately Tudor-style residence, a moth-eaten and mutilated couch abandoned in front of a high-rise, kitschy lawn decorations, and two black boys playing outside their decrepit graffiti-ridden apartment, immediately followed by a shot of a young white boy riding his Big Wheel down the sidewalk of a quiet middle-class neighborhood. The melancholic pulse of Springsteen's guitar strums complements the grey New York City skyline that housing consultant Oscar Newman surveys via helicopter. The montage ends with aerial shots of these homologous homes, the black and white residencies austerely segregated by the Saw Mill River Parkway.

Springsteen's saturnine lyrics connect the original sin of Cain and Abel to a modern scene of domestic violence to suggest that humanity has never escaped the poison and shame of its darker impulses, alluding to the housing protesters' racism passed down from generation to generation. David Simon observes that Nick's bid to appeal the housing is his own "original sin," which he spends the rest of his career atoning for.[5] "Gave it a Name," with its sharp guitars and moody keyboards, sets a solemn tone for the thorny political world Nick inhabits, a dirty business where "nobody gets out clean" dictated by the "twin currencies of money and fear."[6] As one of the politicians says, "You know how you're doing the right thing in Yonkers? They make you pay for it"—and Nick pays with his life.

The introductory montage circumscribes the defining theme of *Show Me a Hero*: the meaning of home, which David Masciotra describes as "inseparable from belonging, community, and the comfort and stability that are only possible in a loving, nurturing environment."[7] For the white homeowners who go on to protest the housing order, their neighborhoods are tranquil spaces where children can freely play outside without danger. They take pride in their homes and adorn them with quaint decorations and flowers. But for those living in the projects of Schlobohm or School Street, home is like a prison. The tall, X-shaped brick buildings resemble something out of an apocalyptic dystopia. Garbage bags and crumbling couches guard the doorways where slews of young men loiter while smoking pot or trading drugs. The interior aesthetics of the projects seem to match the hostility and disquietude of the residents: the walls are lined with hideous yellow ceramic tiles and covered with graffiti. There is also the incessant background din of expletives, racial slurs, barking dogs, and muffled rap music. Black men in hoodies commiserate inside the elevators and "bad stairwells," causing mothers to fearfully lead their children down an alternate—and often more complicated—route to their door. Needles litter the dilapidated playgrounds. Haggis describes these unsightly buildings as warehouses destined to fail, burdened by what Oscar Newman terms a "stigma of ugliness." Constructing the projects to "look as different as possible from its surroundings … marks it off as clearly as if by quarantine," which "not only 'puts the poor in their place' but 'brings their vulnerability to the attention of others.'"[8] In other words, the buildings reflect an "unspoken philosophy that we as a society look down on people who need help paying their rent, and we want their housing to be different."[9]

Although Nick supports the housing initiative, he also considers a good home something to work toward and a space that reflects one's position in life. During the "Gave It a Name" sequence, he peers through the windows of a handsome house on a hill, imagining filling its empty rooms. With its princely porch overlooking the Yonkers cityscape, it is the kind of home built for a future mayor—the home of his dreams. Later in the miniseries, Nick shows Nay the house and envisages raising their children there: "I could walk to work from here. Kids ask, 'Where's Dad?' and you point over there. You're like 'Council meeting's on tonight. See? Lights are on. He's in his office.'" Nick admits that he never questioned the realtor about purchasing the home because he wasn't in a serious romantic relationship at the time and "hadn't done anything to deserve a home like this." To Nick, the house on the hill is a dignified space worthy of the governor or senator he hopes to be one day.

A montage set to Springsteen's sprightly romp "Hungry Heart" signifies Nick's growing desire for professional and personal success. The song begins as diegetic source music after Nick, who as a child was nicknamed "The Mayor," decides to fulfill his destiny and run for office. He saunters over to a diner jukebox and selects the song, much to the chagrin of his brother Michael and friend Jim Surdoval: "Springsteen? This again? Oh, come on," they groan. Disregarding them, Nick bops along to the music and declares it his "theme song." Its jovial, bouncy rhythm juxtaposes the glum narrative of a man who has just abandoned his family. "Hungry Heart" then transfers to non-diegetic score accompanying shots of various hungry hearts in search of love and success, the song's upbeat tempo driving Haggis' swift pace. Nick peeks over his typewriter as he is writing campaign slogans to trade a shy smile with his crush Nay, who works for his colleague Harry Oxman. The future townhouse occupants display different forms of love: Alma opens the furniture store she works at early in the morning to provide for her children, Doreen flirts with her future fiancé, Billie makes out with a ne'er-do-well named Hot, and Norma cares for her patients.

Yonkers politicians (from left) Edwin E. McAmis (Luke Kirby), Neil DeLuca (Saverio Guerra), Nick Wasicsko (Oscar Isaac), Nick Longo (Jim Bracchita), and John Henry Cox (Judge William H. Mulligan) survey where to build the townhouses to spread out affordable housing (www.moviestillsdb.com).

An extremely on-the-nose shot of Oscar Newman sketching his design of the new townhouses just as Springsteen sings of the ubiquitous desire to "have a home" and "a place to rest" encapsulates the dogma of *Show Me a Hero*: everyone—regardless of skin color or class—deserves a decent place to live. The xenophobic protesters may argue that people of color "don't want what we want. They don't live the way we do," but the universality of "Hungry Heart" insists that we *all* long for familial and communal security. Nick echoes Springsteen's sentiment, acknowledging after he purchases his dream house on the hill that supporting the townhouse decree means he is "on the right side of something … people just want a home, right? It's the same for everybody." *Show Me a Hero* presents the repugnant homes that the low-income Yonkers citizens are forced to occupy as detrimental to their well-being: the emergency housing that social services offers Doreen, a seedy motel in a town riddled with KKK members, or the Schlobohm apartments where Carmen ironically pins a "Welcome Home" sign onto the wall for her son while gunshots ring outside. "I thought if I could get a place of my own and a family of my own, everything else would come with that. This was supposed to feel like home for us. This isn't home," Doreen writes about the projects in a letter to her sister.

The character of Mary Dorman transforms from one of the desegregation movement's fiercest objectors to its greatest champion after her perceptions of home and neighborly compassion are challenged. A resolute woman, Mary has a tremendous amount of pride for her home and values the ideal of being a good neighbor. She tells an African American reporter who interviews her about the housing debate that she dreamed of living in this little house on her "favorite block in the whole city." "I always said to my husband, 'Buddy, if I can't have a brick house on Saint John's Avenue, I don't want a house.' I fell in love with it the first time I saw it," she gushes. Parroting the protesters' deflective rhetoric, Mary insists her opposition is not a racial issue but an economic one: "People are worried about their property values."

The reporter responds with a blunt follow-up question: "Do you think the families that might move into these houses—do you think they might see those houses the same way as you see yours?" Mary can only argue that if they had taken care of their homes in the first place, they wouldn't have to move out of the projects. "I just think you shouldn't take people with one lifestyle and put them smack in the middle of a place with a different lifestyle," she sourly concludes. She is outraged by the liberal outsiders trying to impose their will on her community and fears a court-ordered invasion of poor black people in her neighborhood. It is not until Mary sees life in the projects with her own eyes that she undergoes a conversion and understands what Springsteen sings about everyone wanting a home.

When Mary joins the Housing Education Relocation Enterprise program, which assists with the transition to the townhouses, she interviews potential residents in their current homes in the projects. The sights and sounds of a man being arrested by the front door, another sleeping on a stairwell (one that is to be strictly avoided, a woman warns them), eerie flickering lights, and the constant, overbearing thrum of rap music frighten her, but once Mary gets inside the apartments and learns about her potential new neighbors, seeing how pleasant they are and how hard they work to impress her, she recognizes the universal desire for a respectable home. Mary, Nick, and the townhouse residents are inextricably bound by the desire for a home to call their own: the perfect block on St. John's Avenue, the house on the hill, and a townhouse that resembles nothing in the projects. These characters relate to the cozy Springsteenian ideal that "our physical place, home, and 'native soil,' is what defines us."[10]

From Prodigy to Has-Been

Nick has difficulty deciding how to pitch his mayoral campaign against his opponent Antonio Martinelli when they have consistently voted the same until he realizes that, unlike Martinelli, he voted for an appeal to the housing decision—a platform that readily attracts the townhouse protesters. Springsteen's jovial rocker "Ramrod" operates as an emotional signifier for Nick's exultant discovery of his newfound supporters. The song emits from Nick's radio as diegetic source music while he and Nay drive through a neighborhood in Martinelli's district. Much to their surprise, rows of homemade "Vote for Wasicsko" signs adorn the lawns. Clarence Clemons' gleeful saxophone wail aurally denotes Nick's elation, its rousing sound visually articulated through a crane shot that travels from the street up toward the trees that canopy the tranquil neighborhood to gain a wider view of the scattered signs—an ascent that replicates the swelling of Nick's ego and euphoria. The little boy nicknamed "The Mayor" sees his childhood dream come true, becoming the youngest mayor in America and "officially a rising star in the Democratic Party."

On the opposite end of the spectrum, Nick's friend Vinni Restiano loses the election, leaving her adrift and dejected. Even though she tells herself not to take the loss personally, she cannot help but feel as if a part of her life is missing: "It's like your candle goes out, you know? And everyone just moves on to the next candle. And people stop calling and reporters stop trying to reach you and it's back to your life." Vinni's wide eyes shyly dart to the side as she tentatively insinuates having suicidal thoughts: "When they make you walk away, you can think some pretty dark shit." The emotional despair and sense of alienation that she experiences foreshadows Nick's denouement.

Death allusions frequently appear on the Springsteen soundtrack for *Show Me a Hero*, first in Part Two of the series with "All That Heaven Will Allow" from *Tunnel of Love*. When Nick listens to the record on his turntable, it is January 1988 and the album is a little more than a year old. "All That Heaven Will Allow" softly plays while Nick reads the newspaper and Nay unpacks a cardboard box. Springsteen's dulcet tune about the heady first stage of a relationship mirrors Nick and Nay's decision to take their own relationship to the next level and move in together; like the song's couple, they plan to "fill this house" with all their love. This scene presents an image of home life very different from that of the low-income tenants. For them, home is not a sacred space to share with their loved ones, but rather a hotbed of crime, drugs, and other temptations that easily tear lovers and families apart.

Springsteen's sweet serenade is a celebration of coupled bliss. The male subject's deep affection for his new girl has the ability to chase away "dark skies," just as Nay serves as Nick's safe harbor from the tempest of the housing brawls. There are multiple scenes throughout the miniseries that demonstrate Nick's reliance on Nay. When the housing debate incites violence and rage from his former supporters, he clings to her in anxiety and desperation. "Don't leave me…. No matter what happens, all right?" he pleads to Nay one night in bed. During a later scene after the townhouse boycotts worsen, Nick admits to Nay, "I couldn't function without you. You keep me grounded. You keep me organized." Nick fears being exiled from the Yonkers government like Vinni. Losing the prosperous position of his childhood dreams would mean a loss of self, and without Nay as a stabilizing influence by his side, he fears sinking into a gulf of despair from which there is no return. The song's coda, wherein Springsteen's narrator "rejects the rock-and-roll cliché that there is something enviable about dying young and leaving a good-looking corpse,"[11] ironically alludes to Nick's eventual suicide. Rather than idealizing death, Springsteen's male subject insists that his relationship is everything he needs to "set [him] straight" and keep him "walkin' proud." Nick longs for "all the time" in the world to be with his sweetheart, but the addictive games of politics consume him and cause him to lose sight of his marital responsibilities.

Haggis and Simon continually reinforce the intense vehemence Nick faces from the anti-desegregation Yonkers citizens. The scenes of the acrimonious town hall meetings establish the unwavering fortitude it took for Nick to calmly remind his constituents to "uphold and obey the law." Nick's gavel barely registers amid the thundering bedlam of the crowd's hateful rhetoric. Protesters stand on top of court benches and scream at Nick, "To hell with you!" and "Coward!" They congest the frame so densely that it seems as if they are going to burst through the very fabric of the screen. Others threaten Nick's career, warning him, "You're gonna regret the day you went into politics. So enjoy the next two years on the council! They're your last two years!" Mary Dorman makes it personal when she bitterly asserts that Nick's deceased father would be ashamed of him.

An interior shot places a throng of protesters with their backs to the screen in the foreground while Nick and the councilmen sit on their pulpit toward the back. The theoretical authority figures seem tiny among the sea of incensed objectors incessantly jeering. Haggis enables the spectator to inhabit Nick's chaotic political realm by avoiding clean shots, going to "great pains to put wrong things in the shot: people standing in the wrong place or a microphone right in your face, or sometimes a pole in the middle of your face so that you felt like you were there."[12] Nick endures humiliating gibes: one member of the crowd throws diapers at him, christening him "Baby Mayor" (as if he should be ashamed of his remarkable achievement at such a young age), and he is spit on.

Outside the enclosed space of city hall, Nick and Nay face a behemothic crowd that blocks entry to their car. A demonstrator indignantly begs Nick to resign—a heartbreaking moment for the young man who once dreamed of becoming an admirable and beloved political figure. Nick manages to remain composed, calmly expressing his sorrow for letting the man down. Once Nick and Nay manage to get inside the car, the sheer enormity of the mob forces them to drive away at a snail's pace. Haggis' unhinged camera jostles in between the couple's shoulders as objectors pound on the car windows to break the glass, climb onto the hood, and even attempt to lift the car from the ground. The frenetic jump cuts and point-of-view close-ups visually embody Nick and Nay's terror and claustrophobia. As the animosity of Nick's constituents escalates to violence, the mise-en-scène begins to resemble something from the horror genre. Astonishingly, Nick never wavers from his commitment to obey Judge Sand's orders to build the townhouses or outwardly expresses his exasperation and anxiety.

"Brilliant Disguise" accompanies a montage of Nick and Nay moving into the beloved house on the hill. The stirring ballad begins non-diegetically over a shot of the curtained bay window; then the camera pans right, placing the archway in the center of the frame to observe Nick, Nay, and his brother bringing in boxes. Sprightly jump cuts hasten the move-in process, ending with Nick throwing Nay over his shoulder and giving her a kiss. The song's themes of infidelity and suspicion contrast with the scene's jocund mood and the couple's frolicking, its Orbisonian pathos portending the strains their relationship will come to face.[13] Soon Nay will no longer recognize her husband in his egomaniacal pursuit of office and willingness to play political games with their lives. Springsteen's driving pace motivates Haggis' smooth camera movements.

Nick runs for mayor again against Hank Spallone, a boisterous, iconoclastic Donald Trump–esque figure, a bulwark during city hall meetings due to his staunch refusal to vote in favor of the townhouses on any measure. By Part Four, it is 1989, and the townhouses are already being laid in the ground. However, Spallone and his supporters refuse to surrender their fight. Nick hopes that they are merely a "narrow lunatic fringe element" and that there is "a silent majority out there that's ready to put this issue behind them because they know that there's more important issues in this election. But they are being intimidated by the mob which is the loud minority." Nick realizes the loud minority's impact when he sees his "Wasicsko for Mayor" billboard covered with graffiti and Spallone support stickers. Haggis cleverly subverts the "Ramrod" sequence by inserting Springsteen's other roaring hot rod rocker from *The River* album, "Cadillac Ranch," over this defeatist moment in which Nick no longer receives the same support. The Wisconsin-bound rider's celebration of shiny cruisers blares diegetically from Nick's car radio, its exuberant rhythms juxtaposing the narrator's fear of abandonment and death. The song preserves the spirit of the Texan sculpture of ten Cadillacs half-buried nose-first in a wheat field, "a vivid metaphor for the transitoriness of all existence, of how that which was once powerful, and elite, and so very much desired becomes, with the passage of time, obsolete, exhausted, and fully expendable."[14] "Cadillac Ranch" foreshadows Nick's fate after the housing debacle; like the buried cars, he is easily discarded from city hall, tossed asunder because he is deemed worthless—leading to his untimely death.

Springsteen's serene lullaby "Valentine's Day" from *Tunnel of Love* gorgeously underscores an emotional scene between Nick and Nay. The romantic ballad emits from Nick's turntable when Nay tenderly assures him that he can recover from any election loss. Here the soundtrack explicitly voices Nick's interior thoughts: what scares him is losing Nay's love and respect. The narrator's plea for his lover to pledge her steadfast devotion, to "say you're forever mine," mirrors Nick's teary entreaty to Nay: "If I'm not the mayor of Yonkers ... will you still love me?" Like the highwayman of "Valentine's Day," he needs the security of romantic commitment to mollify his anxieties. Oscar Isaac's tremulous reading of this line quavers with a self-pitying vulnerability that perfectly captures the immense pressure Nick puts on himself to succeed and the measured unraveling of his ambition.[15] In the final verse, Springsteen's protagonist imagines himself dying in his dream—another allusion to Nick's fate. In transitioning "Valentine's Day" to a louder non-diegetic score, Haggis connects Nick's emotional life to those of the townhouse residents. The romantic coda of gentle, moony synthesizers overlays a montage of Mary casting her vote, Norma and Carmen working late hours, and a drug-addicted Doreen scrounging the ground for spilled pills. The formal connection of these characters through the use of soundtrack suggests that the racial and class lines that divide Yonkers are only an illusion; they all share the same longing to transcend their current circumstances, for a life "born anew." "Valentine's Day" adds an unremitting sweetness to these everyday scenes.

The loud minority prevails, for Hank Spallone wins solely on the basis of his anti-housing stance. By the end of Part Four, the former miracle candidate and twenty-eight-year-old prodigy has become "the youngest ex-mayor in America" and, in his eyes, a thirty-two-year-old has-been. Waking up at 1:40 in the afternoon next to a half-eaten sandwich and apple core on the nightstand, Nick struggles to fill his days now that he is no longer in office. Out of his customary suit and in a grey sweatshirt and jeans, Nick attempts to occupy himself with renovations on his house. After he carefully lines up his tools on the worktable, he puts his *Born to Run* cassette in the nearby boombox—an album that encapsulates his innocent, carefree youth. The infectious energy of "Tenth Avenue Freeze-Out" buoys the scene's comic temporality in the quick, jaunty cuts of Nick's failures to make house repairs.

Beneath the blithe musicality, however, lies a darker subtext. Springsteen's jovial horn-infused bop acutely captures Nick's feelings of existential loneliness as his narrator finds himself "cut off from his home and the things that once motivated and stimulated him."[16] "Stranded in the jungle" and removed from "the light of the living," both Bad Scooter and Nick Wasicsko long to reassimilate themselves with the rhythms of city life, whether it be camaraderie with fellow musicians or the political arena. Nick's subsequent monologue to his father's headstone incorporates the themes of isolation found in "Tenth Avenue Freeze-Out":

> As miserable as they can make it for you when you're in the middle of things, at least you're in the middle of things, you know? And the thing is, when you lose, people will say, "Oh, it's nothing personal, you know? It was just that issue or this thing that happened." But you know what? People either vote for you or they vote for the other guy. What's more personal than that?

This monologue also mirrors his conversation with Vinni; now their roles are reversed, and he is the exiled one. Like Springsteen's narrator, who cannot find his way home, Nick cannot return to politics, the one place he belongs.

Nick is brightened when he learns he has been nominated for the prestigious John F. Kennedy Profile in Courage Award. The nomination letter praises him for his political courage, leadership, and "unrelenting support for the rights of minorities and the poor" at only twenty-eight years old. "Despite calls for your resignation and threats to your personal safety, you forged a path to equality of opportunity and access to public housing in all parts of Yonkers," it reads. This news lifts Nick out of his depression and emboldens him to run for mayor if he wins the award.

Springsteen's sultry ballad "Secret Garden" serves as non-diegetic accompaniment for a montage centered on Nick and Nay's wedding. The sequence opens with a shot of a beautiful cathedral and then cuts to the townhouses being lifted by cranes and placed onto their foundations. Attendees throw rice in celebration of Nick and Nay's union as they walk toward the limousine. However, the erotic lyrics about suspect partners belie this cheerful celebration and foreshadow Nick and Nay's marital strife after Nick struggles to restore his political career and Vinni accuses him of cheating. Like Springsteen's cryptic woman, Nick will keep secrets from Nay and erect emotional walls to soothe his wounded pride. A montage follows of Carmen sharing supper with her children, Mrs. O'Neal knitting, Billie feeding and playing with her baby, and Doreen calling her mother. Haggis allows the repetitive and lush synthesizer line to mobilize his montage's fluidity. This flowing visual and sonic aesthetic emphasizes the interconnectedness of the characters across racial and class divides. Clemons' sensual saxophone coda gently wafts over the montage's final image: blaring blue and red police car lights bouncing off the townhouses' unfinished siding, now sullied by a racist graffiti manifesto, "No Nigger," "Death to Sands" (a misspelling of Judge Sand's name), and "KKK." The houses may be built, but the war against them isn't over.

A Tragedy

Part Five opens nearly two years later in February 1991. Nick considers his Profile in Courage nomination his ticket back to city hall, but his former right-hand man Jim Surdoval warns Nick that he is "the face of the entire ugly mess." In other words, all voters would be focused on is Nick's association with the townhouse debate. Surdoval argues that Yonkers needs a fresh candidate in order to finally put the housing debacle to rest. So, "for the good of the party," Nick concedes to Terry Zaleski and pursues the minor position of a seat on the council with the promise that he will be Zaleski's confidant if he is appointed mayor. Election night is fraught with tension after Nick is not immediately elected for the council, filling him with immense anxiety: "You lose twice in a row, you're done. You can't run again without looking like an idiot. Nobody will take you seriously. My own fucking council district, what a fucking embarrassment," he explains. While the absentee ballots are counted, Nick attends Zaleski's celebration party, where Zaleski, surrounded by a gaggle of reporters and basking in his glory, walks past Nick as if he was a ghost. Nick eventually wins the council seat but struggles to remain on Zaleski's radar. It is not until Zaleski asks Nick to fire the head of the Parking Authority—coincidentally Nay's boss—that he is finally acknowledged.

Nick revels in the chance to become the mayor's "go-to guy on the council" despite Nay and his brother Michael's protestations. As the first verse of Springsteen's "Racing in the Street" from *Darkness on the Edge of Town* plays on his turntable, he explains to them that Zaleski is "making good on his promise" to value him in the administration. The doleful ballad functions as authorial expressivity, "commenting on characters rather than speaking from their point of view, underlining traits a character may not wish to acknowledge."[17] Just as Springsteen's narrator ineffectively races along the fire roads and interstates, imprisoned by his perennial existential ennui, Nick cannot escape the intoxicating gambits of Yonkers politics. His narcissistic attempt to recapture his political savvy echoes the despondent racer's inadequate resurrection of his hot rodding glory days. The soft piano melody of this lachrymose dirge adds a sense of pitifulness to the scene as Nick fruitlessly tries to scrounge his way back into professional recognition, no matter the cost. He betrays Nay, and nearly destroys her job in the process, by attempting to get her boss fired. The narrator of Springsteen's ballad similarly cares little for his wife's perspective, racing even though she spends her entire night on the porch fretting about whether he will return home alive.

During the final part of the miniseries, which takes place in 1992, Nick observes Zaleski handing the keys to the first five completed townhouses to their new occupants. Nick believes this would have been far more significant had he been elected mayor, because he was the one who sacrificed his political standing for the cause. Nick shows his estrangement by sitting a few empty seats away from his colleagues and haphazardly joining in the applause after everyone else. At the housing lottery that no one at city hall informed him about, Nick scans the politicians on the auditorium stage in a silent prayer for them to acknowledge him. The camera ominously inches toward Nick's vanishing smile surrounded by the joyous reactions of the lottery winners. Soon Nick's fermenting rage explodes, and he shouts in front of Nay that he just wants everyone, especially Zaleski, to know "that I'm still here, goddamnit! I gave him everything he has. I gave him—I pushed the housing through, I gave him the strong-mayor charter, the patronage, the power. I stepped aside to let him be mayor. I did all that, and I paid for it, and I bled for it."

One night, Nick listens to "My Beautiful Reward" from Springsteen's 1992 album *Lucky Town* on his car radio. Although the gentle ballad plays briefly, the first two lines cue the emotions of Nick and the future townhouse residents. Springsteen's description of an illuminated "house on a hill," symbolic of his unattainable fantasies, echoes all of the supporting characters' desire for a townhouse, the "beautiful reward" for their families. Nick is just as lost as the song's narrator, searching for his own reward, not of familial but vocational triumph. The last verse reimagines the narrator as a bird soaring over fields in the afterlife—more death imagery that presages Nick's suicide. The song inspires Nick to visit the residents of the finished townhouses. Most of them remain guarded around white visitors, but Norma recognizes Nick as the mayor she voted for and, much to Nick's embarrassment, the one who was spit on. Nick asks her whether she is "happy with the house … because I like to think it was worth it." Norma slyly replies, "I could ask you the same thing."

Nick's second consecutive loss for a City Council president position to his dear friend Vinni leaves him, "by the rules of the game, done as a candidate," and he returns to city hall with his tail between his legs in search of a job. "You're just gonna, you know, use me up like that?" Nick rages in heartbroken incredulity to Jim Surdoval, who admits that he can offer Nick nothing. The former mayor erupts into a chaotic rampage when he charges Surdoval with falsely accusing him of conspiratorial crimes in an IDA investigation, a narrative bombshell that leaves the spectator just as nonplussed as Nick. News of this sudden witch hunt sinks Nick into a pit of paranoid woe because, as Haggis explains, "from inside that cocoon of 'I don't have an ally and nobody remembers me,' he was a wounded soul. Any suggestion that he was going to be further victimized he took to heart."[18] "I don't have a pot to piss in, Jim! I didn't steal, but you wanna take what's left of my reputation? You wanna tear that down as well?" he cries.

Oskar Eustis, artistic director of the Public Theater, who oversaw Oscar Isaac's performances in Hamlet and Two Gentlemen of Verona, considers the actor's "breathtakingly beautiful" performance in the HBO miniseries "one of the greatest television achievements of the millennium," a conviction made abundantly clear in the final episode.[19] Isaac deftly crafts a humane portrait of a man whose confident bravado withers into a lugubrious self-loathing. Nick's immense sorrow emanates from every molecule in Isaac's body. He exquisitely conveys the former mayor's quiet desperation as he begs his wife to "play hooky" from work and stay home with him. His quivering murmurs and tender, beseeching gestures radiate with a profound anguish that positions Nay's decision as a matter of life and death. When they exit to the diner entryway, Nick clutches Nay's arm in dread, insisting that the current Yonkers administration is "gunning for him" and that his "innocence is no defense. It's politics, Nay. It's a smear job." Haggis frames Nick from the exterior of the diner window, his face obscured by the reflection of vertical blinds to evoke the bars of a jail cell door—symbolic of his fear of imprisonment and the paranoid depression that holds his mind captive. Haggis' unstable camera bobs in between the couple to signify Nick's psychological delirium. Nick cannot heed Nay's advice to "snap out of it," and he returns to city hall to berate his former colleagues for being "out for blood." "By the time the truth comes out, it won't matter," he screams, for his reputation will have already been tarnished by the mere accusation of illegal activity. Back at his home, Haggis frames Nick sitting beside a bay window through a tiny sliver of the staircase bars, a voyeuristic shot that confines his figure to visualize Nick's paralyzing psychological torment. The camera travels alongside Nick when he walks into the nearby attic, mumbling softly to himself and pacing back and forth—the brewing of an emotional breakdown. In the faintest of whispers, Nick feebly calls out to his brother for help before slumping onto the ground. Haggis cuts to an extreme close-up of Nick's red, weeping face; the shot's proximity transmits the enormity of his suffering and displays the breadth of Isaac's devastatingly bravura performance.

Show Me a Hero ends as it began: with a montage set to Springsteen's music. The ethereal and transcendent "Lift Me Up" operates as an elegy for the loss of Nick's promising young life. In the first shot of this sequence, Nick leans against a tree and looks toward the sky above his father's grave, the tranquil sounds of rustling leaves and chirping birds mixing with Springsteen's ominous opening organ chords, heartbeat-style drum loop, and angelic falsetto. With its themes of ascension and grace, "Lift Me Up" anticipates the ensuing scene of Nick's funeral as his soul is lifted into the afterlife. The lyrics of grasping at the last vestiges of faith, unanswered prayers, and rising toward heaven align with the church setting and frame the mourning of Nick's untimely death. Springsteen's rhapsodizing of his lover's body—skin, neck, fingers, heartbeat, and breath—brings to mind Nick's lifeless being and all that he has lost in his suicide. Springsteen's high-pitched voice and the somnifacient instrumentals infuse the devastating sequence with a celestial melancholy.

Haggis pans down from the stained-glass summit of a cathedral to Nick's casket and then intercuts scenes of the townhouse residents enjoying their new homes—particularly highlighting Carmen's joyful tears as she grips the chain-link fence of her long-awaited reward. These shots demonstrate what Nick has paid for with his life. Shots of the funeral procession, attended by Martinelli, Spallone, Vinni, Zaleski, and the majority of the supporting characters, follow. As the sun sets, the hearse drives toward the cemetery led by a motorcade. The incredibly moving "Lift Me Up" montage ends with Nick at the graveyard retrieving his gun from his ankle brace and putting it in his mouth. Springsteen's slow heartbeat-esque drums continuously loop to evoke Nick's waning pulse—an artistic decision made by Haggis not found in the original version of the song. The image and soundtrack abruptly cut to a stark, blackened silence right as Nick puts the gun in his mouth and shoots himself. Nick's story ends with a shot of a "For Sale" sign gently swaying in the breeze in front of his beloved house on the hill, waiting for its next occupants.

The title of *Show Me a Hero* is a reference to F. Scott Fitzgerald's quote, "Show me a hero and I'll write you a tragedy," which contends that heroism necessitates sacrifice and adversity. The character of Michael Sussman echoes this quote in the series when he says, "If there was a hero in any of this, it was Nick." Continuing to champion the marginalized people of Yonkers despite the fact that doing so excommunicates him from the only vocation to which he has ever aspired and mentally destroys him is certainly a mark of his valor, but Nick is not a flawless political paragon. "Do you even believe in anything? Anything other than yourself?" Vinni seethes after he deliberately runs against her. A myopic egotism consumes Nick as he desperately tries to stay in office and begins to lose sight of what he once so firmly believed in: the law's ability to change people's lives for the better. After purchasing the house of his dreams, he understood what the housing decree could provide for the disenfranchised and people of color in Yonkers. Springsteen's music orchestrates Nick's journey, from his staunch refusal to surrender to the housing protesters' pleas to his tragedy when voters, colleagues, and fate itself turn against him.

"There's a place for everyone in Springsteen's America"

In his 2016 speech presenting Springsteen with the Presidential Medal of Freedom, President Barack Obama declared that throughout the rock star's nearly fifty-year musical career, he has captured "the pain and the promise of the American experience ... the reality of who we are and the reverie of who we want to be" in his soulful stories of ordinary people.[20] The New Jerseyan poet laureate envisages his country as "a close-knit national community wherein neighbors take care of one another," a place where "individuals look out for more than themselves by helping their neighbors and respecting the dignity of everyone in the community" regardless of race or background.[21] *Show Me a Hero*'s final shot of Doreen and Mary encapsulates Springsteen's vision of America as a family, which he acknowledges is "naive, maybe sentimental or simplistic, but it's a good idea."[22] Springsteen condemns the institutional forces that deny individuals the chance at social mobility because of their economic circumstances or the color of their skin, championing a democratic ideal of the nation as an equal playing field for all its citizens—the same principles behind the Yonkers housing decree. As Obama concludes his speech, "There's a place for everyone in Springsteen's America,"[23] and he advocates a nation founded on inclusivity and acceptance throughout his oeuvre.

Inspired by Curtis Mayfield's "People Get Ready" and the traditional gospel song "This Train Is Bound for Glory," "Land of Hope and Dreams" draws from Springsteen's credo—"Nobody wins unless everybody wins"—to express the utopian chimera of a truly unified America. Against a rousing mandolin riff and gospel choir, Springsteen sings of a ticketless train that welcomes everyone: saints, sinners, losers, winners, whores, gamblers, fools, and kings of all colors, classes, and creeds. "You can't have a United States if you are telling some folks that they can't get on the train," the anthem proudly insists.[24] The townhouses in *Show Me a Hero* evoke Springsteen's metaphorical train as a space for all citizens to have their piece of the American Dream. For Springsteen, America can only fulfill its promise as the land of hope and dreams, where said dreams are not thwarted and faith is magnificently rewarded, if it fully embraces and supports *all* of its people.

The ebullient Irish jig "American Land" addresses the centuries-long suffering of immigrants and minorities. Springsteen holds up the country's melting pot populace—the blacks, Irish, Italians, Germans, and Jews, the Posalskis, the McNicholases, the Smiths, and the Zerillis—who all "gave a life's worth of tears and sweat and asked only for equal respect and opportunity in return," which they did not receive.[25] The first verses are an Ellis Island–bound immigrant's quixotic imaginings of what the coveted America holds: sweets waiting to be plucked from the trees, gold rushing through the rivers, sparkling diamonds in the sidewalk—a glittering bevy of treasures that any hard-working man can obtain. The second half of the song undercuts the newcomer's idolatry when he discovers the United States' horrific exploitation of foreigners and people of color. His beloved American land desperately wants to keep out the immigrants like him, who cripple their backs gathering food in the fields, callus their hands building towering churches and stately colleges, work themselves to the bone and die in the perilous railroads, blistering cotton fields, and clanging factories. Clinging to the same divisive attitudes on a much smaller scale, the white citizens of Yonkers fight to keep hard-working African Americans and Latinos out of their neighborhoods.

Hundreds of years ago, immigrants died shaping the same country that disdained and repudiated them, and "they're [still] dyin' now," Springsteen growls in the final verse—bridging the historical past to the present and affirming America's perennial xenophobia. As he attests in *Springsteen on Broadway*, Americans are continuously engaged "in an ongoing battle for the soul of our good nation." The fight against the oppression and victimization of the country's marginalized people is far from over. David Simon knew that no matter when he chose to adapt *Show Me a Hero*, "The American racial dynamic wasn't going to go away, and what happened in Yonkers, as a political and social allegory, remained pretty damn timeless. When we came back to [*Show Me a Hero*], we would still be landing it on a country that would still be traveling the same hard road. Recent events in Ferguson, in Baltimore, in Charleston make this all too clear."[26] Both Springsteen's songs about race and *Show Me a Hero* are enduring political parables continually recolored by current events. They hold even more resonance in the Trumpian era fueled by a deep-seated anti-immigrant, anti-minority abhorrence. In a 2018 *Esquire* magazine interview, Springsteen condemned

Trump for having "no interest in uniting the country, really, and actually has an interest in doing the opposite and dividing us, which he does on an almost daily basis. So that's simply a crime against humanity, as far as I'm concerned. It's an awful, awful message to send out into the world if you're in that job and in that position. It's just an ugly, awful message. You are intentionally trying to disenfranchise a large portion of Americans."[27] Springsteen's work and *Show Me a Hero* promote the country's long, enduring struggle against the "folks who are invested in denying the idea of a united America and an America for all."[28]

Springsteen localizes his idealistic vision of America through songs about small-town communities reminiscent of his own quaint hometown of Freehold, New Jersey. Through the narrator's nostalgic memories of his neighborhood's halcyon past, "My Hometown" from *Born in the U.S.A.* considers the post–Fordist lives of the white working-class, characters not unlike the protesters in Yonkers. Springsteen's male subject laments the "fights between the black and white" that have ravaged his cherished hometown, leaving ghostly "whitewashed windows and vacant stores" on the once bustling Main Street. Although Springsteen's protagonist contemplates a white flight to the south, Donald Deardorff argues that when he reprises the paternal ritual of displaying the all-American town of his youth to his son, "listeners are left with the definite impression that one should not run from or ignore the tensions produced by pluralism."[29] Springsteen contends that "[y]ou will always be tempted to head 'south,' but in the end, 'this is your hometown,' and you must help it adjust to new realities."[30] The narrator and his wife want their son to share their roots and pass this legacy down to his offspring and all future generations.

Unlike the couple in "My Hometown," the protesters of *Show Me a Hero* simply cannot adjust to the reality of low-income housing infiltrating their neighborhood. Their resistance reflects "the dynamic we have in this country where we're not quite able to share with people who are the most in need,"[31] one that directly opposes Springsteen's vision of America as a family. "I don't think any of these people understand the simple fact that the law doesn't guarantee that you get to live in a neighborhood that you can't afford," one objector spits out. Carrying signs that read "Pensions Not Projects" and "No Rights for the Whites," the protesters declare the housing decree a hypocritical case of "the rich and the elitists looking down on those who have to work for everything they have"; they view the future townhouse occupants as freeloaders being simply handed their share of the American Dream and conceal their racism behind generic concerns of "public housing people bringing drugs and crime into our neighborhood and ruining our property values!" Spallone goads these anxieties by exhibiting photographs of the ravaged "crack jungles" where people of color "live like animals," the implication being that if they move into his supporters' neighborhoods, they will destroy them as well.

"My Hometown" draws from Springsteen's adolescent experiences with the "presumed and casual" racism of his 1950s youth and the subsequent fallout of the civil rights movement, which he details in his memoir *Born to Run*.[32] Springsteen recalls standing on his front porch observing the riots that decimated his hometown after white officials cancelled a black unity march. On South Street, he saw a black man being thrown out a window and the corner sub shop proprietor rush "into a black crowd wielding a meat cleaver. It was taken from him and it was amazing no one was killed."[33] At the intersection of South Street and Route 33 near his home, "a white youth fired a shotgun into a parked car, costing a black youth an eye," which Springsteen directly references in one of the "My Hometown" lines.[34] At Freehold Regional High School in the mid–1960s, racial tensions exploded into violence. "If you entered the wrong restroom, it was a lights-out beating," Springsteen explains in his memoir.³⁵ When one of his black friends refused to speak to him, young Springsteen realized that "the lines had been drawn, even amongst neighborhood friends."³⁶ Springsteen witnessed the same lines being drawn when a bar skirmish resulted in Clarence Clemons being called "nigger." "I know those guys.... I play football with them every Sunday. Why would they say that?" Clemons sadly asked Springsteen, who was "caught blank, embarrassed by the moment myself, and all I offered up to my friend was a shrug and a mumbled, 'I dunno' … silence."³⁷ Decades later, Springsteen regrets not standing up for his dear friend and saying, "'Because they're subhuman assholes.'"³⁸ By sensitively exploring systematic racism with a self-reflective gaze, Springsteen uses his memoir to contemplate his position as a privileged white American citizen, critique his country's failure to advocate for its people of color, and relates the experiences that have shaped his inclusive political vision and commitment to promoting equality.

"Long Walk Home" from *Magic* is a post–9/11 extension of "My Hometown," a wistful plea to resurrect a town whose homespun splendor has withered away, its Veterans Hall standing "silent and alone" and beloved diner "shuttered and boarded." In one of Springsteen's most poignant lines, he envisions a picturesque American community where "nobody crowds you and nobody goes it alone." "Long Walk Home" reconfigures "the small towns that once were death traps and suicide raps" into "communities of affinity, and models of how a good and altruistic life might be lived," idyllic spaces where everybody has a neighbor, a friend, and a reason to begin again.³⁹ Doreen in *Show Me a Hero* also views suburban neighborhoods as romanticized emblems of interconnectedness, motivating her desire to move into the townhouses. Her friend fears that Doreen will be killed on the east (white) side of town. "You would want to live where people are angry at you?" she asks. Just as Springsteen's title "Long Walk Home" denotes a lengthy journey toward the ideal of an inclusive, caring community, after Doreen moves into the townhouses, she realizes that a "judge can mandate housing remedies, but he cannot mandate a sense of belonging or an essence of neighborhood"—that comes in time.⁴⁰

When the townhouses are first built, someone tries to bomb them and white men fly by in cars screaming, "Go home, niggers! You goddamn porch monkeys!" The night that Doreen and Billie arrive in their new homes, they fear one of the white neighbors has broken in. Billie wakes her children and takes them to her mother's house, while Doreen sleeps with a knife under her pillow and a baseball bat by her side. There are also smaller, less violent instances of racism in the newly desegregated neighborhood: the white residents stare disapprovingly at their new neighbors or ignore them completely and allow their dogs to do their business on the lawns. "Will the white folks learn how to be good neighbors as well? Are they attending a course to learn how to accept us?" Doreen protests during a committee meeting, as the whites are the ones who need this education the most. Within these last two episodes of the new residents struggling to adjust to their dream homes and the white neighbors attempting to overcome their bigotry, *Show Me a Hero* takes care to point out that the construction of the townhouses did not magically put an end to Yonkers' racial tensions—in fact, the policies were not even resolved in court until 2007. Simon notes that other housing fights have occurred since that stir the same fears and promote the same racist rhetoric. Completely disregarding the lessons of Yonkers, these communities continued to protest scattered sites of low-income housing.

In his Broadway introduction to "Long Walk Home," which was later altered when he replaced the song with "The Ghost of Tom Joad," Springsteen alludes to the cataclysmic racial collisions as a result of Trump's identification with the far-right movement during his presidency. Springsteen condemns those "in the highest offices of our land who want to speak to our darkest angels" and attempt to "normalize hatred" (a sly reference to Trump's insistence that members of neo-Nazi groups were "very fine people"). He criticizes the "young men in torch-lit parades calling upon the ugliest and most divisive ghosts of America's past and other sins and they want to destroy the idea of an America for all."[41] These marches include the white supremacist Unite the Right rally at the University of Virginia campus in Charlottesville protesting the removal of a Confederate statue during August 2017. The protesters spewed hateful chants such as "One people, one nation, end immigration," "Jews will not replace us," and "White lives matter." "Suddenly your neighbors and your countrymen can look like complete strangers to you," Springsteen sadly reflects on those haunting images of white men holding flaming torches with their lips curled in contempt. The "Make America Great Again" contingent is founded on the kind of repugnant xenophobic attitudes that directly oppose Springsteen's personal and musical message of equality and an integrated America. "There's a beautiful quote by Dr. King that says, 'The arc of the moral universe is long, but it bends towards justice.' It is important to believe in those words and carry yourself and act accordingly and live with compassion," Springsteen closes the introduction, encouraging his audiences to change the world through the virtues of empathy and righteousness, the same fundamental ethos as Simon's *Show Me a Hero*.

The *Ghost of Tom Joad* album and title song took on new meaning during Springsteen's June 19, 2018, performance of his Broadway show, shortly after President Trump enforced a zero-tolerance policy at southwestern immigration borders, caging and forcing young children—even infants—to be separated from their families for an inordinate amount of time. Departing from the script of 146 previous shows, Springsteen launched into a lengthy monologue brimming with contempt: "[W]e are seeing things right now on our American borders that are so shockingly and disgracefully inhumane and un–American that it is simply enraging. And we have heard people in high position in the American government blaspheme in the name of God and country that it is a moral thing to assault the children amongst us. May God save our souls." In light of such policies, Springsteen's lines about hungry, crying newborns and people "struggling to be free" take on a profound resonance. Like the song's vagrant narrator, Springsteen trumpets the injustices against marginalized communities, those who are "fighting for a place to stand" in America, particularly the Mexican and Latin American community. He added the formidable song to his setlist for the duration of his Broadway run to counter Trump's worsening border policies and anti-immigrant rhetoric.

Springsteen occasionally forsakes his white male subjectivity to inhabit characters of African American or Hispanic descent and address "the suspicion, the reluctance, the rejection, and the violence with which large portions of U.S. society react to and try to repress every attempt by marginalized groups to assert their rights to diversity and equal treatment,"[42] which *Show Me a Hero* represents in the embittered housing battle in Yonkers. Through stark first-person narratives infused with the aesthetics of Woody Guthrie and John Ford's *The Grapes of Wrath*, *The Ghost of Tom Joad* intimately brings Springsteen's listeners into the personal worldview of his destitute subjects, who strive to find a better life for themselves on America's soil. He depicts the dire ramifications of poverty for people of color as they face homelessness, drug addiction, prostitution, and death.

"Sinaloa Cowboys," a soft ballad about brothers Miguel and Luis, who earn more money for their families by cooking meth in an abandoned chicken ranch than by picking orchards, brings to mind the *Show Me a Hero* subplot of Doreen's fiancé Skip, whose only opportunity in the projects is to sell drugs. In the elegiac "Across the Border," Springsteen becomes a Mexican immigrant who fantasizes about traveling to America, where he can build a house for his family that sits high on a grassy hill. He imagines the country as a celestial space that cures all ills. Carmen in *Show Me a Hero* can relate to these utopian reveries. She feels guilty for leaving her children at her birthplace in the Dominican Republic while she labors at a furniture store to scrounge money for a new home. Since the only places outside of the Schlobohm projects that she can afford are "where pigs would live," she idolizes the townhouses; they represent her dream of a proper American life.

The song "Black Cowboys" from *Devils & Dust* also mirrors Doreen's plotline. Through the story of Rainey Williams, a young boy growing up in the Mott Haven projects (à la Yonkers), where "melted candles" and "funeral wreaths" honoring his fallen neighbors—unjustly slain young black men—line the sidewalks, Springsteen explores how poverty affects urban life and devours the hopes and dreams of black youth. Rainey's mollycoddling mother shields her son from the dangers of their neighborhood, riddled with "stray bullets," until she falls under the sway of a drug dealer. In *Show Me a Hero*, after her fiancé unexpectedly passes away, Doreen experiments with drugs, the projects' prevailing currency. The scene in which she nods off at the kitchen table while her baby Jarron cries off screen echoes Springsteen's haunting description of Rainey's intoxicated mother becoming "lost in the days." "Rainey's longing for the ghost inside his mother, the spirit that once gave him everything he needed in a cruel world, is a heart-piercing evocation of the lovelessness that many urban children must bear throughout their lives"[43]— and what Jarron would have had to endure had Doreen not remedied her addiction and moved into the safer townhouses.

Springsteen's most renowned song about race is "American Skin (41 Shots)," inspired by the 1999 murder of Guinean immigrant Amadou Diallo. Police officers wrongly assumed that Diallo was a wanted rapist and shot him forty-one times when he reached into his pocket; only after his death did they realize that he was pulling out his wallet to identify himself. In the chorus, Springsteen repeats the phrase "forty-one shots" a total of twenty-eight times, forcing his listeners to reflect on the overwhelming number of bullets that tore through the body of an innocent man. The song's premiere in Atlanta, Georgia, on June 4, 2000—a state rife with civil rights history—instigated media frenzy and led to a boycott of Springsteen's following ten-night appearance at Madison Square Garden by the New York's Patrolmen Benevolent Association. They assumed the song was an anti-cop anthem, an insipid interpretation that completely ignores Springsteen's empathetic second verse written from the perspective of a policeman regretfully leaning over a victim's body.

Springsteen told Robert Hilburn of the *Los Angeles Times* that the aim of "American Skin (41 Shots)" was to highlight how "people of color are viewed through a veil of criminality and that ultimately means they are thought of as less American than other Americans, therefore people with less rights."[44] He wanted his country to face the idea that people of color are habitually denied full citizenship, as seen in *Show Me a Hero* when they are denied proper housing. "American Skin (41 Shots)" challenges Springsteen's predominantly white, often conservative audiences "to break down our walls of division; look into each other's eyes without prejudices of inferiority, distrust, or a 'veil of criminality,'" as he phrases it.[45] Years after its release, "American Skin (41 Shots)" has taken on new significance in the wake of the #BlackLivesMatter movement. During the *River* tour in 2016, E Street saxophonist Jake Clemons (nephew of the late Clarence Clemons) stood for the entirety of the song (with the exception of his stirring solo) in the "hands up, don't shoot" pose, inspired by the killings of countless other unarmed black men and women such as Trayvon Martin and Philando Castile.

Show Me a Hero addresses this "veil of criminality" ideal when Frank Spallone constructs a narrative that paints all people of color as miscreants for the white audience in court. He and his supporters want to keep people of color on their own side of the Saw Mill River Parkway in the same way that Springsteen's own hometown confined the African American community and other non-whites to the ramshackle west side. The miniseries depicts racial profiling during the "Hungry Heart" montage with a shot of a white officer skeptically eyeing a group of commiserating African American teenagers in an outdoor common area. Spallone manipulates photographs of life in the projects through this veil of criminality in order to goad protesters' fears and intolerance. In a point-of-view shot from the viewfinder of Spallone's camera, we voyeuristically scan the residents outside. Spallone purposefully waits until he can capture a moment that appears incriminating in the black-and-white freeze frame. Therefore, he does not take pictures of mothers playing with their children, but rather Billie giving him the middle finger and a circle of black men gambling. Two boys jocosely prance along the sidewalk, their legs and arms spiraling in midair, but when the shutter clicks and we see the resulting photograph, their play appears as a violent skirmish. Like the police who murdered Philando Castile, the protestors only see what they want to see, ignoring the actual people by focusing exclusively on the color of their skin.

"We Are Alive" from *Wrecking Ball* is one of Springsteen's most poignant songs about American identity and racial politics. The ethereal voices of marginalized figures from the past and present, such as the 1877 railroad strikers in Maryland, the innocent African American child victims of the 1963 Birmingham church bombing, and a Mexican immigrant family whose bodies rot after failing to cross the southern desert, conjoin in the chorus against an uplifting folk rhythm. "We are alive," they proclaim, their voices rising from their dark, worm-infested graves into the moonlit earth's air to valiantly insist that their legacies will not be forgotten. Springsteen conjures these ghosts of our pasts to stand alongside the living in our ongoing fight against injustices that have never been fully put to rest. He professes that these people of color who have been cruelly silenced or erased from history are a fundamental part of the intricate American fabric. Their "voices and spirit and ideas remain with us and go on and on," Springsteen declares. Their sacrifices and triumphs do not die or drift into the ether, but rather guide us toward an inclusive future.[46]

From David Sancious and the E Street Choir of the *Wrecking Ball* and *High Hopes* tours to the predominantly black "Other Band" of the *Human Touch* and *Lucky Town* tours, and, of course, the Big Man himself, Clarence Clemons, Springsteen has always taken care to include people of color in the various incarnations of his legendary E Street Band. His musical companions reflect the multicultural vision he has for his country. "But nobody captured my audience's imagination as much as Clarence," Springsteen proclaims during his Broadway introduction to "Tenth Avenue Freeze-Out." More than mere bandmates and dear friends, Springsteen says that he and Clarence were soul brothers who "told a story that was bigger than any of the ones I'd written in my songs. It was a story where not only did Scooter and the Big Man bust the city in half, but we remade the city into a kind of place where our friendship would not be such a strange thing." This was a story of racial harmony and inclusion crystallized in the juxtaposition of Springsteen's lithe white frame leaning against Clemons' large, hulking black body on the *Born to Run* album cover.

The corporeal performance of their deep relationship during concerts rife with dancing, hugging, leaning, hand holding, and even lying on top of one another's bodies signifies assimilation and effortless integration.[47] The union of their black and white bodies on stage articulates "the noble, utopian fantasy that the inclusive atmosphere at these concerts can serve as a microcosm of a tolerant America emerging," most powerfully symbolized when Springsteen slides across stage to kiss Clemons on the lips during the orgiastic finale of "Thunder Road" or "Rosalita (Come Out Tonight)."[48] This subversive act not only dismantles cultural expectations of heteronormative masculinity but also directly challenges white supremacist ideologies and celebrates integration as an American strength. As music critic Caryn Rose points out, the E Street Band formed shortly after the end of Jim Crow and toured during the racial tensions of the early 1970s, highlighting the importance and risk of this gesture.[49] The tempestuous racial politics of the 1950s and 1960s shaped the progressive ideologies Springsteen would go on to explore in his songwriting, concert performances, and memoir. His sensitive, unremitting artistic contemplation and acceptance of America's subjugated people aligns with the ethos of *Show Me a Hero*.

Heading Home

The Springsteen soundtrack serves as the narrative thrust of *Show Me a Hero* and brings the viewer "more intimately into the story and into knowing who Nick really was," Nay Wasicsko says.[50] More than just a pleasing pop/rock soundtrack, Springsteen's music embodies the thematic spirit of *Show Me a Hero*. His work acutely structures a young man's vanquished ambition and a community's lost integrity. The inclusion of Springsteen on the series' soundscape invites spectators to consider how his extratextual work relates to the series' themes of race, community, and American identity.

Through his decades of songwriting, Springsteen mediates the transgenerational racial and political quandaries encumbering his nation. He inspires his audiences to empathize with those different from themselves and embrace America's diversity, uniting them with "a common vision that we are all living together for the same things: freedom, opportunity, family, safety, and equality … there can be no demonization of 'other sides,' only the realization that we are on the same journey toward the same thing."[51] For Springsteen, we are all on that train bound for glory—black, white, brown, young, old, rich, and poor. In line with *Show Me a Hero*, his work upholds the tenets of justice and inclusivity by exhuming the ghosts of our past so that we may understand, and ultimately transcend, the xenophobic ideologies and racial injustices embedded in America's history.

The protesters in *Show Me a Hero* belie Springsteen's vision of American communities as a space of love, support, and respect. The "social disharmony engineered through racist legacies rests on the shoulders of policymakers" such as Mayor Wasicsko, who fights for unity and inclusion in the city he loves.[52] As Springsteen sings in "We Are Alive," when the uglier ghosts of America's history are resurrected, the legacies of those who stood against injustice, like Nick Wasicsko, persevere. Springsteen and *Show Me a Hero* encourage spectators to recognize our common humanity and take care of each other down our long walk toward the kind of home we want America to be.

American Honey

The poster for Andrea Arnold's *American Honey* (2016) features a young woman sitting on the hood of a car with the wind blowing back her hair à la "Thunder Road." A spacious blue sky superimposed with American flag stars surrounds her. The film's title is set in a rustic-style font emblazoned with an American flag print, bringing to mind the nationalistic aesthetic of Springsteen's *Born in the U.S.A.* era. The girl is Star, a teenage runaway who flees her impecunious home to embark on an odyssey across Midwest America with an obstreperous group of magazine vendors. Along the way, she witnesses the desperate, abject poverty that exists alongside pockets of abundant wealth. *American Honey* explicitly negotiates the minutiae of American life and identity through British director Andrea Arnold's critical outsider's gaze. Arnold says *American Honey* is a mixture of what she witnessed on her own cross-country road trip, "but also what I grew up seeing on films—the mythical America of westerns and road movies."[53] Arnold mobilizes her themes of national identity by using Springsteen, a quintessential American icon, on the soundtrack with his reformulated cover of Suicide's "Dream Baby Dream." With a lush Instagram-hued verité style, *American Honey* contemplates some of the key facets of Springsteen's work: the road and the automobile, young and disenfranchised characters on the run chasing their American Dream, and the pressures of a capitalistic society.

As a road movie influenced by the western genre's American mythology, *American Honey* embodies Springsteen's countless nomadic songs, in which characters use the highway and the act of driving to seek ontological understanding and freedom from institutional oppression. Affected by her own poor, working-class English youth, Arnold authentically captures the same post-economic crisis anxieties that Springsteen bewails on his impassioned album *Wrecking Ball*. At the time of its release, Springsteen notably avowed to reporters, "I have spent my life judging the distance between American reality and the American dream."[54] *American Honey* animates this space within Star's struggle to transcend the hardships of her dire upbringing. Thoroughly Springsteenian ideologies and iconography informed by the road and western film genres suffuse Arnold's luminous epic.

"Dream Baby Dream"

Variety's Guy Lodge describes *American Honey* as "[p]art dreamy millennial picaresque, part distorted tapestry of Americana and part exquisitely illustrated iTunes musical."[55] Soundtrack plays an integral role in *American Honey*, being as much a part of the narrative as the dialogue, and is an inherent part of Arnold's auteurist vision. She told *The Independent*, "Music is a hugely important part of my life. There's not a day goes by where

I don't start by playing music, or have it as some part of my day. Emotionally, it can completely change the way I feel or it can accentuate the way I feel…. So anything I write is always going to have music and dancing because it's just part of my life."[56] Arnold could easily relate to the real-life magazine crew she tailed across the United States in preparation for her film because they "were playing music all the time. It's a huge part of their lives."[57]

In *American Honey*, the soundtrack is interwoven into the crew's identity, capturing "the hope, the fire that burns within them, but also that streak of self-destructive recklessness that comes in our immortal beliefs of youth."[58] Lyrics express their emotional states when they themselves cannot because they guard themselves with juvenile behavior. Music allows the crew to emotionally connect beyond their soulless bacchanalian lifestyle and the loneliness of poverty, uniting them as a community separated from the world's harsh capitalist values. The simplistic pleasure of listening is the only stable, authentic, and joyous aspect of their unhinged lives. Multiple scenes feature the misfit group singing and dancing passionately as their van navigates America's heartland. Arnold cleverly draws from various musical genres—classic rock, country, modern rap, or techno—to construct a soundscape that is as eclectic and complex as the country her characters traverse.

The magazine crew's sing-along sessions are mostly connected to rap and hip-hop tunes that fetishize the ultimate American fantasy: massive amounts of wealth and fame. When Rihanna's "We Found Love" blasts from a Kmart radio, the teenagers transform the mundane, halogen-flared place of business into a ludic wonderland when they stand on check-out counters and spastically boogie through the aisles. The lyrics reflect Star's idealized visions of her romance with Jake: she has also found love in a place without hope. In a similar vein, one of the film's final scenes features the rowdy band of peddlers belting out Lady Antebellum's bucolic "American Honey," a song about the desire to abandon adult life and return to the sweetness of childhood. The mag crew's impoverished lives have caused them to grow up fast, and they navigate the dredges of American society orphaned and alone. The crew often runs into dangerous circumstances, some involving prostitution and drugs. "American Honey" reminds them of the adolescence they never had but secretly yearn for.

American Honey adheres to road movie genre conventions in its heightened use of the soundtrack. The road genre's symbiotic relationship with soundtrack began when Steppenwolf's "Born to Be Wild" blasted over the opening titles of *Easy Rider* (1969). *Easy Rider* was notably the first film to forgo the use of traditional score for popular prerecorded music, straight from director Dennis Hopper and star Peter Fonda's record collection. Whether as diegetic source music blaring from a car radio or as non-diegetic score in a montage, a pop/rock soundtrack in the road genre "[a]urally enhances the mood of the on-screen driving experience" and brings to mind "our own recollections of mobility."[59] The device functions as "another aesthetic expression of the visceral and sensual thrill of driving, of moving at high speed," and often plays during scenes of road travel.[60]

Springsteen's cover of "Dream Baby Dream," the former closer of his *Devils & Dust* tour included on the *High Hopes* album, operates in this manner by appearing diegetically on the radio while Star and a trucker drive through the Midwest. Arnold's camera lingers on the trucker's hanging crosses, adorable Yorkie puppy panting in the backseat, and photographs of his quaint family with beaming smiles. "That's my daughter. She got married last year. I gave her away," the trucker fondly recalls. They are the kind of loving family that Star never had, and she softly replies with envy, "That's sweet." The trucker's kindhearted, pacific demeanor squelches Star's—and, by extension, the audience's—wariness of him, upending the preconceived expectation that a scene involving a young woman alone with a truck driver is insidious in nature.

As soon as Springsteen sings the first moving lines of "Dream Baby Dream," Star breaks into a wide smile and cheerfully exclaims, "I know this one." Earlier in the film, Jake belted out the ballad as he twirled around suburbia's well-manicured lawns; such spontaneity was part of what led Star to fall for the happy-go-lucky, effervescent Jake in the first place. Now Springsteen's mesmeric canticle will forever remind her of him. "The Boss. I love the Boss," the trucker professes. As a middle-aged white man, the trucker fits squarely within Springsteen's demographic, but in this moving scene Arnold insists that Springsteen's appeal is universal because Star, a woman of color, also shares a deep connection to his heartfelt lyrics.

In one of the most poignant moments in the film, Star and the trucker sing along to Springsteen's supplication that they never squelch the burning urgency inside them to make their dreams come true. Moved by the lyrics' seraphic simplicity, the truck driver asks Star, "What's your dream?" Star becomes flustered because no one has ever cared enough to ask her that question before; then she concludes that it is to "have my own place and my own trailer. You know, somewhere with lots of trees, like real big ones. And lots of kids." Springsteen transforms Suicide's jagged electro-punk bop into a hypnotic hymn fueled by the aching sounds of a harmonium. Sung in an impassioned vibrato, Springsteen's reverent mantra begs Star and the trucker to forget the miseries of their arduous daily existence and never stop dreaming of a better future. The use of repetition engenders the forceful fervor of his entreaty. "[T]here's just those few phrases repeated and they are the essence of everything else I'm saying…. It's so purely musical, that's what's beautiful about it, it's so simple and so purely musical," Springsteen reflected to *Mojo*.[61] The minimalist and benevolent lyrics genuflect to the stirring instrumentals of rich cellos and ethereal strings that surround Star and the truck driver, filling them with hope. The soft piano sprinkled throughout sounds like the falling crystals of a thousand wished-upon stars. These heartening sounds drive the sequence's gentle focus on compassion and humanity's innate kindness as Star and the trucker open up their hearts and share their innermost secrets.

Star's rural fantasy mirrors Jake's yearning for his "own spot somewhere in the woods and just fucking … just stay small, you know? Like a little duplex or something. Like the forty acres and a mule, you know? Just some piece of land in the woods somewhere." Jake's reference to the United States' promise to redistribute Confederate property to newly freed black slaves taps into one of the defining thematic preoccupations of *American Honey* and Springsteen's oeuvre: the American Dream. For most Americans, this dream includes homeownership and the ability to support a family through hard work, resolve, and enterprise—no matter what class they occupy. Springsteen believes the American Dream is not for everyone "to make a billion dollars" but to "have an opportunity and the chance to live a life with some decency and some dignity and a chance for some self-respect."[62] However, he and Arnold awaken their audiences "to the emptiness and despair swept under the carpet" of this dream through their protagonists' rejection of a naïve view of America as a utopian space where all hard-working individuals can find prosperity despite their background.[63] Star is repulsed by greedy materialism of the "real wealthy territory" and how the rich ignore the suffering lower classes. During her travels, she witnesses a country where the poor and middle class are drowning in debt and living in derelict conditions while the rich get richer. Like Springsteen's blue-collar workers, the *American Honey* mag crew members are trapped in a lonely and cutthroat capitalistic society that denies them upward mobility.

With just a high school education, Star's only job opportunity is to peddle magazines that no one wants to buy. Springsteen's raw vocals and haunting pump organ score on "Dream Baby Dream" seem to mourn this loss of the American Dream despite the lyrics' plea to dry your tears and persevere with a smile on your face.

The "Dream Baby Dream" scene is Springsteenian in itself because it presents two characters who find a sense of community through the power of music while they barrel down the open road. Arnold uses Springsteen's affective spiritual to demonstrate how music can forge kinship among strangers. As a young woman of color and a middle-aged white man, externally Star and the trucker could not be more different, but they are both ordinary, hard-working Americans straight out of Springsteen's songbook. They heed their working-class hero's call to light a fire within them and bring their wildest dreams to fruition, even if it may be difficult in such a contested and economically divided country.

On the Road

"America is a vast and complicated place filled with all kinds of truths and contradictions and I wanted to find my own emotional connection to it," Arnold reflected on her cross-country road trip as part of her research to inhabit the experiences of her itinerant mag crew subjects.[64] *American Honey* became "a mix of the America I grew up with—which I mostly saw though Hollywood; my romanticised idea of it—and the contemporary America I saw when I did my trips," she told *The Guardian*.[65] Arnold's idealized perception of the United States was shaped by the expansive vistas and roving spirit of the road movie genre. "The road movie is synonymous with American cinema … [and] to some extent defines 'America' itself," having emerged "through the forceful prism of what we might call Eisenhower's Road, a road that celebrates the search for the meaning of America on the highway."[66] The highway and automobile are emblematic American icons because they have adapted to the nation's enormous size and abundant middle class. To accommodate the developing suburbs in the 1950s, President Dwight Eisenhower revitalized the interstate highway system by constructing nearly 40,000 miles of road, thereby enabling motorized mobility to become an object of mass consumption and travel across the United States more accessible.[67] This twentieth-century development cemented road travel as a staple of American life.

Born in 1949, Springsteen entered the world when the production and utilization of the automobile was at its zenith. The hot rod culture of Springsteen's 1950s era upbringing—drag racing around the Circuit in Asbury Park, the "tire-screeching, high-octane heaven" of stock car races at Wall Stadium, his avid consumption of road movies at the Shore Drive-In, and his father's own love of mobility—fueled the car travel motifs that would define his songwriting.[68] Springsteen's image in popular culture has been inextricably tied to the highway and the automobile ever since he found "the key to the universe in the engine of an old parked car" on *Greetings from Asbury Park, N.J.* Most songs in Springsteen's canon incorporate the iconographical and narratological elements of the road movie to simultaneously valorize and critique American ideologies. "Not since Kerouac had a spokesman of American popular culture so clearly recognized the significance of the automobile as a deep icon of our national spirit," Jeffrey Symynkywicz writes.[69] *American Honey*'s inclusion of Springsteen, a quintessentially American icon whose oeuvre embodies the nation's paradigmatic film genre, invites exploration of the road movie's cross-pollination between Arnold's cinematic vision and Springsteen's lyrics.

Out of Springsteen's 318 released songs, 141 reference cars or the road, which translates to almost half of his music.[70] Nearly all of his characters wax poetic about the various streets, roads, turnpikes, and highways they traverse across America—from the pine ridges of South Carolina to the Wisconsin backstreets to New Jersey's Highway 9. The little white lines and rolling blacktop of the open road unfurl a world of boundless possibilities for Springsteen and his characters. Springsteen often frames driving as a baptismal experience with the power to transform his subjects from just another cog in the mundane capitalist machine to emancipated chrome heroes. Conversely, road travel can also be an oppressive action that traps his protagonists in a perpetual quest for insoluble meaning.

Visually, cars appear throughout Springsteen's album covers, promotional photos, and music videos. The *Nebraska* album cover is a point-of-view shot of a car windshield looking out onto a frosty, barren landscape; a single cover of "Dancing in the Dark" features a 1950s-era pink Cadillac (also the title of one of his songs, which equates the female anatomy with that of the rose-colored automobile); and a suit-clad and bolo-tied Springsteen leans up against his 1956 Ford Thunderbird on *Tunnel of Love*. The same Thunderbird is featured in the "I'm on Fire" music video and the ultimate hot rod teen movie, *American Graffiti* (1973). Some other cars that appear in Springsteen's music videos include a 1957 Ford Fairlane Club Sedan ("One Step Up"), a Porsche 550 Spyder ("Better Days"), and a 1962 Chevrolet Biscayne ("Secret Garden"). These classic cars align with the 1950s hot rod aesthetic of Springsteen's early music. Framing Springsteen's body in such close proximity to the cars or inside them further ties him to the object.

Road movie characters often seek the far-reaching road as freedom from oppressive and harrowing social circumstances. Mobility serves as their only means of obtaining personal satisfaction. Disconnection, fragmentation, and isolation are the key motifs "encapsulated in the frequently solitary and often solipsistic figure of the driver [habitually a white male] on the wide and open American road."[71] Springsteen psychically identified with the notorious archetype of the outcast highwayman, one that appears time and time again throughout his oeuvre. He, too, felt alienated from society and had a desire for mobility born from a need to outrun his childhood traumas. Springsteen's chaotic home life with a mentally ill, verbally abusive father indoctrinated the belief that he was undeserving of love. As an adult, he was petrified of intimacy, keeping those around him at a careful emotional distance because the vulnerability of genuinely being loved was strange and overwhelming, causing him to lash out in emotionally brutish behaviors. Springsteen explains in his memoir that he was well suited for an intermittent life on the road as a musician because it enabled him to avoid the oppressive shackles of stability—a long-term relationship, singular home, and nuclear family—that he feared but secretly pined for. Here the significance of his memoir title and magnum opus becomes clear: like a disaffected road movie character, he was a rolling stone "born to run" from mainstream structural comforts.

Arnold similarly describes herself as a "natural roamer" enamored with the immeasurable potentialities of wandering. She would amble around the chalk pits, fields, woods, and motorways that surrounded the tumbledown Dartford, Kent, housing projects where she resided with her single teenage mother.[72] In *American Honey*, Arnold subverts the generic archetype of the white male wanderer that Springsteen avidly adopts throughout his work in her narrative focus on Star, a woman of color. As abandoned children fleeing toxic family situations, Star and the entire mag crew fulfill the road movie character trope of running from the past. The abuses of the foster-care system motivate Star to leave her home and travel across the country with Jake after briefly meeting him in a parking lot. Whatever lies ahead on the distant skyline splayed before the van's dashboard is sure to surpass her current circumstances.

Springsteen's thrumming powerhouses "Born to Run" and "Thunder Road" from *Born to Run* (the album Greil Marcus called "a '57 Chevy running on melted down Crystals records"[73]) are musical road movies. Their widescreen sounds—Clemons' soaring saxophone, the glistening glockenspiel, Springsteen's operatic vocals, layers upon layers of sharp guitars and mighty drums that explode with the walloping force of a thousand coruscating engines—are as massive as the horizon that stretches out before his ramblers. The Technicolor vistas of the hot rod classics from Springsteen's youth inform the vivid grandiosity of these heady anthems. His high-octane lyrics craft imagery that evokes familiar formal qualities of the road genre: a shot of the wind blowing back Mary's wispy hair, panoramic vistas of the expansive two lanes that magically transport the lonely riders to a limitless anywhere, reflections bouncing off the car's windshield, and the sun's glow flaring in the lens. Such iconography appears throughout Arnold's film to suggest how transient characters "become integrated into the moving vehicle (and the moving image)."[74]

Sprung from the cages of their draconian environs, like most road movie characters, Springsteen's tramps regard their mobility with reverence. The road offers them salvation from their "death trap" of a town that grips them in its smothering vise. Springsteen's broken heroes can only know whether love is wild and real if they roar out of the Garden State and leave their sleepy boardwalk town behind in the far distance of their rearview mirror. His music adheres to the generic conventions of the road movie by situating the highway as the manna of redemption, as a space of thrilling urgency and unknown possibility that delivers his despondent subjects to some exhilarating place they've never been before. Star and the mag crew relate to the frustration of Springsteen's protagonists, their desperate need to bolt to a better place, and their idealism—the hope that a prosperous life awaits them on that stretch of the interstate. Arnold expresses this idea in a scene where Star and her friends are in awe of the glistening, silver, "fucking huge" buildings of Kansas City. "I never seen so many tall things in my life.... This is where Superman lives!" one of them exclaims when they enter the city. Compared to the mammoth skylines of New York City, these towers are quite puny, but for Star and the mag crew, who have hardly ventured beyond their insolvent one-story homes, they are a wondrously colossal sight. The excitement of crossing state lines is another road movie genre motif, one that notably appears in Springsteen's "Jungleland." America's rangy spaces offers the road movie characters seen in *American Honey* and Springsteen's music the promise of a better life.

Yet the more Star journeys across America, the more the open road loses its rapturous luster. No longer a gateway to the thrilling unfamiliar, the highway leads her to the same—if not worse—penury she tried to escape from. Arnold once again subverts the road movie genre by reversing the film's earlier idealized visions of mobility. The erosion of Star's nomadic dreams matches the tectonic shift in Springsteen's songwriting within the three-year gap between *Born to Run* and *Darkness on the Edge of Town*. Like Arnold, Springsteen negates his previous romanticism of the road. *Darkness* and the latter half of *American Honey* match the nihilism of 1970s road movies such as *Five Easy Pieces* (1970), *Two-Lane Blacktop* (1971), and *Badlands* (1973), in which chrome-wheeled travel has no significance or capacity for change, characters are no longer motivated by the same sense of purposeful excitement, and the road offers nothing but social disarray and economic devastation.

Financial ruin forces the narrator of Springsteen's dismal "Thunder Road" sequel, "The Promise," to sell the beloved Challenger he painstakingly built with his own two hands, the object that allowed him to escape the oppressive grind of his Darlington job. Racing down Route 9, he followed the dreams of his road movie heroes in his quest for the autonomous freedom that the coveted Thunder Road once offered. Springsteen's warbled intonation and elongation of the phrase "Thunder Road" during the chorus sounds like a requiem for the treasured thruway, the former site of salvation that now harbors dying spirits. "Something in the Night" places Springsteen's subject back in Asbury Park, but instead of leaving the Palace Amusements behind, he aimlessly wanders around the closed loop of the Circuit on Kingsley Avenue, past the familiar two-bit bars and dead ends. The highway was once lit by the resplendent sun, but now he tears into the ravaging guts of the pitch-black night, emblematic of his gloom. He slams his pedal to the floor, speeding off fruitlessly in search of "a moment when the world seems right" out on the expanse of the empty road, but is paralyzed when he reaches the state line, powerless to transcend the boundary of his unendurable hometown. The downtrodden narrator's dreams and hopes for the future are crushed as his former vehicle of redemption explodes into a cinder, leaving him charred and blind—therefore permanently unable to escape. In "Darkness on the Edge of Town," left jobless, penniless, and without a wife, Springsteen's weathered narrator detests those who were "born into a good life" and will never know what it is like to lose their dreams. Racing the trestles no longer liberates the narrator because, as the title indicates, a despairing darkness engulfs the road that leads to the edge of town. For these figures, pulling out of town to win and finding redemption on the open road is not possible.

Star relates to these defeated characters as the struggle of hustling magazines overwhelms her and she becomes a mere pawn of her malicious boss and is forced to sell her body for extra means. Like Springsteen's protagonists, she sadly discovers the more she travels across the Midwest that she cannot afford the luxury of dreaming in her destitute condition. Living from hand to mouth, there seems to be no possible way out for her, no feasible avenue to get back on her feet and live life on her own terms. By the end of *American Honey* and in *Darkness on the Edge of Town*, the automobile and open road are no longer the holy grail of salvation. Arnold and Springsteen cut to the core of contemporary American ennui and disaffection stemming from the pressures of economic oppression and cultural alienation by engaging with the darker ethos of the road movie.

Rebels and Runaways

The ne'er do wells of *American Honey* share a continuity with the hobo, a Depression-era icon who exists outside the law and society. His unattached, rambling lifestyle is an implicit critique of materialism.[75] This figure inspired Jack Kerouac's whiskey-fueled magnum opus *On the Road*, the formative influence of Vietnam-era road movies such as *Easy Rider* (1969) or *Scarecrow* (1973). Arnold's flaneurs relate to the countercultural, anti-establishment protagonists of those films, the drug-addled motorcyclists and vagrant rovers who reject conventional domesticity. As runaways from impoverished backgrounds, the teenagers of *American Honey* "embrace the hobo lifestyle as the debris of a failed economic system."[76] Abandoned by their families, who cannot afford them, they have nowhere else to turn and no other prospects aside from a haphazard trade that defies the nine-to-five paradigm. Star and the mag crew hop from motel to motel and door to door across America to procure an income based purely on happenstance, scrounging for measly cash to hand over to their exploitative boss who divvies up the pay at her own discretion, an amount that fluctuates daily.

Arnold infuses *American Honey* with a Kerouacian beatnik wanderlust through the mag crew's hedonism. "We explore, like, America. We party. A whole bunch of shit. It's cool," one of them brags to Star after she joins the group. They reject monogamy and often trade sexual partners, preferring an unreserved polyamorous expression of physical and romantic attraction. The mag crew's van is a rowdy, lawless space where they are free to drink alcohol, smoke weed, and jam to music while they discover unseen American landscapes. Arnold frames these rambunctious moments with familiar road movie iconography: a tremulous, mobile camera positioned inside the car looking out onto the hood, rear windshields, or rearview mirrors; dynamic montages composed of long takes and long shots that express the traversal of space and time; and a desultory shooting style that gives the spectator a kinetic sense of being on the road. In these wild sequences, *American Honey* shares the infatuation with drug culture and devil-may-care attitudes of the consummate road movie *Easy Rider*.

Star's bacchanalian lifestyle brings to mind Springsteen's colorful portrait of New Jersey nightlife in "Spirit in the Night," a jazzy romp about Crazy Janey, Wild Billy, G-Man, and Hazy Davy hightailing down Route 88 to party at Greasy Lake, mirroring the final scene of *American Honey*, in which the galère drunkenly capers around a lakeside bonfire. The dust in Wild Billy's coonskin cap and bottle of rosé seems to have quite an effect on Springsteen's merrymakers, as their frenzied clowning erupts into the absurd violence of a "stone mud fight" in the same way that the mag crew's parking lot dance-offs often burst into fisticuffs. Crazy Janey's lovemaking in the dirt with her mission man echoes the scene in which Star and Jake have sex in a field of wildflowers. Arnold's decision to use a street cast—a group of non-actors selected after scouting Walmart parking lots and spring break beaches—mobilizes the film's freewheeling aesthetic. Sasha Lane (who plays Star) and the ensemble bring their own grungy, idiosyncratic styles to their loose, improvised performances. The actors' fluid naturalism invokes *American Honey*'s anarchic authenticity in the vein of early road movies.

The open-ended narrative structure of *American Honey* opposes the formulaic architecture of classic cinema. At its heart, *American Honey* is a quest road movie marked by its meandering design that probes the mysterious experience of discovery. A quest narrative carves out a rambling, picaresque path; aimless and fragmented, it does not possess a clear-cut beginning, middle, or end, nor does it point toward a specific destination.[77] This wayward armature embodies the protagonists' carefree nomadic spirits. The filmic body can be thought of a Möbius strip, with repetitive scenes continuously looping in on themselves: the mag crew sings along to music, sells magazines, drives the van to another state, listens to music, hustles magazines, drives to another state, again and again and again. Arnold expresses the tedious futility of Star's quest in the film's wearying three-hour length. Each stop Star makes for her sales never seems to get her any further than where she began. The final shot of Star submerging herself in a lake is purposefully ambiguous, an ending that avoids a neat conclusion of her literal and emotional journey. Although the action can be read as baptismal, a rite of passage in which Star leaves the mag crew behind and is reborn an independent woman, her destiny is ultimately as unknown as the spider web of highways before her.

Into the West

With its emphasis on migration, wandering, and the frontier, the western genre functions as the road movie's grandparent.[78] The cowboy is an earlier incarnation of the hobo archetype, someone whose wings are unclipped by the law and domestic responsibilities and who is free to roam the unpredictable American wilderness. The western genre's lone rider reemerges as the road movie's vagabond, a solitary traveler who traverses America's bucolic terrain in order to abandon modernity and humankind, a conceit reflected in Star and Jake's dreams to live alone in the countryside. Jake has a hefty stash of stolen jewelry and cash that he has hoarded for years to make this wish come true. Star and Jake's pastoral longing is the locus of the western genre and the road movie's ideological "tension between rebellion and conformity."[79] The wayward couple desires "security and enclosure" via place (their dream home) while at the same time needing the freedom and mobility afforded by space (their current life on the road) in the same way that Springsteen's drivers ironically "long for roots and yet feel essentially rootless," a reflection of the cowboy's incongruous internal conflict, seen in characters such as Ethan Edwards of *The Searchers*.[80] Springsteen told Kurt Loder that he personally identified with such tensions: "I don't like feelin' too rooted for some reason. Which is funny, because the things that I admire and the things that mean a lot to me all have to do with roots and home, and myself, personally, I'm the opposite. I'm very rootless in that sense. I never attach myself to any place that I am. I always felt most at home when I was like in the car or on the road, which is, I guess, why I always wrote about it."[81]

The road movie's expansive American vistas "obviously recall the Western's compelling articulation of the frontier."[82] Arnold's Malickian shots capture the Midwest's voluminousness with a breathtaking flourish despite her tightened use of an Instagram-esque full-frame 1.33:1 style. Her gorgeously georgic images have a unique intimate focus on minuscule worldly details—the way a blade of grass sways in the breeze, a flicker of light on the dashboard, how smoke disappears into the black of night. In one scene, Star and the mag crew visit the Badlands National Park in South Dakota, the locale of Springsteen's *Darkness on the Edge of Town* opener named after Terrence Malick's western noir. Arnold's kinetic camera hovers beside Star's shoulders and scans the rocky canyon landscape that stretches as far as the eye can see, the sunset hues softly accentuating the plateau's exquisite grandeur. "I wanted one [moment] where you just think: Wow, this country is amazing. I thought, no wonder people have this sort of huge feeling about America, because, look, it's amazing. I wanted that," Arnold told *Vogue*.[83] Arnold surveys another Springsteenian space when Star and the mag crew visit an oil field, recalling the industrial refineries in songs such as "State Trooper" and "Open All Night." The wide cornflower blue sky blends into the pale dirt as Star dances for the scruffy hard-hat workers on their break.

Arnold's sprawling, arcadian American landscapes recall Springsteen's monologue before his performance of "The Promised Land" in *Springsteen on Broadway*. Before the song, he describes his three-day trip to a midnight New Year's Eve gig in Big Sur, California, when he saw the United States "at its fullest and I was overwhelmed by its beauty." Springsteen continues, adapting from a poetic passage in his memoir:

> The country was beautiful and I felt a great elation at the wheel as we crossed the western desert at dawn, the deep blue and purple shadowed canyons, pale yellow morning sky with all its color drawn out, leaving just the black silhouetted mountains behind us…. Morning woke the Earth into muted color, then came the flat light of the midday sun, and everything stood revealed as pure horizon low-

ering on two lanes of blacktop and disappearing into… nothing—my favorite thing. Then the evening, with the sun burning in your eyes, dropping gold into the western mountains. It all felt like home and I fell into a lasting love affair with the desert.[84]

Springsteen invokes the western genre by leaving his familiar New Jersey milieu for sprawling deserts and wild prairies on the albums *Darkness on the Edge of Town*, *Nebraska*, *The Ghost of Tom Joad*, and *Devils & Dust*. His characters bask in the tranquility of nature—auburn skies, grassy hills draped with sweet blossoms, stone rivers bubbling along the Mexican border, the mesquite rustling in the wind, Cassiopeia and Orion sparkling in the spacious sky, the cool blues of the towering Sierra Madres. Such gorgeous visions of earthly beauty run throughout *American Honey* and are part of its western-inspired romanticization of the wilderness.

Below Banker's Hill

John Ford's Great Depression tone poem *The Grapes of Wrath*—the inspiration for Springsteen's stark *The Ghost of Tom Joad* album, which tackles Midwestern poverty, Mexican immigration, and the increasing epidemic of homelessness in the United States during the 1990s—is a precursor to the road movie genre. *The Grapes of Wrath* chronicles the Joad family's journey to California in search of a new livelihood after the devastation of the Dust Bowl, while *American Honey* surveys America in the aftermath of another great depression: the financial crisis of 2008. Like Star and her band of misfits, the Joads are victims of a cruel capitalistic system. Their road trip is made under duress, marked by an incessant worry over limited resources—food, money, gas—and the journey leads them to one bad situation after another in the same way that Star and the mag crew escape toxic family situations only to be placed in dangerous circumstances and dilapidated spaces while they scrounge for paltry means each day.

In "The Ghost of Tom Joad," Springsteen transforms the highway—his "iconic symbol of hope rooted in the American tradition of exploration and progression"—into a "structural manifestation of division, inequality and inaccessible opportunity. The highway may lead to transference from one location to another, but not to transcendence from the inescapable and hellacious conditions that define their lives as social misery."[85] Mobility only plunges his protagonists into further economic despair. Scores of homeless men who warm themselves next to campfires, walk along abandoned railroad tracks, and wait in a line around the block for shelter, lest they be forced to rest their heads on asphalt or in a cardboard box, populate America's heartland. Families with no homes or jobs sleep in cars, and babies cry from hunger pangs. This is "the new world order." The west that was once a land of hope and promise, and a symbol of meritocracy and Manifest Destiny, is now a ravaged wasteland. The ghost of Tom Joad, someone who once stood against human injustices, haunts this ruined country where the American Dream is proven a lie.

The devastated landscape of Springsteen's haunting ballad anticipates Star's environment in *American Honey*. Much like the Joads, the destitute mag crew are refugees fleeing from their impecunious homes and "forced to view society from the enlightening distance instability affords."[86] During their westward journey, they witness the affluent upper echelons of society who willingly turn a blind eye and refuse to aid the families struggling beneath them. Each space they visit in *American Honey*—the middle-class homes, the oil fields, the sprawling mansions—highlights their proletarian strata and stands in stark contrast to the dreadfully poverty-stricken areas nearby. Along their travels, they critique America's cruel capitalistic society and the modern economic crisis' deadly ramifications on families. "I really wish I could meet the motherfucker that invented selling dirt," one of them chides with envy. Such observations are drawn from Arnold's own experience during her cross-country road trip.

The distressing circumstances Arnold witnessed during her travels belied the glamorous portraits of the United States found in mainstream cinema: "I grew up with a lot of Hollywood films. Cozy farmhouses, cowboys, nice flats in New York ... you know, I grew up seeing farmhouses on the prairie. Then when we go there, a lot of the farmhouses are run down," Arnold said.[87] "I was quite upset about some of the towns I went to, and some of the poverty I saw. It seemed really different to me than in the UK," she explained in another interview.[88] She expressed concern for the United States' lack of universal health care, high rates of drug addiction, and shortage of jobs in small towns where "there's not a lot of industries if you're coming out of school and need to work. A lot of the opportunities were working in fast food restaurants. That seemed quite sad to me."[89] Many of the places Arnold visited (such as Muskogee, Oklahoma, one of the poorest towns in America) were far too bleak to be shown in her film. "Some of the things I saw, with people in poverty, the film doesn't go anywhere near it. If I had, people's eyes would open even wider. The reaction to the film would be completely different," she reveals.[90]

It is difficult to imagine the severity of the neglect that Arnold witnessed because *American Honey* features some incredibly destitute places. Arnold's camera lingers closely on various grimy objects in domestic spaces so that spectators may identify with the unpleasant sensorial experience of being inside these locales. In Star's home, unwashed plates and overfilled ashtrays sit on tables; ants crawl around a group of leftover French fries on the countertop; one of the children stabs a chicken with a fork, its pale red blood spilling on the coffee-colored stained tile floor, where two large pit bulls roam nearby; and the wallpaper peels behind a refrigerator that holds only beer and soda. Later in the film, Star stumbles upon a crumbling house with filthy, broken shutters, corroded planks, and beams shedding their white paint. Inside, three moppet children, all under the age of seven, sit alone among a gallimaufry of damaged toys and furniture and a sink stockpiled with dirty dishes. Star spies the mother passed out on the bed with a crack pipe beside her—a reminder of her own mother, who died of a meth addiction.

Growing up in working-class Freehold, New Jersey, inside a tumble-down home with no hot water and heated by a single kerosene stove, Springsteen was no stranger to such conditions. "We only bathed a few times a week because the ritual of my mother heating up pots of water on the gas stove, then carrying them up, one by one, to slowly fill the upstairs bath was too much," Springsteen writes in his memoir.[91] The unauthorized biography *Point Blank* by Christopher Sandford claims that young Springsteen "haunt[ed] the dustbins at the Borough Hall soup kitchen."[92] As a child, he watched his father bounce from one grinding, soul-crushing blue-collar job to the next, from taxi driver to prison guard to rug mill worker, assembly lineman, and bus driver—wearying jobs "that take everything from you and give you barely nothing back."[93] During his late teens and early twenties as a struggling musician, Springsteen lived hand to mouth while either shacked up in the back of a surfboard factory or shuffling from couch to couch on the verge of homelessness. All of these experiences honed Springsteen's artistic focus on people living in the shadow of the American Dream.

American Honey's opening scene immediately places the spectator within Star's arrested youth and tumultuous upbringing when she scrounges in a dumpster to feed her small, grubby-faced foster siblings. At home, her foster mother's boyfriend begs her to "dance with Dad." Arnold uses suffocating close-up shots to convey Star's profound discomfort when "Dad" grabs her buttocks, licks her neck, and forces her to slow dance amid the haze of cigarette smoke and littered debris of empty beer cans. After she agrees to join the mag crew, Star drops off her foster siblings with their belligerent mother at a bar—interrupting her drunken line-dancing routine. With raccoon eyes from smudged mascara and rumpled clothing stretched over her flabby belly, Star's lewd foster mother scorns her offspring with a deep-seated hatred, flippantly dismissing them as objects to be pawned off on Star while she engages in her own frivolous affairs. "I can't have them.... Fuck you, bitch," she childishly hisses. Perhaps that is why Star dreams of having children of her own—she wants to break the cycle and provide a better life for them. Star is determined to rise from the ashes of these derelict conditions like a phoenix.

Arnold's focus on the quotidian existence of people struggling in vain to make ends meet is in line with the songs of Springsteen's canon, as the majority of his characters are working class or poor. As Deardorff argues, "If there is one condition that informs all the other social maladies under which Springsteen's characters and millions of Americans suffer, it is poverty. From his very first album, Springsteen has populated his songs with tired people so poor that they can barely afford to die," including firemen, gas station workers, dockworkers, mechanics, coal miners, car washers, foremen, and factory workers.[94] Throughout his oeuvre, Springsteen chronicles the oppression, exploitation, and neglect of hard-working American people buckling under post–Fordist economics. The taut lyrics and scorching guitar solos on *Darkness on the Edge of Town* craft an arid soundscape that matches the album's Midwestern backdrop and the characters' primal instincts to survive; *Born in the U.S.A.* envelops somber stories of characters facing unemployment and the degradation of their once idyllic hometowns in buzzing pop hooks; *The Ghost of Tom Joad* is a granular portrait of the harrowing 1990s immigration crisis. The acoustic masterpieces found on the latter album unflinchingly unveil the country's dark realities by intimately examining the lives of extremely destitute characters, many of whom are homeless. "Balboa Park," a half-whispered ode about a homeless Mexican huffer named Spider who transports cocaine and cohabitates with young male prostitutes, echoes *American Honey* in its examination of poverty's devastating effects on children and teenagers, especially those who are orphaned.

However, it is what Donald Deardorff calls the "'angriest album' of his career" that directly informs *American Honey*'s milieu.[95] *Wrecking Ball* is an apoplectic vilification of "the first major recession of the twenty-first century, an economic disaster largely caused by individual and corporate greed that left the swelling ranks of the poor even poorer and the shrinking middle class ever more pressed while the wealthy emerged relatively unscathed."[96] Springsteen uses violent, evocative imagery to condemn the bourgeoisie, likening them to ravenous, flesh-eating vultures that play God by obliterating community-sustaining factories and beloved homes. They are gambling men who haphazardly roll the dice and let the working man face the dangerous consequences, irresponsible figures who leisurely pass time on banker's hill while leaving the shackled lower classes to starve, criminals who freely roam the streets. In the somber "Jack of All Trades," a weary husband assures his timorous wife that his tactile work—harvesting crops and repairing cars, drains, and roofs—will see them through the economic drought, but internally he suppresses a morose desire to "find the bastards and shoot 'em on sight," the higher-ups who have left him in dire straits. Springsteen transforms the automobile, the seminal icon of his lyrical palate and potent symbol of freedom, into a broken, unstable object during the second verse when the narrator boasts of his ability to repair his car engine.

In "We Take Care of Our Own," Springsteen rebukes America for failing as a nation to care for its struggling people, thereby betraying its constitutional dogma. The vigorous pounding drums and ringing chimes are at odds with Springsteen's growled search for merciful hearts to ameliorate the lower classes' anguish. "In the beginning, the idea [of America] was that we all live here a little bit like a family, where the strong can help the weak ones.… We're slowly getting split up into two different Americas. Things are being taken away from the people that need them and given to the people that don't," Springsteen told Geoffrey Himes.[97] Now he cries out for a country that has abandoned such ideals of familyhood, its "good intentions … gone dry as bone." The lower classes are nothing more than invisible objects to those who sit on gilded thrones built by their broken backs. Their hearts have been turned to stone in their futile search for enlivening work to occupy their hands, engage them with the world at large, and set their souls free.

Both Springsteen and Arnold examine the cavernous chasms between America's rich, middle class, and poor in the wake of the 2008 financial crisis. When Star traverses across America, she witnesses how, like Springsteen's characters, those in need have been abandoned by the upper classes, left without proper homes, education, and food. She sees this reality in her own trailer park community, the ramshackle motels she and the mag crew stay in, and the decrepit Mexican neighborhood that appears at the end of the film with unsupervised children aimlessly roaming the overgrown weeds in their front yards. Star and her companions observe how the other half lives—the "rich motherfuckers," they call them—sitting "fat and easy up on banker's hill," as Springsteen sings. Arnold frames the "nice-ass neighborhood[s]" from behind the van's windows to symbolize the mag crew's demarcation from the upper fringes of society. They stick out like sore thumbs on the bright green lawns of the cyclopean mansions with their craggy clothing, dyed hair, and smattered tattoos.

By narrowly focusing on spaces and objects in subjective shots, Arnold heightens the spectators' awareness of how her characters perceive the world around them. We register Star's discomfort when she and Jake enter one of the suburban palaces. On the outside, sparkling gold horse-shaped knockers guard the forest green door—its color symbolizing the family's wealth. Inside, an incandescent chandelier hangs from a towering ceiling, posh modern art and gold-framed mirrors adorn the walls, vases of fresh flowers sit on ornate tables beside a massive stone fireplace, and a puppy prances on the white and grey marble floors. A cornucopia of birthday presents, including social media mogul Kim Kardashian's book of selfies, lies on the center coffee table above a sprawling, intricate Kashan rug.

Star is insulted by the rich woman's judgment and Jake's groveling as he tries to sell her the remnants of a dying industry. Jake pretends that the magazine sales are part of a program to pay for his first year of college and the woman's purchase would be "more about sponsoring impoverished youths, so that they can chase their dreams and actually make something of their lives." He continues, "I come from nothing, ma'am. Like, I'm an impoverished youth, bottom barrel, and this would be my chance to, like, achieve something more with myself." His Oliver Twist–esque performance upsets Star because she does not want to lie, be ashamed of her background, or have to ingratiate herself with the upper classes who have taken so much from people like her.

In Search of America

During one of the last scenes, Star meets a trio of men in cowboy hats who live in an elegant stone mansion with chestnut horses roaming free on the grassy outskirts. They agree to purchase her magazines because they "ain't got nothing better to spend our time and money on." Jake arrives and pulls Star along to steal their Cadillac, reclaiming the epitomized object of American wealth and fantasy. With her back toward the camera, Star sits on top of the stolen Cadillac and stretches her arms out into the howling wind. The expansive blue sky and billowing white clouds consume the frame as she screams in elation, "I feel like I'm fucking America!" She has just made her first magazine sale and earned four hundred dollars, more money than she has ever seen at once in her entire life. For the first time, the country's promise of upward mobility seems obtainable. But the allure of Star's earnings quickly collapses under the immense pressures of impoverished living. The tagline of *American Honey*—"Travel across the vast emptiness of the American dream"—affirms that in modern society, America's golden promises of prosperity are ultimately meaningless for those already in the vise-like grip of destitution. Determination and initiative are futile when the gap between the lower and upper classes is constantly widening. No matter how far her travels take her, Star will never be able to escape the cycle of poverty.

The dominant thematic icons of Springsteen's music—the road, the car, and America itself—define *American Honey*. Like Arnold, Springsteen tells stories that are typically hidden from American life "because they contradict the cozy Horatio Alger tales of 'rugged individualism' that take place in a 'land of opportunity' where supposedly anyone can succeed without significant obstruction if he or she is willing to work hard."[98] From Arnold's restless mag crew and oil workers to Springsteen's disillusioned dockworkers and garage mechanics, both artists chronicle lower-class characters' dreams of transcending the perennial rhythms of penury that compel them to hit the highway in search of "a place to call their own and a chance for economic and emotional satisfaction" through a comfortable home and decent, dignified employment.[99] Arnold's and Springsteen's road movie narratives informed by western genre mythology conclude that the quest for the fabled American Dream is fractured and hard to reconcile with across the boundless landscape of a divided country.

Chapter Notes

Preface

1. Jon Landau, in e-mail discussion with the author, July 11, 2018.
2. Ibid.
3. Bruce Springsteen, "Chords for Change," *New York Times*, August 5, 2004, https://www.nytimes.com/2004/08/05/opinion/chords-for-change.html.
4. Colleen Sheehy, *Springsteen: Troubadour of the Highway* (Seattle: Frederick R. Weisman Art Museum, 2002).

Introduction

1. Meg Guroff, Jim Jerome, and Lyndon Stambler, "Glory Days: Friends of the Boss Share Their Most Intimate Insights," *AARP The Magazine* (September 2009), https://www.aarp.org/entertainment/music/info-07-2009/springsteen_glory_days.html.
2. Jon Landau, in e-mail discussion with the author, July 11, 2018.
3. Ariel Swartley, "*The Wild, the Innocent and the E Street Shuffle*: Bruce Springsteen (Columbia 32432) 1974," in *Stranded: Rock and Roll for a Desert Island*, edited by Greil Marcus (Boston: Da Capo Press, 2007), 55.
4. David Burke, *Heart of Darkness: Bruce Springsteen's Nebraska* (London: Cherry Red Books, 2011), 73.
5. Chet Flippo, *Musician* (November 1984).
6. Paul Nelson, "Springsteen Fever," *Rolling Stone*, July 13, 1978, https://www.rollingstone.com/music/music-news/springsteen-fever-178757/.
7. Debbie Miller, "Bruce Springsteen in the Heartland," *Rolling Stone*, August 16, 1984, https://www.rollingstone.com/music/live-reviews/bruce-in-the-heartland-19840816.
8. Dave Marsh, *Two Hearts: The Story* (New York: Routledge, 2003), 146.
9. Robert Hilburn, *Springsteen* (New York: Scribner, 1985), 121.
10. Ibid.
11. Judith Skinner Sawyers, "Introduction," in *Racing in the Street: The Bruce Springsteen Reader*, edited by Judith Skinner Sawyers (London: Penguin Books, 2004), 22.
12. Caryn Rose, "All 314 Bruce Springsteen Songs, Ranked from Worst to Best," *Vulture*, September 13, 2016, http://www.vulture.com/2016/06/every-bruce-springsteen-song-ranked.html.
13. Bruce Springsteen, *Born to Run* (New York: Simon & Schuster, 2016), 431.
14. Nicholas Dawidoff, "The Pop Populist," *New York Times Magazine*, January 26, 1997.
15. Ibid.
16. Springsteen, *Born to Run*, 296.
17. Ibid.
18. Ibid.
19. Landau, e-mail discussion with the author.
20. Giaco Furino, "Does Bruce Springsteen Love B-Movies?" *Tribeca Shortlist*, April 29, 2017, https://outtake.tribecashortlist.com/does-bruce-springsteen-love-b-movies-d4873ed9abfb.
21. Ibid.
22. Bruce Springsteen, *Songs* (New York: HarperCollins, 2003), 44.
23. Furino, "Does Bruce Springsteen Love B-Movies?"
24. Landau, e-mail discussion with the author.
25. Ibid.
26. Flippo, *Musician*.
27. Burke, *Heart of Darkness*, 74.
28. Pauline Reay, *Music in Film: Soundtracks and Synergy* (New York: Wallflower Press, 2004), 31.
29. Jeff Smith, *The Sounds of Commerce: Marketing Popular Film Music* (New York: Columbia University Press, 1998), 164.
30. Anahid Kassabian, *Hearing Film: Tracking Identifications in Contemporary Hollywood Film Music* (New York: Routledge, 2000).
31. Will Percy, "Rock and Read: Will Percy Interviews Bruce Springsteen," *DoubleTake* (Spring 1998).
32. Ibid.
33. David R. Shumway, "Rock 'n' Roll Sound Tracks and the Production of Nostalgia," *Cinema Journal* 38, no. 2 (Winter 1999), 36.
34. John Sayles, *Thinking in Pictures: The Making of the Movie Matewan* (Boston: Da Capo Press, 2003), 109.
35. John Sayles, in phone discussion with the author, May 23, 2018.
36. Claudia Gorbman, "Why Music? The Sound Film and Its Spectator," in *Movie Music, the Film Reader*, edited by Kay Dickinson (London: Routledge, 2003), 58.

Baby It's You

1. After *Baby It's You*, Springsteen would go on to write "Lift Me Up" for the end credits of Sayles'

Limbo (1999). His ethereal use of falsetto and the transcendental lyrics are perfectly suited for the film's enigmatic ending, with the protagonists looking heavenward in hopes of being rescued or in fear of meeting their death. The abrupt cut to black that follows fixes them in an eternal limbo.

2. Cynthia Baron, "Sales Between the Systems: Bucking 'Industry Policy and the Indie Apolitical Chic,'" in *Sayles Talk: New Perspectives on Independent Filmmaker John Sayles*, edited by Diane Carson and Heidi Kanaga (Detroit: Wayne State University Press, 2006), 41.

3. John Sayles, in phone discussion with the author, May 23, 2018.

4. Alex Woloch, "Breakups and Reunions: Late Realism in Early Sayles," in *Sayles Talk: New Perspectives on Independent Filmmaker John Sayles*, edited by Diane Carson and Heidi Kanaga (Detroit: Wayne State University Press, 2006), 70.

5. Baron, "Sales Between the Systems," 38.

6. Osborne, David. "John Sayles: From Hoboken to Hollywood—And Back," *American Film*, October 1982.

7. Bruce Springsteen, *Born to Run* (New York: Simon & Schuster, 2016), 222.

8. *Ibid.*, 170.

9. Sayles, phone discussion with the author.

10. Elizabeth M. Seymour, "'Where Dreams Are Found and Lost': Springsteen, Nostalgia, and Identity," in *Bruce Springsteen, Cultural Studies, and the Runaway American Dream*, edited by Kenneth Womack, Jerry Zolten, and Mark Bernhard (New York: Routledge, 2016), 66.

11. Springsteen, *Born to Run*, 77.

12. *Ibid.*, 76.

13. *Ibid.*

14. *Ibid.*, 74.

15. Jack Ryan, *John Sayles, Filmmaker: A Critical Study and Filmography* (Jefferson, NC: McFarland, 2010), 74.

16. Springsteen, *Born to Run*, 192.

17. Sayles, phone discussion with the author.

18. There is one scene featuring the Ratmobile that frames the automobile in the same vein as Springsteen's songs, where cars are an incredible source of pride for men, an extension of their virility, and a flashy toy used to impress girls. After school, Sheik takes Jill for a hypersonic joy ride in the Ratmobile, a possession he has borrowed to dazzle his upper-class girlfriend. Wielding it at such a breakneck pace demonstrates his strength and control. The manic absurdity of "Surfin' Bird," its rapid instrumentation and repetitive, nonsensical lines sung in a silly, high-pitched voice, fuels Sheik's roller-coaster ride down one-way streets, over and under bridges, and past a lumber mill. Sayles quickly intercuts between wide shots of the car blazing down the Jersey streets and close-up interiors of Jill and Sheik looking out the window over the dashboard in exhilaration. After Sheik returns Jill to the school parking lot, he disappears like a mysterious magician in a puff of smoke to the sound of squealing tires. This scene has the same freewheeling exuberance as Springsteen's countless rockers about cars.

19. Keith Phipps, "The Semi-Lost Brilliance of John Sayles' 'Baby It's You,'" *Oscilloscope Musings*, July 21, 2015, http://musings.oscilloscope.net/post/124673064816/the-semi-lost-brilliance-of-john-sayles-baby.

20. David Osborne, "John Sayles: From Hoboken to Hollywood—and Back," in *John Sayles: Interviews*, edited Diane Carson (Jackson: University of Mississippi Press, 1999), 35.

21. Gavin Smith, *Sayles on Sayles* (London: Faber and Faber, 1998), 99.

22. John Sayles, phone discussion with the author.

Mask

1. Thomas J. Harris, *Bogdanovich's Picture Shows* (Metuchen, NJ: Scarecrow Press, 1990), 245.

2. Bogdanovich also protested the removal of two integral scenes whose absence completely disrupts the film's mood and temporal logic. These scenes are restored on the DVD "Director's Cut" along with the Springsteen soundtrack. In the first, Rocky and his mother perform a song and dance routine to "Little Egypt (Ying Yang)" by the Coasters. This sequence not only gave star Cher the chance to display her renowned singing skills but also was "designed as a high in the middle of the picture to imbue a sense of fun," according to Bogdanovich on the DVD commentary. "Without it, you have miserable scenes one after the other," he continued. This scene served as an interlude that split *Mask* into two acts, with the latter segment focused on Rocky's troubles with girls and romance. The second cut scene was the funeral of Red, Rocky's biker friend. Rocky's exchange with his mother after the burial gave the spectator a glimpse into Rocky's enlightened perspective on death and foreshadowed his own fate. Rocky comforts Rusty by telling her that Red is not in a grave; rather, "He's everywhere now. It's like he used to say, Mom, 'Nobody ever really dies.'" Later, in the film's denouement, these soothing words reassure Rusty that although her son has passed away, she will always carry his spirit with her. Yet when this moving moment with Rocky is erased in the theatrical version, her reference to his monologue—"Now you can go anywhere you want, baby"—does not carry the same dramatic weight.

3. Harris, *Bogdanovich's Picture Shows*, 209.

4. Andrew Yule, *Picture Shows: The Life and Films of Peter Bogdanovich* (New York: Limelight Editions, 1992), 210.

5. Harris, *Bogdanovich's Picture Shows*, 210.

6. "Feature Commentary with Director Peter Bogdanovich," *Mask: Director's Cut*, directed by Peter Bogdanovich (Universal City, CA: Universal Pictures Home Entertainment, 2004), DVD.

7. Harris, *Bogdanovich's Picture Shows*, 211.

8. *Ibid.*, 209.

9. "Feature Commentary with Director Peter Bogdanovich," *Mask: Director's Cut*, DVD.

10. *Ibid.*

11. *Ibid.*

12. *Rolling Stone*, "Bruce Springsteen Honored at Kennedy Center by Mellencamp, Vedder, Sting," December 30, 2009, https://www.rollingstone.com/music/music-news/bruce-springsteen-honored-at-kennedy-center-by-mellencamp-vedder-sting-254744/.

13. Ann V. Bliss, "Growin' Up to Be a Nothing Man: Masculinity, Community, and the Outsider in Bruce Springsteen's Songs," in *Reading the Boss: Interdisciplinary Approaches to the Works of Bruce Springsteen*, edited by Roxanne Harde and Irwin Streight (Lanham, MD: Lexington Books, 2010), 141.

14. Christopher Sandford, *Springsteen: Point Blank* (Boston: Da Capo Press, 1999), 146.

15. Mark Hagen, "The Midnight Cowboy," in *Talk about a Dream: The Essential Interviews of Bruce Springsteen*, edited by Christopher Phillips and Louis P. Masur (New York: Bloomsbury Press, 2013), 254.

16. Peter Ames Carlin, *Bruce* (New York: Simon & Schuster, 2012), 12.

17. Eric Alterman, *It Ain't No Sin to Be Glad You're Alive: The Promise of Bruce Springsteen* (New York: Back Bay Books, 2001), 16.

18. Bruce Springsteen, *Born to Run* (New York: Simon & Schuster, 2016), 15.

19. *Ibid*.

20. *Ibid.*, 16.

21. *Ibid*.

22. Sandford, *Springsteen: Point Blank*, 146.

23. Bruce Springsteen, *Songs* (New York: HarperCollins, 2003), 26.

24. Harris, *Bogdanovich's Picture Shows*, 254.

25. "Feature Commentary with Director Peter Bogdanovich," *Mask: Director's Cut*, DVD.

26. Harris, *Bogdanovich's Picture Shows*, 247.

27. *Ibid.*, 253.

28. *Ibid.*, 255.

29. Mikal Gilmore, "Bruce Springsteen: Voice of the Decade," *Rolling Stone*, November 15, 1990, https://www.rollingstone.com/music/music-news/bruce-springsteen-voice-of-the-decade-192581.

30. Harris, *Bogdanovich's Picture Shows*, 268.

31. "Feature Commentary with Director Peter Bogdanovich," *Mask: Director's Cut*, DVD.

32. *Ibid*.

33. *Ibid*.

34. Harris, *Bogdanovich's Picture Shows*, 272.

35. "Feature Commentary with Director Peter Bogdanovich," *Mask: Director's Cut*, DVD.

36. *Ibid*.

37. *Ibid*.

38. *Ibid*.

39. David Masciotra, *Working on a Dream: The Progressive Political Vision of Bruce Springsteen* (New York: A&C Black, 2010), 243.

40. Harris, *Bogdanovich's Picture Shows*, 266.

41. *Ibid.*, 245.

In Country

1. Bobbie Ann Mason, *In Country* (New York: Harper Perennial, 1985), 123.

2. *Ibid.*, 124.

3. *Ibid.*, 122.

4. I've always found this plot line very uncomfortable in the film version, perhaps because Emily Lloyd's Sam has such a wide-eyed naiveté, while Mason's novel paints her as more of a grungy rebel.

5. Mason, *In Country*, 123.

6. Kurt Loder, "The Rolling Stone Interview: Bruce Springsteen on 'Born in the U.S.A.,'" *Rolling Stone*, December 7, 1984, https://www.rollingstone.com/music/news/the-rolling-stone-%20interview-bruce-springsteen-on-born-in-the-u-s-a-19841206.

7. *Ibid*.

8. Roger Scott and Patrick Humphries, *HotPress*, November 2, 1984.

9. *Ibid*.

10. George Will, "A Yankee Doodle Springsteen," *Washington Post*, September 13, 1984.

11. David Masciotra, *Working on a Dream: The Progressive Political Vision of Bruce Springsteen* (New York: A&C Black, 2010), 11.

12. Jefferson Cowie and Lauren Boehm, "Dead Man's Town: 'Born in the USA,' Social History, and Working-Class Identity," in *Bruce Springsteen, Cultural Studies, and the Runaway American Dream*, edited by Kenneth Womack, Jerry Zolten, and Mark Bernhard (New York: Routledge, 2016), 31.

13. Masciotra, *Working on a Dream*, 68.

14. Cowie and Boehm, "Dead Man's Town," 38.

15. Eric Alterman, *It Ain't No Sin to Be Glad You're Alive: The Promise of Bruce Springsteen* (New York: Back Bay Books, 2001), 157.

16. Chet Flippo, *Musician* (November 1984).

17. Loder, "The Rolling Stone Interview."

18. Michael D. Dwyer, *Back to the Fifties: Nostalgia, Hollywood Film, and Popular Music of the Seventies and Eighties* (New York: Oxford University Press, 2015), 31.

19. *Ibid.*, 34.

20. During my interview with John Sayles on *Baby It's You*, we also discussed the making of the "Born in the U.S.A." video. Sayles said, "[Springsteen] wanted something a little grittier for 'Born in the U.S.A.' and I said, 'Well, I can do gritty,' and so we shot it in 16mm.... We had shot all the documentary stuff, some of it, in Jersey. We actually went out to a Vietnamese neighborhood in Los Angeles. I got a couple of shots there. It was just kind of like this impressionistic, what's this song really about? What are the images that the songs really about?" Sayles' shots juxtapose the idyllic pre–Vietnam America with the present: men toiling inside factories or waiting in line for food stamps, children of the 1950s at a birthday party, a couple on their way to the prom, a whirling Himalaya ride at an amusement park, soldiers' graves lining the grass like rows of small teeth. It is also worth mentioning that Springsteen's music video for his cover of "War" has lots of Vietnam War iconography. The opening shot is a theatrical tableau with a black background and bright white overhead lighting centered on a father and son at the dinner table watching television. They watch a newscaster announce that President Johnson has increased the

American fighting forces in Vietnam War. The camera zooms into the black-and-white footage and then out onto the Vietnam War come to life in a collage of harrowing photographs and videos: men climbing out of helicopters, crying Vietnamese villagers, bombs falling onto the jungle, and soldiers trampling through rivers where dead bodies lie. The video somberly ends with the father sitting alone across from his son's empty chair, the war having claimed yet another young man's soul.

21. Loder, "The Rolling Stone Interview."
22. Susan Jeffords, *The Remasculinization of America: Gender and the Vietnam War* (Bloomington: Indiana University Press, 1989), 175.
23. Ronald Reagan, "The President's News Conference April 4, 1984," in *Public Papers of the Presidents of the United States: Ronald Reagan, 1984, Book I: January to June 29, 1984* (Washington, DC: Government Printing Office, 1984), 465, 467.
24. Will, "A Yankee Doodle Springsteen."
25. Mason, *In Country*, 125.
26. Jonathan D. Cohen, "Lost in the Flood: Bruce Springsteen's Political Consciousness and the Vietnam War, 1968–2014," in *Bruce Springsteen and Popular Music: Rhetoric, Social Consciousness, and Contemporary Culture*, edited by William I. Wolff (New York: Routledge, 2017), 21.
27. Phil Sutcliffe, "You Talkin' to Me?" in *Talk about a Dream: The Essential Interviews of Bruce Springsteen*, edited by Christopher Phillips and Louis P. Masur (New York: Bloomsbury Press, 2013), 306.
28. Bruce Springsteen, *Born to Run* (New York: Simon & Schuster, 2016), 100.
29. Ibid., 101.
30. Ibid., 100.
31. Ibid.
32. Ibid.
33. Jim Cullen, *Born in the U.S.A.: Bruce Springsteen and the American Tradition* (Middletown, CT: Wesleyan University Press, 2005), 89.
34. Known as Monmouth University since 1995.
35. Azzan Yaddin-Israel, *The Grace of God and the Grace of Man: The Theologies of Bruce Springsteen* (Highland Park, NJ: Lingua Press, 2016), 38.
36. This monologue is an excerpt from the January 9, 2018, bootleg of *Springsteen on Broadway*.
37. Johanna Pirttijärvi, online transcript of Bruce Springsteen concert, August 20, 1981, Los Angeles Memorial Sports Arena, Los Angeles, California, https://brucebase.wikispaces.com/1981-08-20%20-%20LOS%20ANGELES%20MEMORIAL%20SPORTS%20ARENA%2C%20LOS%20ANGELES%2C%20CA.
38. Ibid.
39. Dave Marsh, *Two Hearts: The Story* (New York: Routledge, 2003), 233.
40. Ibid., 236.
41. Ibid., 237.
42. Masciotra, *Working on a Dream*, 63.
43. Barbara Tepa Lupack, "History as Her-Story: Adapting Bobbie Ann Mason's *In Country* to Film," in *Vision/Re-Vision: Adapting Contemporary American Fiction by Women in Film*, edited Barbara Tepa Lupack (Bowling Green, KY: Bowling Green State University Popular Press, 1996), 176.
44. See "A Long Walk Home: The Role of Class and the Military in the Springsteen Catalogue" by Robert M. Citino for more analysis regarding Springsteen's representation of veterans from the Vietnam, Gulf, and Iraq wars.

Philadelphia

1. Including Grammy Awards for Best Song of the Year, Best Rock Song, Best Rock Vocal Performance, and Best Song Written Specifically for a Motion Picture or Television.
2. "Audio Commentary," *Philadelphia*, directed by Jonathan Demme (Culver City, CA: Sony Pictures Home Entertainment, 2002), DVD.
3. Ibid.
4. Larry Kramer, "Playwright and Gay Activist Larry Kramer Explains Why He Hated Jonathan Demme's 'Philadelphia,'" *Los Angeles Times*, January 10, 1994, https://www.latimes.com/entertainment/movies/la-et-archives-jonathan-demme-philadelphia-20170426-story.html.
5. One particular point of critical contention was the scene in which Gumb dresses up and poses in front of a mirror with his penis tucked between his legs while Catherine Martin screams for help from the bottom of the well. The combination of this sound and imagery distorts Gumb's action of empowerment into something sinister and perverted.
6. Barbara Caroline Mennel, *Queer Cinema: School Girls, Vampires, and Gay Cowboys* (New York: Columbia University Press, 2012), 69.
7. Ibid., 26.
8. D.A. Miller, "Anal Rope," in *Inside/Out: Lesbian Theories, Gay Theories*, edited by Diana Fuss (New York: Routledge, 1991), 123.
9. Harry M. Benshoff and Sean Griffin, "General Introduction," in *Queer Cinema: The Film Reader*, edited by Harry M. Benshoff and Sean Griffin (New York: Routledge, 2004), 8.
10. *One Foot on a Banana Peel, the Other Foot in the Grave* has none of the big-budget artifice of Demme's *Philadelphia*, inviting audiences to experience the day-to-day tribulations of living with AIDS as a gay man with startling frankness.
11. "People Like Us: Making *Philadelphia*," *Philadelphia*, directed by Jonathan Demme (Culver City, CA: Sony Pictures Home Entertainment, 2002), DVD.
12. Ibid.
13. Anthony DeCurtis, "The Rolling Stone Interview: Jonathan Demme on 'Philadelphia,' Tom Hanks, Homophobia," *Rolling Stone*, March 24, 1994, https://www.rollingstone.com/movies/movie-features/the-rolling-stone-interview-jonathan-demme-on-philadelphia-tom-hanks-homophobia-62429/.
14. Emmanuel Levy, *Gay Directors, Gay Films? Pedro Almodóvar, Terence Davies, Todd Haynes, Gus Van Sant, John Waters* (New York: Columbia University Press, 2015), 167.

15. "Audio Commentary," *Philadelphia*, DVD.
16. "People Like Us: Making *Philadelphia*," *Philadelphia*, DVD.
17. There is an intra-diegetic connotation of Andrew's queerness when he hides his sexuality from his co-workers, but even when the film is outside of such white-collar, staunchly masculine spaces, Andrew's characterization mostly adheres to a conventional straightness.
18. Kramer, "Playwright and Gay Activist Larry Kramer Explains Why He Hated Jonathan Demme's 'Philadelphia.'"
19. Judy Wieder, "Bruce Springsteen: The Advocate Interview," *The Advocate*, April 2, 1996.
20. DeCurtis, "The Rolling Stone Interview."
21. Bryan Garman, "The Ghost of History: Bruce Springsteen, Woody Guthrie, and the Hurt Song," *Popular Music and Society* 20, no. 2 (1996), 108.
22. Wieder, "Bruce Springsteen: The Advocate Interview."
23. DeCurtis, "The Rolling Stone Interview."
24. "Audio Commentary," *Philadelphia*, DVD.
25. Azzan Yaddin-Israel, *The Grace of God and the Grace of Man: The Theologies of Bruce Springsteen* (Highland Park, NJ: Lingua Press, 2016), 178.
26. Ibid., 176.
27. The original title of the film was *People Like Us* to emphasize how those in the LGBTQ community are no different from any other American.
28. In his 2008 speech for Obama's election campaign rally in Philadelphia, Springsteen described the city as the space where the American promise to "do your best to make these things real: opportunity, equality, social and economic justice, a fair shake for all of our citizens, was handed down to us from our founding fathers.... These are the things that give our lives hope, shape, and meaning. They are the ties that bind us together and give us faith in our contract with one another."
29. Bruce Springsteen, interview by Scott Pelley, *60 Minutes*, NBC, October 7, 2007.
30. Richard C. Cante, "HIV, Multiculturalism, and Popular Narrativity in the United States," *Narrative* 7, no. 3 (1999), 246.
31. Ibid.
32. Ibid., 247.
33. David Masciotra, *Working on a Dream: The Progressive Political Vision of Bruce Springsteen* (New York: A&C Black, 2010), 74.
34. Robert Kirkpatrick, *The Words and Music of Bruce Springsteen* (Westport, CT: Greenwood, 2006), 130. The song was actually inspired by Kristen Ann Carr (the late daughter of Springsteen's manager Barbara Carr and biographer Dave Marsh), who died of Sarcoma cancer in 1993.
35. Mennel, *Queer Cinema*, 95.
36. *The Celluloid Closet*, Sony Pictures Home Entertainment, 2001.
37. Masciotra, *Working on a Dream*, 74.
38. Nathan Smith, "Remembering the Streets of Philadelphia," *Out*, November 5, 2015, https://www.out.com/entertainment/2015/11/05/remembering-streets-philadelphia.
39. Larry Kramer condemned the portrayal of Andrew's family in the *Washington Post*: "No family like this exists in the entire world. Every single one of them is supportive, loving, proud of Tom, just thrilled he's gay." Janet Maslin of the *New York Times* felt that "the screenplay's tendency to evade and overgeneralize is not helped by the depiction of gay men as gentle souls, straight men as bigots, and Andrew's large family as a monolithic, enlightened entity." Nyswaner and Demme countered these criticisms of sugarcoating with the idea that it was more "courageous to say that people love each other and support their gay children." Andrew was already surrounded by homophobia, so giving him an equally homophobic family would have been overkill. Furthermore, Demme wanted to salute the families out there who were accepting, even if they were in the minority.
40. Statistics taken from the American Psychological Association and FACT: Fighting AIDS Continuously Together.
41. Masciotra, *Working on a Dream*, 74.
42. Yaddin-Israel, *The Grace of God and the Grace of Man*, 143.
43. Roger Ebert, "Philadelphia," RogerEbert.com, January 14, 1994, https://www.rogerebert.com/reviews/philadelphia-1994.
44. "Audio Commentary," *Philadelphia*, DVD.
45. Wieder, "Bruce Springsteen: The Advocate Interview."
46. Bruce Springsteen, interview by Jimmy Fallon, *The Tonight Show Starring Jimmy Fallon*, NBC, December 17, 2015.
47. Rosalie Zdzienicka Fanshel, "Beyond Blood Brothers: Queer Bruce Springsteen," *Popular Music* 32, issue 3 (2013), 360.
48. Edward U. Murphy, "'The Country We Carry in Our Hearts Is Waiting': Bruce Springsteen and the Art of Social Change," in *Bruce Springsteen, Cultural Studies, and the Runaway American Dream*, edited by Kenneth Womack, Jerry Zolten, and Mark Bernhard (New York: Routledge, 2016), 198.
49. Martha Nell Smith, "Sexual Mobilities in Bruce Springsteen: Performance as Commentary," in *Present Tense: Rock and Roll Culture*, edited by Anthony DeCurtis (Durham, NC: Duke University Press Books, 1992), 209.
50. Wieder, "Bruce Springsteen: The Advocate Interview."
51. Ibid.
52. In the narrator's eyes, Mary is not a *real* woman, a perspective that completely demonizes those who identify as transgender, men and women who are unequivocally the gender they identify as.
53. Fanshel, "Beyond Blood Brothers," 361.
54. Ibid., 367.
55. Christopher Phillips, liner notes to *Tracks*, Bruce Springsteen, CD, 2010.
56. Fanshel, "Beyond Blood Brothers," 365.
57. Ibid., 372.
58. John Lombardi, "St. Boss," *Esquire*, December 1, 1988.
59. Fanshel, "Beyond Blood Brothers," 374.
60. Kate Dailey, "Bruce Springsteen Comes Out

in Support of NJ's Gay Marriage Bill," *Newsweek*, December 9, 2009, https://www.newsweek.com/bruce-springsteen-comes-out-support-njs-gay-marriage-bill-222096.

61. Curtis Wong, "Bruce Springsteen Stars in Gay Marriage Social Media Campaign," *Huffington Post*, October 2, 2012.

62. Bruce Springsteen, "A Statement from Bruce Springsteen on North Carolina," *BruceSpringsteen.net*, April 8, 2016, http://brucespringsteen.net/news/2016/a-statement-from-bruce-springsteen-on-north-carolina.

63. Ibid.

64. Another small moment worth noting occurred during the March 28, 2008, concert in Portland, Oregon, when Springsteen replaced "Germans" in "Land of Hope and Dreams" with "lesbians" to honor a group of women in the pit wearing shirts that read "Lesbians [heart] Bruce."

65. Wieder, "Bruce Springsteen: The Advocate Interview."

66. Ibid.

67. Fanshel, "Beyond Blood Brothers," 378.

68. Bruce Springsteen, "Music and Lyric by Bruce Springsteen Academy Awards Acceptance Speech" (Los Angeles, CA, March 21, 1994), Academy Awards Acceptance Speech Database, http://aaspeechesdb.oscars.org/link/066-15/.

Dead Man Walking

1. "Director's Commentary," *Dead Man Walking*, directed by Tim Robbins (Beverly Hills, CA: MGM Home Entertainment, 2001), DVD. Robbins provided script and film footage for other musicians he admired, such as Patti Smith, Johnny Cash, and Tom Waits, who composed songs from other characters' perspectives. For example, Suzanne Vega's "Women on the Tier (I'll See You Through)" expresses Sister Helen's internal thoughts, while Steve Earle Ellis penned "Unit One" to provide the prison guard's point of view.

2. Bruce Springsteen, *Born to Run* (New York: Simon & Schuster, 2016), 7.

3. Bruce Springsteen, interview by Elvis Costello, *Spectacle*, Sundance, September 25, 2009.

4. Azzan Yaddin-Israel, *The Grace of God and the Grace of Man: The Theologies of Bruce Springsteen* (Highland Park, NJ: Lingua Press, 2016), 86.

5. David Thurmaier, "'The Country We Carry in Our Heart Is Waiting': Bruce Springsteen, Franklin Delano Roosevelt, and the Search for Human Rights in America," in *Popular Music and Human Rights*, Volume I: *British and American Music*, edited by Ian Peddie (Farnham, UK: Ashgate, 2011), 151.

6. "Director's Commentary," *Dead Man Walking*, DVD.

7. Ibid.

8. Ibid.

9. Springsteen repurposes his "Downbound Train" line in this song.

10. "Director's Commentary," *Dead Man Walking*, DVD.

11. Ibid.
12. Ibid.
13. Ibid.
14. Ibid.

15. Andrew Cohen, "The Problems with the Death Penalty Are Already Crystal Clear," *The Atlantic*, May 5, 2014, https://www.theatlantic.com/politics/archive/2014/05/we-already-know-whats-wrong-with-the-death-penalty/361635/.

16. Ibid.

17. Yaddin-Israel, *The Grace of God and the Grace of Man*, 75.

18. Frank Fury, "'Deliver Me from Nowhere': Place and Space in Bruce Springsteen's *Nebraska*," in *Reading the Boss: Interdisciplinary Approaches to the Works of Bruce Springsteen*, edited by Roxanne Harde and Irwin Streight (Lanham, MD: Lexington Books, 2010), 86.

19. Ibid.

20. Masciotra, *Working on a Dream*, 105.

21. Robert Kirkpatrick, *The Words and Music of Bruce Springsteen* (Westport, CT: Greenwood, 2006), 82.

22. Jim Cullen, *Born in the U.S.A.: Bruce Springsteen and the American Tradition* (Middletown, CT: Wesleyan University Press, 2005), 169. See my chapter on *The Wrestler* for more information on Springsteen's relationship with religion.

23. "Director's Commentary," *Dead Man Walking*, DVD.

24. Terry Gross, "On Jersey, Masculinity and Wishing to Be His Stage Persona," *Fresh Air*, September 15, 2017, https://www.npr.org/2017/09/15/551112185/bruce-springsteen-on-jersey-masculinity-and-wishing-to-be-his-stage-persona.

25. Ibid.

26. Springsteen, *Born to Run*, 17.

27. Jon Pareles, "Bruce Almighty," *New York Times*, April 24, 2005, https://www.nytimes.com/2005/04/24/arts/music/bruce-almighty.html; Springsteen, *Born to Run*, 17.

28. Springsteen, *Born to Run*, 15.

29. Johanna Pirttijärvi, online transcript of Bruce Springsteen concert, November 29, 1984, the Summit, Houston, Texas, https://brucebase.wikispaces.com/1984-11-29+-+THE+SUMMIT%2C+HOUSTON%2C+TX.

30. Springsteen, *Born to Run*, 17.

31. Ibid.
32. Ibid.
33. Ibid.

34. Ibid. For more on Springsteen's relationship with Catholicism, I highly recommend Azzan Yaddin-Israel's *The Grace of God and the Grace of Man*.

35. Ibid., 7.

36. "Director's Commentary," *Dead Man Walking*, DVD.

No Looking Back

1. Marya Morris, "From 'My Hometown' to 'This Hard Land': Bruce Springsteen's Use of Geography,

Landscapes, and Places to Depict the American Experience," *Interdisciplinary Literary Studies* 9, no. 1 (2007), 10.

2. Edward Burns, interview with Mike Vaccaro, Tribeca Film Festival 2018, New York City, April 27, 2018.

3. "Director's Commentary," *No Looking Back*, directed by Edward Burns (Century City, CA: 20th Century Fox, 2002), DVD; Bruce Springsteen, *Born to Run* (New York: Simon & Schuster, 2016), 222.

4. Stephen Holden, "Film Review: Blue Collars and Miseries by the Sea," *New York Times*, March 27, 1998, https://www.nytimes.com/1998/03/27/movies/film-review-blue-collars-and-miseries-by-the-sea.html.

5. Morris, "From 'My Hometown' to 'This Hard Land,'" 3.

6. Jeffrey Symynkywicz, *The Gospel According to Bruce Springsteen: Rock and Redemption, from Asbury Park to Magic* (Louisville: Westminster John Knox Press, 2008), 16.

7. Burns' Springsteen fandom appears throughout his canon. His second film, *She's the One* (1996), is named after the *Born to Run* song and the album can be seen in the background on his lead character's bookshelf. Also, in *Sidewalks of New York* (2001), Dave Krumholtz stars as an aspiring musician who declares *Greetings from Asbury Park, N.J.* one of the greatest debut albums of all time.

8. "Director's Commentary," *No Looking Back*, DVD.

9. Ibid.

10. Ibid.

11. Holden, "Blue Collars and Miseries by the Sea."

12. "Director's Commentary," *No Looking Back*, DVD.

13. Ibid.

14. Azzan Yaddin-Israel, *The Grace of God and the Grace of Man: The Theologies of Bruce Springsteen* (Highland Park, NJ: Lingua Press, 2016), 67; "Director's Commentary," *No Looking Back*, DVD.

15. Kenneth Womack, "'Who's That Girl?' Nostalgia, Gender, and Springsteen," in *Reading the Boss: Interdisciplinary Approaches to the Works of Bruce Springsteen*, edited by Roxanne Harde and Irwin Streight (Lanham, MD: Lexington Books, 2010), 128.

16. Burns purposefully shot on cloudy days to solidify the town's dismalness.

17. Jim Cullen, *Born in the U.S.A.: Bruce Springsteen and the American Tradition* (Middletown, CT: Wesleyan University Press, 2005), 144.

18. "Director's Commentary," *No Looking Back*, DVD.

19. Ibid.

20. Samuele F.S. Pardini, "Bruce Zirilli: The Italian Sides of Bruce Springsteen," in *Bruce Springsteen, Cultural Studies, and the Runaway American Dream*, edited by Kenneth Womack, Jerry Zolten, and Mark Bernhard (New York: Routledge, 2016), 103. See also Katherine Parkin's "The Key to the Universe: Springsteen, Masculinity, and the Car," in *Bruce Springsteen and the American Soul: Essays on the Songs and Influence of a Cultural Icon*, edited by David Garrett Izzo (Jefferson, NC: McFarland, 2011), for more on how Bruce Springsteen perpetuates the American cultural notion of driving as a predominantly masculine pursuit.

21. Gareth Palmer, "Bruce Springsteen and Masculinity," in *Sexing the Groove: Popular Music and Gender*, edited by Sheila Whiteley (New York: Routledge, 1997), 105.

22. Pamela Moss, "Still Searching for the Promised Land: Placing Women in Bruce Springsteen's Lyrical Landscapes," *Cultural Geographies* 18, issue 3 (2011), 351–355.

23. Pardini, "Bruce Zirilli," 108.

24. Palmer, "Bruce Springsteen and Masculinity," 105.

25. For more on this idea, see my chapter on *High Fidelity*.

26. Rebecca Bohanan, "The Only Three Women in Bruce Springsteen's Music," *Jezebel*, March 15, 2012, https://jezebel.com/5893602/the-only-three-women-in-bruce-springsteens-music.

27. Lisa Zitelli, "'Like a Vision She Dances': Re-Visioning the Female Figure in the Songs of Bruce Springsteen," in *Reading the Boss: Interdisciplinary Approaches to the Works of Bruce Springsteen*, edited by Roxanne Harde and Irwin Streight (Lanham, MD: Lexington Books, 2010), 155.

28. Ibid.

29. Lisa Delmonico, "Queen of the Supermarket: Representations of Working Class Women," in *Bruce Springsteen and the American Soul: Essays on the Songs and Influence of a Cultural Icon*, edited David Garrett Izzo (Jefferson, NC: McFarland, 2011), 47.

30. Ibid.

31. Ibid., 48.

32. Bohanan, "The Only Three Women in Bruce Springsteen's Music."

33. See also "My Lover Man," "Countin' on a Miracle," and "Devil's Arcade."

34. Delmonico, "Queen of the Supermarket," 47.

The Sopranos

1. Maurice Yacowar, *The Sopranos on the Couch: The Ultimate Guide* (London: Continuum, 2006), 172.

2. Ellen Willis, "Our Mobsters, Ourselves," *The Nation*, April 2, 2001, https://www.thenation.com/article/our-mobsters-ourselves/.

3. Franco Ricci, *The Sopranos: Born Under a Bad Sign* (Toronto: University of Toronto Press, 2014), 11.

4. Ibid., 264.

5. See Brett Martin's *Difficult Men: Behind the Scenes of a Creative Revolution: From The Sopranos and The Wire to Mad Men and Breaking Bad* and Alan Sepinwall's *The Revolution Was Televised: The Cops, Crooks, Slingers, and Slayers Who Changed TV Drama Forever* for more on television's twenty-first-century renaissance.

6. Willis, "Our Mobsters, Ourselves."

7. Ricci, *The Sopranos: Born Under a Bad Sign*, 18.

8. Ken Tucker, "The Sopranos," *Entertainment*

Weekly, April 2, 1999, http://ew.com/article/1999/04/02/sopranos-7/.

9. Allen Rucker, *The Sopranos: A Family History* (New York: New American Library Trade, 2001).

10. Lance Strate, "No(rth Jersey) Sense of Place: The Cultural Geography (and Media Ecology) of *The Sopranos*," in *This Thing of Ours: Investigating The Sopranos*, edited by David Lavery (New York: Wallflower Press, 2002), 265, note 2.

11. Marc Peyser, "HBO'S Godfather," *Newsweek*, March 4, 2001, https://www.newsweek.com/hbos-godfather-148803.

12. Brett Martin, *Difficult Men Behind the Scenes of a Creative Revolution: From The Sopranos and The Wire to Mad Men and Breaking Bad* (London: Penguin Group, 2013), 66.

13. Frank DiGiacomo, "Steven Van Zandt Discusses 'Soulfire,' Springsteen, Republicans," *Billboard*, May 16, 2017, https://www.billboard.com/articles/columns/rock/7793162/steven-van-zandt-relationship-bruce-springsteen-solo-album-soulfire.

14. Ricci, *The Sopranos: Born Under a Bad Sign*, 23.

15. *Ibid.*, 26.

16. Rucker, *The Sopranos: A Family History*.

17. Kevin Fellezs, "Wiseguy Opera: Music for *The Sopranos*," in *This Thing of Ours: Investigating The Sopranos*, edited by David Lavery (New York: Wallflower Press, 2002), 163.

18. Maureen Droney, "Lots of Music, No Composer," *Mix*, April 1, 2001, https://www.mixonline.com/recording/lots-music-no-composer-372146.

19. *Ibid.*

20. Annette Davison, "The End Is Nigh: Music Postfaces and End-Credit Sequences in Contemporary Television Serials," *Music, Sound, and the Moving Image* 8, issue 2 (2014), 196.

21. *Ibid.*, 198.

22. Martin, *Difficult Men Behind the Scenes of a Creative Revolution*, 288.

23. Davison, "The End Is Nigh," 203.

24. Tucker, "The Sopranos."

25. Frank DeCaro, "The Mob Squad," *TV Guide*, January 8–12, 2000, 24.

26. Willis, "Our Mobsters, Ourselves."

27. Yacowar, *The Sopranos on the Couch*, 169.

28. *Ibid.*, 170.

29. *Ibid.*

30. Pussy's fish-like appearance is a reference to the infamous *Godfather* line: "Luca Brasi sleeps with the fishes." In the tenth episode of Season Three, "… Save Us All from Satan's Power," Tony receives the novelty gift Big Mouth Billy Bass for Christmas, an animatronic fish mounted onto a wooden plank that sings kitschy cover songs. It unsettles Tony because it reminds him of his "Funhouse" dream and Pussy's watery death, which Chase sardonically punctuates when the toy gives an enthusiastic rendition of Al Green's "Take Me to the River."

31. Austin Bogues, "$1 Billion Rebirth: Changing Face of Asbury Park," *Asbury Park Press*, January 26, 2017, https://www.app.com/story/insider/extras/2017/01/26/asbury-park-gentrification-population-tourism/91219354/.

32. *Ibid.*

33. *Ibid.*

34. Ron Bernard, "Funhouse (2.13)," *Sopranos Autopsy: Examining TV's Greatest Series*, 2014, https://sopranosautopsy.com/season-2-3/funhouse-draft/.

35. *Ibid.*

36. Martin, *Difficult Men Behind the Scenes of a Creative Revolution*, 91.

37. Willis, "Our Mobsters, Ourselves."

38. Ricci, *The Sopranos: Born Under a Bad Sign*, 165.

39. Bruce Springsteen, *Born to Run* (New York: Simon & Schuster, 2016), 298–299.

40. Ricci, *The Sopranos: Born Under a Bad Sign*, 126.

41. Springsteen, *Born to Run*, 288.

42. Frank Fury, "'Deliver Me from Nowhere': Place and Space in Bruce Springsteen's *Nebraska*," in *Reading the Boss: Interdisciplinary Approaches to the Works of Bruce Springsteen*, edited by Roxanne Harde and Irwin Streight (Lanham, MD: Lexington Books, 2010), 88.

43. Samuel J. Levine, "Portraits of Criminals on Bruce Springsteen's *Nebraska*: The Enigmatic Criminal, the Sympathetic Criminal, and the Criminal as Brother," *Widener Law Journal* 14, no. 3 (2005).

44. Per Dave Marsh in interviews after the publication of David Remnick's 2012 profile in the *New Yorker*.

45. Springsteen, *Born to Run*, 499.

46. *Ibid.*

47. Phil Sutcliffe, "You Talkin' to Me?" In *Talk about a Dream: The Essential Interviews of Bruce Springsteen*, edited by Christopher Phillips and Louis P. Masur (New York: Bloomsbury Press, 2013), 315.

48. Martin, *Difficult Men Behind the Scenes of a Creative Revolution*, 288.

49. Christopher Orr, "David Chase Just Ruined the Finale of *The Sopranos*," *The Atlantic*, April 19, 2015, https://www.theatlantic.com/entertainment/archive/2015/04/david-chase-just-ruined-the-finale-of-the-sopranos/390879/.

50. *Ibid.*

High Fidelity

1. Nick Hornby is a long-time fan of Springsteen. See *Songbook*, his collection of essays on songs and musical artists that have a particular emotional resonance for him. "Thunder Road" ranks as #2. Growing up in a small English countryside town with the ambition of becoming a writer, he related to Springsteen's escapist longing and hunger for artistic success. Joe Leydon, "High Fidelity—'High Fidelity' Turns Up the Volume for Romantic Laffer," *Variety*, March 19, 2000, https://variety.com/2000/film/reviews/high-fidelity-high-fidelity-turns-up-the-volume-for-romantic-laffer-1200461104/.

2. Kristin Nelson, *Narcissism in High Fidelity* (Bloomington: iUniverse, 2004), 110; Tom Brown, *Breaking the Fourth Wall: Direct Address in Cinema* (Edinburgh: Edinburgh University Press, 2013), 126.

3. Brown, *Breaking the Fourth Wall*, 127.
4. *Ibid.*, 124.
5. *Ibid.*, 137.
6. *Ibid.*, 136.
7. Neil Strauss, "Human Touch: Bruce Springsteen Reflects on His Music, Life Without the E Street Band, and the Glory of Rock and Roll," *Guitar World* (September 1995).
8. The musical version of *High Fidelity*, with lyrics by Amanda Green and music by Tom Kitt, parodies Springsteen and the "Bobby Jean" scene. A bandana-clad and gravelly-voiced actor impersonates a fairy godmother-esque Springsteen in "Goodbye and Good Luck," comparing Rob's girlfriends to ghosts that haunt a steel town with a factory that has been shut down since Veterans' Day. It's absolutely hilarious.
9. Kenneth Womack, "'Who's That Girl?' Nostalgia, Gender, and Springsteen," in *Reading the Boss: Interdisciplinary Approaches to the Works of Bruce Springsteen*, edited by Roxanne Harde and Irwin Streight (Lanham, MD: Lexington Books, 2010), 122.
10. "Conversations with Writer/Co-Producer John Cusack and Director Stephen Frears," *High Fidelity*, directed by Stephen Frears (Burbank, CA: Buena Vista Pictures, 2000), DVD.
11. Owen Gleiberman, "Review: High Fidelity," *Entertainment Weekly*, March 24, 2000, http://ew.com/article/2000/03/24/high-fidelity-8/.
12. Jen Aswad, "Bruce Springsteen Takes Us on a Tour of His iTunes Playlist," *Variety*, October 4, 2017, https://variety.com/2017/music/news/bruce-springsteen-a-guided-tour-of-his-itunes-foldeplaylist-1202580076/.
13. Womack, "'Who's That Girl?'" 122.
14. Johanna Pirttijärvi, online transcript of Bruce Springsteen concert, June 29, 1985, Parc de la Courneuve, Paris, France, https://brucebase.wikispaces.com/1985-06-29+-+PARC+DE+LA+COURNEUVE%2C+PARIS%2C+FRANCE.
15. Christopher Sandford, *Springsteen: Point Blank* (Boston: Da Capo Press, 1999), 147.
16. Bruce Springsteen, *Born to Run* (New York: Simon & Schuster, 2016), 331.
17. Brown, *Breaking the Fourth Wall*, 127.
18. *Ibid.*
19. This monologue is a bit of a tall tale because Springsteen could not drive and did not have a license until he was in his twenties. Johanna Pirttijärvi, online transcript of Bruce Springsteen concert, July 25, 1988, Parken Stadium, Copenhagen, Denmark, https://brucebase.wikispaces.com/Story+-1988-07-25+Copenhagen%2C+Denmark.
20. *Ibid.*
21. *Ibid.*
22. Brown, *Breaking the Fourth Wall*, 130.
23. A confession included in a deleted scene from the DVD and Blu-ray special features.
24. Lisa Delmonico, "Queen of the Supermarket: Representations of Working Class Women," in *Bruce Springsteen and the American Soul: Essays on the Songs and Influence of a Cultural Icon*, edited by David Garrett Izzo (Jefferson, NC: McFarland, 2011), 54.
25. Gareth Palmer, "Bruce Springsteen and Masculinity," in *Sexing the Groove: Popular Music and Gender*, edited by Sheila Whiteley (New York: Routledge, 1997), 112.
26. Lisa Zitelli, "'Like a Vision She Dances': Re-Visioning the Female Figure in the Songs of Bruce Springsteen," in *Reading the Boss: Interdisciplinary Approaches to the Works of Bruce Springsteen*, edited by Roxanne Harde and Irwin Streight (Lanham, MD: Lexington Books, 2010), 153.
27. Springsteen, *Born to Run*, 275.
28. Delmonico, "Queen of the Supermarket," 50.
29. Palmer, "Bruce Springsteen and Masculinity," 104.
30. Jeffrey Symynkywicz, *The Gospel According to Bruce Springsteen: Rock and Redemption, from Asbury Park to Magic* (Louisville, KY: Westminster John Knox Press, 2008), 63.
31. David Burke, *Heart of Darkness: Bruce Springsteen's Nebraska* (London: Cherry Red Books, 2011), 120.
32. *Ibid.*
33. Kirkpatrick, *The Words and Music of Bruce Springsteen*, 130.
34. Burke, *Heart of Darkness*, 26.
35. Nelson, *Narcissism in High Fidelity*, 119.
36. Springsteen, *Born to Run*, 33.
37. *Ibid.*, 413.
38. Peter Ames Carlin, *Bruce* (New York: Simon & Schuster, 2012), 290.
39. Springsteen, *Born to Run*, 413.
40. Carlin, *Bruce*, 290.
41. Springsteen, *Born to Run*, 413.
42. Carlin, *Bruce*, 88.
43. Lynn Goldsmith, *Photodiary* (New York: Random House, 1995).
44. Springsteen, *Born to Run*, 272.
45. *Ibid.*, 358.
46. *Ibid.*, 272.
47. *Ibid.*, 273.
48. *Ibid.*, 380.
49. Brian Hiatt, "True Bruce: Springsteen Goes Deep, from Early Trauma to Future of E Street," *Rolling Stone*, October 5, 2016, https://www.rollingstone.com/music/music-features/true-bruce-springsteen-goes-deep-from-early-trauma-to-future-of-e-street-106550/.
50. Donald L. Deardorff II, *Bruce Springsteen: American Poet and Prophet* (Lanham, MD: Scarecrow Press, 2014), 82.
51. *Ibid.*
52. Zitelli, "'Like a Vision She Dances,'" 166.
53. Deardorff, *Bruce Springsteen: American Poet and Prophet*, 82.
54. Springsteen, *Born to Run*, 273.

Prozac Nation

1. John Rockwell, "Springsteen's Rock Poetry at Its Best," *New York Times*, August 29, 1975.
2. *Vermouth Pinetree*, January 18, 2009, http://jackdeyoung-blog.tumblr.com/post/71427207/i-hate-elizabeth-wurtzel-but-i-love-bruce.

3. Elizabeth Wurtzel (@elizabethwurtzel), "Here We Are after #springsteen on #broadway," Instagram photo, December 10, 2017, https://www.instagram.com/p/BchudW5F11o/?hl=en&taken-by=elizabethwurtzel/.

4. Elizabeth Wurtzel, *Prozac Nation: Young and Depressed in America* (New York: Riverhead Books, 1994), 60.

5. The *Tunnel of Love* poster is an anachronism because Elizabeth Wurtzel was a freshman at Yale University in 1985, two years prior to the album's 1987 release.

6. When discussing Elizabeth Wurtzel in the context of the film adaptation, I will refer to her as Elizabeth.

7. Wurtzel, *Prozac Nation*, 34.

8. Jocelyn Gecker, "Bruce Springsteen on His Depression, Family, and New Memoir," *Boston Globe*, October 6, 2016, https://www.bostonglobe.com/arts/2016/10/06/bruce-springsteen-his-depression-family-and-new-memoir/tCVn8Qm3xYV7Asb9r1EvxN/story.html.

9. Vermouth Pinetree.

10. Wurtzel, Prozac Nation, 50.

11. Ibid., 50–51.

12. Ibid., 51.

13. Vermouth Pinetree.

14. Bruce Springsteen, Born to Run (New York: Simon & Schuster, 2016), 36.

15. Dave Marsh, Two Hearts: The Story (New York: Routledge, 2003), 16.

16. Ibid., 19.

17. Springsteen, Born to Run, 6.

18. Ibid., 10.

19. Ibid.

20. Ibid., 29.

21. Ibid.

22. Ibid., 179.

23. Ibid., 28.

24. Ibid.

25. Ibid., 409.

26. Louis P. Masur, Runaway Dream: Born to Run and Bruce Springsteen's American Vision (London: Bloomsbury Press, 2009), 22.

27. Springsteen, Born to Run, 414.

28. Terry Gross, "On Jersey, Masculinity and Wishing to Be His Stage Persona," Fresh Air, September 15, 2017, https://www.npr.org/2017/09/15/551112185/bruce-springsteen-on-jersey-masculinity-and-wishing-to-be-his-stage-persona.

29. David Kamp, "Cover Story: The Book of Bruce Springsteen," Vanity Fair, September 6, 2016, https://www.vanityfair.com/culture/2016/09/bruce-springsteen-cover-story.

30. Springsteen, Born to Run, 11.

31. Ibid.

32. David Remnick, "We Are Alive: Springsteen at Sixty-Two," New Yorker, July 30, 2012, https://www.newyorker.com/magazine/2012/07/30/we-are-alive.

33. Springsteen, Born to Run, 414.

34. Ibid., 26.

35. Robert Kirkpatrick, The Words and Music of Bruce Springsteen (Westport, CT: Greenwood, 2006), 122.

36. Springsteen, Born to Run, 412.

37. Cecilia Walden, "Elizabeth Wurtzel: 'Getting Married for the First Time at 47 Is My Real Mistake,'" The Telegraph, June 22, 2015, https://www.telegraph.co.uk/women/mother-tongue/11687854/Elizabeth-Wurtzel-Getting-married-for-the-first-time-at-47-is-my-real-mistake.html.

38. Bruce Springsteen, interview by Jimmy Fallon, Late Night with Jimmy Fallon, NBC, March 10, 2012.

39. Springsteen, Born to Run, 305.

40. Ibid.

41. Ibid., 306.

42. Ibid., 498.

43. Michael Hainey, "Beneath the Surface of Bruce Springsteen," Esquire, November 27, 2018.

44. Ibid.

45. Bruce Springsteen, interview by Will Gompertz, BBC News, BBC, November 6, 2016.

46. Wurtzel, Prozac Nation, 317. This chapter heading was the original title of the book.

47. Springsteen, Born to Run, 309.

48. Ibid., 484.

49. Springsteen, interview by Will Gompertz.

50. Springsteen, Born to Run, 499.

51. Ibid., 217.

52. Ibid., 485.

53. Ibid.

54. Ibid., 312.

55. Marc Eliot, Down Thunder Road: The Making of Bruce Springsteen (New York: Simon & Schuster, 1992), 218.

56. Ibid., 222.

57. Wurtzel, Prozac Nation, 61.

58. Ibid.

59. Ibid.

60. Ibid., 63.

61. Elizabeth Wurtzel, More, Now, Again: A Memoir of Addiction (New York: Simon & Schuster, 2001), 210.

62. David Burke, Heart of Darkness: Bruce Springsteen's Nebraska (London: Cherry Red Books, 2011), 122.

63. Wurtzel, Prozac Nation, 327.

64. Vermouth Pinetree.

65. David Masciotra, Working on a Dream: The Progressive Political Vision of Bruce Springsteen (New York: A&C Black, 2010), 26.

66. Elizabeth Wurtzel, "Bruce Almighty," The Guardian, June 22, 2008, https://www.teguardian.com/music/2008/jun/22/popandrock.culture4.

67. Ibid.

68. Ibid.

69. Vinciguerra, Thomas, "For Author of 'Prozac Nation,' Film Is a Downer," The New York Times, November 9, 2003.

70. Ed Gonzalez, "Prozac Nation Film Review," Slant Magazine, June 14, 2004, https://www.slantmagazine.com/film/review/prozac-nation.

71. Ibid.

72. Wurtzel, "Here We Are after #springsteen on #broadway."

73. Wurtzel, Prozac Nation, 359.

Reign Over Me

1. Stephen Farber, "9/11 Is Sneaking onto a Screen Near You," *New York Times*, March 13, 2005, https://www.nytimes.com/2005/03/13/movies/911-is-sneaking-onto-a-screen-near-you.html.
2. Bruce Springsteen, *Born to Run* (New York: Simon & Schuster, 2016), 443.
3. Terence McSweeney, *The "War on Terror" and American Film: 9/11 Frames per Second* (Edinburgh: Edinburgh University Press, 2016), 12, 27.
4. Guy Westwell, *Parallel Lines: Post-9/11 American Cinema* (New York: Wallflower Press, 2014), 112.
5. McSweeney, *The "War on Terror" and American Film*, 4.
6. John Markert, *Post-9/11 Cinema: Through a Lens Darkly* (Lanham, MD: Scarecrow Press, 2011), 45.
7. A.O. Scott, "The Poet Laureate of 9/11," *Slate*, August 2, 2002, https://www.slate.com/articles/arts/music_box/2002/08/the_poet_laureate_of_911.html; "Album of the Month," *Uncut* (September 2002).
8. Robert Kirkpatrick, *The Words and Music of Bruce Springsteen* (Westport, CT: Greenwood, 2006), 143.
9. Springsteen, *Born to Run*, 443.
10. *Ibid*.
11. Brad Yates, "Healing a Nation: Deconstructing Bruce Springsteen's *The Rising*" (paper presented at Glory Days: A Bruce Springsteen Symposium, Monmouth University, Long Branch, NJ, September 2005), 5.
12. McSweeney, *The "War on Terror" and American Film*, 4.
13. Rhys Tranter, "American Cinema in the Shadow of 9/11," *RhysTranter* (blog), November 10, 2016, https://www.rhystranter.com/2016/11/10/terence-mcsweeney-american-cinema-in-the-shadow-of-911/.
14. McSweeney, *The "War on Terror" and American Film*, 34.
15. *Ibid*., 35.
16. Kurt Loder, "Bruce Springsteen: The Rising," *Rolling Stone*, July 30, 2002, https://www.rollingstone.com/music/albumreviews/the-rising-20020730.
17. Kirkpatrick, *The Words and Music of Bruce Springsteen*, 188.
18. McSweeney, *The "War on Terror" and American Film*, 4.
19. David Browne, "The Rising," *Entertainment Weekly*, August 2, 2002, https://ew.com/article/2002/08/02/rising-4/.
20. Directed by Mark Pellington, the "Lonesome Day" music video is riddled with post–9/11 iconography, such as the silhouette of a man rising out of a cloud of smoke, American flags waving in the breeze, and a firetruck flying down the street. In one shot, Springsteen stands in an abandoned building that resembles the Twin Tower ruins while holding his hands up toward the sky as a benediction for peace and healing. The video opens with the sound of distant ocean waves and the soft clinking of Springsteen's glass while he sits alone at a beachside cafe. Flickering orange flames obscure the title card, evoking the horrible explosions that stole so many lives. During his lonesome day, Springsteen wanders the vacant, wind-swept Asbury Park boardwalk and beach, a metaphoric backdrop for America's emptiness in the wake of September 11. The music video ends with a quick-paced, kaleidoscopic collage of juxtapositional images defined by peace or destruction: a house explodes, an old man in a Yankees cap passes by, an American flag on the side of a looming city skyscraper gently sways in the breeze, blood drips from the tip of a knife, and china plates on a dining room table burn. Pellington crafts a bold and viscerally impressionistic video that reflects a haunted post–9/11 society.
21. David Burke, *Heart of Darkness: Bruce Springsteen's Nebraska* (London: Cherry Red Books, 2011), 144.
22. Springsteen, *Born to Run*, 442.
23. David Masciotra, *Working on a Dream: The Progressive Political Vision of Bruce Springsteen* (New York: A&C Black, 2010), 141.
24. Springsteen, *Born to Run*, 442.
25. Adam Sweeting, "Bruce Springsteen: 'I Think I Just Wanted to Be Great,'" *Uncut* (September 2002), https://www.uncut.co.uk/features/bruce-springsteen-i-think-i-just-wanted-to-be-great-part-1-21634.
26. Roxanne Harde, "'May Your Hope Give Us Hope': *The Rising* as a Site of Mourning," in *Reading the Boss: Interdisciplinary Approaches to the Works of Bruce Springsteen*, edited by Roxanne Harde and Irwin Streight (Lanham, MD: Lexington Books, 2010), 253.
27. Donald L. Deardorff II, *Bruce Springsteen: American Poet and Prophet* (Lanham, MD: Scarecrow Press, 2014), 21.
28. Harde, "'May Your Hope Give Us Hope,'" 246.
29. John Mead, "9/11, Manhood, Mourning, and the American Romance," in *Reframing 9/11: Film, Popular Culture and the "War on Terror"*, edited by Jeff Birkenstein, Anna Froula, and Karen Randell (New York: Continuum, 2010), 65.
30. Harde, "'May Your Hope Give Us Hope,'" 246.
31. McSweeney, *The "War on Terror" and American Film*, 19.
32. Melanie Henwood, "Wrecking Ball: Hard Times, Loss and Renewal; The Lifetime Conversation" (paper presented at Glory Days: A Bruce Springsteen Symposium, Monmouth University, Long Branch, NJ, September 2005), 5.
33. Harde, "'May Your Hope Give Us Hope,'" 246.
34. In order to universalize his songs about grief on *The Rising* (i.e., "Mary's Place," "You're Missing," and "Into the Fire"), Springsteen does not delineate the genders of his protagonists. I have chosen to assign gender-specific pronouns in order to read the song from Charlie's point of view, but there is nothing in the text to prevent listeners from interpreting the song from a female perspective. With "Mary's Place," the reference made to a photograph kept in a locket makes me initially think of a woman, but it could be a locket that the deceased woman left behind for the male narrator. The beauty of Springsteen's music is that you can interpret it however you like.

35. Azzan Yaddin-Israel, *The Grace of God and the Grace of Man: The Theologies of Bruce Springsteen* (Highland Park, NJ: Lingua Press, 2016), 125.

36. Harde, "'May Your Hope Give Us Hope,'" 260.

37. Masciotra, *Working on a Dream*, 136.

38. McSweeney, *The "War on Terror" and American Film*, 125.

39. Adam Sandler is a Springsteen fan and makes this fact clear in his comic writing. In the 1980s-set *The Wedding Singer*, "Hungry Heart" plays while Sandler's Robbie Hart nurses his recent breakup at a bar. *The Grown-Ups 2* portrays Sandler as a fumbling father who dresses as Springsteen from the *Born in the U.S.A.* cover for his 1980s-themed party. When his son doesn't recognize his costume, Sandler sadly sighs, "My own son doesn't know the Boss? I've failed as a father." During his stint as a *Saturday Night Live* cast member, Sandler frequently impersonated Springsteen. Most notably, he re-created the "Dancing in the Dark" video with host Courtney Cox and performed a "She's the One"–esque Thanksgiving song aptly titled "The Thanksgiving Song."

40. Springsteen, *Born to Run*, 438.

41. Ibid., 439.

42. McSweeney, *The "War on Terror" and American Film*, 40.

43. Jeffrey Symynkywicz, *The Gospel According to Bruce Springsteen: Rock and Redemption, from Asbury Park to Magic* (Louisville: Westminster John Knox Press, 2008), 145.

44. "My City of Ruins" was originally written in November 2000 for a Christmas benefit show promoting the revitalization of Asbury Park, NJ. The ballad took on a whole new meaning in light of the September 11 attacks and became an anthem for the ravaged New York City.

45. *25th Hour* (2002) is Spike Lee's operatic valentine to New York City. More than any film during that time period, it deftly captures the existential malaise of post-9/11 America. Springsteen's magnetic end-credits song "The Fuse" simmers with the same electric tension and sense of finite time that looms over Lee's grieving metropolis and the leading character Montgomery, who has twenty-four hours before he is sent to jail for seven years. Lee boldly defied other filmmakers who tried to conceal any references to 9/11. The tragedy is immediately felt in the haunting low-angle opening shots of the Tribute of Light. The racist rant that Montgomery unfurls is a soliloquy of Shakespearean heights, a poignant manifestation of the vitriol and misery that plagued New York in the wake of that devastating September morning. Much like *The Rising* (and very unlike *Reign Over Me*), *25th Hour* unflinchingly delves into the heated racial politics and profound grief of the post–9/11 zeitgeist.

46. Harde, "'May Your Hope Give Us Hope,'" 244.

The Wrestler

1. Garth Bardsley, "How Mickey Rourke Got Bruce Springsteen's 'Wrestler' Song—for Free," *MTV*, January 12, 2009, http://www.mtv.com/news/1602516/how-mickey-rourke-got-bruce-springsteens-wrestler-song-for-free/.

2. As of 2019, Springsteen's longest concert is four hours and six minutes at the Olympic Stadium in Helsinki, Finland, on July 31, 2012, the final European show of the *Wrecking Ball* tour.

3. When "Sweet Child O' Mine" by Guns N' Roses plays in a bar, Cassidy and Randy wax poetic about the 1980s, a decade Randy calls the "best shit ever." Randy admired the hypermasculinity of heavy metal musicians such as Guns N' Roses and Def Leppard until "that Cobain pussy had to come around and ruin it all. Like there's something wrong with wanting to have a good time." Both Cassidy and Randy agree that the "nineties fuckin' sucked" and the 1980s was their heyday.

4. Jadranka Skorin-Kapov, *Darren Aronofsky's Films and the Fragility of Hope* (London: Bloomsbury Academic, 2015), 83.

5. Bruce Springsteen, *Born to Run* (New York: Simon & Schuster, 2016), xvi.

6. Jay Cocks, "Rock's New Sensation: The Backstreet Phantom of Rock," *Time*, October 27, 1975, http://content.time.com/time/subscriber/article/0,33009,913583,00.html (page 2).

7. Ibid. (page 1).

8. Although Springsteen's madcap stage antics seem deliriously improvised, many of his actions, movements, and song transitions are premeditated and rehearsed. In the same vein, Randy discusses the maneuvers in advance with his fellow wrestlers, making them appear raw and unplanned during the fight.

9. David Remnick, "We Are Alive: Springsteen at Sixty-Two," *New Yorker*, July 30, 2012, https://www.newyorker.com/magazine/2012/07/30/we-are-alive.

10. Michael Hann, "Bruce Springsteen: 'You Can Change a Life in Three Minutes with the Right Song,'" *The Observer*, October 30, 2016, https://www.theguardian.com/music/2016/oct/30/bruce-springsteen-interview-born-to-run-change-someones-life-right-song-donald-trump.

11. Ibid.

12. Fred Schruers, "Bruce Springsteen: The Boss Is Back," *Rolling Stone*, November 27, 1980, https://www.rollingstone.com/music/music-news/bruce-springsteen-the-boss-is-back-178801/.

13. Springsteen, *Born to Run*, 414.

14. Fred Goodman, *The Mansion on the Hill: Dylan, Young, Geffen, Springsteen, and the Head-On Collision of Rock and Commerce* (New York: Times Books, 1997), 294.

15. Gareth Palmer, "Bruce Springsteen and Masculinity," in *Sexing the Groove: Popular Music and Gender*, edited by Sheila Whiteley (New York: Routledge, 1997), 109.

16. Ibid.

17. Tarja Laine, *Bodies in Pain: Emotion and the Cinema of Darren Aronofsky* (New York: Berghan Books, 2015), 20.

18. Ibid., 114.

19. Cocks, "Rock's New Sensation" (page 2).

20. This idea that Springsteen could overwork

himself so much on stage that it would induce a heart attack brings to mind the ending of *The Wrestler*.

21. David Kamp, "Cover Story: The Book of Bruce Springsteen," *Vanity Fair*, September 6, 2016, https://www.vanityfair.com/culture/2016/09/bruce-springsteen-cover-story.
22. Ibid.
23. Remnick, "We Are Alive."
24. Springsteen, *Born to Run*, 304.
25. Hann, "Bruce Springsteen."
26. Springsteen, *Born to Run*, 305.
27. Remnick, "We Are Alive."
28. Skorin-Kapov, *Darren Aronofsky's Films and the Fragility of Hope*, 87.
29. Ibid., 90.
30. Remnick, "We Are Alive."
31. Springsteen, *Born to Run*, 466.
32. Kamp, "Cover Story."
33. *The Wrestler* is not Rourke's only appearance in Asbury Park. The gritty drama *Homeboy* (1988), about a self-destructive boxer (another self-reflexive role for Rourke), features fights inside Convention Hall, Rourke walking along the (at the time) seedy Cookman Avenue, and a boardwalk carousel specially built for the film.
34. *The Wrestler (Behind the Scenes)*, directed by Noah Hunter (released on iTunes).
35. Ibid.
36. Keri Walsh, *Mickey Rourke* (London: British Film Institute, 2014), 157.
37. Springsteen, *Born to Run*, 326.
38. This is a self-reflexive reference to actor Mickey Rourke's own misshapen face, adding to the film's documentary realist aesthetic. Art imitates life in *The Wrestler* through Rourke's casting because he was a former sex symbol who fell out of the public eye after having lots of plastic surgery following a motorcycle accident. Jadranka Skorin-Kapov further examines the intertextual relationship between Rourke's star image and his role as Robin Ramzinski in her book *Darren Aronofsky's Films and the Fragility of Hope*.
39. Aronofsky reinforces the importance of this fight by shooting in an elegant old-fashioned theater instead of the garish fluorescent-lit high school gyms of previous scenes.
40. Bruce Springsteen, interview by Stephen Colbert, *The Late Show with Stephen Colbert*, CBS, September 24, 2016.
41. Ibid.
42. David Garrett Izzo, "Introduction," in *Bruce Springsteen and the American Soul: Essays on the Songs and Influence of a Cultural Icon*, edited by David Garrett Izzo (Jefferson, NC: McFarland, 2011), 2.
43. Roxanne Harde and Irwin Streight, "Introduction," in *Reading the Boss: Interdisciplinary Approaches to the Works of Bruce Springsteen*, edited by Roxanne Harde and Irwin Streight (Lanham, MD: Lexington Books, 2010), 7.
44. Peter Ames Carlin, "Two Truths and a Lie," Keynote Address, Bruce Springsteen's *Darkness on the Edge of Town*: An International Symposium, Monmouth University, Long Branch, NJ, April 14, 2018. A recurring skit on *The Ben Stiller Show*, "Legends of Springsteen," pokes fun at popular culture's perception of Springsteen. After performing every song he ever wrote for fifteen hours, Stiller's Springsteen mops the bar floor, refills ketchup bottles, and then helps a waitress deliver her baby and rescues the patrons from intergalactic aliens.
45. Deardorff, *Bruce Springsteen: American Poet and Prophet*, 80.
46. John J. Sheinbaum, "'I'll Work for Your Love': Springsteen and the Struggle for Authenticity," in *Reading the Boss: Interdisciplinary Approaches to the Works of Bruce Springsteen*, edited by Roxanne Harde and Irwin Streight (Lanham, MD: Lexington Books, 2010), 224.
47. James Henke, "Bruce Springsteen Leaves E Street: The Rolling Stone Interview," *Rolling Stone*, August 6, 1992, https://www.rollingstone.com/music/music-news/bruce-springsteen-leaves-e-street-the-rolling-stone-interview-172718/.
48. Terry Gross, "On Jersey, Masculinity and Wishing to Be His Stage Persona," *Fresh Air*, September 15, 2017, https://www.npr.org/2017/09/15/551112185/bruce-springsteen-on-jersey-masculinity-and-wishing-to-be-his-stage-persona.
49. Henke, "Bruce Springsteen Leaves E Street."
50. Springsteen, *Born to Run*, xvi.
51. Ibid.
52. Springsteen, interview by Stephen Colbert.

Show Me a Hero

1. Chris Ryan, "Show Me a Boss: The Use of Bruce Springsteen in 'Show Me a Hero,'" *Grantland*, August 26, 2015, http://grantland.com/hollywood-prospectus/show-me-a-boss-the-use-of-bruce-springsteen-in-show-me-a-hero/.
2. Liz Shannon Miller, "'Show Me a Hero': David Simon and Paul Haggis Might Have Made This Year's Most Important Miniseries," *IndieWire*, August 12, 2015, https://www.indiewire.com/2015/08/show-me-a-hero-david-simon-and-paul-haggis-might-have-made-this-years-most-important-miniseries-59397/.
3. Nay Wasicsko-McLaughlin, in e-mail discussion with the author, August 30, 2017.
4. Ibid.
5. "HBO Miniseries: Show Me a Hero Inside the Series Parts One and Two (HBO)," YouTube Video, August 16, 2015, https://www.youtube.com/watch?v=oksclThb3fw.
6. Lisa Belkin, *Show Me a Hero: A Tale of Murder, Suicide, Race, and Redemption* (Boston: Little, Brown, 1999), xiv.
7. David Masciotra, *Working on a Dream: The Progressive Political Vision of Bruce Springsteen* (New York: A&C Black, 2010), 25.
8. Belkin, *Show Me a Hero*, 118.
9. Ibid.
10. Marya Morris, "From 'My Hometown' to 'This Hard Land': Bruce Springsteen's Use of Geography, Landscapes, and Places to Depict the American

Experience," *Interdisciplinary Literary Studies* 9, no. 1 (2007), 15.

11. Alex Pitofsky, "Springsteen's Imitations of Mortality," in *Bruce Springsteen and the American Soul: Essays on the Songs and Influence of a Cultural Icon*, edited by David Garrett Izzo (Jefferson, NC: McFarland, 2011), 229

12. "HBO Miniseries: Show Me a Hero Inside the Series Parts One and Two (HBO)."

13. Caryn Rose, "All 314 Bruce Springsteen Songs, Ranked from Worst to Best," *Vulture*, September 13, 2016, http://www.vulture.com/2016/06/every-bruce-springsteen-song-ranked.html.

14. Jeffrey Symynkywicz, *The Gospel According to Bruce Springsteen: Rock and Redemption, from Asbury Park to Magic* (Louisville: Westminster John Knox Press, 2008), 67.

15. *Show Me a Hero* is not Oscar Isaac's only connection to Springsteen. Brian Hiatt's 2016 *Rolling Stone* article "Oscar Isaac: The Internet's Boyfriend Becomes a Leading Man" compared his look to the musician's: "He's wearing a thin white T-shirt, loose at the neck, which, combined with his ropy physique, dark good looks, and the sideburns he's grown for his *Star Wars* part as Poe Dameron, gives him a distinct Springsteen-in-'78 vibe. (He doesn't deny that he'd be good casting for a Bruce biopic, but adds, 'Wouldn't you rather just see Springsteen for real?')"

16. Symynkywicz, *The Gospel According to Bruce Springsteen*, 31.

17. Jeff Smith, *The Sounds of Commerce: Marketing Popular Film Music* (New York: Columbia University Press, 1998), 169.

18. "HBO Miniseries: Show Me a Hero Inside the Series Parts Five and Six (HBO)," YouTube Video, August 23, 2015, https://www.youtube.com/watch?v=G2yqAl519H4.

19. Oskar Eustis, "Artistic Director Note," program notes for *Hamlet*, Public Theater, August 23, 2017.

20. Barack Obama, "Remarks by the President at the Presidential Medal of Freedom" (speech, Washington, DC, November 22, 2016), White House: President Barack Obama, https://obamawhitehouse.archives.gov/the-press-office/2016/11/22/remarks-president-presentation-presidential-medal-freedom.

21. Jonathan D. Cohen, "'This Depression': The 2008 Financial Crisis and the Betrayal of America in Bruce Springsteen's *Wrecking Ball*" (paper presented at Glory Days: A Bruce Springsteen Symposium, Monmouth University, Long Branch, NJ, September 2012), 2; Jason P. Stonerook, "Springsteen's Search for Individuality and Community in Post-1960s America," in *Bruce Springsteen, Cultural Studies, and the Runaway American Dream*, edited by Kenneth Womack, Jerry Zolten, and Mark Bernhard (New York: Routledge, 2016), 216.

22. Mikal Gilmore, "Bruce Springsteen: Voice of the Decade," *Rolling Stone*, November 15, 1990, https://www.rollingstone.com/music/music-news/bruce-springsteen-voice-of-the-decade-192581.

23. Obama, "Remarks by the President at the Presidential Medal of Freedom."

24. Fiachra Gibbons, "Bruce Springsteen: 'What Was Done to My Country Was Un-American,'" *The Guardian*, February 12, 2012, https://www.theguardian.com/music/2012/feb/17/bruce-springsteen-wrecking-ball.

25. Masciotra, *Working on a Dream*, 205.

26. Daniel Calvisi, "David Simon Interview 'SHOW ME A HERO' on HBO," *Act Four Screenplays*, August 11, 2015, http://actfourscreenplays.com/screenwriting-blog/david-simon-interview-show-me-a-hero-on-hbo.

27. Michael Hainey, "Beneath the Surface of Bruce Springsteen," *Esquire*, November 27, 2018.

28. *Ibid.*

29. Donald L. Deardorff II, *Bruce Springsteen: American Poet and Prophet* (Lanham, MD: Scarecrow Press, 2014), 112.

30. *Ibid.*

31. HBO, "HBO Miniseries: Show Me a Hero Inside the Series Parts Three and Four (HBO)," YouTube, August 30, 2015, https://www.youtube.com/watch?v=3GNCZLfDkO8.

32. Bruce Springsteen, *Born to Run* (New York: Simon & Schuster, 2016), 52.

33. *Ibid.*, 53.

34. *Ibid.*, 345.

35. *Ibid.*, 52.

36. *Ibid.*

37. *Ibid.*, 245.

38. *Ibid.*

39. Masciotra, *Working on a Dream*, 159.

40. Belkin, *Show Me a Hero*, 255.

41. These quotes are an amalgamation of the "Long Walk Home"/"The Ghost of Tom Joad" monologue from a January 9, 2018, bootleg of *Springsteen on Broadway* and the final Netflix version directed by Thom Zimny.

42. Antonella D'Amore, "Meeting the Other: Bruce Springsteen's Community Ideal after September 11" (paper presented at the 27th International AISNA Conference, Rome, Italy, November 6, 2008), 182.

43. Masciotra, *Working on a Dream*, 108.

44. Robert Hilburn, "Under the Boss' Skin," *Los Angeles Times*, April 1, 2001.

45. Masciotra, *Working on a Dream*, 61.

46. Jon Stewart, "Bruce Springsteen's State of the Union," *Rolling Stone*, March 29, 2012, https://www.rollingstone.com/music/music-news/bruce-springsteens-state-of-the-union-172644/.

47. Rob Horning, "Bruce Springsteen and the E Street Band," *PopMatters*, August 19, 2003, https://www.popmatters.com/springsteen-bruce-030724-2496080883.html.

48. *Ibid.*

49. Caryn Rose (@carynrose), "this is a great thread. but let's remember that the E Street Band came together not long after the end of Jim Crow & they were touring at a time when people were still not thrilled that there was a black dude in the band. The kiss was SUBVERSIVE," Twitter, December 23, 2017, https://twitter.com/carynrose/status/944615730447872000.

50. Nay Wasicsko-McLaughlin, e-mail discussion with the author.

51. Deardorff, *Bruce Springsteen: American Poet and Prophet*, 100.
52. Masciotra, *Working on a Dream*, 201.

American Honey
53. Sean O'Hagan, "Andrea Arnold: 'I Always Aim to Get Under the Belly of a Place,'" *The Observer*, October 9, 2016, https://www.theguardian.com/film/2016/oct/09/andrea-arnold-interview-american-honey-shia-labeouf-sasha-lane.
54. Fiachra Gibbons, "Bruce Springsteen: 'What Was Done to My Country Was Un-American,'" *The Guardian*, February 12, 2012, https://www.theguardian.com/music/2012/feb/17/bruce-springsteen-wrecking-ball.
55. Guy Lodge, "Film Review: 'American Honey,'" *Variety*, May 14, 2016, https://www.variety.com/2016/film/reviews/american-honey-review-shia-labeouf-1201774708/.
56. Clarisse Loughery, "Andrea Arnold Interview: On *American Honey*, Chasing People in Walmart, and the Power of Rihanna," *The Independent*, October 12, 2016, https://www.independent.co.uk/arts-entertainment/films/features/american-honey-interview-andrea-arnold-a7358326.html.
57. Ibid.
58. Ibid.
59. David Laderman, *Driving Visions: Exploring the Road Movie* (Austin: University of Texas Press, 2006), 16.
60. Ibid.
61. Phil Sutcliffe, "You Talkin' to Me?" in *Talk about a Dream: The Essential Interviews of Bruce Springsteen*, edited by Christopher Phillips and Louis P. Masur (New York: Bloomsbury Press, 2013), 318.
62. Andy Gill, "Bruce Springsteen: The Man, the Music, the Politics … the Boss," *The Independent*, June 25, 2009, https://www.independent.co.uk/arts-entertainment/music/features/bruce-springsteen-the-man-the-music-the-politicsthe-boss-1719354.html.
63. Stephen Maher, "Springsteen's Wrecking Ball and the Plague of the 99%," *Monthly Review: An Independent Socialist Magazine*, December 1, 2012, https://monthlyreview.org/2012/12/01/springsteens-wrecking-ball-and-the-plague-of-the-99/.
64. O'Hagan, "Andrea Arnold."
65. Catherine Shoard, "Andrea Arnold in Cannes: I Was Shocked and Upset by the Poverty I Saw in the US," *The Guardian*, May 15, 2016, https://www.theguardian.com/film/2016/may/15/andrea-arnold-in-cannes-i-was-shocked-and-upset-by-the-poverty-i-saw-in-the-us.
66. Neil Archer, *The Road Movie: In Search of Meaning* (New York: Wallflower Press, 2016), 11; Laderman, *Driving Visions*, 40.
67. Archer, *The Road Movie*, 14.
68. Bruce Springsteen, *Born to Run* (New York: Simon & Schuster, 2016), 28.
69. Jeffrey Symynkywicz, *The Gospel According to Bruce Springsteen: Rock and Redemption, from Asbury Park to Magic* (Louisville: Westminster John Knox Press, 2008), 26.
70. To gather this data, I consulted Bobby Olivier's complete list of Springsteen's officially released work (https://www.nj.com/entertainment/music/index.ssf/2017/10/bruce_springsteen_songs_ranked_springsteen_on_broa.html) and Caryn Rose's ranking of all Springsteen songs (https://www.vulture.com/2016/06/every-bruce-springsteen-song-ranked.html). Special thanks to Kate French-Morris for her assistance.
71. Archer, *The Road Movie*, 18.
72. Loughery, "Andrea Arnold Interview"; Sophie Elmhirst, "Andrea Arnold's Immersive Cinema," *New Yorker*, October 8, 2016, https://www.newyorker.com/culture/persons-of-interest/andrea-arnolds-immersive-cinema.
73. Greil Marcus, "Born to Run," *Rolling Stone*, October 9, 1975, https://www.rollingstone.com/music/music-album-reviews/born-to-run-87675/.
74. Laderman, *Driving Visions*, 30.
75. Ibid., 19.
76. Ibid., 17.
77. Ibid., 23.
78. Ibid.
79. Ibid.
80. Frank Fury, "'Deliver Me from Nowhere': Place and Space in Bruce Springsteen's *Nebraska*," in *Reading the Boss: Interdisciplinary Approaches to the Works of Bruce Springsteen*, edited by Roxanne Harde and Irwin Streight (Lanham, MD: Lexington Books, 2010), 91; Judith Skinner Sawyers, "Introduction," in *Racing in the Street: The Bruce Springsteen Reader*, edited by Judith Skinner Sawyers (London: Penguin Books, 2004), 15.
81. Kurt Loder, "The Rolling Stone Interview: Bruce Springsteen on 'Born in the U.S.A,'" *Rolling Stone*, December 7, 1984, https://www.rollingstone.com/music/news/the-rolling-stone-%20interview-bruce-springsteen-on-born-in-the-u-s-a-19841206.
82. Laderman, *Driving Visions*, 9.
83. Julia Felsenthal, "*American Honey* Is Like Nothing You've Ever Seen Before," *Vogue*, September 29, 2015, https://www.vogue.com/article/american-honey-andrea-arnold-interview.
84. Springsteen, *Born to Run*, 127.
85. David Masciotra, *Working on a Dream: The Progressive Political Vision of Bruce Springsteen* (New York: A&C Black, 2010), 77.
86. Laderman, *Driving Visions*, 29.
87. Esther Zuckerman, "Andrea Arnold on Her Mesmerizing Party on Wheels, *American Honey*," *The AV Club*, September 30, 2016, https://film.avclub.com/andrea-arnold-on-her-mesmerizing-party-on-wheels-ameri-1798252554.
88. Shoard, "Andrea Arnold in Cannes."
89. Ibid.
90. Tasha Robinson, "Director Andrea Arnold on the Cross-Country Party that Produced American Honey," *The Verge*, September 29, 2016, https://www.theverge.com/2016/9/29/13109072/american-honey-movie-director-interview-andrea-arnold-tiff-2016.
91. Springsteen, *Born to Run*, 261.
92. Christopher Sandford, *Springsteen: Point Blank* (Boston: Da Capo Press), 16.

93. Dave Marsh, *Glory Days: Bruce Springsteen in the 1980s* (New York: Thunder's Mouth Press, 1988), 87.

94. Donald L. Deardorff II, *Bruce Springsteen: American Poet and Prophet* (Lanham, MD: Scarecrow Press, 2014), 117.

95. *Ibid.*, 62.

96. *Ibid.*

97. Geoffrey Himes, *Bruce Springsteen's Born in the U.S.A. (33 1/3)* (London: Continuum, 2005), 111.

98. Masciotra, *Working on a Dream*, 80.

99. Jonathan D. Cohen, "'This Depression': The 2008 Financial Crisis and the Betrayal of America in Bruce Springsteen's *Wrecking Ball*" (paper presented at Glory Days: A Bruce Springsteen Symposium, Monmouth University, Long Branch, NJ, September 2012), 4.

Bibliography

"Album of the Month." *Uncut* (September 2002).

Alterman, Eric. *It Ain't No Sin to Be Glad You're Alive: The Promise of Bruce Springsteen*. New York City: Back Bay Books, 2001.

Archer, Neil. *The Road Movie: In Search of Meaning*. New York: Wallflower Press, 2016.

Aswad, Jen. "Bruce Springsteen Takes Us on a Tour of His iTunes Playlist." *Variety*, October 4, 2017. https://variety.com/2017/music/news/bruce-springsteen-a-guided-tour-of-his-itunes-folder-playlist-1202580076/.

Bardsley, Garth. "How Mickey Rourke Got Bruce Springsteen's 'Wrestler' Song—for Free." *MTV*, January 12, 2009. http://www.mtv.com/news/1602516/how-mickey-rourke-got-bruce-springsteens-wrestler-song-for-free/.

Baron, Cynthia. "Sayles Between the Systems: Bucking 'Industry Policy and the Indie Apolitical Chic.'" In *Sayles Talk: New Perspectives on Independent Filmmaker John Sayles*, edited by Diane Carson and Heidi Kanaga, 16–50. Detroit: Wayne State University Press, 2006.

Belkin, Lisa. *Show Me a Hero: A Tale of Murder, Suicide, Race, and Redemption*. Boston: Little, Brown, 1999.

Benshoff, Harry M., and Sean Griffin. "General Introduction." In *Queer Cinema: The Film Reader*, edited by Harry M. Benshoff and Sean Griffin, 1–15. New York: Routledge, 2004.

Bernard, Ron. "Funhouse (2.13)." *Sopranos Autopsy: Examining TV's Greatest Series*. 2014. https://sopranosautopsy.com/season-2-3/funhouse-draft/.

Bliss, Ann V. "Growin' Up to Be a Nothing Man: Masculinity, Community, and the Outsider in Bruce Springsteen's Songs." In *Reading the Boss: Interdisciplinary Approaches to the Works of Bruce Springsteen*, edited by Roxanne Harde and Irwin Streight, 133–150. Lanham, MD: Lexington Books, 2010.

Bogdanovich, Peter. "Feature Commentary with Director Peter Bogdanovich." *Mask: Director's Cut*. Directed by Peter Bogdanovich. Universal City, CA: Universal Pictures Home Entertainment, 2004. DVD.

Bogues, Austin. "$1 Billion Rebirth: Changing Face of Asbury Park." *Asbury Park Press*, January 26, 2017. https://www.app.com/story/insider/extras/2017/01/26/asbury-park-gentrification-population-tourism/91219354/.

Bohanan, Rebecca. "The Only Three Women in Bruce Springsteen's Music." *Jezebel*, March 15, 2012. https://jezebel.com/5893602/the-only-three-women-in-bruce-springsteens-music.

Brown, Tom. *Breaking the Fourth Wall: Direct Address in Cinema*. Edinburgh: Edinburgh University Press, 2013.

Browne, David. "The Rising." *Entertainment Weekly*, August 2, 2002. https://ew.com/article/2002/08/02/rising-4/.

Burke, David. *Heart of Darkness: Bruce Springsteen's Nebraska*. London: Cherry Red Books, 2011.

Burns, Edward. "Director's Commentary." *No Looking Back*. Directed by Edward Burns. Century City, CA: 20th Century Fox, 2002. DVD.

———. Interview with Mike Vaccaro. Tribeca Film Festival 2018. New York City, April 27, 2018.

Calvisi, Daniel. "David Simon Interview 'SHOW ME A HERO' on HBO." *Act Four Screenplays*, August 11, 2015. http://actfourscreenplays.com/screenwriting-blog/david-simon-interview-show-me-a-hero-on-hbo.

Cante, Richard C. "HIV, Multiculturalism, and Popular Narrativity in the United States." *Narrative* 7, no. 3 (1999): 239–258.

Carlin, Peter Ames. *Bruce*. New York: Simon & Schuster, 2012.

———. "Two Truths and a Lie." Keynote Address, Bruce Springsteen's *Darkness on the Edge of Town*: An International Symposium, Monmouth University, Long Branch, NJ, April 14, 2018.

The Celluloid Closet. Directed by Rob Epstein and Jeffrey Friedman. Culver City, CA: Sony Pictures Home Entertainment, 2001.

Citino, M. Robert, and Michael Neiberg. "A Long Walk Home: The Role of Class and the Military in the Springsteen Catalog." *The Biannual-Online Journal of Springsteen Studies* 2, issue 1 (2016): 42–63.

Cocks, Jay. "Rock's New Sensation: The Backstreet Phantom of Rock." *Time*, October 27, 1975. http://content.time.com/time/subscriber/article/0,33009,913583,00.html.

Cohen, Anthony. "The Problems with the Death Penalty Are Already Crystal Clear." *The Atlantic*, May 5, 2014. https://www.theatlantic.com/politics/archive/2014/05/we-already-know-whats-wrong-with-the-death-penalty/361635/.

Cohen, Jonathan D. "Lost in the Flood: Bruce Springsteen's Political Consciousness and the Vietnam War, 1968–2014." In *Bruce Springsteen and Popular Music: Rhetoric, Social Consciousness, and Contemporary Culture*, edited by William I. Wolff, 17–30. New York: Routledge, 2017.

———. "'This Depression': The 2008 Financial Crisis and the Betrayal of America in Bruce Springsteen's *Wrecking Ball*." Paper presented at Glory Days: A Bruce Springsteen Symposium, Monmouth University, Long Branch, NJ, September 2012.

Cowie, Jefferson, and Lauren Boehm. "Dead Man's Town: 'Born in the USA,' Social History, and Working-Class Identity." In *Bruce Springsteen, Cultural Studies, and the Runaway American Dream*, edited by Kenneth Womack, Jerry Zolten, and Mark Bernhard, 25–44. New York: Routledge, 2016.

Cullen, Jim. *Born in the U.S.A.: Bruce Springsteen and the American Tradition*. Middletown, CT: Wesleyan University Press, 2005.

Dailey, Kate. "Bruce Springsteen Comes Out in Support of NJ's Gay Marriage Bill." *Newsweek*, December 9, 2009. https://www.newsweek.com/bruce-springsteen-comes-out-support-njs-gay-marriage-bill-222096.

D'Amore, Antonella. "Meeting the Other: Bruce Springsteen's Community Ideal after September 11." Paper presented at the 27th International AISNA Conference, Rome, Italy, November 6, 2008.

Davison, Annette. "The End Is Nigh: Music Postfaces and End-Credit Sequences in Contemporary Television Serials." *Music, Sound, and the Moving Image* 8, issue 2 (2014): 195–215.

Dawidoff, Nicholas. "The Pop Populist." *New York Times Magazine*, January 26, 1997.

Deardorff, Donald L., II. *Bruce Springsteen: American Poet and Prophet*. Lanham, MD: Scarecrow Press, 2014.

DeCaro, Frank. "The Mob Squad." *TV Guide*, January 8–12, 2000.

DeCurtis, Anthony. "The Rolling Stone Interview: Jonathan Demme on 'Philadelphia,' Tom Hanks, Homophobia." *Rolling Stone*, March 24, 1994. https://www.rollingstone.com/movies/movie-features/the-rolling-stone-interview-jonathan-demme-on-philadelphia-tom-hanks-homophobia-62429/.

Delmonico, Lisa. "Queen of the Supermarket: Representations of Working Class Women." In *Bruce Springsteen and the American Soul: Essays on the Songs and Influence of a Cultural Icon*, edited by David Garrett Izzo, 45–55. Jefferson, NC: McFarland, 2011.

Demme, Jonathan, and Ron Nyswaner. "Audio Commentary." *Philadelphia*. Directed by Jonathan Demme. Culver City, CA: Sony Pictures Home Entertainment, 2002. DVD.

Demme, Jonathan, et al. "People Like Us: Making *Philadelphia*." *Philadelphia*. Directed by Jonathan Demme. Culver City, CA: Sony Pictures Home Entertainment, 2002. DVD.

DiGiacomo, Frank. "Steven Van Zandt Discusses 'Soulfire,' Springsteen, Republicans." *Billboard*, May 16, 2017. https://www.billboard.com/articles/columns/rock/7793162/steven-van-zandt-relationship-bruce-springsteen-solo-album-soulfire.

Droney, Maureen. "Lots of Music, No Composer." *Mix*, April 1, 2001. https://www.mixonline.com/recording/lots-music-no-composer-372146.

Dwyer, Michael D. *Back to the Fifties: Nostalgia, Hollywood Film, and Popular Music of the Seventies and Eighties*. New York: Oxford University Press, 2015.

Ebert, Roger. "Philadelphia." *RogerEbert.com*, January 14, 1994. https://www.rogerebert.com/reviews/philadelphia-1994.

Eliot, Marc. *Down Thunder Road: The Making of Bruce Springsteen*. New York: Simon & Schuster, 1992.

Elmhirst, Sophie. "Andrea Arnold's Immersive Cinema." *New Yorker*, October 8, 2016. https://www.newyorker.com/culture/persons-of-interest/andrea-arnolds-immersive-cinema.

Eustis, Oskar. "Artistic Director Note." Program notes for *Hamlet*, Public Theater, August 23, 2017.

Fanshel, Rosalie Zdzienicka. "Beyond Blood Brothers: Queer Bruce Springsteen." *Popular Music* 32, issue 3 (2013): 359–383.

Faraci, Devin. "TWO LANE BLACKTOP Is The Picture." *Birth.Movies.Death.*, March 25, 2015. https://birthmoviesdeath.com/2015/03/25/two-lane-blacktop-is-the-picture.

Farber, Stephen. "9/11 Is Sneaking onto a Screen Near You." *New York Times*, March 13, 2005. https://www.nytimes.com/2005/03/13/movies/911-is-sneaking-onto-a-screen-near-you.html.

Fellezs, Kevin. "Wiseguy Opera: Music for *The Sopranos*." In *This Thing of Ours: Investigating The Sopranos*, edited by David Lavery, 162–177. New York: Wallflower Press, 2002.

Felsenthal, Julia. "*American Honey* Is Like Nothing You've Ever Seen Before." *Vogue*, September 29, 2015. https://www.vogue.com/article/american-honey-andrea-arnold-interview.

Flippo, Chet. *Musician* (November 1984).

Frears, Stephen, and John Cusack. "Conversations with Writer/Co-Producer John Cusack and Director Stephen Frears." *High Fidelity*. Directed by Stephen Frears. Burbank, CA: Buena Vista Pictures, 2000. DVD.

Furino, Giaco. "Does Bruce Springsteen Love B-Movies?" *Tribeca Shortlist*, April 29, 2017. https://outtake.tribecashortlist.com/does-bruce-springsteen-love-b-movies-d4873ed9abfb.

Fury, Frank. "'Deliver Me from Nowhere': Place and Space in Bruce Springsteen's *Nebraska*." In *Reading the Boss: Interdisciplinary Approaches to the Works of Bruce Springsteen*, edited by Roxanne Harde and Irwin Streight, 79–94. Lanham, MD: Lexington Books, 2010.

Garman, Bryan. "The Ghost of History: Bruce Springsteen, Woody Guthrie, and the Hurt Song." *Popular Music and Society* 20, no. 2 (1996): 69–120.

Gecker, Jocelyn. "Bruce Springsteen on His Depression, Family, and New Memoir." *Boston Globe*, October 6, 2016. https://www.bostonglobe.com/arts/2016/10/06/bruce-springsteen-his-depression-family-and-new-memoir/tCVn8Qm3xYV7Asb9rIEvxN/story.html.

Gibbons, Fiachra. "Bruce Springsteen: 'What Was

Done to My Country Was Un-American.'" *The Guardian*, February 12, 2012. https://www.theguardian.com/music/2012/feb/17/bruce-springsteen-wrecking-ball.

Gill, Andy. "Bruce Springsteen: The Man, the Music, the Politics ... the Boss." *The Independent*, June 25, 2009. https://www.independent.co.uk/arts-entertainment/music/features/bruce-springsteen-the-man-the-music-the-politicsthe-boss-1719354.html.

Gilmore, Mikal. "Bruce Springsteen: Voice of the Decade." *Rolling Stone*, November 15, 1990. https://www.rollingstone.com/music/music-news/bruce-springsteen-voice-of-the-decade-192581/.

Gleiberman, Owen. "Review: High Fidelity." *Entertainment Weekly*, March 24, 2000. http://ew.com/article/2000/03/24/high-fidelity-8/.

Goldsmith, Lynn. *Photodiary*. New York: Random House, 1995.

Gonzalez, Ed. "Prozac Nation Film Review." *Slant Magazine*, June 14, 2004. https://www.slantmagazine.com/film/review/prozac-nation.

Goodman, Fred. *The Mansion on the Hill: Dylan, Young, Geffen, Springsteen, and the Head-On Collision of Rock and Commerce*. New York: Times Books, 1997.

Gorbman, Claudia. "Why Music? The Sound Film and Its Spectator." In *Movie Music, the Film Reader*, edited by Kay Dickinson, 37–48. London: Routledge, 2003.

Gross, Terry. "On Jersey, Masculinity and Wishing to Be His Stage Persona." *Fresh Air*, September 15, 2017. https://www.npr.org/2017/09/15/551112185/bruce-springsteen-on-jersey-masculinity-and-wishing-to-be-his-stage-persona.

Guroff, Meg, Jim Jerome, and Lyndon Stambler. "Glory Days: Friends of the Boss Share Their Most Intimate Insights." *AARP The Magazine* (September 2009). https://www.aarp.org/entertainment/music/info-07-2009/springsteen_glory_days.html.

Hagen, Mark. "The Midnight Cowboy." In *Talk about a Dream: The Essential Interviews of Bruce Springsteen*, edited by Christopher Phillips and Louis P. Masur, 233–257. New York: Bloomsbury Press, 2013.

Hainey, Michael. "Beneath the Surface of Bruce Springsteen." *Esquire*, November 27, 2018.

Hann, Michael. "Bruce Springsteen: 'You Can Change a Life in Three Minutes with the Right Song.'" *The Observer*, October 30, 2016. https://www.theguardian.com/music/2016/oct/30/bruce-springsteen-interview-born-to-run-change-someones-life-right-song-donald-trump.

Harde, Roxanne. "'May Your Hope Give Us Hope': *The Rising* as a Site of Mourning." In *Reading the Boss: Interdisciplinary Approaches to the Works of Bruce Springsteen*, edited by Roxanne Harde and Irwin Streight, 243–266. Lanham, MD: Lexington Books, 2010.

Harde, Roxanne, and Irwin Streight. "Introduction." In *Reading the Boss: Interdisciplinary Approaches to the Works of Bruce Springsteen*, edited by Roxanne Harde and Irwin Streight, 1–22. Lanham, MD: Lexington Books, 2010.

Harris, Thomas J. *Bogdanovich's Picture Shows*. Metuchen, NJ: Scarecrow Press, 1990.

"HBO Miniseries: Show Me a Hero Inside the Series Parts One and Two (HBO)." YouTube Video, August 16, 2015. https://www.youtube.com/watch?v=oksclThb3fw.

"HBO Miniseries: Show Me a Hero Inside the Series Parts Three and Four (HBO)." YouTube Video, August 23, 2015, https://www.youtube.com/watch?v=3GNCZLfDkO8.

Henke, James. "Bruce Springsteen Leaves E Street: The Rolling Stone Interview." *Rolling Stone*, August 6, 1992. https://www.rollingstone.com/music/music-news/bruce-springsteen-leaves-e-street-the-rolling-stone-interview-172718/.

Henwood, Melanie. "Springsteen: Growin' Up, Growing Older: A Route Map for the Long Walk Home." In *Bruce Springsteen and the American Soul: Essays on the Songs and Influence of a Cultural Icon*, edited by David Garrett Izzo, 233–244. Jefferson, NC: McFarland, 2011.

_____. "Wrecking Ball: Hard Times, Loss and Renewal; The Lifetime Conversation." Paper presented at Glory Days: A Bruce Springsteen Symposium, Monmouth University, Long Branch, NJ, September 2005.

Hiatt, Brian. "Oscar Isaac: The Internet's Boyfriend Becomes a Leading Man." *Rolling Stone*, May 18, 2016. https://www.rollingstone.com/culture/culture-news/oscar-isaac-the-internets-boyfriend-becomes-a-leading-man-204043/.

_____. "True Bruce: Springsteen Goes Deep, from Early Trauma to Future of E Street." *Rolling Stone*, October 5, 2016. https://www.rollingstone.com/music/music-features/true-bruce-springsteen-goes-deep-from-early-trauma-to-future-of-e-street-106550/.

Hilburn, Robert. *Springsteen*. New York: Scribner, 1985.

_____. "Under the Boss' Skin." *Los Angeles Times*, April 1, 2001.

Himes, Geoffrey. *Bruce Springsteen's Born in the U.S.A. (33⅓)*. London: Continuum, 2005.

Holden, Stephen. "Film Review: Blue Collars and Miseries by the Sea." *New York Times*, March 27, 1998. https://www.nytimes.com/1998/03/27/movies/film-review-blue-collars-and-miseries-by-the-sea.html.

Horning, Rob. "Bruce Springsteen and the E Street Band." *PopMatters*, August 19, 2003. https://www.popmatters.com/springsteen-bruce-030724-2496080883.html.

Izzo, David Garrett. "Introduction." In *Bruce Springsteen and the American Soul: Essays on the Songs and Influence of a Cultural Icon*, edited by David Garrett Izzo, 1–5. Jefferson: McFarland, 2011.

Jeffords, Susan. *The Remasculinization of America: Gender and the Vietnam War*. Bloomington: Indiana University Press, 1989.

Kamp, David. "Cover Story: The Book of Bruce Springsteen." *Vanity Fair*, September 6, 2016. https://www.vanityfair.com/culture/2016/09/bruce-springsteen-cover-story.

Kassabian, Anahid. *Hearing Film: Tracking Identifications in *Contemporary Hollywood Film Music*. New York: Routledge, 2000.

Kirkpatrick, Robert. *The Words and Music of Bruce Springsteen*. Westport, CT: Greenwood, 2006.

Kramer, Larry. "Playwright and Gay Activist Larry Kramer Explains Why He Hated Jonathan Demme's 'Philadelphia.'" *Los Angeles Times*, January 10, 1994. https://www.latimes.com/entertainment/movies/la-et-archives-jonathan-demme-philadelphia-20170426-story.html.

Laderman, David. *Driving Visions: Exploring the Road Movie*. Austin: University of Texas Press, 2006.

Laine, Tarja. *Bodies in Pain: Emotion and the Cinema of Darren Aronofsky*. New York: Berghan Books, 2015.

Levine, Samuel J. "Portraits of Criminals on Bruce Springsteen's *Nebraska*: The Enigmatic Criminal, the Sympathetic Criminal, and the Criminal as Brother." *Widener Law Journal* 14, no. 3 (2005): 767–785.

Levy, Emmanuel. *Gay Directors, Gay Films? Pedro Almodóvar, Terence Davies, Todd Haynes, Gus Van Sant, John Waters*. New York: Columbia University Press, 2015.

Leydon, Joe. "High Fidelity—'High Fidelity' Turns Up the Volume for Romantic Laffer." *Variety*, March 19, 2000. www.variety.com/2000/film/reviews/high-fidelity-high-fidelity-turns-up-the-volume-for-romantic-laffer-1200461104/.

Loder, Kurt. "Bruce Springsteen: The Rising." *Rolling Stone*, July 30, 2002. https://www.rollingstone.com/music/albumreviews/the-rising-20020730.

———. "The Rolling Stone Interview: Bruce Springsteen on 'Born in the U.S.A.'" *Rolling Stone*, December 7, 1984. https://www.rollingstone.com/music/news/the-rolling-stone-%20interview-bruce-springsteen-on-born-in-the-u-s-a-19841206.

Lodge, Guy. "Film Review: 'American Honey.'" *Variety*, May 14, 2016. https://www.variety.com/2016/film/reviews/american-honey-review-shia-labeouf-1201774708/.

Lombardi, John. "St. Boss." *Esquire*, December 1, 1988.

Loughrey, Clarisse. "Andrea Arnold Interview: On *American Honey*, Chasing People in Walmart, and the Power of Rihanna." *The Independent*, October 12, 2016. https://www.independent.co.uk/arts-entertainment/films/features/american-honey-interview-andrea-arnold-a7358326.html.

Lupack, Barbara Tepa. "History as Her-Story: Adapting Bobbie Ann Mason's *In Country* to Film." In *Vision/Re-Vision: Adapting Contemporary American Fiction by Women in Film*, edited by Barbara Tepa Lupack. Bowling Green, KY: Bowling Green State University Popular Press, 1996.

Maher, Stephen. "Springsteen's Wrecking Ball and the Plague of the 99%." *Monthly Review: An Independent Socialist Magazine*, December 1, 2012. https://monthlyreview.org/2012/12/01/springsteens-wrecking-ball-and-the-plague-of-the-99/.

Marcus, Greil. "Born to Run." *Rolling Stone*, October 9, 1975. https://www.rollingstone.com/music/music-album-reviews/born-to-run-87675/.

Markert, John. *Post-9/11 Cinema: Through a Lens Darkly*. Lanham, MD: Scarecrow Press, 2011.

Marsh, Dave. *Glory Days: Bruce Springsteen in the 1980s*. New York: Thunder's Mouth Press, 1988.

———. *Two Hearts: The Story*. New York: Routledge, 2003.

Martin, Brett. *Difficult Men Behind the Scenes of a Creative Revolution: From The Sopranos and The Wire to Mad Men and Breaking Bad*. London: Penguin Group, 2013.

Masciotra, David. *Working on a Dream: The Progressive Political Vision of Bruce Springsteen*. New York: A&C Black, 2010.

Maslin, Janet. "Review/Film: 'Philadelphia'; Tom Hanks as an Aids Victim Who Fights the Establishment." *New York Times*, December 22, 1993.

Mason, Bobbie Ann. *In Country*. New York: Harper Perennial, 1985.

Masur, Louis P. *Runaway Dream: Born to Run and Bruce Springsteen's American Vision*. London: Bloomsbury Press, 2009.

McSweeney, Terrence. *The "War on Terror" and American Film: 9/11 Frames per Second*. Edinburgh: Edinburgh University Press, 2016.

Mead, John. "9/11, Manhood, Mourning, and the American Romance." In *Reframing 9/11: Film, Popular Culture and the "War on Terror"*, edited by Jeff Birkenstein, Anna Froula, and Karen Randell, 57–68. New York: Continuum, 2010.

Mennel, Barbara Caroline. *Queer Cinema: School Girls, Vampires, and Gay Cowboys*. New York: Columbia University Press, 2012.

Miller, D.A. "Anal Rope." In *Inside/Out: Lesbian Theories, Gay Theories*, edited by Diana Fuss, 119–141. New York: Routledge, 1991.

Miller, Debbie. "Bruce Springsteen in the Heartland." *Rolling Stone*, August 16, 1984. https://www.rollingstone.com/music/live-reviews/bruce-in-the-heartland-19840816.

Miller, Liz Shannon. "'Show Me a Hero': David Simon and Paul Haggis Might Have Made This Year's Most Important Miniseries." *IndieWire*, August 12, 2015. https://www.indiewire.com/2015/08/show-me-a-hero-david-simon-and-paul-haggis-might-have-made-this-years-most-important-miniseries-59397/.

Morris, Marya. "From 'My Hometown' to 'This Hard Land': Bruce Springsteen's Use of Geography, Landscapes, and Places to Depict the American Experience." *Interdisciplinary Literary Studies* 9, no. 1 (2007): 3–18.

Moss, Pamela. "Still Searching for the Promised Land: Placing Women in Bruce Springsteen's Lyrical Landscapes." *Cultural Geographies* 18, issue 3 (2011): 343–362.

Murphy, Edward U. "'The Country We Carry in Our Hearts Is Waiting': Bruce Springsteen and the Art of Social Change." In *Bruce Springsteen, Cultural Studies, and the Runaway American Dream*, edited by Kenneth Womack, Jerry Zolten, and Mark Bernhard, 177–198. New York: Routledge, 2016.

Nelson, Kristin. *Narcissism in High Fidelity*. Bloomington: iUniverse, 2004.

Nelson, Paul. "Springsteen Fever." *Rolling Stone*, July 13, 1978. https://www.rollingstone.com/music/music-news/springsteen-fever-178757/.

Obama, Barack. "Remarks by the President at the Presidential Medal of Freedom." Speech, Washington, DC, November 22, 2016. White House: President Barack Obama. https://obamawhitehouse.archives.gov/the-press-office/2016/11/22/remarks-president-presentation-presidential-medal-freedom.

O'Hagan, Sean. "Andrea Arnold: 'I Always Aim to Get Under the Belly of a Place.'" *The Observer*, October 9, 2016. https://www.theguardian.com/film/2016/oct/09/andrea-arnold-interview-american-honey-shia-labeouf-sasha-lane.

Orr, Christopher. "David Chase Just Ruined the Finale of *The Sopranos*." *The Atlantic*, April 19, 2015. https://www.theatlantic.com/entertainment/archive/2015/04/david-chase-just-ruined-the-finale-of-the-sopranos/390879/.

Osborne, David. "John Sayles: From Hoboken to Hollywood—and Back." In *John Sayles: Interviews*, edited by Diane Carson, 27–36. Jackson: University of Mississippi Press, 1999.

Palmer, Gareth. "Bruce Springsteen and Masculinity." In *Sexing the Groove: Popular Music and Gender*, edited by Sheila Whiteley, 100–118. New York: Routledge, 1997.

Pardini, Samuele F.S. "Bruce Zirilli: The Italian Sides of Bruce Springsteen." In *Bruce Springsteen, Cultural Studies, and the Runaway American Dream*, edited by Kenneth Womack, Jerry Zolten, and Mark Bernhard, 97–110. New York: Routledge, 2016.

Pareles, Jon. "Bruce Almighty." *New York Times*, April 24, 2005. https://www.nytimes.com/2005/04/24/arts/music/bruce-almighty.html.

Percy, Will. "Rock and Read: Will Percy Interviews Bruce Springsteen." *DoubleTake* (Spring 1998).

Peyser, Marc. "HBO'S Godfather." *Newsweek*, March 4, 2001. https://www.newsweek.com/hbos-godfather-148803.

Phillips, Christopher. Liner notes to *Tracks*. Bruce Springsteen. CD. 2010.

Phipps, Keith. "The Semi-Lost Brilliance of John Sayles' 'Baby It's You.'" *Oscilloscope Musings*, July 21, 2015. http://musings.oscilloscope.net/post/124673064816/the-semi-lost-brilliance-of-john-sayles-baby.

Pitofsky, Alex. "Springsteen's Imitations of Mortality." In *Bruce Springsteen and the American Soul: Essays on the Songs and Influence of a Cultural Icon*, edited by David Garrett Izzo, 226–232. Jefferson, NC: McFarland, 2011.

PT Staff. "Prozac Nation with Christina Ricci." *Psychology Today*, March 1, 2003. https://www.psychologytoday.com/us/articles/200303/prozac-nation-christina-ricci.

Reagan, Ronald. "The President's News Conference April 4, 1984." In *Public Papers of the Presidents of the United States: Ronald Reagan, 1984, Book I: January to June 29, 1984*. Washington, DC: Government Printing Office, 1984.

Reay, Pauline. *Music in Film: Soundtracks and Synergy*. New York: Wallflower Press, 2004.

Remnick, David. "We Are Alive: Springsteen at Sixty-Two." *New Yorker*, July 30, 2012. https://www.newyorker.com/magazine/2012/07/30/we-are-alive.

Ricci, Franco. *The Sopranos: Born Under a Bad Sign*. Toronto: University of Toronto Press, 2014.

Robbins, Tim. "Director's Commentary." *Dead Man Walking*. Directed by Tim Robbins. Beverly Hills, CA: MGM Home Entertainment, 2001.

Robinson, Tasha. "Director Andrea Arnold on the Cross-Country Party that Produced American Honey." *The Verge*, September 29, 2016. https://www.theverge.com/2016/9/29/13109072/american-honey-movie-director-interview-andrea-arnold-tiff-2016.

Rockwell, John. "Springsteen's Rock Poetry at Its Best." *New York Times*, August 29, 1975.

Rolling Stone. "Bruce Springsteen Honored at Kennedy Center by Mellencamp, Vedder, Sting." December 30, 2009. https://www.rollingstone.com/music/news/bruce-springsteen-honored-at-kennedy-center-by-mellencamp-vedder-sting-254744.

Rose, Caryn. "All 314 Bruce Springsteen Songs, Ranked from Worst to Best." *Vulture*, September 13, 2016. http://www.vulture.com/2016/06/every-bruce-springsteen-song-ranked.html.

Rucker, Allen. *The Sopranos: A Family History*. New York: New American Library Trade, 2001.

Ryan, Chris. "Show Me a Boss: The Use of Bruce Springsteen in 'Show Me a Hero.'" *Grantland*, August 26, 2015. http://grantland.com/hollywood-prospectus/show-me-a-boss-the-use-of-bruce-springsteen-in-show-me-a-hero/.

Ryan, Jack. *John Sayles, Filmmaker: A Critical Study and Filmography*. Jefferson, NC: McFarland, 2010.

Sandford, Christopher. *Springsteen: Point Blank*. New York: Da Capo Press, 1999.

Sawyers, Judith Skinner. "Introduction." In *Racing in the Street: The Bruce Springsteen Reader*, edited by Judith Skinner Sawyers, 1–25. New York: Penguin Books, 2004.

Sayles, John. *Thinking in Pictures: The Making of the Movie Matewan*. Boston: Da Capo Press, 2003.

Schruers, Fred. "Bruce Springsteen: The Boss Is Back." *Rolling Stone*, November 27, 1980. https://www.rollingstone.com/music/music-news/bruce-springsteen-the-boss-is-back-178801/.

Scott, A.O. "The Poet Laureate of 9/11." *Slate*, August 2, 2002. https://www.slate.com/articles/arts/music_box/2002/08/the_poet_laureate_of_911.html.

Scott, Roger, and Patrick Humphries. *HotPress*, November 2, 1984.

Seymour, Elizabeth M. "'Where Dreams Are Found and Lost': Springsteen, Nostalgia, and Identity." In *Bruce Springsteen, Cultural Studies, and the Runaway American Dream*, edited by Kenneth Womack, Jerry Zolten, and Mark Bernhard, 61–78. New York: Routledge, 2016.

ShainaTV. "Oscar Isaac, David Simon and More Talk 'Show Me a Hero.'" YouTube Video, August 16, 2015. https://www.youtube.com/watch?v=G2yqAl519H4.

Sheehy, Colleen. *Springsteen: Troubadour of the Highway*. Seattle: Frederick R. Weisman Art Museum, 2002.

Sheinbaum, John J. "'I'll Work for Your Love': Springsteen and the Struggle for Authenticity." In *Reading the Boss: Interdisciplinary Approaches to the Works of Bruce Springsteen*, edited by Roxanne Harde and Irwin Streight, 223–242. Lanham, MD: Lexington Books, 2010.

Shoard, Catherine. "Andrea Arnold in Cannes: I Was Shocked and Upset by the Poverty I Saw in the US." *The Guardian*, May 15, 2016. https://www.theguardian.com/film/2016/may/15/andrea-arnold-in-cannes-i-was-shocked-and-upset-by-the-poverty-i-saw-in-the-us.

Shumway, David R. "Rock 'n' Roll Sound Tracks and the Production of Nostalgia." *Cinema Journal* 38, no. 2 (Winter 1999): 36–51.

Skorin-Kapov, Jadranka. *Darren Aronofsky's Films and the Fragility of Hope*. London: Bloomsbury Academic, 2015.

Smith, Gavin. *Sayles on Sayles*. London: Faber & Faber, 1998.

Smith, Jeff. *The Sounds of Commerce: Marketing Popular Film Music*. New York: Columbia University Press, 1998.

Smith, Martha Nell. "Sexual Mobilities in Bruce Springsteen: Performance as Commentary." In *Present Tense: Rock and Roll Culture*, edited by Anthony DeCurtis, 196–218. Durham, NC: Duke University Press Books, 1992.

Smith, Nathan. "Remembering the Streets of Philadelphia." *Out*, November 5, 2015. https://www.out.com/entertainment/2015/11/05/remembering-streets-philadelphia.

Springsteen, Bruce. *Born to Run*. New York: Simon & Schuster, 2016.

———. "Chords for Change." *New York Times*, August 5, 2004. https://www.nytimes.com/2004/08/05/opinion/chords-for-change.html.

———. Interview with Elvis Costello. *Spectacle*. Sundance. September 25, 2009.

———. Interview with Jimmy Fallon. *Late Night Show with Jimmy Fallon*. NBC. March 10, 2012.

———. Interview with Jimmy Fallon. *The Tonight Show Starring Jimmy Fallon*. NBC. December 7, 2015.

———. Interview with Scott Pelley. *60 Minutes*. NBC. October 7, 2007.

———. Interview with Stephen Colbert. *The Late Show with Stephen Colbert*. CBS. September 24, 2016.

———. Interview with Will Gompertz. *BBC News*. BBC. November 6, 2016.

———. "Music and Lyric by Bruce Springsteen Academy Awards Acceptance Speech." Los Angeles, California, March 21, 1994. Academy Awards Acceptance Speech Database. http://aaspeechesdb.oscars.org/link/066-15/.

———. *Songs*. New York: HarperCollins, 2003.

———. "A Statement from Bruce Springsteen on North Carolina." *BruceSpringsteen.net*, April 8, 2016. https://www.brucespringsteen.net/news/2016/a-statement-from-bruce-springsteen-on-north-carolina.

Stewart, Jon. "Bruce Springsteen's State of the Union." *Rolling Stone*, March 29, 2012. https://www.rollingstone.com/music/music-news/bruce-springsteens-state-of-the-union-172644/.

Stonerook, Jason P. "Springsteen's Search for Individuality and Community in Post-1960s America." In *Bruce Springsteen, Cultural Studies, and the Runaway American Dream*, edited by Kenneth Womack, Jerry Zolten, and Mark Bernhard, 199–228. New York: Routledge, 2016.

Strate, Lance. "No(rth Jersey) Sense of Place: The Cultural Geography (and Media Ecology) of *The Sopranos*." In *This Thing of Ours: Investigating The Sopranos*, edited by David Lavery, 178–194. New York: Wallflower Press, 2002.

Strauss, Neil. "Human Touch: Bruce Springsteen Reflects on His Music, Life Without the E Street Band, and the Glory of Rock and Roll." *Guitar World* (September 1995).

Sutcliffe, Phil. "You Talkin' to Me?" In *Talk about a Dream: The Essential Interviews of Bruce Springsteen*, edited by Christopher Phillips and Louis P. Masur, 300–319. New York: Bloomsbury Press, 2013.

Swartley, Ariel. "*The Wild, the Innocent and the E Street Shuffle*: Bruce Springsteen (Columbia 32432) 1974." In *Stranded: Rock and Roll for a Desert Island*, edited by Greil Marcus, 49–57. Boston: Da Capo Press, 2007.

Sweeting, Adam. "'Bruce Springsteen: 'I Think I Just Wanted to Be Great.'" *Uncut* (September 2002). https://www.uncut.co.uk/features/bruce-springsteen-i-think-i-just-wanted-to-be-great-part-1-21634.

Symynkywicz, Jeffery. *The Gospel According to Bruce Springsteen: Rock and Redemption, from Asbury Park to Magic*. Louisville: Westminster John Knox Press, 2008.

Thurmaier, David. "'The Country We Carry in Our Heart Is Waiting': Bruce Springsteen, Franklin Delano Roosevelt, and the Search for Human Rights in America." In *Popular Music and Human Rights, Volume I: British and American Music*, edited by Ian Peddie, 143–156. Farnham, UK: Ashgate, 2011.

Tranter, Rhys. "American Cinema in the Shadow of 9/11." *RhysTranter* (blog), November 10, 2016. http://www.rhystranter.com/2016/11/10/terence-mcsweeney-american-cinema-in-the-shadow-of-911/.

Tucker, Ken. "The Sopranos." *Entertainment Weekly*, April 2, 1999. http://ew.com/article/1999/04/02/sopranos-7/.

Vinciguerra, Thomas. "For Author of 'Prozac Nation,' Film Is a Downer." *The New York Times*, November 9, 2003.

Walden, Cecilia. "Elizabeth Wurtzel: 'Getting Married for the First Time at 47 Is My Real Mistake.'" *The Telegraph*, June 22, 2015. https://www.telegraph.co.uk/women/mother-tongue/11687854/Elizabeth-Wurtzel-Getting-married-for-the-first-time-at-47-is-my-real-mistake.html.

Walsh, Keri. *Mickey Rourke*. London: British Film Institute, 2014.

Westwell, Guy. *Parallel Lines: Post-9/11 American Cinema*. New York: Wallflower Press, 2014.

Wieder, Judy, "Bruce Springsteen: The Advocate Interview." *The Advocate*, April 2, 1996.

Will, George. "A Yankee Doodle Springsteen." *Washington Post*, September 13, 1984.

Williams, Deane. *The Cinema of Sean Penn: In and Out of Place*. New York: Wallflower Press, 2015.

Willis, Ellen. "Our Mobsters, Ourselves." *The Nation*, April 2, 2001. https://www.thenation.com/article/our-mobsters-ourselves/.

Woloch, Alex. "Breakups and Reunions: Late Realism in Early Sayles." In *Sayles Talk: New Perspectives on Independent Filmmaker John Sayles*, edited by Diane Carson and Heidi Kanaga, 51–78. Detroit: Wayne State University Press, 2006.

Womack, Kenneth. "'Who's That Girl?' Nostalgia, Gender, and Springsteen." In *Reading the Boss: Interdisciplinary Approaches to the Works of Bruce Springsteen*, edited by Roxanne Harde and Irwin Streight, 121–132. Lanham, MD: Lexington Books, 2010.

Wong, Curtis. "Bruce Springsteen Stars in Gay Marriage Social Media Campaign." *Huffington Post*, October 2, 2012.

Wurtzel, Elizabeth. "Bruce Almighty." *The Guardian*, June 22, 2008. https://www.theguardian.com/music/2008/jun/22/popandrock.culture4.

———. *More, Now, Again: A Memoir of Addiction*. New York: Simon & Schuster, 2001.

———. *Prozac Nation: Young and Depressed in America*. New York: Riverhead Books, 1994.

——— (@elizabethwurtzel). "Here We Are after #springsteen on #broadway." Instagram, December 10, 2017. https://www.instagram.com/p/BchudW5Fl1o/?hl=en&taken-by=elizabethwurtzel/.

Yacowar, Maurice. *The Sopranos on the Couch: The Ultimate Guide*. London: Continuum, 2006.

Yaddin-Israel, Azzan. *The Grace of God and the Grace of Man: The Theologies of Bruce Springsteen*. Highland Park, NJ: Lingua Press, 2016.

Yates, Brad. "Healing a Nation: Deconstructing Bruce Springsteen's *The Rising*." Paper presented at Glory Days: A Bruce Springsteen Symposium, Monmouth University, Long Branch, NJ, September 2005.

Yule, Andrew. *Picture Shows: The Life and Films of Peter Bogdanovich*. New York: Limelight Editions, 1992.

Zitelli, Lisa. "'Like a Vision She Dances': Re-Visioning the Female Figure in the Songs of Bruce Springsteen." In *Reading the Boss: Interdisciplinary Approaches to the Works of Bruce Springsteen*, edited by Roxanne Harde and Irwin Streight, 151–176. Lanham, MD: Lexington Books, 2010.

Zuckerman, Esther. "Andrea Arnold on Her Mesmerizing Party on Wheels, *American Honey*." *The AV Club*, September 30, 2016. https://film.avclub.com/andrea-arnold-on-her-mesmerizing-party-on-wheels-ameri-1798252554.

Index

"Across the Border" 8, 188
"Adam Raised a Cain" 28-9, 139
The Advocate 64, 71-2
Alabama 3, 104
"All Man the Guns" 56
All That Heaven Allows (film) 9
"All That Heaven Will Allow" (song) 9, 125, 177
Allen, Woody 91, 129
Altman, Robert 9
"America Under Fire" 56, 60
American Cinema 9
American Film 18
American Graffiti 17
American Honey 190-204
"American Honey" 192
American Land" 184
American Madness 9
"American Skin" (41 Shots) 188
Andrea Chenier (opera) 69
Angels from Hell 46
The Animals 28
Antholis, Kary 173
Appel, Mike 10, 142-3
Arnold, Andrea 190-204
Aronofsky, Darren 159-172
Ashby, Hal 33

Baby It's You 15, 17-32
Back to the Future 17
"Backstreets" 13, 73, 129
Badlands (film) 13, 82, 196
"Badlands" (song) 32, 36-8, 99, 161
"Balboa Park" 202
"Ballad of Jesse James" 6
"Ballad of the Self-Loading Pistol" 7
"Be True" 13, 129
The Beatles 120, 156
Belkin, Lisa 173
Bernard, Ron 109
"Better Days" 126, 195
Big Man: Real Life & Tall Tales 12
Billy the Kid 6
Binder, Mike 148-58
Birth.Movies.Death 11
Bittan, Roy 50, 161, 163
"Black Cowboys" 7, 188
"Blinded by the Light" 107, 132
Blue Collar 12-3
"Bobby Jean" 119-20
Bogdanovich, Peter 33-42, 46, 104
Bohanan, Rebecca 98

Bonds, Gary U.S. 162
Bonnie and Clyde 10
"Book of Dreams" 126
Boorman, John 9
Born in the U.S.A. (album) 13, 41, 44, 47, 50, 52, 54, 58-9, 61, 72, 75, 77, 119-120, 160, 163, 173, 185, 191, 202
"Born in the U.S.A." (song) 13, 41, 44, 47, 49, 52, 61
The Born Losers 46
Born on the 4th of July 57
"Born to Be Wild" 192
Born to Run (album) 8, 10, 19, 24, 31, 73, 91-3, 100, 122, 171, 179, 189
Born to Run (book) 2, 9, 19, 117, 124, 132, 137, 140-1, 156, 170, 185
"Born to Run" (song) 31, 38, 73, 91-3, 95-8, 101-2, 107-8, 196
Borzage, Frank 9
Bowie, David 54
Bracken, Pam 128
Brando, Marlon 5, 11, 20, 122, 129
Brave Cowboy Bill 6
"Brilliant Disguise" 144, 170, 178
"Brothers Under the Bridge" 59
Brown, Tom 117, 121, 123
Bruce 34, 127
Bruce Springsteen & The E Street Band: Live in New York City 168
Bruestle, Martin 103
The Bull-Dogger 7
Burke, David 5
Burns, Edward 91-101

"Cadillac Ranch" 124, 179
Cain, James M. 5
Callas, Maria 70
"Camilla Horn" 13
"Candy's Room" 124
Capra, Frank 9
"Car Wash" 100
Carlin, Peter Ames 34, 127
Cassavetes, John 33
"Cautious Man" 8, 13, 87
The Celluloid Closet (film) 64, 68
Chanko, Kenneth M. 18
"Chapel of Love" 18
Chase, David 102-16
Cichon, Walter 54, 60
Clemons, Clarence 12, 73-4, 120, 153-4, 163, 177, 180, 186, 188-9, 196

Clemons, Jake 188
"Clouds" 57
Cockfighter 12
Cocks, Jay 161-2
Cohen, Andrea 82
Colbert, Stephen 169, 171
Cooper, Gary 114
Coppola, Francis Ford 33
Coulter, Allen 109-10
"Cowboys of the Sea" 6
Cream 114
The Crimson Skull 7
Crisp, Quentin 68
Cruising 63
"Crush on You" 124
Cusack, John 118-9
"Cynthia" 124

"Dancing in the Dark" 13, 132, 173, 195
D'Angerio, Alan 68
Darkness on the Edge of Town (album) 9-11, 13, 19, 28, 31-2, 91, 93, 122, 124, 132-3, 140, 142, 161, 181, 196-7, 190-200, 202
"Darkness on the Edge of Town" (song) 12, 197
Dassin, Jules 10
Davison, Annette 104
Dawidoff, Nicholas 7
Dayak, Kathryn 103-4
Dead End Street 9
Dead Man Walking (film) 76-90
"Dead Man Walking" (song) 1, 76-81
Dean, James 11, 13, 20, 122, 129
Deardorff, Donald L. 129, 185, 202
de Caro, Frank 106
DeCurtis, Anthony 64
The Deer Hunter 167
Delmonico, Lisa 125
Demme, Jonathan 5, 63-75
Demme, Ted 67
De Niro, Robert 5, 12
DePalma, Brian 13
Devils & Dust (album) 7, 89, 167, 188, 200
"Devils & Dust" (song) 87
DiGiacomo, Frank 103
Diner 17
The Dixie Cups 18

Index

"Don't Stop Believing" 115-6
The Doors 108
Double Indemnity 10
"Dream Baby Dream" 191-4
Dressed to Kill 63
"Drive All Night" 73, 155-57
Dylan, Bob 118

"E Street Shuffle" 21
East of Eden 138-9
Easy Rider 192, 197-8
Ebert, Roger 69
The Elephant Man (film) 36
"Empty Sky" 150-2
Eternal Love 13
Eustis, Oskar 182
"Evacuation of the West" 6

"Factory" 47
"Fade to Black" 13
Fallon, Jimmy 79, 139
Fanshel, Rosalie Z. 71-4
Faraci, Devin 11
Farrow, Mia 129
Fast Times at Ridgemont High 18
Faust 13
Federici, Danny 56, 125
Fellini, Federico 103, 106
Films in Review 18
"Fire" 122
Five Easy Pieces 196
Flippo, Chet 6, 13, 51
Fonda, Peter 192
"For You" 133, 143-4
Ford, John 6-8, 187, 200
4th of July, Asbury Park (Sandy) 23, 72, 107
Fox, Michael J. 13
Frankenstein (film) 36
Frears, Stephen 63, 117-131
Freebie and the Bean 63
"Freehold" 35
Fugate, Caril Ann 13, 82-3
"Fugitive's Dream" 72-3
Fullerton, Carl 68
Fury, Frank 113

"Galveston Bay" 77
Gandolfini, James 106
Garbo, Greta 13
"Gave It a Name" 173-4
The Ghost of Tom Joad (album) 2, 10, 59, 77, 187, 200, 202
"The Ghost of Tom Joad" (song) 186, 200
Gibson, Mel 169
"Gloria's Eyes" 126-7
"Glory Days" 17, 92, 120, 173
Godard, Jean-Luc 103
Goldsmith, Lynn 128
Gompertz, Will 141
Gorbman, Claudia 13, 16
Gould, Elliot 9
The Grapes of Wrath (film) 187
Grease 17
Greetings from Asbury Park, N.J. 2, 8, 19-20, 24, 57, 72, 107, 194
Gross, Terry 137, 170

Gun Crazy 10
Guthrie, Woody 5, 187

Haggis, Paul 173-190
Hainey, Michael 140
Hammersmith Odeon London '75 143
Hanks, Tom 64, 68-9
Harde, Roxanne 3, 154
Harlem on the Prairie 7
Harris, Thomas J. 38
Haynes, Bart 49, 54, 60
Haynes, Todd 63
Hellman, Monte 11-2
High Fidelity 103, 117-131
High Hopes (album) 60, 164, 189
"Highway Patrolman" 59
"Highway 29" 10
Hilburn, Robert 188
Hines, Geoffrey 203
History Is Made at Night 9
"The Hitter" 167
Holden, Stephen 91
Hopper, Dennis 192
Hopper, Edward 105
Hornby, Nick 117
Horne, Camilla 13
How the West Was Won 7
Hughes, Howard 6
Human Touch (album) 126, 131, 173, 189
"Human Touch" (song) 126
"Hungry Heart" 175-6, 189
Huston, John 13

"I Feel Free" 114
"I Wanna Marry You" 125
"I Wish I Were Blind" 87
"Iceman" 91, 99
"If I Should Fall Behind" 126
"If I Was the Priest" 86
"I'll Work for Your Love" 100
"I'm a Big Girl Now" 98
"I'm a Rocker" 129
"I'm on Fire" 17, 44-5, 47, 95, 97, 195
"Incident on 57th Street" 72
"Independence Day" 139
"Into the Fire" 156
Isaac, Oscar 179, 182
"It's Hard to Be a Saint in the City" 20-1, 29
"It's My Life" 28
Izzo, David Garrett 169

"Jack of All Trades" 202
"James Lincoln Deere" 84
Jefferson Airplane 112
Jeffords, Susan 53
"Jesse" 170
Jesus Was an Only Son 89
Jett, Joan 13
Jewison, Norman 43-62
"Johnny 99" 82-3
Joplin, Janis 108
Journey 103, 115
"Jungleland" 21, 24, 196

Kassabian, Anahid 15
Kazan, Elia 46
Keruoac, Jack 197
King, Ben E. 21
Kirkpatrick, Robert 67
"The Klansman" 77
Kovic, Ron 57-8
Kramer, Larry 63-4
Kubrick, Stanley 103

Lady Antebellum 192
Lake, Veronica 9
"Land of Hope and Dreams" 89, 184
Landau, Jon 1, 5, 8-9, 12, 113, 140-2
The Last American Virgin 18
The Last Temptation of Christ 89
The Last Waltz 136
Late Night with Jimmy Fallon 139
Late Show with Stephen Colbert 169
Laverne & Shirley 17
"Leap of Faith" 168
The Left Handed Gun 6
Leone, Sergio 7
"Let's Be Friends (Skin to Skin)" 154
Levine, Samuel J. 113
"Life Itself" 87, 127
"Lift Me Up" 182-3
Light of Day (film) 13
"Light of Day" (song) 13
Lilyhammer 103
Live 1975/1985 54-5, 72
"Living Proof" 87
Loder, Kurt 49, 52, 150, 199
Lodge, Guy 191
Lofgren, Nils 106
Lombardi, John 74
The Lone Ranger 114
"Lonesome Day" 107, 150
The Long Goodbye 9
"Long Walk Home" 186
"Loose Ends" 103
Lopez, Vinnie "Mad Dog" 55, 60
"Lost in the Flood" 57, 72, 86
Lubitsch, Ernst 13
Lucas, George 17
Lucky Town (album) 126, 181, 189

Magic 100, 186
Malick, Terrence 13, 82, 199
"La Mamma Morta" 69
"Man's Job" 126
"Mansion on the Hill" 13, 112
Marcus, Griel 196
Marsh, Dave 58
Martin, Brett 110, 115
"Mary Lou" 14, 129
"Mary Louise Watson" 86
"Mary Queen of Arkansas" 72
"Mary's Place" 154
Mascriota, David 174
Mask 1, 33-42
Mason, Bobbie Ann 43, 47
Mayfield, Curtis 184
"Meeting Across the River" 10, 24
Miller, Paul 146

Index

Mitchum, Robert 10
More, Now, Again 132-3, 144
Morricone, Ennio 7
Moss, Pamela 98
Muller, Bob 57-8
Mulligan, Robert 13
"Murder Incoporated" 9
Murnau, F.W. 13
My Beautiful Laundrette 63
"My Beautiful Reward" 181
"My City of Ruins" 157-8
"My Father's House" 139
"My Hometown" 185-6
"My Lover Man" 73
"My Lucky Day" 127
My Own Private Idaho 63

Nebraska (album) 2, 13, 50, 58-9, 76, 82, 84, 102, 104, 112-4, 195, 200
"Nebraska" (song) 13, 82
Night and the City 10
Nighthawks 105
No Looking Back 91-101
No Nukes: The Muse Concerts for a Non-Nuclear Future 128, 132, 162
"Nothing Man" 59
Nyswaner, Ron 63-4, 70-1

Obama, Barack 184
Obsession 13
On the Road 197
Once Upon a Time in the West 7
"One Step Up" 94, 195
"Open All Night" 99, 199
Orbison, Roy 24, 34
Out of the Past 10
"Out in the Street" 153-4
The Outlaw 6
"Outlaw Pete" 7

Pacino, Al 103
Palmer, Gareth 98, 124-5
"Paradise" 150-1
Pardini, Samuele F.S. 98
"Part Man, Part Monkey" 87
"Party Lights" 99
The Passion of the Christ 169
The Patty Duke Show 18
Pelley, Scott 66
Penn, Arthur 10
Penn, Sean 78-9
Penn, William 66
Percy, Will 15
Philadelphia 63-75
Phillips, Julianne 120, 125-6
"Pink Cadillac" 87
Point Blank (book) 201
"Point Blank" (song) 9, 99
Poison 63
Porky's 18
The Postman Always Rings Twice 10
Presley, Elvis 5, 24, 120
Price, Frank 33
"The Price You Pay" 86
Prince 54
"The Promise" 12-3, 129, 132-5, 142, 146, 197

"The Promised Land" 12, 39, 41-2, 99, 199
Prozac Nation (book) 132-147
Prozac Nation (film) 132-147
Psycho 63
Purple Rose of Cairo 129

"Quarter to Three" 162
"Queen of the Supermarket" 100

"Racing in the Street" 11, 31, 38, 100, 143, 181
Rambo: First Blood 53
"Ramrod" 9, 124, 177, 179
Reading the Boss 2
Reagan, Ronald 44-5, 50-54
"Real Man" 126-7
Rebel Without a Cause 11, 13, 24, 31, 122
Reign Over Me 148-158
Remnick, David 139, 163-4
"Resurrection" 86
Ricci, Christina 146
Ricci, Franco 102
Rihanna 192
Ripley, Arthur 10
The Rising (album) 59, 148-9, 152-3, 157-8
The River (album) 9, 40, 103, 121, 124-5, 129, 131-2, 148, 152-3, 155, 188
"The River" (song) 54-5, 117, 121, 150
Robbins, Tim 76-90
Robinson, Smokey 154
"Rock and Roll Never Forgets" 39
"Rocky Ground" 87
"Roll Me Away" 41
"Romeo" 95
"Rosalita (Come Out Tonight)" 73, 91, 190
Rose, Caryn 7, 190
Roslin, "Little" Vinnie 55, 60
Rourke, Mickey 159, 164-66
Rucker, Allen 104
Rumble Doll 97
"Rumble Doll" 97

"Sad Eyes" 73
"Saga of the Architect Angel" 7
Sancious, David 24, 189
Sandford, Christopher 35, 201
Sandler, Adam 155
Sandler, Cruise 1; *see also* Sobel, Phillip
Sant, Gus Van 63
Saroyan, William 26
Sarris, Andrew 9
Sayles, John 15, 17-32, 95
Scarecrow 197
Scarface 13
Schrader, Paul 12-3
Scialfa, Patti 8, 71, 74, 95, 97-8, 126-7, 129, 165, 170
Scorsese, Martin 46, 89
The Searchers 7-8, 12, 199
"Secret Garden" 180, 195
Seger, Bob 33, 39, 41

Sheehy, Colleen 2
Sheen, Martin 13
"Sherry Darling" 124
She's the One 24-6, 124
The Shooting 12
Shumway, David R. 15
"Shut Out the Light" 47, 49, 59
Silence of the Lambs 63
Simon, David 173-4, 184, 186
Sinatra, Frank 18, 20, 22-3, 26
"Sinola Cowboys" 187
"Sister Thersea" 86
Skjoldbjærg, Erik 132-147
Smith, Jeff 13, 15
Smith, Nathan 69
Sobel, Phillip 1; *see also* Sandler, Cruise
"Something in the Night" 107, 143, 197
Songs 9
The Sopranos 102-116
The Sopranos: A Family History 102
Southside Johnny 106
Spector, Phil 24
"Spirit in the Night" 198
Springfield, Dusty 18
Springsteen, Adele 28, 34-5, 129, 136-7
Springsteen, Alice 137
Springsteen, Douglas 28, 55, 137-9, 162
Springsteen on Broadway 2, 52, 54, 57, 61, 88, 137, 139, 170-1, 184, 187, 189, 199
Stallone, Sylvester 53
"Stand by Me" 21
Starger, Martin 33, 42
Starkweather, Charles 13, 82-3
"State Trooper" 102, 104-5, 111, 113-4, 116, 199
Steppenwolf 192
"Stolen Car" 100, 145
Stolz, Eric 36
"Stop in the Name of Love" 18
"Strangers in the Night" 23, 32
"Streets of Fire" 1, 12, 143
"Streets of Philadelphia" 63, 65, 67-71, 75
Streight, Irwin 3
Suicide 191, 193
The Supremes 18
Sutcliffe, Phil 54
"Swallowed Up (In the Belly of the Whale)" 88
Swartley, Ariel 5
Symykywicz, Jeffery 125, 194

Tallent, Garry 163
Targets 46
Taxi Driver 12, 45-6
"Tenth Avenue Freeze-Out" 161, 179, 180, 189
"This Depression" 145
"This Hard Land" 7, 72
"This Life" 127
"This Train Is Bound for Glory" 184
Thompson, Jim 5

Index

Thunder Road (film) 10
"Thunder Road" (song) 8, 10, 31, 38-40, 86, 91-3, 95, 97-8, 100, 101, 134, 190-1, 197
Thurmaier, David 78
The Ties That Bind (film) 131
"The Ties That Bind" (song) 124-5
The Time of Your Life 26
To Kill a Mockingbird (film) 13
The Tonight Show with Jimmy Fallon 79
"Tougher Than the Rest" 71, 125
Tourneur, Jacques 10
Tracks 7, 87, 173
Troche, Rose 64
"Trouble in Paradise" 131
Tunnel of Love (album) 44, 74, 87, 91, 94, 101, 125-6, 132, 139, 144, 177, 179, 195
"Tunnel of Love" (song) 36, 107-8, 167
23rd Street Lullaby 95
"Two Faces" 110, 144
"Two Hearts" 125
Two Lane Blacktop 11, 196
Tyrell, Soozie 150

"Unchained Melody" 21
Unheard Melodies: Narrative Film Music 13
"Unsatisfied Heart" 72

The Untouchables 13
"Used Cars" 13, 112

"Valentine's Day" 95-7, 125, 179
Van Zandt, Maureen 103
Van Zandt, Steven 74, 103, 106
Vh1 Storytellers 89, 170
"Vietnam" 49
The Visitors 46

"Waiting on a Sunny Day" 154, 161
"Walk Like a Man" 139
"The Wall" 60
"The War Is Over" 56
Washington, Denzel 64
Wasiscko, Nay 173, 190
Wayne, John 7, 12
"We Are Alive" 139, 189-190
"We Found Love" 192
"We Take Care of Our Own" 203
Weinberg, Max 50, 135, 154, 161-2
Whale, James 36
"What Love Can Do" 127
"White Rabbit" 112
The Who 108
The Wild and the Innocent (film) 9
"Wild Billy's Circus Story" 35
The Wild One 11, 122
The Wild, the Innocent, and the E Street Shuffle (album) 8, 19, 20-1, 24

Wilder, Billy 33
Will, George 50, 51, 54
Willis, Ellen 102, 106
"Wings for Wheels" 10
Wise Blood 13
"The Wish" 35
"With Every Wish" 126
"Woke Up This Morning" 104
Woloch, Alex 17
Wonder, Stevie 120
Working on a Dream (album) 7-8, 100, 127
"Worlds Apart" 150
Wrecking Ball (album) 87, 145, 164, 189, 191, 202
The Wrestler 159-172
"The Wrestler" 159-60, 164, 166, 171
Wurtzel, Elizabeth 132-147

Yacowar, Maurice 102
Yosha, Yaky 9
"You Can Look (But You Better Not Touch)" 122
"You Don't Have to Say You Love Me" 18
Young, Neil 65
"Youngstown" 47
"You're Missing" 157

Zitelli, Lisa 99, 124
Zorzi, William 173

www.ingramcontent.com/pod-product-compliance
Ingram Content Group UK Ltd.
Pitfield, Milton Keynes, MK11 3LW, UK
UKHW050532150426
5217IPUK00026B/1909